WINDOWS NT SERVER 4

No experience required.

WINDOWS NT® SERVER 4

No experience required.™

Robert Cowart   Boyd Waters

SYBEX®

San Francisco • Paris • Düsseldorf • Soest

Associate Publisher: Gary Masters
Acquisitions Manager: Kristine Plachy
Acquisitions & Developmental Editor: Richard Mills
Editor: Marilyn Smith
Project Editor: Alison Moncrieff
Technical Editor: Kevin Summers
Book Designers: Cătălin Dulfu and Patrick Dintino
Graphic Illustrator: Patrick Dintino
Electronic Publishing Specialist: Kate Kaminski
Production Coordinator: Michael Tom
Indexer: Nancy Guenther
Cover Design: Ingalls & Associates

Screen reproductions produced with Collage Complete.
Collage Complete is a trademark of Inner Media Inc.

SYBEX is a registered trademark of SYBEX Inc.

TRADEMARKS: SYBEX has attempted throughout this book to
distinguish proprietary trademarks from descriptive terms by
following the capitalization style used by the manufacturer.

Library of Congress Card Number: 97-65359
ISBN: 0-7821-2081-4

Manufactured in the United States of America

10 9 8 7 6 5 4 3 2 1

To my electronics professor, Gary Svihula, for his support in the nascent stages of my career—Bob

To Lisa—Boyd

Acknowledgments

Robert Cowart wishes to thank all the folks at Sybex who worked so diligently to get this book to press in a timely fashion. Editing, typesetting, printing, and distributing high-quality computer books in roughly the time it takes to publish a magazine is truly an art form, and Sybex has mastered it. In the years that I've been publishing with Sybex, this has been proven time and again.

Particular thanks to Richard Mills for developmental editing; to Alison Moncrieff for project coordination; to Marilyn Smith our primary editor, who toiled numerous hours filling in various holes in the manuscript and fixing the language; to Wendy Ray for administrative coordination; and to technical editor Kevin Summers for ensuring accuracy. Also thanks to Kate Kaminski, electronic publishing specialist; Michael Tom, production coordinator; and Patrick Dintino, illustrator. And finally to the Sybex marketing and sales departments, responsible for getting this book on the bookstore shelves around the world.

Boyd Waters wishes to thank Roger Jacob, MIS Director of the White Mountain Apache Tribe, and David Waters, for letting me use their computer systems during the course of creating the book. Also thanks to Dave Dhillon (Chiron Corporation) and Bill Woodcock (Zocalo Engineering) for their insight into some of the networking optimization issues. Thanks to Lisa and Dweezil for giving me the space I needed to complete this project. Much thanks to the editing and production team at Sybex.

Contents at a Glance

Table of Contents

Introduction

Welcome to *Windows NT Server 4: No experience required*, a book written from the ground up to help you get moving with this product ASAP. As you undoubtedly know, NT Server 4 is a complex—even monumental—product.

Not only is it an extremely rich operating system for high-powered PCs, but it's also a networking product, and even an Internet product. In the olden (DOS) days, it would have taken three books to deal with what a good NT book should address: one on DOS, one on Windows, and a third to cover a network operating system such as Novell's NetWare. Maybe even a fourth book in the suite would cover stuff like hot-rodding your PC or information about RAS (Remote Access Service), IIS (Internet Information Server), and various Internet-related topics. So writing any book on Windows NT (especially the Server version) is by definition an ambitious undertaking.

What's Special about This Book?

So what is this book all about? Obviously it's not one of those gigantic books that details every hive in the NT Registry. No, this isn't a book intended to cover all aspects of NT, or serve as your doorstop. Based on our research, there is a growing class of professional folks (and you're probably one of them) who need to get up and running with NT immediately. Typically, you're working for a corporation or small business that is converting from a NetWare network, or at least wants to add a bunch of NT boxes—for development platforms, applications servers, or possibly as Web servers. Should you be forced to pore over some 1000-page tome just to figure out how to configure NT, set up some servers, and assign some group privileges? No.

This book takes you quickly through explanations of what NT Server does, on to "back-of-the-envelope" decisions about your hardware and network topology, right through installation and getting up and running. But unlike some "basics" books, this is not a "dummies" concept. The assumption is that you know what you're doing with PC operating systems, just not with NT.

Here's what's *not* in this book:

- Hand-holding. We skip this, assuming you know what a mouse is, what a network is, and even what a Web server is.

- Huge lists of command references, API calls, or regurgitated Help files that you can find on your own.

- Unnecessary trivia.

- Boring language. We use lots of computer lingo and slang like *disk-hit*, *crash*, *bomb*, *gonzo*, and *bozo*. Something may be lost when this book is translated into Chinese, but hey, this is the American English version.

What you *will* find is:

- Basic nuts-and-bolts theory about what NT Server is, how it's constructed, and what's new in version 4.

- Lots of seat-of-the-pants, how-to information, such as how to install NT, how to ensure systems integrity and security, and how to find and eliminate network bottlenecks.

- Worksheets to fill out. These worksheets are similar to tax forms and will help you get your head straight about your hardware choices, your network load, and NT efficiency tweaking.

- Real-world optimization secrets, tips, tricks, and warnings. When do you really need Fast/Wide SCSI and RAID? What about using Pentium Pro, MIPS, Power PC, or Alpha boxes? Which network protocol is fastest? How many users should be on a network branch? What about routers? We give you that sort of stuff.

Fifteen Minutes to the Future

The Big Hassle about Windows NT is that it forces you to make some fundamental design decisions with your very first server, immediately when you start to install. These decisions will influence the shape of your network down the road. Even if you're an experienced LAN administrator, some core NT competency is crucial with that very first box.

As it goes with Windows NT, so it goes with this book. You'll find a lot of cross-references in the material. We've tried to weave this tapestry of concepts into the book you hold in your hand, but don't take the sequential nature of the page numbers too seriously (if we were going to read this book, we would start with Skill 12!). Often, you'll be asked questions we haven't given the answers to yet. That's okay—as a computer professional, you're always living fifteen minutes in the future anyway, right? You're presented with challenges all the time. When we get to a concept that branches off into other areas, there are pointers to related sections of the book.

Don't be afraid to follow these pointers; don't be afraid to wander around. What we've really created here is an Easter egg hunt by taking two tons of candy eggs and dumping them on the soccer field. You can run around as fast as you want to, and you'll discover treasures everywhere you go—you'll find lots of stuff in here.

Bringing Order out of Chaos— How to Read This Book

Here's the basic lowdown on how to read this book. First, take a look at the TOC to get an idea of the different topics and parts. Then, as mentioned above, you might want to take a quick look at Skill 12 right off the bat, to get a quick overview of basic system design concepts. That will help you sort out your thoughts about the nature of the systems you're going to set up.

Next, you'll want to go back to the beginning and start delving into Part I: Starting Out. Skills 1 through 5 discuss the theory and internals of NT functionality and architecture. Here, you'll get some perspective on this operating system, its mission, and how it's built to do what it was designed to do. By the end of this part, you'll understand what NT is and where it came from. You'll also have your server hardware set up and the software installed. Because the best way to learn about Windows NT is to actually set it up and go, we get you started as soon as possible. There are lots of forward references in this section, so you can use this section as a "Start button" for the rest of the book.

Part II: Components of a Solid NT Server System is where we go beyond the basics of Windows NT design and focus on building the best possible Windows NT systems that provide a high degree of performance and reliability. Skill 6 presents an overview of how to build a solid NT Server system, not just get NT installed in a box. In Skill 7, you'll learn about scaling up your NT system—this is what NT is all about. Next, in Skill 8, we'll talk exclusively about local- and wide-area networks, and how to optimize them for the greatest throughput and the easiest management and administration.

Worried about power failures? You should be. Skill 9 discusses the essentials of determining what you need in a UPS (uninterruptible power supply) system and how to use NT's UPS features. The crux of any server system is mass storage. In Skill 10, we look at the variety of mass-storage systems in the market today, RAID technology, SCSI drives, striping, mirroring, and other stuff you need to consider when setting up servers. For mission-critical sites, backups are just as important as primary storage; read Skill 11 to learn how to establish efficient backup systems and strategies. Finally, Skill 12 will recap the entire part with a design review (and worksheets) to help you take down some notes and actually design your server system.

Part III: Networking and Security goes into detail about networking. If you're already a network admin type, you know that heavy networking is a black art. We've done a lot of the homework for you, tested NT Server in a large corporation, and have much to say about Do's and Don't's. Skill 13 explains the not-so-easy-to-grasp concept of NT domains, complete with pictures to help you decide which system works best for your network. Then we cover the setups for various network clients, beginning with Microsoft Windows clients in Skill 14, and then Mac clients in Skill 15. Then in Skill 16, we'll talk about the big question: What about Novell's NetWare and NT? How well do they work together? How do you integrate them? Skill 17 sums it all up with ten steps to bring your network plan together.

Just in case you don't think there's a method to all this madness, note that we're building toward networked business solutions, which is why you are installing Windows NT Server in the first place. That's where Part IV: BackOffice and Internet Systems comes in. In Skills 18 and 19, we present some client/server intranet systems that can be built on top of a Windows NT Server network using BackOffice and other client/server software platforms. We'll build a practical example that will get you on the right track to designing your own solutions.

Notes, Tips, Warnings, and Sidebars

Throughout the book, you'll find a lot of extras. When there is something more that goes along with the discussion at hand, but maybe is incidental, more detailed, or just an interesting aside, it appears as a note. If there is a neat trick or shortcut, it's in the book as a tip. And when it is something you need to watch out for, it's a warning, usually with a way to avoid the potential problem.

Along the way, you'll find sidebars scattered throughout. These contain related but separate information, lengthier than the notes, tips, and warnings. For example, in a sidebar, we'll tell you that Microsoft's Visual Test utility, which lets you "record" windows operations and then play them back, can be a great tool for network administrators.

Our goal is to help you get the most out of NT Server 4, without slogging through pages of information you don't need. Best of luck in your work with NT. We hope this book will serve as not only an introductory guide, but as a future reference when troubleshooting or upscaling your network to accommodate growth.

PART I

Starting Out

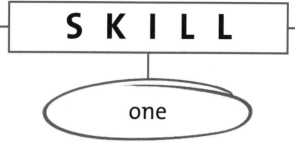

SKILL

one

1

Evaluating NT Server's Capabilities

- ❑ Features of Windows NT Server 4.0
- ❑ NT compared with other desktop operating systems
- ❑ NT compared with other network servers
- ❑ NT and client/server computing

NT—why is everyone talking about it? Well, or course, there's critical mass—everyone is talking about it because everyone is talking about it. But don't dismiss NT by assuming that it's all hype. I assure you, in the case of NT Server, there's a *there* there!

The *NT* in Windows NT stands for (according to the official party line from Microsoft) *New Technology*. In reality, of course, very little about NT is really very new. Most of the technologies in NT are about ten years old. This is not bad news—it means that you can wrap your brains around NT pretty quickly, if you already have experience with other, more-established operating systems. So by way of introduction, we'll compare NT to a number of other products, to see how NT measures up.

Don't get me wrong—there actually *is* a new technology to NT. We all know the genius of Microsoft does not lie in the ability to innovate fundamental technologies, but rather to bring together effective technologies, make them more accessible to business folks, put shrink-wrap around the bundle, and then make megabucks by hawking it cheap to everyone on the planet.

Let's see what this is all about!

What NT Is All About

Perhaps the most significant "new" thing about NT is that it lets you set up a reliable, secure, multithreaded, symmetric-processing, client/server system in about four hours, with modest hardware. Let's take a look at each of these points:

- **Reliable:** NT is made up of a series of separate subsystems; so one program, for example, can't crash the whole system. NT also supports fault-tolerant devices like redundant disk arrays.

- **Secure:** Both users and processes must have permission to access resources. All accesses are logged by the system.

- **Multithreaded and symmetric-processing:** NT can handle many "trains of thought" simultaneously. If your system has more than one CPU, NT will distribute tasks among all the available processors. It's fast!

- **Client/server:** NT Server supports a wide range of network protocols and RPC (Remote Procedure Call) communications, making it easy for programmers to create distributed applications.

- **Ease of use:** For all its power and complexity, NT is easy to set up and maintain. Most administrative functions can be performed with the powerful graphical tools provided.

- **Wide range of hardware support:** NT was designed from "Day One" to be a portable operating system. These days, you can run NT Server on Intel, DEC Alpha, MIPS, and PowerPC computers, ranging from a simple 486 desktop all the way up to a 128-processor monster computer. You can find the system that meets your needs.

We'll go into more detail on these points in Skill 3, which covers NT's internal architecture.

What's New with 4.0

The main new features in this version of NT Server are optimized performance, a new user interface, distributed OLE (object linking and embedding) support, and built-in Internet access. Let's see what these features do for your work with NT.

Performance Optimizations

Perhaps the most controversial change in NT 4.0 is the reorganization of the Win32 subsystem and the Graphics Device Interface, or GDI. Much of the Win32 subsystem and all of the User and GDI systems have been moved to the Windows NT Executive, which runs in kernel mode.

What?

NT owes much of its much-vaunted reliability to the fact that most of NT runs in a special processor mode (*kernel mode*), which protects the system (by using the CPU chip hardware) and prevents applications from stomping on it. Anything that lives down there in kernel mode with the rest of NT had better not crash; if it does, the whole system is going down with it.

Before NT 4.0, the Win32 subsystem, which processes all Windows function calls, and the User and GDI systems, which draw everything on the screen, were completely separated from the core operating system. These systems were up there in user mode, away from the sensitive parts of NT. But *every* time a Windows function call happened, or something updated the screen, the system had to switch modes: from user to kernel and back again. This operation was time-consuming, and it was happening all the time.

The trade press took Microsoft to task on moving the User and GDI systems to run in kernel mode in NT 4.0, claiming that NT's stability was being compromised by this change. In theory, this design change does indeed compromise the pristine nature of the Windows NT kernel-mode system. In fact, though, the user/kernel separation was never that pristine.

NOTE   If you're interested in this kind of stuff, see Skill 3 for a more in-depth discussion of Windows NT internal architecture. I'll even show you how to crash a Windows NT 3.51 system by nuking its Win32 subsystem—something that should not happen in theory. But there's more to this story...

Of Course, the Windows 95 Interface

The most obvious change in NT 4.0 is the integration of a user interface that looks pretty much like Windows 95. This dramatic change is causing Microsoft to refer to this release as the SUR, for Shell Update Release (the *shell* is the part of the operating system that interacts with the user). Figure 1.1 shows some of the windows you'll see in NT 4.0.

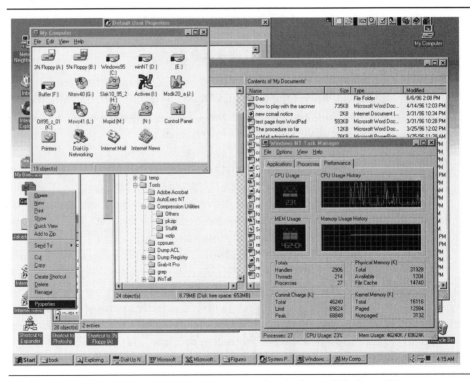

FIGURE 1.1:   Windows NT Server 4.0 looks similar to Windows 95.

It isn't exactly Windows 95, however. Most of the Control Panels are different, which is to be expected. NT Server's networking model is very different from Windows 95, so of course the Network Control Panel isn't the same. And since NT doesn't support Plug-and-Play hardware (yet), the System Control Panel reminds you that this isn't Windows 95, as you can see in Figure 1.2.

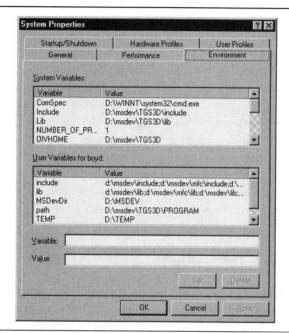

FIGURE 1.2: The NT Server System Control Panel has an Environment tab for controlling system and user variables.

 NOTE   In previous versions of NT, you could type "control <control panel name>" at a command prompt, and the specified Control Panel would pop right up. This now works with only a few Control Panels.

Distributed OLE for Client/Server Applications

NT Server's primary mission is to be the best client/server platform for corporate LANs. As a network designer, I haven't paid much attention to all the talk about

OLE—until now. Today, I'm scrambling to catch up, and maybe you should, too. Because with Distributed OLE, as well as Microsoft's Internet strategy, OLE is becoming pervasive.

Usually, each process running on the computer will have its own protected area, which other processes cannot see. But it's often desirable for processes to exchange information. OLE is a protocol that allows processes to exchange data. For example, a user can embed an object into a Word document, and Word will talk to Excel via OLE to render the spreadsheet on the screen.

In the past, OLE data exchange has been limited to processes running on a single computer. With Distributed OLE, those software components no longer have to be on the same machine. Consider the power of embedding an Excel spreadsheet into your Word document, when the Excel spreadsheet is running on the symmetric-multiprocessing server in the next building! Distributed OLE makes it easier for programmers to create ever more powerful distributed applications.

Perhaps the easiest way to understand why Distributed OLE is interesting is to realize its specification reads like the design of the Java language. And unless you've been hiding under a rock all summer, you know that *everyone* thinks that Java is cool. You don't need to worry about Distributed OLE too much right now. Just know that it's there.

NT Means iNTerNeT

One of the best things about Microsoft people is the cute way that they are running scared all the time. They're the 800-pound gorilla of the entire industry right now, and they're convinced that if they stop running flat out, they'll be besieged by a screaming horde of rabid monkeys.

And they're right.

The Internet didn't happen overnight, of course, but it sometimes feels that way. And Microsoft managers had to turn their ship around to handle it. Well, the aircraft carrier U.S.S. Enterprise can move at freeway speeds on the water, even though it's the size of a couple of Empire State Buildings. It's the same with Microsoft.

In NT 4.0, there's the stamp of Internet standards all over the place. There's the Internet Explorer on the Desktop, and there's the Internet Information Server

embedded into the system setup. By default, you're asked if you want to create a Web server each time you install NT. Every file in the entire system is associated with a MIME (Multimedia Internet Mail Extension) type, as shown in Figure 1.3.
   The Internet is everywhere. In this book, it's in Skill 19.

How NT Stacks Up

We'll talk about the particular features of NT in Skill 3, but let's set the stage for that discussion by cutting to the results first (kind of like looking at the answers in the back of the book). Here are a few tables that give a crude comparison of the various operating systems. Table 1.1 shows how NT compares with Windows 95 and OS/2 Warp. Table 1.2 shows how NT compares with other network server systems: Unix, VMS, and Novell's NetWare. If you need more information about what's in the tables, read on.

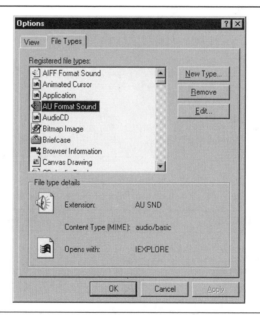

FIGURE 1.3 : NT associates files with its registered file types, including the MIME type, which opens files in Internet Explorer.

T A B L E 1 . 1 : Comparison of Desktop Operating Systems

FEATURE	NT 4.0	Win95	OS/2 Warp
386 support		✔	✔
Minimum RAM for a workable system	24 MB	16 MB	16 MB
Addressable memory	4 GB	4 GB	4 GB
Application code size	2 GB	2 GB	512 MB
Multiprocessor support	2	No	Not yet
Multithreading support	✔	✔	✔
Multiple message queues	✔		No, but after a period of time, the system will flush the message queue if it is locked.
Preemptive multitasking of Win32 apps	✔	✔	
Preemptive multitasking of Win16 apps	✔	✔	
C2-level security	✔		
Plug and Play		✔	
Windows 95 interface	✔	✔	
Internet integration	✔	✔	✔

T A B L E 1 . 2 : Comparison of Network Application Servers

FEATURE	NT 4.0	Unix (HP)*	VMS	NetWare
Addressable memory	4 GB**	4 GB	8 TB**	4 GB
Maximum file size	17 TB	128 GB	10 TB	4 GB
Total disk storage	408 TB	NA	NA	32 TB
"Journaling" file system	✔	✔	✔	✔
Disk quotas	3rd party	✔	✔	✔
Protected memory	✔	✔	✔	
C2-level security	✔	✔	✔	✔
Multiprocessor support	32	14	✔	2
Multithreaded	✔	✔	✔	

TABLE 1.2 CONTINUED: Comparison of Network Application Servers

FEATURE	NT 4.0	Unix (HP)*	VMS	NetWare
Server clustering	Planned	✔	✔	
RAID fault-tolerance	✔	✔	✔	✔
Database server speed	Getting better	Fast	Way fast	OK
Intel	✔			✔
DEC Alpha	✔		✔	
HP PA-RISC		✔		
PowerPC	✔			
MIPS	✔			

* For this comparison, I had to pick a flavor of Unix to illustrate. I chose Hewlett-Packard's (HP's) Unix, because it's well regarded as a solid business system. You can find a Unix for just about any hardware platform, but it won't necessarily have all the features indicated in this table.

** GB means gigabyte, and TB means terabyte. A gigabyte is (of course) 1,073,741,824 bytes. A terabyte is 1024 gigabytes, or 1,099,511,627,776 bytes.

NT versus Windows 95 or OS/2: An Advanced Workstation

Many companies are still agonizing over the decision to upgrade their vast sea of PCs to the next generation of Windows. What's it going to be, Windows 95 or Windows NT? Or will you split the difference, and go with OS/2 Warp?

On one hand, Windows 95 preserves backward compatibility while giving people a really nice-looking user interface, Internet support, and Plug-and-Play hardware support.

On the other hand, NT provides the advanced, protected-memory, client/server platform that more fully supports typical business applications. With NT 4.0, you get the Windows 95 user interface, so what's stopping you from choosing NT?

- **Hardware requirements:** Many companies still have a large installed base of 386 computers or 486 machines with only 8 MB or less of RAM in them. You won't be able to install NT on those systems.

- **Plug and Play:** I don't think the lack of Plug and Play in NT is a big deal. I think that most companies have standardized their hardware to the point where they support only one or two kinds of PCs, anyway. (But my computer support tech friends tell me I've been in the LAN lab too long, and offer to increase the oxygen supply to my obviously atrophied brain with a hit from the compressed-air can they always tote around in their tool kits.) Standardization issues aside, if you have a portable notebook or laptop computer, NT's support of PCMCIA and other hardware still lags behind Windows 95.

- **Legacy code:** Some DOS and Windows programs won't run under NT, because they were written to access the system hardware directly, or expect to do things to memory a certain way. But you'll have tested all your critical programs against all possible operating systems before you upgrade, right? Right?

NOTE   Interesting point: The Windows 95 Team at Microsoft is now working under the Windows NT Team. Of course, Microsoft wants these teams to cross-pollinate, to create the ideal system.

I prefer NT, but I have Windows 95 on my computer. I have done this so I'll be able to run any PC program I might need. With the focus on delivering products for Windows 95, and the requirement that programs operate under NT to get the Windows 95 certification from Microsoft, you might think that every program in the world will run under NT by next year. Well, they might, but there's running and then there's *running*. One program (a Microsoft program, with a Windows 95 logo) that I have will run under NT 4.0, all right—it brings up a beautiful warning box that explains that it does not work under Windows NT, and then gracefully quits.

NT Advantages

If you look back at the desktop comparisons in Table 1.1, you'll see that NT on the desktop can be described as the operating system that has all the advanced features of OS/2 Warp and Windows 95 combined. NT can run Win32 and (well-behaved) Win16 applications in their own memory space, switching between these tasks with complete control and grace. NT has these advantages:

- **Preemptive multitasking:** NT can switch among multiple programs "preemptively," which means that NT can force the switch to occur without waiting for the program to relinquish control of the system. You care about this if you want to continue working in your word processing program while the computer formats a floppy disk for you.

- **Multiple message queues:** With graphic, windowing user interface systems, a "message" is any action that the program needs to know about: You pressed a key, moved the mouse, or spoke a voice command. In previous versions of Windows, and in the current version of OS/2, there is only one big stream of these messages for the whole system. The problem is that a berserk program could go haywire by spewing messages, or could grab all the input and prevent any other program from knowing that you were trying to get the system's attention.

- **Protected memory:** Under NT, a program can't trash the whole system when it crashes.

- **Security:** There is extensive security support in NT. All you need to do to gain access to the local computer under Windows 95 is hit Cancel at the Windows login screen. OS/2 Warp desktop security falls in between (again). You can't control access to individual files on the local computer as finely with OS/2 as you can with NT.

Skill 3 discusses all the "non-security" stuff in more detail. For an in-depth discussion of NT security features, see Skill 13.

NT versus Unix or VMS: A Scalable Applications Platform

Under the hood, NT is similar to a "mainframe" operating system: there are multiple subsystems that run in a special, protected processor mode. Many programs are running at once, and each program is isolated from all the others. Security is everywhere; something is always asking for permission before accessing different parts of the system.

VMS Heritage

None of this is surprising, given NT's heritage. In 1988, David Cutler, the primary designer of the VMS operating system, left Digital Equipment Corporation (DEC) to begin work at Microsoft, designing a modern operating system that would run on the emerging generation of PCs—desktop computers that promised to rival the power of the large refrigerator-sized DEC VAX systems. Quarterdeck was selling 1-pound cards that brought your PC up to an amazing 4 MB of RAM.

NT shares some design concepts with VMS. In fact, the VMS folks at my company are sometimes in the position of explaining some esoteric tidbit or another to the trainer who has been brought in to teach them all about NT! Based on their experience, if you're comfortable with VMS and Windows 95, you'll get along with NT. Indeed, some of the best technical material I've run across on NT is from *Digital News & Review*, a newsletter for DEC professionals.

 NOTE   Most VMS applications vendors know a market opportunity when they see it, and they are porting their programs to NT. DEC is leading the porting effort in order to generate sales for its (pretty impressive) Alpha AXP-based systems. At my company, it's getting hard to tell the difference, just peeking into the data center, between the Alpha VMS computers and the departmental NT servers. The operators have had to label the boxes to keep them straight. We may well move all of our financial and manufacturing applications over to NT in the next ten months.

With all that, NT is (of course) *not* VMS. After all, this was Dave's second system. He had already designed VMS, and now he had a chance to do it right. So NT incorporates a lot of the most advanced operating system theory from the time, throwing in sophisticated thread scheduling (from the Mach operating system at Carnegie-Mellon University), hardware independence, a self-healing file system, 32-bit memory access, and even the emulation of other operating environments.

NT Supports Many Unix Features

Many of the freely available Unix tools are moving over to NT as well, thanks to market demand and cheap licensing that Microsoft is providing to universities. Also, porting many Unix programs to NT is no more difficult that porting to Unix on a new hardware platform. This is because NT supports a subset of the standard Unix API (Application Program Interface), POSIX (Portable Operating System Interface Extension), which allows "straight" POSIX programs to be ported to NT with a simple recompile operation.

Figure 1.4 shows popular Unix programs that have been ported to Win32. But as a first cut, programmers can recompile some POSIX-compliant programs to run under NT.

NT supports most of the operating system features that you would want in a Unix system: security, protected memory, long filenames, virtual memory, and remote procedure calls. We'll talk about all these features in Skill 3.

NTFS, the NT file system, does not yet support soft links. However, POSIX programs will be able to create and manage hard links on NTFS.

 TIP

You can also purchase an enhanced POSIX subsystem from Softway Systems (http://www.softway.com/OpenNT).

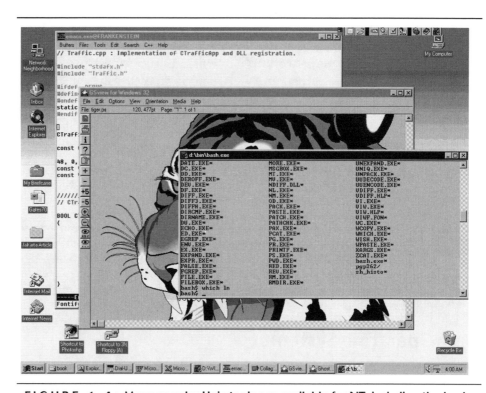

FIGURE 1.4: Many popular Unix tools are available for NT, including the bash shell, the Ghostscript Postscript interpreter, and the GNU Emacs editor.

Being a Unix type myself, one of the first things I did with my NT system was configure it to run all my familiar Unix tools: Emacs, the bash shell, perl, and so on. Surprisingly, this didn't last too long. I found that it was like trying to speak a foreign language by constantly translating everything first. However, the transition was fairly easy to make. And I still use the ls command instead of DIR.

Can NT Compete with the Big Iron?

The word on the street is that NT is still not as scalable as Unix or VMS. I believe that this is a function of the maturity of VMS and some commercial Unix systems. Developers have been tuning their systems to run Oracle (for example) really, really fast for a really, really long time.

Another issue is that you might treat VMS as a turn-key, dedicated database platform. That is, you could point to your glorious cluster of AlphaServer 8100s and say, "That's the database." If a computer system is tuned to do one thing, it will probably be able to do that one thing pretty well.

For simple network applications, it has been my experience that Unix can sometimes outperform NT, presumably because the Unix box is doing less. It's not drawing pretty screens; it's doing just one thing. My Unix-based Web server is plenty fast on modest hardware, and it takes a more powerful box to do the same job with NT. But you know, it took me two weeks to configure the Unix machine, but only one day to set up the NT box.

The bottom line: I think that as the Alpha and other RISC (reduced instruction set computing) platform vendors gain experience with NT, we'll continue to see performance improvements.

 TIP

If you are considering replacing your VMS or Unix system with NT, memorize Part 2 of this book first. In particular, you'll want to see Skill 7, which covers scaling up NT servers and networks.

NT versus NetWare: An Enterprise Network Operating System

NT Server is being positioned as a file and print server to rival NetWare and Banyan Vines. You can see by the comparison of network applications servers shown in Table 1.2 that NT and NetWare have some of the same broad characteristics. But are the two really comparable?

The Big News about NT, relative to NetWare, is NT's lack of a true network directory system. Microsoft knows this and is feverishly at work on the next release of NT, which is supposed to solve this problem once and for all. For now, there is a way to centralize the management of your user accounts with an NT enterprise network, but you must set up your network correctly to do it, and it is not at all obvious how to do that. (That's okay—you've got this book, so you're covered.)

But if you have 10,000 happy people on a NetWare network, with directory services going on just fine, and your 500 NetWare administrators are able to take vacations once a year—oh, I don't know—I wouldn't touch it. Of course, if you're doing your job that well, you're probably going to get outsourced to EDS next month anyway, so you'll need to know about NT to get your next job. (Huh, you think I'm joking?)

NT can coexist in a NetWare environment, and given NT's talent as an applications platform, this is a good thing. There are two primary ways to get NT and NetWare to interoperate:

- As a gateway between a Microsoft and NetWare network

- As a native NetWare server

Gateway Services: NT As Network Glue

Gateway service enables an NT Server machine to connect to a NetWare machine and share as a *client*, then turn around and publish that as a *server* for the rest of the Microsoft-based network. That is, you can have a non-NetWare network client connect to NetWare resources through an NT gateway, or a *proxy*. This is useful if lots of your users don't have a NetWare client on their computer for some reason. The application that occurs to me is a way to connect Macintoshes to the NetWare server cheaply. But, of course, you lose some functionality.

NetWare File and Print Services for NT

The Real Cool Way to get NT to exist in your Novell NetWare environment is to set up NT to be a NetWare server. Then you can just forget about it. Well, almost—you'll be reminded because your server retains all of the features of NT and can run all the NT programs.

Migration Utilities

Of course, Microsoft wants you to move from Novell and buy truckloads of NT Server packages. You'll find a utility for importing NetWare user names into your NT domain. We'll talk all about NetWare-to-NT interoperability issues in Skill 16.

Bottom Line: NT and NetWare Compared

NT is the better applications server, but until directory services come along, NetWare will hold the lead as a straight-ahead file and print server.

However, it has been my experience that for small networks, NT is easier to administer. The tools are better, and more stuff is included. Every NT server comes with Macintosh support, for example, and this makes me happy (as a Macintosh integration specialist).

From a single-server performance standpoint, on the same hardware, it's a wash: NT and NetWare are pretty much the same. However, keep in mind that NetWare is bound to Intel servers; NT can scale up to multiprocessor RISC machines.

NT Is New Technology

The goal of the designers of NT Server was to create a general-purpose operating system that is particularly suited for distributed, client/server application development and implementation. Just as Unix is a networking and computing horse, and VMS is the database monster, so NT Server is the client/server master—both as the client on the desktop and as the server on the back end.

The BackOffice Connection

Microsoft has positioned NT Server as a member of a whole line of client/server support applications, called BackOffice. Microsoft added distributed inter-process communications to Visual Basic and to NT 4.0, so folks who once programmed the mainframe in COBOL can now do the proper 90's thing, and reimplement those systems in Visual Basic, using NT as the back end.

Think about this for a second: You'll be able to walk up to my mainframe cluster and fire up Doom! Okay, so maybe the big boxes won't have a joystick port, but they *will* be able to run Visual Basic and Microsoft Office. You will be able to create enterprise applications by scaling up the desktop technologies in a networked environment. And these applications will run on every computer in your enterprise network, from the Intel-based desktop systems to the multiple-Alpha servers in the machine room.

If you're familiar with three-tier client/server design, the wheels in your head are already turning. But if not, it's easier to show you than to tell you. So here's an example.

Wrap-Up Example: An Enterprise-Wide, Client/Server Intranet System

A couple of things happened in computing over the past decade. We witnessed the development of object-oriented methods of application design, with the paradigm of a community of software components performing tasks by sending messages among themselves. And we saw the explosive arrival of computer networking, first transforming business communications and now affecting our larger culture as the Internet avalanche comes roaring down around us.

The synergy between these two revolutionary technologies is striking. If my program is simply a community of software components that talk to one another, why can't they live on various computers and use my network to do the talking? This idea is more than traditional client/server computing; it's a fully distributed model for program design. Put the arithmetic functions on the fastest computer. Put the data-lookup functions on the biggest computer, the one with the huge disk farm on it. Put the front-end servers, the intranet Web servers, on every departmental file server, where they are close to the users. And put the nice interactive front end right there on the desktop.

This is client/server computing as of 1997. NT is the enabling technology that was designed to get you there. In order to show you how, we're going to take a peek at the final part of the book, in which we develop just this sort of distributed, client/server system.

Our simple example is an employee database system that helps employees find car-pool partners. Those employees who want to participate in the ride-sharing program can have their home address made available to other employees in the program. See Figure 1.5 for a screenshot of the Web-based query tool in action.

Our example will use a SQL Server database and Web server running on NT to maintain and distribute employee data. The database runs on a huge computer somewhere, the Web server on a smaller departmental server, and the Web browsers (the clients) on the desktop computers, whatever they may be.

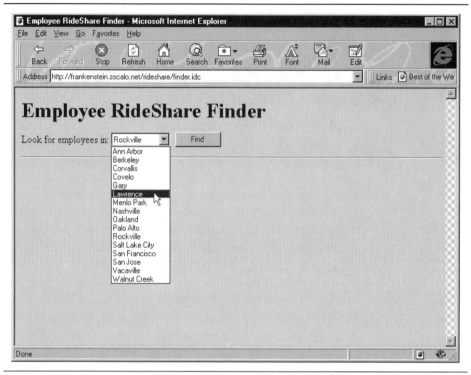

FIGURE 1.5: The Web-based front end of our client/server example application, developed in Skill 19.

Are You Experienced?

Now you know...

☑ **NT Server's interface resembles Windows 95, but NT is a completely different operating system, which happens to run most Windows software**

☑ **NT version 4.0 has many improvements, including tighter integration of Internet technologies, and performance optimizations**

☑ **NT Server performs well as an applications server in a LAN environment**

☑ NT can be incorporated in a NetWare environment, either as a gateway or as a native NetWare server

☑ NT Server is particularly suited for distributed, client/server application development

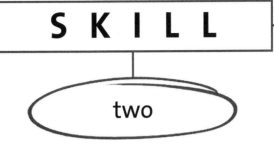

SKILL

2

two

Working from the NT Server Desktop

- ❑ The NT graphical user interface
- ❑ How to run Windows and DOS applications
- ❑ How to work with files and folders
- ❑ NT's administrative tools

Before going on to the more "high-end" skills related to network design, system installation, performance tuning, and administration, you need to master the basic skill of getting around in the Windows NT interface. Even if you're an experienced NT 3.*x* or Windows 3.*x* user, NT 4.0's interface will be new to you. If you have used Windows 95, the GUI will be more familiar, but there are still some notable differences.

Here, you will learn how to run programs from the Desktop, switch between tasks, create shortcuts to applications, and work with files and folders. You'll also be introduced to NT Server's main system administration tools.

Running Applications under NT Server

When it comes to running applications, some significant differences exist between NT 4.0 and 3.*x*. However, NT's new approach is almost identical to that of Windows 95. The following sections explain the various ways that you can run applications under NT Server 4.0 and some things you should know about running DOS programs.

What Can and Can't Be Run

NT was designed to be *backward compatible* with Windows 3.*x* and DOS programs, and to be *forward compatible* with most 32-bit programs. Although Windows 95 may be the best of all worlds when it comes to running your existing programs due to its high compatibility with "legacy" software, NT is no slouch either. You can pretty much bet that much of your existing software arsenal will run under NT Server.

However, it is wiser not to run too many applications on a server in the first place, especially if your network traffic load is high. Why? An NT server can be too busy dealing with resource sharing, authentication, remote access services, and other high-end services to be bothered running typical "productivity" applications like word processors. Your NT Server station probably shouldn't be thought of as a "workstation." You'll need it to administer the network, so you'll be running a variety of NT network utilities, such as monitoring programs and user and disk administration programs. And as you'll see later in the book, for some NT network adminstration tasks, you'll need to be running NT Server, *not* NT Workstation. We always recommend that NT network adminstrators have a fast deskop computer on their desk, running NT Server software.

One word of warning: Remember that certain older 16-bit programs (both DOS and Windows ones) can't be run under NT. NT will simply trap any calls that some wily old programs make directly to hardware or the hard disk. For example, some old disk utilities (such as Norton Utilities for DOS and Windows 3.*x*) were designed to read and write directly to the hard disk. NT's security subsystem doesn't allow this. As a rule, don't try to run utility programs that haven't been written for at least NT 3.*x* or Windows 95. They should preferably be written for NT 4.0.

Techniques for Running Programs

Launching an application in NT can be done in myriad ways. In fact, there are so many ways to run programs and open documents that it's a little mind-boggling. Microsoft developers outdid themselves making the new interface almost too flexible. Anyway, here's the basic list of ways to run programs:

- Choose the desired application from the Start button menu. Just click on Start, choose Programs, walk through the cascading menus until you see the program you want, and then click on it. Gone too far in the menus? Press Escape to back up one level, or click somewhere outside the menu to close it and then click on Start to try again from the beginning.

- Open My Computer, click on the disk containing the program, and walk your way through directories until you find the application's icon. Then double-click on it.

- Run the NT Explorer by clicking on Start, choosing Programs, and then choosing Windows NT Explorer. Find the application's icon and double-click on it. Another way to run Explorer is to right-click on My Computer or a drive's icon in the My Computer window and choose Explore.

 NOTE   If you're a diehard Windows 3.*x* user, you can use the good old File Manager, which is also included with NT. To run File Manager, just click on Start, then Run. Type **winfile** and press Enter.

- Click on the Start button, choose Find, and then File or Folders. Then enter the application's name (or portion thereof) and click on Find Now. When the application is found, double-click on its name in the Find box.

- Choose Start, then Run, enter the name of the program, and hit Enter. Note that you can use this method to start any type of program that NT is capable of running, such as DOS, POSIX, or Windows types. Entering Start alone will open a DOS window (actually called a Command Line Prompt window since it's not actually running DOS and isn't limited to DOS programs) from which you can enter Start commands. For help on the marvels of the Start command, check the NT Help file. But the catch is that Run requires the program to be in the DOS search path.

- Locate a document that was created with the application in question and double-click on it. This will run the application and load the document into it. This works only if the document type has an associated application (for example, DOC files are associated with WordPad or Word).

 NOTE

In NT, there are five kinds of executable (applications) file types: Those with extensions of EXE, COM, BAT, CMD, and PIF. (CMD files are like DOS batch files, but written for NT.) If you double-click on any other type, it either will not run or will run its associated program and load into it. For example, files with the extension BMP are graphics. Double-clicking on such a file (for example, arches.bmp) will run the Paint program and load the graphic into the Paint window for editing.

- Right-click on the Desktop or in a folder and choose New. (Right-click means to click the right mouse button on the item, not the usual left button.) Then choose a document type from the menu that appears. This creates a new document of that type, which you can double-click on to run the application.

- Click on the Start button, choose Documents, and choose the document from the list of recently edited documents. This will open the document in the appropriate application.

For many folks, the last three approaches in this list will make the most sense, because they deal with the document itself instead of the application that created it. Want to edit that letter to Aunt Jenny? Just find and open the folder it's stored in, then double-click on the document. NT's document-centricity makes this approach straightforward. For more veteran users, the familiar approach of running an application first, then loading in a document will have more appeal. And for the old-timers who prefer to type in commands from the keyboard, well, that's possible too. Just use the Start button's Run command and enter the name of the application manually. But even old-timers will soon discover that it really does make sense to organize your documents into folders, give them long names that you recognize, and simply double-click on them when you want to edit, view, or print them.

When you aren't going directly to a document, running a program from the Start button is the way to go. When you install a new program, the program's name is added to the Start button's Program menu. Then you just find your way to the program's name and choose it.

WARNING   When you want to run a program or open a document by clicking on it, don't double-click on its name slowly! If you do, this tells NT that you want to change the object's name. Just press Escape to get out of editing mode. This is a great feature when you want to rename a file or folder, but not when you're trying to run a program or open a folder. To be safe, it's better to click on any item's little icon (the picture portion) when you want to run it. In short, stay away from clicking on an object's name unless you want to change the name.

If you like using the My Computer approach to getting into your hard disk, fine. Many prefer to use the Windows Explorer, which is basically the old File Manager on steroids. But My Computer can quickly lead you to some important items such as Printers, Dial-up Networking, and the Control Panel. And some folks like the windowing approach that it uses. A good way to minimize all open windows and see the Desktop (and thus the My Computer icon) is to right-click on the clock in the Taskbar and choose Minimize All Windows. You can later choose Undo Minimize All to reverse the effect.

TIP   If you don't like seeing a new window for each folder you explore from My Computer, Choose View, then Options, and then Browse Folders Using a Single Window. When you're browsing through the directory tree, you can use the Backspace key to back up a level to a folder's parent.

When you are working with folder windows, you may want to turn on the toolbar or alter the way files and folders are displayed. Check out the View menu for these options. Choose Small Icons, List, or Details. The Details view is helpful when you're looking for a specific file or folder. It shows the sizes of files, the dates they were created, their types, and other information about the files.

Normally, files with certain filename extensions (the last three letters of a file's name) are hidden from display in your folder windows. For example, files with DLL, SYS, VXD, 386, DRV, and CPL extensions will not be listed. This way, your display isn't cluttered with essentially useless files that perform duties for the operating system but not directly for users. If you want to see all the files in a folder, open the View menu in the folder's window, choose Options, and select the File Types tab. Then turn on the appropriate checkbox option.

TIP If you've done a multi-boot install, remember that some programs require that you reinstall them under NT to get them to work correctly. You won't be able to just install them under, say Windows 95 in the Explorer or Find box, and then launch them by double-clicking from NT. You'll typically be told that some DLL files are missing and the program won't run. You must reinstall the program(s) in question, while running NT. The programs can actually be installed in the same directory they were in before (overwriting the old files), which will save you some disk space. The reinstallation process is necessary to get DLLs in the right directories and to update the NT Registry with details about the applications.

More about File Registration

As explained earlier, some documents will open when you double-click on their icons—whether those icons are in the Find box, a folder, File Manager, Explorer, or wherever. Only special documents do this—ones that are *registered*. NT has an internal registry (basically just a list) of filename extensions that it knows about. Each registered file type is matched with a program that it works with. When you double-click on any document, NT scans the list of registered file types to determine what it should do with it.

By default, filename extensions of registered files are not displayed on screen. This cuts down on visual clutter, letting you see simple names that make sense, such as 1995 Report instead of 1995 Report.wk3. You can change this by choosing Options from the View menu in Explorer or any folder window. If you choose to see filename extensions, it will be easier to change an extension. Sometimes, changing an extension can be useful, such as when you want to open a document with an application other than the normally registered one.

How Do File Types Become Registered?

You may be wondering how documents with certain extensions become registered so they will run an application when you double-click on them. Some types are set up by NT when you install it. For example, HLP files (such as paint.hlp) are Help files and will open up in an appropriate window. Likewise, TXT files will open in Notepad, PCX files in Paint, DOC files in WordPad, and so on.

In addition to those extensions that are automatically established when you install NT, some others might have been imported into your system from an earlier version of Windows. If you upgraded to NT 4.0 from NT 3.*x*, any previous associations will be migrated to the new version.

Some programs register their file type when you install the program. So, for example, when you install Word, NT changes the registration list so that DOC files will be opened by Word instead of by WordPad.

 NOTE   With NT, you can type the path to a file in the Run dialog box or on a command line, and if that file type is registered, NT will launch the appropriate program and open the document. For example, if you type the path to a Word document, ups.doc, in the Run dialog box, Word will fire up with the document. With Windows 95, if you want to open a text file, you would need to type "notepad foo.txt" in the Run dialog box. With NT, you simply type "foo.txt," and the system will figure out which program to use to open it.

Running DOS Programs

DOS applications are by no means the preponderant genre of PC programs being sold today, but they were for many years. Consequently, thousands of useful and interesting programs exist for the IBM PC DOS environment. Many of these programs are not easily replaced with popular Windows programs, simply because they are specialized programs, custom designed for vertical market uses such as point-of-sale, transaction processing, inventory, scientific data gathering, and so on. As a result, much of the code that was written five to ten years ago that ran in DOS programs is still doing its job in companies and other institutions today.

For these reasons, NT runs DOS programs. You can run a DOS program these ways:

- Click on the Start button, choose Programs, and look for the program on the submenus.

- Double-click on the program's name in a folder, Explorer, File Manager, or Find box.

- Click on Start, choose Run, enter the program's name into the Run box, and press Enter.

- Open a Command Prompt window (DOS session), type in the program's name at the DOS prompt, and press Enter.

- Double-click on a document file with an extension that you've manually associated with the DOS program.

The Command Prompt window in NT is not DOS, but rather a full 32-bit program that understands almost all the DOS commands, plus many more. You can even launch POSIX and Windows programs from this window. For information about available commands, simply type **Help** at the prompt and press Enter. Note that both short and long filenames are shown in this new version of DOS. Long filenames are in the rightmost column, with corresponding short filenames over on the left.

You also get the line-editing capabilities of the DOSKEY command built right in; you can repeat previous commands by pressing the up arrow, and you can edit the current command line with the arrow, Insert, and Delete keys before pressing the Enter key.

Adjusting the Command Prompt Window

While running a DOS session, there are several easy adjustments you can make (more complex adjustments are described in the next section), which are either cosmetic or actually affect the performance of the program. You make these changes from the Command Prompt window's Control menu (click on the little icon in the upper-left corner of the window). Just open that menu and choose Properties. You'll see the dialog box shown in Figure 2.1.

In the Properties dialog box, you can adjust these settings:

- Toggle the DOS session between full screen and windowed.

- Adjust the font and colors.

- Resize the DOS window.

- Set the number of command lines that will be buffered for later recall.

- Change the cursor size.

- Determine some details about cutting and pasting, and decide whether the DOS session should take over the computer's resources when in the foreground.

TIP   To quickly toggle a Command Prompt window between full screen and windowed, press Alt+Enter. Most DOS applications will run in a window. Some won't, however; you'll be advised if this is the case.

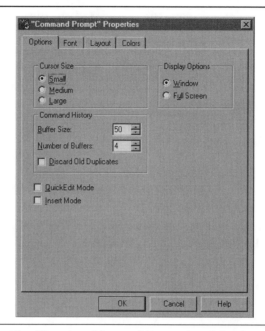

F I G U R E   2 . 1 :   The "Command Prompt" Properties dialog box lets you control some aspects of your DOS session.

Advanced DOS Session Settings

NT offers additional advanced settings for optimizing DOS applications running in the NT environment. They may be necessary for MS-DOS programs of various types—whether a traditional program, a pop-up program, or another type of TSR (terminate-and-stay resident) program.

Unlike Windows applications, DOS programs were designed to run one at a time, and they are usually memory hogs. They often need at least 640 KB of RAM, and some may require expanded or extended memory to perform well. Under Windows, when you switch from one running DOS program to another, intelligent memory reallocation is essential, or the DOS programs will hog precious system resources. Since DOS programs don't really "know" that other programs are running, they expect to have direct access to all the computer's resources, such as RAM, printer, communications ports, screen, and so on. In most cases, NT does pretty well at faking out the DOS program without your help, using various default settings and its own memory-management strategies. However, you may occasionally experience the ungracious shutting down of a program under NT with a message about attempts to corrupt "system integrity."

You may know that in previous versions of Windows, you could fine tune settings for a given DOS application by creating a PIF (Program Information File) for it. When you ran the PIF, the memory and other settings went into effect. In Windows 95 and NT 4.0, PIFs are replaced by Properties. The Properties dialog box for an MS-DOS program replaces PIFEdit (PIF Editor). If you are accustomed to using a PIF with your DOS programs, you can continue doing so with NT 4.0, but the new approach is easier. A PIF is now created anytime you create a shortcut or modify the default properties of an MS-DOS program. From then on, those settings go into effect whenever you run the program from within NT.

What Do PIFs Do?

First off, PIFs are used only with DOS programs. PIFs are short files, typically 1 KB. They're stored on disk, usually in the same directory as the program or in the NT System directory (usually WINNT of the boot drive). The settings affect many aspects of the program's operation, such as the following:

- Filename and directory of the program

- File attributes

- Font and window size

- Directory that becomes active once a program starts

- Memory usage, including conventional, expanded, extended, and protected mode

- Multitasking priority levels

- Use of keyboard shortcut keys

- Foreground and background processing
- Toolbar display
- Program termination options

PIFs generally have the same first name as the program, but have PIF as the extension. Thus, the PIF for WordStar (WS.EXE) is typically named WS.PIF, although you can name it whatever you like.

Aside from the active directory, only directories listed in the search path (set up by your AUTOEXEC.BAT file) are examined for PIFs. If a PIF isn't found when a program is double-clicked, it won't be loaded. NT's default PIF settings are then used with the DOS program.

You can run a program directly from its PIF by clicking on the PIF file icon in a folder, Explorer, or a Find box. You can also add a PIF to the Start menu, or type its full name into the Run dialog box (as you would to run any program). Running directly from a PIF is useful when the PIF isn't in the current search path or when you have more than one PIF for a program, each with its own settings.

 NOTE   PIFs are one of two types of shortcut files. Shortcuts for Windows applications and documents are given the LNK extension. Only shortcuts for DOS applications actually are given the PIF extension. Even if you select to display MS-DOS extensions of all files (through the Options command on the View menu in Explorer or a folder), you won't see the PIF extension in listings. Use the Find utility to look for PIFs by extension, if you need to.

Making PIF Settings for a Program

Before you make PIF settings for a program, consider that there may be an easier approach: you can set some options on the fly from the Command Prompt window's Control menu, as explained earlier. Check there if the feature you want to change isn't among the advanced Properties settings.

To get to the more advanced settings, right-click on the DOS program's icon (EXE or COM file) and choose Properties. You'll see the Properties dialog box, as shown in Figure 2.2.

Editing the CONFIG.NT and AUTOEXEC.NT Files

You can also modify the configuration of the DOS environment by setting up two files that act much like CONFIG.SYS and AUTOEXEC.BAT do in normal DOS on a PC. These files are called CONFIG.NT and AUTOEXEC.NT. They're loaded when NT senses that you're running a DOS application.

When you run a DOS application, NT creates a DOS VDM (Virtual DOS Machine) by loading the DOS environment subsystem and sort of "booting up" DOS. In the process, it reads in settings from CONFIG.NT and AUTOEXEC.NT in the same way real DOS does when it boots. The only differences are the filenames and the file locations. In this case, the files are in the \SYSTEM32 directory (usually \WINNT\SYSTEM32 or \WINDOWS\ SYSTEM32) instead of the root directory.

By editing these two files, you can set up the DOS environment used by every DOS application. The great thing about this is that you can change the settings, and when you rerun a program, the new settings are read and put into effect. It's like rebooting DOS after fine tuning CONFIG.SYS and AUTOEXEC.BAT, only faster.

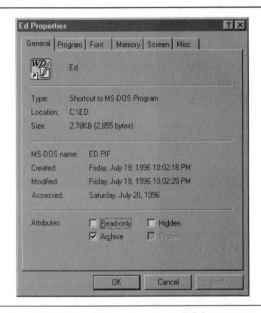

FIGURE 2.2: The Properties dialog box for a DOS program. These tab pages replace the old Windows NT 3.x PIF Editor. If you make changes to the default settings, a PIF for the program will be created.

 TIP   Although it might sound strange at first, you can set the properties for batch files, too. (A batch file is a group of commands that executes DOS commands in sequence for you, without you typing them in.) When the batch file is run from its PIF, all the settings come into play, and they will affect all the programs in the batch file.

Closing a Command Prompt Window

Enter the command **exit** when you're finished running non-Windows NT programs or executing DOS or other (such as NT) commands from a Command Prompt window. This will close the DOS window and end the session. If no DOS program is actually running, clicking on the DOS window's Close button will also end the DOS session. If a DOS program is running, you'll see a message prompting you to quit the DOS program first.

Task Switching

When you run a new program or open a folder, the Taskbar gets another button on it. Just click on a Taskbar button to switch tasks. Simply clicking on a button switches you to that program or folder.

For the first several programs, the buttons are long enough to read the names of the programs or folders. As you run more programs, the buttons automatically get shorter, so the names are truncated, like this:

You can resize the Taskbar to give it an extra line or two of buttons, if you want to see the full names. Just grab the upper edge of the Taskbar, as though it were a regular window you wanted to resize, and release. Position the cursor so that it turns into a double-headed arrow first, then drag it upwards. Here's a Taskbar with another line added:

Note that as you increase the size of the Taskbar, you decrease the effective size of your work area. To save space, you can set the Taskbar to disappear until you move the mouse pointer down to the bottom of the screen. This way, you sacrifice nothing in the way of screen real estate until you actually need the Taskbar. You do this via the Taskbar's Properties settings. Just right-click on an empty part of the Taskbar and choose Properties. Then set Auto Hide on.

If you prefer, you can also position the Taskbar on the right, left, or top of the screen. Just click on any part of the Taskbar other than a button, and then drag it to the edge of your choice.

If you are a habituated Windows 3.x user, you may prefer using Alt+Tab to switch between tasks. Each press of the this key combination will advance to the next task. Shift+Alt+Tab moves in the opposite direction. Note that the name of the program or folder is displayed at the bottom of the box, which is especially useful when choosing folders, since all folders look the same.

NOTE   In Windows 3.*x*, pressing Ctrl+Escape brought up the Task List. It does not do this in NT 4.0. Ctrl+Escape simply opens the Start menu, as though you clicked on the Start button. And don't try double-clicking on the Desktop, because this won't bring up the Task List either. You may want to see the Task Manager (essentially the Task List on steroids) to deal with a runaway or dead application, or check which processes are running. Right-click on the Taskbar and choose Task Manager to start it. The Task Manager is covered later in this Skill.

Shortcut Primer

In addition to Properties, a major new feature in NT 4.0 is *shortcuts*. Shortcuts are alias icons (icons that represent other icons). You can have them almost anywhere, such as in folders or on the NT Desktop. Because a shortcut is really only a link or pointer to the real file or application it represents, you can create as many as you want without fear of duplicating your data or executable files unnecessarily. You just create aliases for them. So, for example, you can have shortcuts to all your favorite programs right on the Desktop while still keeping the programs' executables in their rightful folders. Then you can run them from there, without needing to click on the Start button, walk through the Program menus, and so on.

The trick is knowing how to create shortcuts. Then you need to know how to cut, copy, and paste shortcuts, and how to place them in the Start button groupings so they are right there on the first menu you see when you click on Start.

TIP   A quick way to modify the contents of the Start button menus is to right-click on the Start button and choose Explore.

Adding Shortcuts to the Start Button Menu

The first place you'll want to drop shortcuts is on the Start button menu, so you can easily run the programs you use most. For example, as an administrator, you might run the same utilities day in and out. Cruising through all of the cascading menus from the Start menu is a hassle. So instead, you can drag documents and applications right to the Start button's first menu level. True, you can put your programs, folders, and documents right on the Desktop, and just double-click on them to use them. But sometimes it's a hassle to get back to the Desktop, particularly when it's obscured by whatever windows you might have open. The Start menu shown here is an example of one with added shortcuts.

As with most operations in Windows, there are several ways to add items to the Start menu. The easiest is to locate the document or executable file (EXE, COM, BAT, or CMD) and drag it to the Start button. When the file is positioned over the button, a little arrow appears under the icon to let you know that you're creating a shortcut.

Another way to manage the items on the Start menu—rearrange them, delete existing ones, and add new items—is through the Taskbar's Settings dialog box. From the Start menu, choose Settings, then Task Bar. Click on the Start Menu tab, which includes options for adding and removing items from the Start menu.

Clicking on Advanced brings up the whole hierarchy of programs in a two-paned "File Manageresque" arrangement. You can drag, drop, and select multiple items; right-click on things; and cut, copy, or paste them at will.

Broken Shortcuts

Unlike on the Mac or in OS/2, NT shortcuts can be broken fairly easily. If you move the actual item to another drive or computer on the LAN, the operating system doesn't update the alias. Double-clicking on the shortcut results in a message like the one shown here.

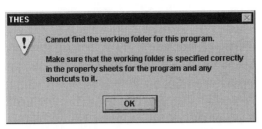

In some cases, NT will scan your computer looking for the item—a gracious gesture—and repair the pointer successfully. Other times, it won't succeed. There will no doubt be times when you'll want to remove an item from one of your Start button menus, such as when you've removed a program or no longer use it often enough to warrant its existence on the menu.

You can examine or repair a shortcut by displaying it with Explorer, right-clicking on it, and choosing Properties. Or you can delete it and create a new one—perhaps a more efficient method.

NOTE   In case you're wondering where the Start button shortcuts are and how the groupings are organized, here's how it works. This whole menu thing is based on directories, with LNK (link) files for the shortcuts. Check out the directory structure under this path: \winnt\profiles\administrator\start menu\. You'll find directories that correspond to each menu, with LNK files for each shortcut. Each user on the server will have a directory under Profiles, which contains that user's Start menu settings.

It's important for Unix and Mac folks to understand that Windows shortcuts are *not* soft links (Unix) or aliases (Mac). In many cases, the file system will *not* recognize a shortcut to a folder as a valid path. For example, consider a directory c:\users, which contains the directories default, alice, and bob. A shortcut to the folder c:\users\bob is created in Alice's directory as c:\users\alice\shortcut.lnk. The file c:\users\bob\text.doc *cannot* be opened by typing c:\users\alice\shortcut\text.doc. The shortcut to Bob's folder does not act like a folder, as a Unix soft link or Mac alias would; it's a file. Windows programs will see it as such and probably won't open it. And unlike Mac aliases, shortcuts to files on remote volumes don't work unless the remote server volume is already mounted.

Working with Files and Folders

By now, you get the idea about the NT folder system. You know that folders are, technically speaking, disk directories, and that directories hold files (programs and documents are the main two types of files) and subdirectories.

Of course, being a system administrator type, you also know that you need to keep your files organized systematically, in folders. Now in addition to the normal folders, you have the Desktop to play with. Actually, the Desktop is a folder under the \winnt\profiles directory.

There are a few more things to know about how the folder system works. Here, we'll cover these topics:

- Making new folders

- Copying and moving items between folders

- Deleting items, including folders

- Putting items on the Desktop

- Copying files to and from floppy disks

- Setting viewing options for folders

- Checking the trashcan folder

WARNING   **Be careful not to put a lot of important work in folders within Desktop folders. Why? Suppose you decide to erase the winnt directory to do a fresh install. You'll lose everything on each user's Desktop. For this reason, you might consider keeping your work in directories below the user directory, rather than below the winnt directory.**

Organizing files was a bit difficult with the Windows 3.*x* interface. You really had to understand how to use the File Manager to create new directories, move files around, rename them, erase them, and so on. With NT, you have two file-management choices: the folder system and Explorer. The folder system is more Mac-like. Explorer is more File Manager-like. You choose. Either way works, and the techniques are much the same.

Once you have the basics of the folder system or Explorer under your belt, working with your files and folders is a piece of cake. As mentioned earlier, since everything in NT's new interface is object-oriented, you just drag, drop, cut, copy, and paste objects where you want them. It's straightforward.

Making New Folders

If you need to create a new folder, first get the destination location in view. It may be the Desktop or it might be another folder, either on the local computer or on another computer. You can use Explorer, Network Neighborhood, or My Computer to browse to the destination. Once there, right-click in the destination location and choose New, then Folder. A new folder appears, called New Folder. Its name is highlighted and ready for editing. Whatever you type will replace the current name.

Moving and Copying Items

The techniques for moving and copying folders are important because they are the basis for managing all your NT objects—shortcuts, files, documents, executables, folders, and so on—within NT.

Let's say you want to pull several of your existing Desktop folders into a single new folder to reduce clutter. It's as simple as dragging and dropping. Begin by opening the destination folder's window. (Actually you don't even need to open the destination folder, but what you're about to do is more graphically understandable with that folder open.) Then size and position the destination folder's window so you can see the folder(s) you want to put in it. Now you can drag folders from the Desktop inside the perimeter of the destination folder's window. Figure 2.3 illustrates the process.

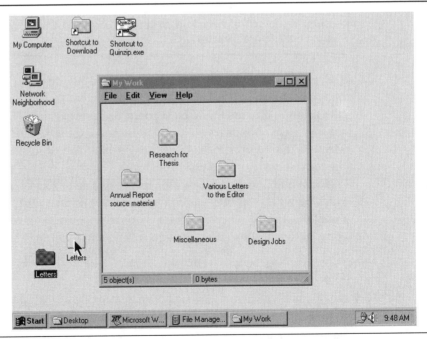

FIGURE 2.3: Working with folder windows and objects is as simple as dragging and dropping. Rearranging your work is as simple as organizing your desk drawer.

You can drag and drop most objects in NT using this same scheme. Every effort has gone into designing a uniform approach for manipulating objects on your screen. In general, if you want something placed somewhere else, you can drag it from the source to the destination.

About Moving versus Copying

When you drag an item from one location to another, NT does its best to figure out if you intend to copy it or move it. The general rule about moving versus copying is simple. When you move something by dragging, the mouse pointer keeps the shape of the moved object, as in the top example shown here. But when you copy, the cursor takes on a + sign, as in the bottom example shown here. To switch between copying and moving, press the Ctrl key as you drag. In general, holding down the Ctrl key causes a copy to be made. The + sign will show up in the icon, so you know you're making a copy.

 **WARNING** When dragging and dropping, be careful where you are aiming before you release the mouse button. If you drop an object too close to another object (or on top of it), it can be placed *inside* of that object. For example, when moving folders around, or even repositioning them on the Desktop, watch that a neighboring folder doesn't become highlighted. If something other than the object you're moving becomes highlighted, that means it has become the target for the object. If you release at that time, your object will go inside the target. If you accidentally do this, just open the target and drag the object out again, or click on *any* folder window's Edit menu and choose Undo.

If you just can't remember whether to use Ctrl, Shift, or Alt, no problem. Here's a great little trick. The easiest way to fully control what's going to happen when you drag an item around—from folder to folder, to and from the Desktop, within the Explorer, from the Find box, and so on—is to right-click drag (just use the right mouse button when you drag). When you drop the object, you'll see a pop-up menu of choices, similar to the one shown here.

Selecting a number of objects can be useful when you want to move, copy, delete, or make shortcuts out of them in one fell swoop. Just draw a box around multiple items to select them (start in the upper left and drag down to the lower right). Once objects are selected as a group, you can then drag them or right-click and choose a command. All the selected items will be affected.

WARNING Many "big time" programs, like those in Microsoft Office, Borland's office suite, database packages, and communications packages, are "installed" into NT. Almost any program that you actually install with an Install or Setup program will register itself with NT, indicating its location on the hard disk. Such files typically don't like to be moved around. Moving the program around after that (actually copying it rather than creating shortcuts that point to it) will bollix up something somewhere, unless the program actually comes with a utility program for relocating it. The bottom line? Use caution when relocating executable files.

Deleting Items

Of course, there will be times when you'll want to delete items, such as that old report from last year or all those old GIF or TIF files that take up so much space on your hard disk. Regular file deletion is very important if you don't want to become like everyone else—strapped for disk space. This is especially imperative on servers. You should know how to delete files and folders. As with moving and copying, the same deletion techniques apply to other objects (such as printers and fax machines) as well, because all objects are treated much the same way, regardless of their type or utility.

NT has a trashcan (much like the Mac) that lets you recover stuff you accidentally delete—until you empty the trash, that is. It's called the Recycle Bin. When you delete something (except from an external drive such as a floppy, or on another computer), that's where it goes. Before deleting an item, you're prompted to confirm your action. There is no way around this other than by dragging something directly into the Recycle Bin.

If you realize you made a mistake after you've confirmed a deletion, just open the Recycle Bin, find the item you want to reclaim, and choose Restore. That's about it. You can find the Recycle Bin on the Desktop or in the Explorer, down at the bottom of the directory tree. The Recycle Bin is a hidden system resource (one for each hard disk on each computer). Good luck finding it in File Manager or as a folder. The only way I know to find it in NT is via the icon itself.

NOTE In Windows 95, the Recycle Bin is only one level deep. It doesn't store or display deleted folders. When you delete a folder in Windows 95, the folder's contents are dumped individually into the Recycle Bin, appearing as files. Trying to retrieve the folder is a hassle, because it doesn't appear as a single entity. In NT, this isn't the case. It's easy to restore a whole folder since you can see it.

Emptying the Recycle Bin

Once in a while, you will want to empty the Recycle Bin. You've probably already noticed the command that empties the Recycle Bin, since it's on the File menu. But the easiest way to empty the trash is to clear the Desktop (by right-clicking on an empty portion of the Taskbar), then right-click on the Recycle Bin and choose Empty Recycle Bin.

When you want to free some disk space and are sure that all the contents of the Recycle Bin can be dispensed with, go ahead and empty it. It's always a good idea to have plenty of free disk space for NT Server (in fact, you should have as much available disk space as possible!). Regularly emptying the trash, just like at home, is a good practice.

 TIP   The Recycle Bin has a few properties worth noting by system administrators. Be sure to right-click on it at some point and check them out. Most notable is the amount of the disk that is dedicated to trash.

Copying Files and Folders to and from Floppy Disks

As you might expect, there are a number of ways to copy files to and from floppies. You can use any of these paths:

- My Computer
- Explorer
- File Manager
- Command Prompt window
- Right-click menu (choose Send To, then Floppy Disk)

Explorer is the choice of most experienced NT users. Unlike File Manager, Explorer shows the floppies on the same tree as the hard disks. Just scroll up to the top of the tree in the left pane and drag stuff to the floppy. If you prefer, open My Computer, double-click on the floppy drive, and you have a window showing the contents of the floppy. You can drag stuff in and out of the floppy from there.

Of course, you can resort to the old File Manager if you want. You can even run a DOS session (from the Command Prompt window, described earlier) and issue ye olde DOS commands, such as COPY, DIR, and DEL.

Note that when you drag a file to or from a floppy's window, NT assumes that you want to copy the file, not move it. (This is true of any external drive, such as a Syquest or a network drive, too.) For example, if you drag an item from the floppy's window to the Desktop, you'll be making a copy of the file and placing the copy on the Desktop. If you actually want to *move* the file rather than *copy* it, just hold down the Shift key while dragging, or use the right-click-drag approach.

When you replace one floppy diskette with another, the computer doesn't know about it automatically, as it does on the Mac. After you change the disk, the contents of an open floppy disk window will still be the same, even though the disk holds a completely different set of files. To update the contents of the floppy disk's window, press the F5 key. (This same technique is needed with File Manager and Explorer, incidentally, whenever you change a floppy.)

TIP   To see how much room is left on any disk drive, including a floppy, right-click on the drive's icon in My Computer or Explorer and choose Properties. You'll see a display of your disk's free and used space.

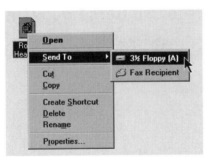

Realizing that people frequently wanted an easy way to copy a file or folder to a floppy disk, Microsoft provided a cute little shortcut to the interface that does this from almost anywhere. Just right-click on any file or folder icon that's on your Desktop—in a folder, networked shared folder, in the Find box, or wherever. Then choose the Send To option as shown here. Insert a floppy disk that has some free space on it, and choose the desired drive. The item will be copied to the drive you specify. Your choices on the Send To list depend on your computer's setup. You'll probably have at least one floppy destination, and possibly two.

NOTE   As you know, disks must be formatted before you can write to them. You format a floppy disk by inserting the diskette, right-clicking on the drive icon, and choosing Format. You'll see options for the drive. You can only format floppies as FAT drives, not NTFS.

The Send To option is very handy. Note that it can also send something to the Briefcase (a little program for helping you synchronize files between multiple computers) or to a mail recipient. You can even customize the Send To list, adding other destinations, such as for sending a file to a viewer program, to the Desktop, to a file compression program, to a network destination, and so on. Look for the Send To directory under \winnt\profiles. Put shortcuts into the directory, and they'll show up in the Send To list.

Using the Cut, Copy, and Paste Commands with Files and Folders

An interesting NT feature is its inclusion of the Cut, Copy, and Paste commands when browsing folders, files, and other objects (such as printers, fax machines, fonts, and so on). To a veteran Windows user, these commands don't make sense at first. You might wonder how *cutting* a file would differ from *deleting* it. However, once you know how these commands work, you may find them very useful.

As we mentioned earlier, the Desktop is a useful temporary storage medium when copying or moving objects between windows or folders. Having the Desktop available means you don't need to arrange *both* the source and destination windows on screen at once to make the transfer. Well, the Cut, Copy, and Paste commands do the same thing, without needing the Desktop.

Here's how it works:

1. When you want to copy a file or directory, simply click on it (or select multiple items by drawing a box around them). To select noncontiguous items, such as files in Details view in Explorer, hold down the Ctrl key and click on each object you want to select. To select a range of items, click on the first item you want to select, hold down the Shift key, and click on the last item you want to select.

2. Right-click and choose the appropriate command: Copy if you want to make a duplicate, Cut if you plan to move the item, or Delete if you want to send it to the Recycle Bin.

3. Adjust your screen so you can see the destination window, folder, Desktop, or wherever. Now right-click on the destination and choose Paste from the menu.

That's all there is to it. This is a powerful function. A great place to use it is in Explorer. Rather than first arranging your windows for a move by dragging (as you do in File Manager), just cut and paste.

Skill 2

NOTE   If when you go to paste, the Paste command is grayed out, this means you didn't properly cut or copy anything first. You must use the Cut or Copy commands on a file or other object *immediately* before using the Paste command, or it won't work. That is, if you go into, say, a word processor, and use the Cut or Copy commands there, then the Paste command as it applies to your files or other objects will be grayed out and won't work.

Administrative Tools

The NT 4.0 Start menu organizes a complex array of tools, which is great news for the system administrator. You need lots of tools to do your job, and organization is key to finding the right tool for the right job. NT helps out; most of the key system administration tools are organized under the Programs submenu of the Start menu, in the Administrative Tools (Common) submenu, shown here.

Because this menu is common, it will show up for each person that logs into the NT server console; that is, if you have physical access to the NT server, and you log in right at that machine locally, you'll get the Administrative Tools list. Remote users won't be able to get to these tools from their Start menu. This works pretty well, because in practice, the people with physical access to your server should be trusted server operators and administrators.

Let's take a look at each of the commands on the Administrative Tools menu.

Administrative Wizards

The Administrative Wizards command opens up a "dashboard" for the server administrator, which lists many common tasks, such as adding new users. Figure 2.4 shows the main Administrative Wizards window. When you click on one of the tasks, a scripted series of forms—a *wizard*, in Microsoft parlance—will guide you through the process.

As checklists, these wizards are great. You can use the wizards to perform the first couple of user installations, or to add your first printer. Running through them can be a good way to get a feel for the kind of information that you'll need to have organized before starting a task. For example, the Add User Account Wizard, shown in Figure 2.5, lets you know that you need a full name, user name, description, domain name, password, and other optional information for a new user.

However, once you're familiar with an administrative process, you will probably want to use the proper tool for the job, because you'll move more quickly and have more control over what you're doing. For example, you can use the User Manager for Domains tool to create and manage users.

FIGURE 2.4 : The Administrative Wizards window is the dashboard for administering your server.

TIP   You may want to go ahead and take a look at all the Administrative Wizards now. Be careful, and don't do anything on a real server until you know what you're doing, but mouse around in there.

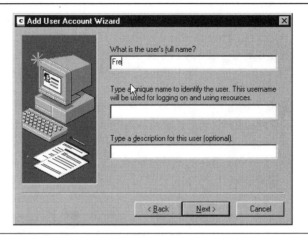

FIGURE 2.5 : The wizard for setting up new accounts on the server can help you remember to enter specific information about each user.

Backup

The Backup program lets you manage tape backups. You can select volumes for dumps to tape, or you can explore a tape to find files that you might want to restore. Figure 2.6 shows an example of the Drives and Tapes windows in this utility. We'll talk about using the Backup program in detail in Skill 11.

Domain Name Service Manager

The Domain Naming Service (DNS) is the network service that you use to map TCP/IP addresses to host names. DNS is a standard Internet service, so it is in common use on computers that use the TCP/IP Internet networking protocol. NT Server 4.0 includes a DNS server service, so your NT server can provide names to any TCP/IP client that needs to look up TCP/IP hosts.

You can manage every NT-based DNS server in your enterprise with one easy-to-use graphical tool, the DNS Manager. For the uninitiated, this sure beats standard Unix DNS administration! Even if you're experienced with Unix, having a DNS server service on an NT server (which can be managed remotely) gives you some interesting options. Figure 2.7 shows an example of a Server Statistics display in the Domain Name Service Manager window. We talk about DNS and the Domain Name Service Manager in Skill 8, and also in Skill 19, where we cover design considerations for Internet and intranet systems.

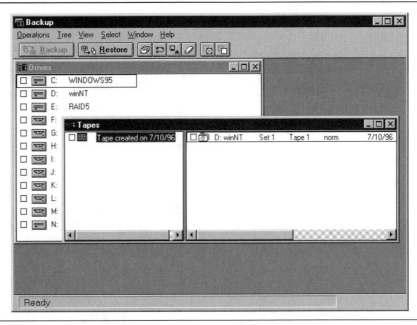

FIGURE 2.6: The Backup program takes some pain out of tape backups.

Event Viewer

As we've said, NT has support for auditing, and it logs system events as they occur. The Event Viewer allows you to look at the NT internal system logs. There are three main log areas:

- **System:** For events relating to the NT system services.

- **Security:** For events relating to access of system resources.

- **Application:** For events relating to high-level services, such as network backup or printer spooling.

The Event Viewer can be one of your primary troubleshooting tools. It's great for those next-day postmortem analyses. Since the events are logged, the Event Viewer can tell you what happened after the fact. Figure 2.8 shows an example of an Event Viewer window with a Security Log listing. We talk about using the Security Log and Event Viewer in Skill 13.

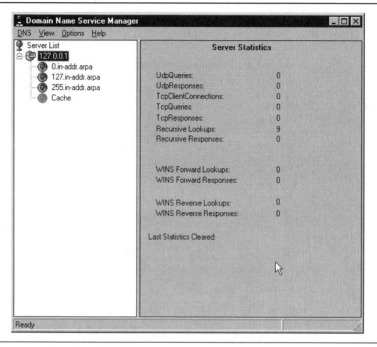

FIGURE 2.7: The Domain Name Service Manager is important for TCP/IP work.

Date	Time	Source	Category	Event	User	Computer
7/16/96	4:09:41 PM	Security	Detailed Tracking	592	boyd	FRANKENSTEIN
7/16/96	4:09:34 PM	Security	Detailed Tracking	593	boyd	FRANKENSTEIN
7/16/96	4:09:02 PM	Security	Detailed Tracking	593	boyd	FRANKENSTEIN
7/16/96	4:07:06 PM	Security	Detailed Tracking	593	boyd	FRANKENSTEIN
7/16/96	4:07:00 PM	Security	System Event	515	SYSTEM	FRANKENSTEIN
7/16/96	4:06:59 PM	Security	Detailed Tracking	592	boyd	FRANKENSTEIN
7/16/96	4:06:59 PM	Security	Logon/Logoff	529	SYSTEM	FRANKENSTEIN
7/16/96	4:06:57 PM	Security	System Event	515	SYSTEM	FRANKENSTEIN
7/16/96	4:06:36 PM	Security	Detailed Tracking	592	boyd	FRANKENSTEIN
7/16/96	4:06:33 PM	Security	Detailed Tracking	593	boyd	FRANKENSTEIN
7/16/96	4:05:35 PM	Security	Detailed Tracking	592	boyd	FRANKENSTEIN
7/16/96	4:04:48 PM	Security	Detailed Tracking	593	boyd	FRANKENSTEIN
7/16/96	4:04:36 PM	Security	Detailed Tracking	592	SYSTEM	FRANKENSTEIN
7/16/96	4:04:26 PM	Security	Detailed Tracking	593	SYSTEM	FRANKENSTEIN
7/16/96	4:04:05 PM	Security	Detailed Tracking	592	boyd	FRANKENSTEIN
7/16/96	4:00:57 PM	Security	Privilege Use	577	boyd	FRANKENSTEIN
7/16/96	4:00:34 PM	Security	Detailed Tracking	593	boyd	FRANKENSTEIN
7/16/96	3:49:18 PM	Security	Detailed Tracking	592	boyd	FRANKENSTEIN
7/16/96	3:48:28 PM	Security	Detailed Tracking	592	boyd	FRANKENSTEIN

FIGURE 2.8: The Event Viewer lets you see NT logs. This is an example of Security Log information.

License Manager

With the License Manager, you'll be able to track the client licenses for NT Server and BackOffice programs, such as Microsoft's SQL Server database. Microsoft requires that you purchase a license for each client that you want to connect to an NT server. This makes sense; you pay more for the servers that are used by more people. In practice, tracking software licenses can get to be a big headache. The License Manager can track the client licenses that are actually being used on every server in your enterprise, enabling you to make informed decisions about the nature and number of licenses to purchase. Figure 2.9 shows an example of a Purchase History window in the License Manager.

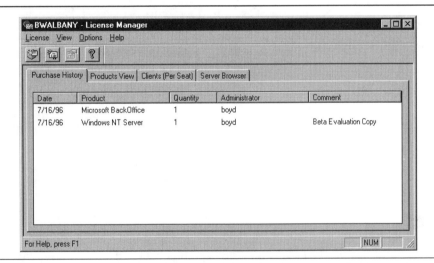

FIGURE 2.9: The License Manager helps you keep track of software licenses.

You can also set up licensing on your server in the Licensing Control Panel. We talk about this in detail in Skill 4.

NOTE   Microsoft has been working with other software vendors to standardize the tracking of software licenses on a network. This work comes out of Microsoft's Systems Management Server (SMS), which lets network administrators keep detailed tabs on their computer equipment inventory on the network ("Which programs are installed on the PCs in the Finance Department right now?"). The License Manager, now a standard part of NT Server, benefits from this work.

Migration Tools for NetWare

You tie one end of the Migration Tools for NetWare tool to a NetWare server, and you tie the other end to an NT server. You pull the chain to fire it up, the sparks fly, and BAM! Your NT server now has a bunch of user accounts, all filled in from the NetWare registry and ready to go.

There's at least a little NetWare LAN lurking in almost every company. It's no surprise that Microsoft wants to make it as easy as possible for you to purchase more NT servers, and fewer NetWare servers. But the reality is that Novell owns the market. Most NT servers will find themselves trying to live as good citizens within the context of a NetWare LAN. Migration Tools for NetWare makes it that much easier. Figure 2.10 shows an example of a Servers for Migration list in this tool. NT and NetWare interoperability is discussed in detail in Skill 16.

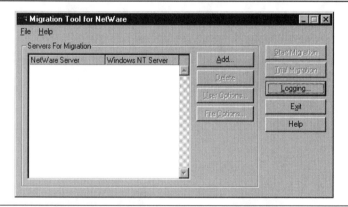

FIGURE 2.10: The Migration Tool for NetWare program is the key to integrating your server with a NetWare LAN.

Network Client Administrator

Windows for Workgroups and Windows 95 clients need some extra software enabled on them in order to be able to connect to your NT server. Normally, when you start up Windows 95, your computer just starts up, or it asks you for a password so it knows which Desktop to display. With the Network Client for Microsoft Networks software enabled on the computer, the user name and password that you enter at your Windows 95 computer can be granted access to your entire NT enterprise.

Use the Network Client Administrator to create installer floppies for the Network Client for Microsoft Networks software, or to create installer floppies for a version of the Windows NT Server administration tools that can be run under Windows 95 (User Manager for Domains and Server Manager only). Figure 2.11 shows the Network Client Administrator window. We discuss Windows clients for NT Server in Skill 14. (Macintosh clients don't use this software at all; they use a different method of connecting to NT servers, discussed in Skill 15.)

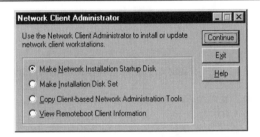

FIGURE 2.11: The Network Client Administrator lets you administer the Windows clients in an NT network.

Performance Monitor

Just as you use the Event Viewer the morning after the server crashed to review what went wrong, you use the Performance Monitor to see what's happening with your server in real time, right as it occurs. Think of the Event Viewer as the doctor writing your case up for your file, late at night. The Performance Monitor is that same doctor, taking your pulse and sticking...well, you get the picture.

Because of the Performance Monitor's immediate, real-time nature, you can see the performance counters change in response to server activity; and after a while, you can get a feel for what to look for and what to monitor. If you prefer to be proactive in your troubleshooting, the Performance Monitor can show you stuff in that trajectory, on its way to hit the fan. Plus, all those squiggly lines look exactly like a computer monitor should, as you can see in Figure 2.12.

Seriously, you can get some critical information about the health of every server on your network right in one place: in the Performance Monitor. We discuss the use of the Performance Monitor to identify performance bottlenecks in Skill 7.

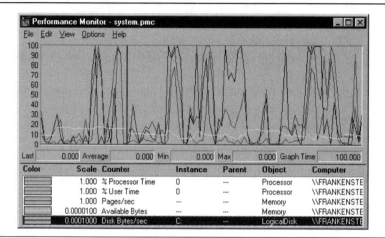

FIGURE 2.12: The Performance Monitor lets you see real-time activity on your server.

Remote Access Admin

Your NT server can be used as a dial-in server, enabling properly configured remote computers to dial up through a modem, ISDN, or X.25 connection and hop onto your network, just as if they were physically in the office. In this brave new world, where everybody's mom is starting a dial-up Internet access company, this concept should hold little mystery. It's just one more way that NT can be used to build flexible, useful networks.

The Remote Access Admin tool lets you manage the Remote Access Service on your server, keeping tabs on connections—who has dialed in, for how long, at what times, and at what speeds. Figure 2.13 shows an example of a Remote Access Admin dialog box for starting remote access to a server. We discuss this tool in Skills 8 and 19.

Server Manager

By now, you're getting the idea that NT has a great system for administering a network. The Server Manager tool lets you manage every NT server on your network (if you have the appropriate access privileges, of course).

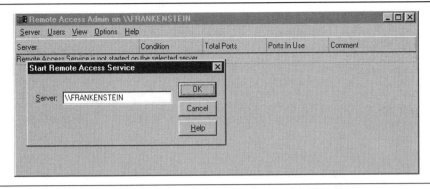

FIGURE 2.13: The Remote Access Admin tool lets you manage Remote Access Service on your computer.

The Server Manager displays a list of all the servers in your domain, as shown in Figure 2.14. When you double-click on a server in the list, that server's Server Control Panel appears, letting you manage file sharing and users connected to the server. You can manage the server's services remotely, so that you can stop and restart that cranky printer spooler, for example. And if you're running the Server Manager from an NT server that has the Services for Macintosh feature installed, you'll be able to administer all the NT-based Macintosh servers on your network, too. We discuss network server administration in Skill 13.

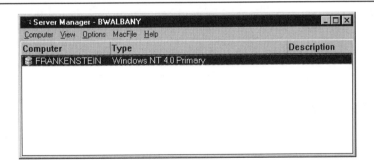

FIGURE 2.14: The Server Manager lets you manage every NT server on your network.

System Policy Editor

System Policies were introduced in Windows 95 as a way of managing complex, graphically rich network clients. Now that NT computers essentially share the same user interface, System Policies have found their way into NT.

Have you ever wished you could set a corporate standard for the contents of the Start menu? How would you like it if your network administrators' computers automatically configured themselves with a locking screen saver and distinctive background wallpaper? You could tell by glancing at the computer that the machine was a possible danger, and that danger would be minimized with the lock on the screen saver. You can set up all this kind of stuff and more with the System Policy Editor. Figure 2.15 shows an example of defaults set up in the System Policy Editor.

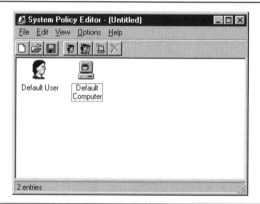

FIGURE 2.15: The System Policy Editor lets you manage standard configurations for your network.

User Manager for Domains

The User Manager for Domains is the tool you use to manage all of your users and groups on your NT Server network. You can create new users, change passwords, set the profiles, audit security, and set up groups with this tool.

Figure 2.16 shows an example of a User Manager window that lists the user name, full name, and description, as well as user group names and their descriptions. We talk about the User Manager in Skill 13.

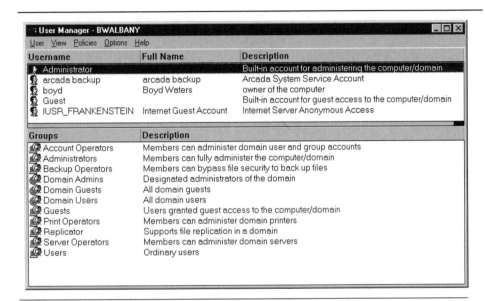

Figure 2.16: The User Manager for Domains tool lets you manage your network users and groups.

NT Server Diagnostics

The NT Diagnostics tool gives you a great deal of information about resource usage on your server. For example, you can get a listing of every DMA (direct memory access) line and every I/O port being used on your server.

With this tool, you can go a long way toward resolving hardware conflicts on your server or another server on the network. You can also get quick-and-dirty counts of memory utilization and network statistics. Figure 2.17 shows an example of Resources information in an NT Diagnostics window. We'll talk about the use of the NT Diagnostics tool for network troubleshooting in Skill 8.

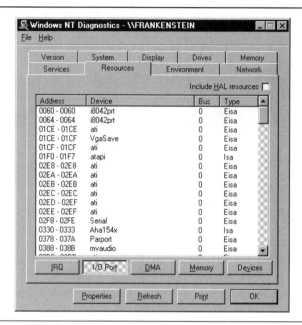

FIGURE 2.17: The NT Server Diagnostics program lets you see a lot of information about resource usage on your server.

The Task Manager

NT is a multitasking system, and lots of stuff is happening all the time. If you're trying to use an NT computer, and it's acting really slow for no apparent reason, it might be helpful to get a quick snapshot of everything that the server is doing. NT provides a tool that does just that: the Task Manager.

The Task Manager was originally conceived for use with Windows NT Workstation, where a user would be sitting at the computer for long periods of time, wondering why the computer is suddenly sluggish. But as a system administrator, you might find the Task Manager a great tool for getting a list of the active processes running on the server. In a pinch, you can even destroy processes that have gone berserk.

The Task Manager can't be used from the network; you can't kill a process on a remote server from your desktop computer using the Task Manager. But if you're at the console of an NT server, and you want an immediate measurement of memory and CPU load, simply right-click in the Taskbar and select Task Manager from the pop-up menu. You'll get answers, right away, without the need to resort to setting up counters in the Performance Monitor.

You can see all the programs that are running on the computer by clicking on the Applications tab in Task Manager. Figure 2.18 shows an example of this list.

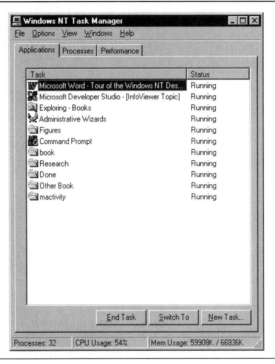

FIGURE 2.18: The Task Manager displays all the applications currently running.

TIP   Look for programs that have a status of "Not Responding." You'll probably need to kill these.

What's better, you can get an excruciatingly detailed listing of every process currently executing on the system. Click on the Processes tab to see a screen similar to the one shown in Figure 2.19.

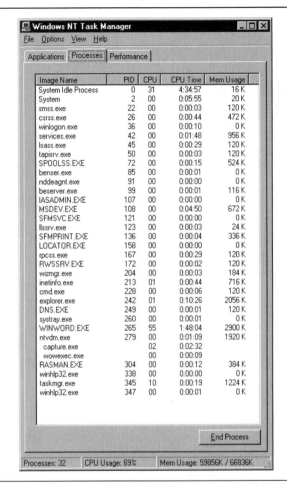

Image Name	PID	CPU	CPU Time	Mem Usage
System Idle Process	0	31	4:34:57	16 K
System	2	00	0:05:55	20 K
smss.exe	22	00	0:00:03	120 K
csrss.exe	26	00	0:00:44	472 K
winlogon.exe	36	00	0:00:10	0 K
services.exe	42	00	0:01:48	956 K
lsass.exe	45	00	0:00:29	120 K
tapisrv.exe	50	00	0:00:03	120 K
SPOOLSS.EXE	72	00	0:00:15	524 K
benser.exe	85	00	0:00:01	0 K
nddeagnt.exe	91	00	0:00:00	0 K
beserver.exe	99	00	0:00:01	116 K
IASADMIN.EXE	107	00	0:00:00	0 K
MSDEV.EXE	108	00	0:04:50	672 K
SFMSVC.EXE	121	00	0:00:00	0 K
llssrv.exe	123	00	0:00:03	24 K
SFMPRINT.EXE	136	00	0:00:04	336 K
LOCATOR.EXE	158	00	0:00:00	0 K
rpcss.exe	167	00	0:00:29	120 K
RWSSRV.EXE	172	00	0:00:02	120 K
wizmgr.exe	204	00	0:00:03	184 K
inetinfo.exe	213	01	0:00:44	716 K
cmd.exe	228	00	0:00:06	120 K
explorer.exe	242	01	0:10:26	2056 K
DNS.EXE	249	00	0:00:01	120 K
systray.exe	260	00	0:00:01	0 K
WINWORD.EXE	265	55	1:48:04	2900 K
ntvdm.exe	279	00	0:01:09	1920 K
capture.exe		02	0:02:32	
wowexec.exe		00	0:00:09	
RASMAN.EXE	304	00	0:00:12	384 K
winhlp32.exe	338	00	0:00:00	0 K
taskmgr.exe	345	10	0:00:19	1224 K
winhlp32.exe	347	00	0:00:01	0 K

Processes: 32   CPU Usage: 69%   Mem Usage: 59856K / 66836K

FIGURE 2.19: The Task Manager can even display all the "processes" that are running in the machine, including elements of the NT operating system as well as programs.

TIP   Look for processes that are swallowing large chunks of memory and CPU time. You can click on the CPU heading to sort by percentage of CPU time, and you can click on the Mem Usage Heading to sort by process memory utilitzation.

Exiting NT Server

Exiting NT properly is very important. You can lose your work, lose work of others who are logged in to your server, or otherwise foul up the NT Registry or other settings if you don't shut down NT correctly before turning off your computer.

To exit NT properly, choose Shut Down from the Start menu. Switch to the Program Manager window and double-click on its Control box. You will be asked whether you want to shut down the computer, restart the computer, or log on as a different user. But before you do this, you should warn users who are using resources on your server that you are about to shut down.

Are You Experienced?

Now you can...

- ☑ run Windows and DOS applications from the Desktop
- ☑ adjust the settings for running a DOS session
- ☑ switch between tasks using the Taskbar or keyboard
- ☑ add shortcuts to the Start button menu
- ☑ create, move, and copy folders to organize your files
- ☑ find all of NT Server's main tools for system administration on the Administrative Tools menu

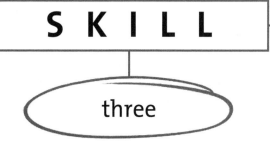

S K I L L

three

Understanding the Anatomy of NT Server 4

3

In Skill 1, we talked quite a bit about NT Server's advanced technology. Here, you'll learn how NT delivers these features, so that you'll be able to understand how NT gets the job done. Armed with this knowledge, you'll be able to make better design decisions (how much memory do I need?) and to troubleshoot problems more effectively (why is my server slowing down?). In short, this is really good stuff to know.

First, we'll take a look at the basic software model under NT: the concept of processes and threads. NT is, after all, a piece of software, so this is a good place to start. Once we review the fundamental building blocks of a program running under NT, we'll take NT apart and see how the various processes that compose NT work together.

The Big Picture

What anatomy course would be complete without a lurid, colorful diagram of the whole thing, in all its gloriously hopeless complexity? Well, take a look at Figure 3.1.

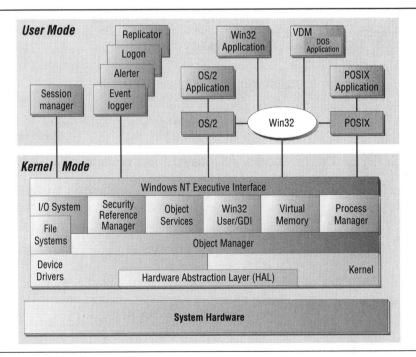

FIGURE 3.1: NT is a complex system comprised of many cooperating software subsystems.

We'll take care of most of these pretty quickly, starting at the lower levels, and working our way up.

Processes and Threads

The first thing you notice about the diagram is how many little boxes there are. What are those boxes, anyway? Most of them are subsystem *processes*.

At the most fundamental level, NT uses a software design to protect subsystems from one another. These subsystem boundaries are defined by processes. All NT software (including NT itself) is made up of a series of processes, which in turn is composed of a collection of *threads*. So we'll talk about processes and threads first. The main things to keep in mind is that *processes* own system resources, and *threads* perform tasks.

Processes: Thread and Storage Management

Processes are collections of system resources that get a particular job done. A process is made up of threads and their associated storage. My word processor, with all of its watching-me-type and correcting-my-spelling threads and memory storage, is one process.

The system keeps track of which memory belongs to which process, so that one process's threads are not allowed to manipulate the memory of another's. Generally speaking, one process may not be aware that any other process is running on the system, because it cannot see any other process's memory.

When a process needs to do something, it creates a thread to do it, and requests more memory from the system to allocate to that thread. When a process terminates, all of the threads in that process go away, and the RAM storage is made available for something else.

Threads Are the Computer's Trains of Thought

A thread is a continuous stream of computer instructions that performs a specific function. In my word processor right now, one thread is blinking the cursor, while another thread is watching me type, while another is looking up words in a dictionary to make sure that I don't misspell anything.

In order for a thread to execute, it needs two things: *system time* and *system space*. The thread must be able to grab the system CPU long enough to move forward a bit, and it needs storage space—a place to keep its data.

When lots of threads are running pell-mell through your computer, a couple of interesting problems need to be solved:

- Each thread must be given enough system time and space to run.

- Threads must be kept from stomping on one another.

To solve these two problems, the following parts of NT work together:

- **Process Manager:** Creates and destroys threads.

- **Kernel:** Allocates CPU time to threads. Threads are *scheduled* for execution.

- **Virtual Memory Manager:** Allocates space for threads.

- **Security Reference Monitor:** Ensures that threads do not interfere with one another's storage by making sure that each access to memory is authorized.

 NOTE   Usually, when a process terminates, the threads associated with that process go away. However, it's possible for one process to refer to another process's threads. In fact, this is how OLE works: one program calling another one's functions, asking its threads to do something. The system keeps track of thread references and does not terminate a thread until nothing is using it.

You Unix folks might be thinking of parent and child processes at this point. Nope. Within NT, there is no concept of a hierarchy of processes. Processes are certainly able to spawn other processes in order to get work done, but when the original process terminates, the other spawned processes are not automatically terminated. However, the POSIX subsystem will maintain a record of process-hierarchy relationships "by hand," and POSIX applications that spawn processes will have those processes terminated when the parent process exits. But the POSIX subsystem doesn't get much help from the NT Process Manager to accomplish this tracking.

How NT Allocates Process Memory

A process is in charge of its storage. When a process is started, the system hands it some memory that it can use. When a process starts under NT, it's able to access about 2 GB of memory of its own. The process accesses a particular piece of data in this chunk of memory by looking at that data's *memory address*. The set of all memory addresses that a process can look at is called that process's *address space*.

In NT, each process gets a 4 GB address space. All this means is that a process has a choice of 4,294,967,296 distinct bytes it can look at. It does *not* mean that you need 4 GB of RAM to start a process! Almost all of those locations (those addresses) don't point to any actual RAM storage at all.

In the United States, we have ten-digit phone numbers. One valid phone number is 800-555-1212. There are 10,000,000,000 distinct phone numbers that are possible—ten billion of them! But there are only millions of phone numbers. Most phone numbers have not been assigned yet. The "phone number space" is much larger than the set of all real phone numbers. It's the same with NT: Each process's address space is far larger than its actual memory requirements.

Earlier, I said that a process gets 2 GB of its very own, inside a 4 GB address space. What happened to the other 2 GB? The upper half of the process address space, the top 2 GB, is where the NT system is loaded, and the process cannot touch it. So when all the protected memory is taken into account, an NT process has 4 GB: 2 GB–2×64 KB = 2,147,352,576 bytes of storage available. This is illustrated in Figure 3.2.

Some phone numbers are invalid. Try calling 000-000-0000 sometime. You'll get a message asking you what you're trying to do. It's the same with NT. One of the most common mistakes that happens in programming is using data before it has been assigned to anything. If that (null) data is used as a memory address, you'll end up looking at address 0 when you really intended to look at something real. To trap this mistake, NT makes the first 64 KB of storage in the address space invalid. For similar reasons, NT locks out addresses whose top or bottom halves are all ones.

Why not just lock out address 0? NT wants to trap if either of the pieces—the top half or the bottom half—is zero. If the bottom 64 KB is restricted, then NT can trap a reference to memory address 0000ABCD as invalid, because the top half of the address is zero, even if the bottom half is not. This kind of thing often happens when the processor is really confused, and is reading misaligned information. For example, in memory we have the following stream of numbers: ...0000ABD1FE0C0000... Say the program is supposed to start reading the data starting with the *A*, to read in a memory address of ABD1FE0C, but instead starts reading the data with the first *0*, by mistake getting 0000ABD1. NT won't let a process use this memory location.

Process Virtual Memory

When a process actually needs real storage, it asks the system to give it some. Now, with each process getting its own 4 GB address space, of which almost 2 GB is usable by that process, we can certainly see that there will be multiple processes out there trying to use memory address 00010ABC. So which process gets the "real" memory at that location?

FIGURE 3.2: An NT process address space—the top 2 GB are reserved for use by the system.

When each process requests some memory, the system allocates some memory from the global system pool, which could be anywhere, and hands it to the process at a certain address in that process's address space. The actual bits might be physically stored on that first RAM chip on your system, which has a physical memory address of, for example, 000000BC, but the system will translate this memory into the process address space at a valid address, like 0001F012.

So somewhere, the system is keeping track of what physical memory is allocated to which process at what process address. Keeping track of all this is the task of the Virtual Memory Manager.

In addition to managing memory among the various processes, the Virtual Memory Manager uses disk storage to supplement physical RAM in a transparent fashion. As portions of memory become inactive, they are swapped out to disk, and then swapped back in again as needed. Typically, NT appears to have a memory capacity that's 150 to 300 percent of the physical RAM installed.

Multithreading and Multiprocessing

You can think about more than one thing at a time, and so can your computer, thanks to NT. NT allows multiple threads to run at the same time.

To support multithreading of processes, the NT kernel is in charge of deciding which thread is going to run, and for how long that thread will have the CPU. The thread might get pulled at any time. Only the kernel knows for sure. This is the crucial property of a *preemptive* multitasking system: The operating system is in charge of which process gets to run. Period.

Contrast this to a cooperative multitasking system, like Windows 3.1 or the Macintosh OS (System 7). These systems are able to run more than one program at a time, but only because each program in the system was explicitly instructed by its creators to periodically relinquish control of the computer, typically to wait for the next user-input event. Such an operating system depends on every program running to be well-behaved. If one program goes berserk, it might not ever give up control of the system. Your only alternative is to attempt to force the program to quit with the old three-finger salute (Ctrl+Alt+Delete).

In NT, a thread might sometimes need to run until it gets to a stopping place. If a thread is in charge of writing some data to a disk, for example, it might need to write a whole block of data before it can safely let go of the CPU. Such a thread is "locked," and the kernel won't kick it off the CPU until the critical operation is completed.

Therefore, the "multithreaded-ness" of a process depends on how that program's code was written and on what that process needs to do. There may be places in the code where threads are locked in a critical operation, or where a thread might be manipulating global data that all the other threads in the process need to access before they can run. Such places in the program are called "regions of the code that are not thread-safe." But fortunately, most areas of code written for NT are thread-safe.

With multithreading, we get multiprocessing for free. If your system has more than one CPU, the kernel will distribute threads among all available processors, so that your system with four CPUs will run four times faster (almost) than a single-CPU system. Generally speaking, there are no "multiprocessing" versions of the programs; NT takes care of it for you, invisibly.

 NOTE One could, of course, write two versions of a program: one that's okay for a single processor and one that's really optimized to run in parallel. NT does not prevent you from doing this.

Kernel Mode and User Mode

The second thing you notice about Figure 3.1 is that the subsystems are split up into two broad classes: user mode and kernel mode subsystems. Just as NT uses the software design of processes to protect subsystems from one another, NT makes use of the CPU hardware to absolutely protect critical subsystems from being harmed by less-critical systems or by user programs.

Computer processors support various modes of operation. *Kernel mode* refers to the most "liberal" mode that the processor provides: no memory location is kept from use, and the entire CPU instruction set is enabled. User mode is the least permissive mode that the CPU provides; memory access must be validated, and some CPU instructions may not be available at all.

Even though computer-chip manufacturers have been building multiple modes into their CPUs for more than a decade, microprocessor operating systems have typically used only the kernel mode. Everything in Windows 95, for example, runs in kernel mode on the Intel CPU. So any process might have unrestricted access to the hardware or to any memory location. Virus programmers love this. They hate NT.

 WARNING Each of the items in kernel mode shares this protected mode with all of the kernel mode items. So if, for example, a device driver crashes, kernel mode won't protect your system. However, the number of items that are in kernel mode is relatively small, and they are part of the NT distribution, which has been tested extensively.

In NT, the critical, low-level parts of NT upon which the rest of the system depends, like hardware control and memory management, run in kernel mode, and are considered part of the NT Executive.

The items in user mode are the higher-level subsystems that provide system services for executing programs. These high-level systems depend on the NT Executive services in order to operate; they are clients of the NT Executive server. The NT designers referred to this split as a client–server architecture, but not in any sense of networked distributed applications. Rather, they wanted to empha-size the fact that NT is a cooperating collection of systems, some of which are clients to the services of the others.

NT 4.0 is unusual in its kernel and user mode allocations. Most operating sys-tems (like VMS or Unix) run entirely in kernel mode. The NT designers took a look at the parts of the NT system that might crash without bringing the entire system down, and moved those less-critical items to user mode. So if the DOS environment goes down, the rest of the operating system will continue working. The DOS environment can't affect the NT Executive, because a user mode process is restricted by the computer hardware from manipulating the systems that oper-ate in kernel mode.

All this provides some very solid hardware-level protection for the core of the NT system.

Kernel Mode Systems

We've pretty much covered most of the NT Executive already, just by talking about processes, threads, and memory. But let's walk through each of the sys-tems, one by one. You'll notice how the processes are interrelated.

Object Manager

The Object Manager is one of the most fundamental of the Executive sub-systems. The Object Manager is responsible for managing the creation and destruction of system objects. System objects include the following types:

- **Event:** User input (like a mouse-moved message) or a signal from an appli-cation (like a disk-full message).

- **File:** A bit of data on a hard disk.

- **Thread:** The Process Manager uses the Object Manager to create and main-tain threads.

- **Mutex:** An object that indicates the execution status of a thread, helping a thread of execution to synchronize with other, dependent threads.

- **Named Pipe:** A connection from one process to another; a way for two processes to communicate.

- **File Mapping:** An object that offers a way to treat a file on the disk drive like RAM. This is a generalization of virtual memory, and another easy way for two processes to communicate. They create some shared storage as a file, and each of them maps this file into their address space. When one of the processes writes to a mapped memory address, the other process will instantly see that change in its own memory space at the same address. The Object Manager calls the Virtual Memory Manager to maintain these objects.

Once an object is created, the Object Manager keeps track of how often that object is referenced. For example, a File Mapping object might be used among ten different processes. We say that the "reference count" of that File Mapping object is 10. The Object Manager will keep track of the requests to release this object, and only when it has received such a request from all ten processes will it go ahead and delete the object.

Process Manager

The Process Manager creates new processes and assigns each one its own unique process ID. The Process Manager does not schedule the processes; it simply provides them upon request.

Kernel

The kernel is responsible for scheduling threads, keeping the system CPUs as busy as possible. When the kernel runs out of threads to feed the CPU, it schedules the *idle thread*, which does nothing.

Virtual Memory Manager

The Virtual Memory Manager is responsible for maintaining the address translation between physical storage (like RAM and the hard disk) and process address spaces. The Virtual Memory Manager also keeps track of which memory sections are actively used enough to stay in RAM, and which ones should be swapped out to disk.

Security Reference Monitor

The Security Reference Monitor, or SRM, verifies that other processes have permission to access the systems they are trying to get to. Perhaps the NT system diagram, shown earlier in this chapter, should have depicted the SRM as a huge squid, its tentacles wrapped around everything. Any time the Object Manager calls the Virtual Memory Manager, the SRM makes sure that's okay. Any time a process tries to signal another one through a named pipe, there's a security check.

I/O Manager

The I/O Manager takes care of input and output to the system via the communications ports. Your printer or modem data flows through the I/O Manager before getting out to the actual hardware. These data flows are in the form of I/O request packets, or IRPs. The communications application will probably talk to the NT Executive interface, which will in turn send an IRP to the I/O Manager, which will send a command to the appropriate device driver, which will talk to the I/O port, which will move the data in or out of your system—with access being validated all the way.

File Systems

File systems maintain the physical organization of data on the disks. NT supports installable file systems, which means that you're free to write your own, which will add to NT's functionality across the board. All other services must go through the file system service to get out to the disk, so as long as you've got a file system service that will read your hard disk, you're in business.

Currently, there are three major file systems supported by NT 4.0:

- FAT (File Allocation Table) file system, which is the same file system used by Windows 95

- NTFS (NT File System), which supports security and fault-tolerance

- CDFS (CD File System), which is used to access CD-ROMs written in the industry-standard ISO-9660 format

We'll talk about the use of each of these file systems in Skill 10.

Skill 3

Device Drivers

Device drivers interact with the hardware to get the job done. Device drivers exist for tape devices, sound cards, SCSI controllers, network interfaces, and other hardware.

Hardware Abstraction Layer

The Hardware Abstraction Layer, or HAL, is where a great deal of the low-level hardware particulars are dealt with. There are HALs that deal with single-processor systems, HALs that deal with multiple-processor systems, HALs that work around the Pentium floating-point error, and so on.

You almost never talk to your HAL. But when you're booting up NT, that friendly blue screen that you get before the log-on screen appears—that's HAL. Whenever your system crashes and you get the Blue Screen of Death, with pages of arcane process status information—that's HAL.

User Mode Environment Subsystems

The NT Executive provides all of the low-level computer operations support for the user-level subsystems that actually interact with the applications. This permits the NT team to write a variety of emulation modules, called Environment subsystems. These provide an operating environment that models a popular operating system, allowing NT to run programs that were originally intended for other operating systems! There are some limitations to what the non-Windows/DOS subsystems provide, but the functionality is there.

Let's take a look at how NT executes various types of applications.

THE CONTROVERSIAL USER/GDI MOVE IN NT 4.0

The design change that has caused the most controversy in the trade press is this: The Win32 User and GDI have been moved to the NT Executive with the release of NT 4.0.

The GDI, or Graphics Device Interface, is responsible for everything that you see on the screen: every pixel, every change, everything. It supports operations like drawing boxes, clipping regions, and off-screen bitmaps. This includes all the stuff you need to operate a bitmapped graphics display. The Win32 User subsystem is responsible for rendering windows on the screen. Think of it as at a little bit higher level than the GDI, with support for backing store, double-buffering, and the like.

You need the Win32 User and GDI to see stuff on the screen. There is no text-only mode to NT, as there is for DOS or Windows 95.

Now, from a reliability standpoint, the fewer things you have in kernel mode the better—to some extent. Anything that's in kernel mode is not restricted by the CPU hardware, so it can do anything it can get away with. So when folks learned that the NT design team had moved such a large subsystem as the GDI/User into kernel mode, they assumed that the integrity of NT must have been compromised.

Well, in theory, yes, but there's more to this story. It turns out that, in versions of NT prior to 4.0, although the Win32 subsystem was out there in user mode, the NT Executive depended upon it for much of its internal operation! So much for complete iron walls between user and kernel modes.

To prove this to yourself, you can perform the following experiment under Windows NT 3.51 if you have the Windows NT 3.51 Resource Kit. These steps will kill the Win32 subsystem, and crash you computer immediately.

WARNING: When I say this will crash your computer, I mean it. Don't do this on a production system. (Or you can just take my word for it and not do it on any system.)

There are two files that you need, which are distributed in the Windows NT 3.51 Resource Kit or the Win32 SDK. The first tool is located at \i386\kill.ex_ (or in the respective directory for your CPU's architecture).

You'll need to expand this utility to kill.exe, using the command shell's expand utility, in order to get it to run. The other tool you'll need is the special version of pview.exe, the Process Viewer, which is located on your ResKit CD in \perftool\meastool\pview.ex_. You'll need to expand this utility as well. Since kill.exe takes a pid for an argument, you'll need pview to get the pid for csrss.exe, which is the process name of the Win32 subsystem. You'll also need to use this special pview to give yourself permission to kill the csrss.exe process. Once you've done that, at the command prompt type **kill csrss.exe**, and watch your computer die!

Okay, enough fun…

Win32 Subsystem

The most significant of the Environment subsystems is the Win32 subsystem. The Win32 subsystem not only provides the operating environment for all applications written to the Windows 32 specification, but also manages all user input.

The other subsystems piggyback on the Win32 subsystem to receive user input from the keyboard or mouse.

With the migration of significant portions of the Win32 User and GDI to the NT Executive, the Win32 subsystem is not as big as it once was. Indeed, in many cases, the functions in the Win32 subsystem are simply pointers to the actual functions in the NT Executive.

MS DOS VDM

DOS programs launch into the Virtual DOS Machine, or VDM. Inside the VDM, the DOS program thinks it has an entire IBM PC to play with. Of course, lots of the hardware is not directly accessible, so programs like Norton Utilities won't run (since they try to access the hard disk directly). However, other aspects of DOS are faithfully emulated, including IRQ 21 services and other standard DOS hardware like the serial ports.

If a DOS program tries to access the hardware in the proper, well-behaved way, via DOS, and the user running the program has permission to use that hardware, then the program will run. For example, you can run some DOS communications packages on NT, and the modem dials just fine. The Gorillas game works beautifully under QuickBasic, with all the sound and the fury.

In our diagram in Figure 3.1 (shown earlier), we indicate just one DOS VDM. The VDM is itself a Win32 process, acting as a wrapper around the DOS program. By default, all DOS programs run on the *same* VDM process, so if one of them crashes, they all die.

WOW

WOW stands for Windows 16 on Win32. The WOW subsystem provides a complete Windows environment for 16-bit Windows applications. The WOW system works much like the DOS VDM, emulating an IBM PC inside NT.

You can instruct NT to fire up a separate WOW subsystem for a DOS program. This will permit the program to be preemptively multitasked, just like all other Win32 programs, at the expense of carrying around an entire extra virtual machine. If another DOS program crashes, your DOS program with its own VDM won't be affected. As shown in Figure 3.3, you can tell NT to create a separate instance of WOW for a 16-bit process by checking the Run in Separate Memory Space checkbox in the Run dialog box.

FIGURE 3.3: You can tell NT to create a separate instance of WOW for a 16-bit process by checking the Run in Separate Memory Space checkbox in the Run dialog box or on the Properties sheet for the executable file.

Realize that the DOS VDM and the WOW subsystems work on the RISC platforms, too—not just the Intel platform. In fact, on a fast DEC Alpha, the DOS programs really scream!

The significant new feature to NT Server 4.0 here is that the WOW and VDM systems now emulate an Intel 486 processor, so you can run programs like Visual Basic on your Alpha or MIPS-based NT box.

OS/2 Subsystem

The OS/2 subsystem is provided as a migration bridge for people with legacy OS/2 applications. The OS/2 subsystem provides support for only OS/2 1.*x* character-based applications. A Presentation Manager add-on for OS/2 1.*x* is available from Microsoft.

The OS/2 subsystem does not run OS/2 2.*x* or OS/2 Warp applications. With the support for the HPFS (High Performance File System) dropped in NT 4.0, the OS/2 subsystem seems of little real utility.

POSIX Subsystem

The big hassle about Unix is that there are too many "standards." The closest the Unix community has come to a pervasive standard is the POSIX set of function calls, which states that if a system supports a list of functions as defined in the POSIX specification, then POSIX applications should be able to run with a simple recompilation.

To that end, NT comes with a simple POSIX subsystem. Unix programs written to the POSIX.1 specification will recompile under NT with little problem, and will run under the POSIX subsystem.

 WARNING   Do not attempt to run POSIX programs against files on non-NTFS volumes. Bad things will happen.

A third-party vendor has released a more fully featured, POSIX.2 subsystem. Various companies have ported Unix toolkits for NT, which come with all the standard Unix command-line tools, like sh, ls, vi, and so on.

Are You Experienced?

Now you know...

- ☑ processes are collections of system resources for performing a particular job

- ☑ a process is made up of threads, which each perform a specific function

- ☑ NT's Process Manager, kernel, Virtual Memory Manager, and Security Reference Monitor work together to manage threads and allow multi-threading and multiprocessing

- ☑ the critical, low-level parts of NT, such as hardware control and memory management, run in kernel mode and are considered part of the NT Executive

- ☑ higher-level functions, such as the Explorer and print spooler, run in NT's user mode

Designing Your
NT Server

- ❑ Server software design
- ❑ Server CPU architecture
- ❑ Server memory requirements
- ❑ Server disk storage requirements
- ❑ Server hardware compatibility
- ❑ System component records

In this skill, you'll discover many of the design options available to you, and get started on making the right choices. You'll notice that most of the material is devoted to hardware issues. This is because it takes the rest of the book to really do the software justice.

You probably want to jump right in, but the best thing to do at this point is to study up, make all the decisions in the comfort and quiet safety of your own cube, on paper, before entering the wild fray of server setup and installation. You'll be making decisions that will require you to reinstall from scratch if you change your mind. So it's better to change your mind on paper, where it's easy, rather than go through the hassle of stripping your server down for the fifth time in a row. And it's cheaper to make a simple mark with your pencil on the design review than it is to order some hardware, unpack it, and then have to send it back.

Don't get too worried. You'll be up to your armpits in computer guts in just a moment. Anticipation makes it all the better.

NT Server Software Design

What do you want to do with your server? Once you have an idea about what role your NT server is going to play on your network, you'll be able to determine the nature of the software that will be required. And once you know which software will be running on your system, you can provide for the computing resource requirements with an adequate hardware design.

In the following sections, we'll deal with these questions:

- Which client licensing option should I choose for my server software?

- What role should my server play on the NT network?

- What services will my server provide to my users?

- What components of NT Server software will be required?

- What other software will I need?

Once you finish designing your server software, designing your hardware will be a snap. And your NT installation will be that much easier.

 **WARNING**   If you blow off the design of your server, you will die. Okay, maybe you won't die, but you will be sorry. Even if you're getting a server handed to you, ready to go, you'll have a chance to be the captain of your fate when it comes to the NT software setup. Server design is for everyone!

Which Client Licensing Option?

Every computer that connects to an NT server must have a license to do so from Microsoft. You have two choices when determining the number of client licenses to purchase: Per Server and Per Seat.

Per Server Licensing

With Per Server licensing, you can buy client licenses when you purchase the NT Server software, in effect buying a version of NT that will permit, say, 1000 simultaneous connections. This makes sense if you don't have a lot of control over the number of clients that are going to connect to the computer, if the clients do not otherwise have an NT client license, or if the connections are not permanent.

For example, you might opt for the Per Server licensing on a server in a company that has a Novell NetWare network, but needs a network application that's based on SQL Server and requires NT. Since you don't already have an NT network, your client licenses would get you access to only one computer—your NT box. And since the clients aren't using the server as a permanent-connection file server, you can probably get away with a smaller number of simultaneous licenses, rather than buy one license for each computer that is going to ever hit the server. In this particular example, it's unlikely that everyone will connect at the same time.

Per Seat Licensing

With Per Seat licensing, you may purchase a client license once for each client computer that needs to connect to NT servers. This makes sense if you've got lots of NT servers, and you're using them for file services. The computers that need the NT servers need them for long periods of time, so it's possible that everyone will be logged on to a server at the same time. Also, the client license is a right granted to the client computer, which means that it has a license to connect to an NT server, or any NT server on your network.

Skill 4

If you have many NT servers, or anticipate having many, you probably don't want to pay for lots of client licenses on each machine. Instead, just take care of it at one time, and purchase enough licenses for all your users.

What Role Should My NT Server Play?

This is a very critical question; you must know the answer before installing NT. NT servers can play three different roles in an NT network:

- Stand-alone server

- Primary domain controller

- Backup domain controller

Which of these roles your NT server is playing on the network determines a great deal of that server's core system behavior. For this reason, changing the role of an NT server requires that you reinstall the software from scratch! Since setting up a server is a complex task, you really don't want to do this more than necessary. Make sure you understand the implications of your decision about your server's network role. For a discussion of NT Server network roles, see Skill 13, which covers the basics of NT networking and security.

What Services Will My Server Provide?

Why are you purchasing your server? Is your server going to be a database server? Are you installing this server because your users need a central file server for their area? Or maybe you're installing the server to run that new order-entry system?

You can think of an NT server as a hard disk that happens to be in a remote location somewhere—a file server—or you can think of your server as a thing that can manipulate data in sophisticated ways in order to answer your questions—a compute or applications server. We talk about file and print services in Part 3, "Networking and Security." Using an NT server as an applications server is discussed in Part 4, "BackOffice and Internet Systems."

What Server Software Components Will Be Required?

NT is a modular server system, allowing you to add software components to expand the functionality of your server. You will want to install some of these components when you set up your NT server for the first time. Most services can be easily installed after the system is up and running. Your installation plan should take into account the services that are available with NT.

You might be surprised at the functionality that the NT Server package provides out of the box, with no further software purchase necessary. Here are some of the services that the standard NT Server 4.0 distribution provides:

- **Internet Information Server:** Turns any NT Server into a Web server. See Part 4, "BackOffice and Internet Systems."

- **Services for Macintosh:** Provides full interoperability with Macintosh networks, including AppleShare file services running on the NT server and print queue services. See Skill 15, which covers setting up Macintosh clients for NT Server.

- **Gateway Services for NetWare:** NT can integrate your Microsoft LAN Manager, Windows for Workgroups, and Windows NT networks with your Novell LAN, by acting as a gateway between the Microsoft and NetWare LAN environments. See Skill 16, which is about NetWare and NT interoperability.

Network Protocols

The network protocols supported by NT Server are components that can be installed independently of the core server software. While some higher-level services might require a particular network protocol, there's nothing about NT that will absolutely die if you don't install the NetBEUI stack, for example. There's no "native" or privileged protocol.

NOTE   See Skill 8, "Optimizing Your Network Design," to get an idea about the network protocols that are needed for different services.

What Other Software Will I Need?

Although you get a great deal of functionality out of the box, some pieces must be added separately:

- **Database systems:** If you are setting up your server to be a database server, you'll need to purchase one of the commercial database systems, such as Oracle, Sybase, or Microsoft SQL Server.

- **NetWare file and print services:** Full integration with Novell NetWare networks might require the File and Print for NetWare package, which is an add-on package available from Microsoft.

- **E-mail and groupware:** NT is a good choice for a platform for a Notes server or for Microsoft Exchange.

While it's impossible to enumerate the requirements of every different possible software server platform in this book, in the following hardware design section, we'll indicate some requirements for components of the Microsoft BackOffice suite to give you a starting place. Consult your software system vendors to get some real numbers for your system.

Server Software Design Worksheet

The best way to capture all the information about the NT Server software choices is to document your choices in a worksheet. You'll find those choices in Worksheet 4.1, complete with references to where you'll find more information.

NT Server Hardware Design

Consider the modern LAN server box. Believe it or not, even desktop PCs these days carry all the traits of the huge computers of just a few years ago. I mean, who thought they would be agonizing over how much level 2 cache to add to the motherboard? Strange to consider that one of my hard disks has four times the RAM on it—just on the disk controller card on the hard disk—than my most powerful computer of seven years ago had for system RAM. And so on.

These days, server systems designers are faced with choices about the various subsystems of their servers that were once only the realm of the main-frame acolytes. While the blaring magazine advertisements have made such terms as "Extended Data Out RAM" part of our vernacular, it's good to take a look at the design of a modern server, to make sure we understand how the pieces fit together.

WORKSHEET 4.1   Server Software Design

See Also	Software Design Decision	Choice
	Server licensing (choose one)	Per Seat Per Server
Skill 13	Network role (choose one)	PDC (Primary Domain Controller) BDC (Backup Domain Controller) Stand-Alone Server
	Are you installing optional components of NT Server?	Yes or No
	Are you installing the Exchange Client?	Yes or No
Skill 19	Are you installing Internet Information Server?	Yes or No
Skill 8 and Skill 13	Network protocols (circle all that apply)	NetBEUI IPX/SPX TCP/IP
	Other applications to be installed on this server (list all, e.g., Notes, SQL Server, SMS, etc.)	

Servers are essentially a CPU, the computer chip, moving data along the system bus between the disk storage system and the network interface. To make things work well, the system needs lots of fast local storage for data, operating system, and cache, so there's lots of RAM in there, too. Other communications ports, for modems and the like, might be indicated. And of course, in order to make the system work, you'll need a video controller, monitor, keyboard, and mouse. Here are the questions we're going to answer in the following sections:

- What kind of CPU should I use for my server application?
- How many CPUs should be in my server?
- What kind of system bus should I use for a server these days?

- How much RAM do I need?

- What's the difference between SIMMs, DIMMs, EDO, and all that?

- What kind of disk controller should I use?

- What kind of hard disks should I use?

- How much hard disk storage should I have?

- How many hard disks should I have?

- Do I need a CD-ROM drive?

- What kind of network interface do I need?

- What kind of video system should I have on a server? Do I care?

- What about the keyboard and mouse?

- What kind of serial ports do I want on my server? How many?

- What other components should I have?

What Kind of CPU?

NT gives you a choice of CPU architectures. At the time of this writing, NT supports Intel *x*86, DEC Alpha AXP, MIPS RISC, and PowerPC-based systems. Apple has announced support for NT Server on its server hardware line. DEC Alpha minicomputer clusters are running NT alongside OpenVMS. NCR/AT&T will sell you an Intel-based box about twice the size of my (large) refrigerator that sports 16 processors, all screaming along in parallel. It's a wild world of CPUs out there.

The Case for Intel

For most folks, the question boils down to Intel or non-Intel CPUs. There's no denying that sticking with an Intel-based server is generally considered a safe bet; a quick scan of the NT hardware compatibility list shows most device drivers available for Intel platforms. And so far, Intel has shown a stubborn tenacity when it comes to performance; the high-end Intel Pentium Pro CPUs are still holding their own against the mainstream RISC systems.

Intel 386

With the release of NT 4.0, the Intel 386 is no longer supported. Attempts to install NT 4.0 on an Intel 386 computer will fail.

Intel 486

The Intel 486 is showing its age, and is probably too slow for your server. You can breathe more life into an aging 486 server in two ways: add another processor, if your server supports a dual-CPU design, or add an OverDrive Pentium upgrade. (You won't be able to do both, because timing issues preclude the possibility of multiprocessing with OverDrive processors.) Neither of these options is really satisfactory, but if I had to choose, I would probably opt for the dual 486 if possible. Since NT is multitasking and multithreaded, you can see an almost-linear performance increase with the addition of a second processor.

But with Pentium systems so cheap these days, that nice 486 server is probably a good test machine, but not a great candidate for a production environment.

Pentium 60 and 66 MHz

The 60 MHz and 66 MHz are the first-generation Pentiums. They are 5-volt chips, and they dissipate a respectable amount of heat during operation. What's more, the first few of these chips to be released included a bug in some floating-point division code, providing a public-relations free-for-all when this model first appeared. NT can detect this bug (using the PENNT utility shown in Figure 4.1) and refuse to use the floating-point unit on the chip; but again, why settle for this when there are other cheap Pentiums out there?

Contemporary Pentiums: 75 MHz to 166 MHz

Systems built around these second-generation Pentium CPUs are generally pretty solid. If you have a choice of CPU speed, faster is better, of course. But beware—you also want to maximize your system bus speed, which is the speed at which the data moves through the computer. The system bus speeds of the Pentium chips are shown in Table 4.1.

You can see that a 133 MHz Pentium system should be faster than a 120 MHz system, with everything else being equal. But you might not notice much of a performance difference between a 133 MHz and a 150 MHz system, because the difference in processor speed is offset by the slower system bus. As always, testing is the best way to make these decisions.

Skill 4

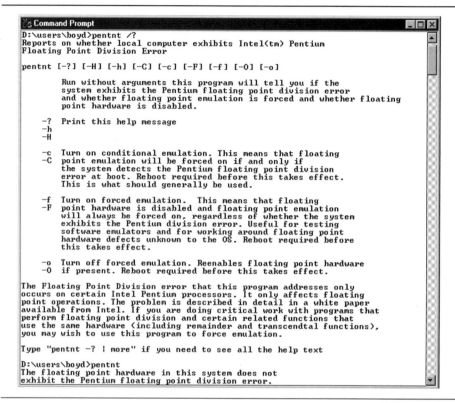

```
Command Prompt                                                    _ □ ×
D:\users\boyd>pentnt /?
Reports on whether local computer exhibits Intel(tm) Pentium
Floating Point Division Error

pentnt [-?] [-H] [-h] [-C] [-c] [-F] [-f] [-O] [-o]

          Run without arguments this program will tell you if the
          system exhibits the Pentium floating point division error
          and whether floating point emulation is forced and whether floating
          point hardware is disabled.

    -?    Print this help message
    -h
    -H

    -c    Turn on conditional emulation. This means that floating
    -C    point emulation will be forced on if and only if
          the system detects the Pentium floating point division
          error at boot. Reboot required before this takes effect.
          This is what should generally be used.

    -f    Turn on forced emulation.  This means that floating
    -F    point hardware is disabled and floating point emulation
          will always be forced on, regardless of whether the system
          exhibits the Pentium division error. Useful for testing
          software emulators and for working around floating point
          hardware defects unknown to the OS. Reboot required before
          this takes effect.

    -o    Turn off forced emulation. Reenables floating point hardware
    -O    if present. Reboot required before this takes effect.

The Floating Point Division error that this program addresses only
occurs on certain Intel Pentium processors. It only affects floating
point operations. The problem is described in detail in a white paper
available from Intel. If you are doing critical work with programs that
perform floating point division and certain related functions that
use the same hardware (including remainder and transcendtal functions),
you may wish to use this program to force emulation.

Type "pentnt -? | more" if you need to see all the help text

D:\users\boyd>pentnt
The floating point hardware in this system does not
exhibit the Pentium floating point division error.
```

FIGURE 4.1 : The PENTNT utility for dealing with the Pentium floating-point division error

TABLE 4.1 : System Bus Speed of Pentium Processors

Bus Speed	CPU Chips
50 MHz	75 MHz
60 MHz	90 MHz, 120 MHz, 150 MHz
66 MHz	100 MHz, 133 MHz, 166 MHz

Pentium Pro

The newest chip out from Intel, the Pentium Pro, is a nice piece of work. Although criticized because of its lack of significant performance gain over the high-end Pentium when running Windows 95, the Pentium Pro makes a great difference when running a real 32-bit operating system like NT.

The thing to look out for here is the size of the on-chip, level 2 cache. Chips with the more generous 512 KB level 2 cache are starting to appear, and they offer increased performance. For NT servers, the Pentium Pro makes a lot of sense.

The Case for Alpha

For the absolutely highest performance, the RISC systems may have something to offer over the Intel platforms. Microsoft's alliance with DEC shouldn't be ignored, and as we discussed in Skill 1, NT and DEC's VMS share some history. If you can afford it, those Alpha systems sure are nice, especially for those of us used to servers that have the heritage of the scaled-up PC. At the high end, the RISC systems share the heritage of the scaled-down mainframe, and the difference in design philosophy shows. Unfortunately, the quality evidenced in this design philosophy comes hand-in-hand with the legacy of proprietary hardware culture. They're getting much better, but there it is: High-end hardware is likely to be more proprietary and more difficult to obtain skilled support for.

There are currently two choices of Alpha CPUs: the 21064 and the 21164.

Alpha 21064

The Alpha AXP 21064 chip was the first of the Alpha chips in wide distribution. You can get some of these systems cheap these days, and they still run faster than many Pentium-based servers. The early models of these chips dissipated an amazing amount of heat during operation, so be sure you get a server system that has been engineered from the ground up for reliability and accommodation of excess heat. Skimping on the case, power supply, or cooling fans won't do.

Alpha 21164

The Alpha 21164 is a significant step forward for Alpha chips, offering parallel, speculative execution, out-of-order execution, and all sorts of other modern chip tricks to squeeze the maximum performance possible out of the silicon. These chips are fast. The 21164 also sports the on-chip level 2 cache, much like the Pentium Pro. For these reasons, the 21164 is significantly more powerful that its 21064 predecessor, and it tends to command the price premium to match.

The Case for Other RISC Architectures

The other RISC architectures besides the Alpha, the MIPS, and the PowerPC might be interesting choices, if you already have server hardware based on these

Skill 4

chips that matches the NT hardware compatibility list. But none of these types of systems have really taken off in the NT world as of yet.

The MIPS chip family was the first mainstream commercial RISC chip widely available. It showed tremendous promise when NT was first being developed, and it was the central CPU in an industry initiative called ACE (for Advanced Computing Environment). And then MIPS ran out of money and was bought by Silicon Graphics. The current crop of high-end MIPS chips are optimized for parallel processing of floating-point operations that most often occur in 3-D modeling. Their integer performance has not been as nifty. You might do well with a MIPS server, depending on your application, but most folks don't need lots of floating-point math in their servers. However, there are some beautiful computers being built based on MIPS, and the MIPS server story may be stronger by the time you read this.

The PowerPC-based computers are an unknown at the time of this writing. Certainly, virtually all Apple computers being shipped right now are PowerPC-based, so there are millions of them out there. Apple has started shipping PowerPC-based NT servers, based on a system that originally ran the AIX flavor of Unix. Apple's stellar reputation for brilliant industrial design is well-deserved, and these servers are really nice boxes. But price/performance versus a dual-processor Pentium Pro server? Hmm…

A Word About RISC and Software Compatibility

NT 4.0 includes an Intel 486 emulator for the RISC architectures, so that when the server is executing software that has not yet been ported to the RISC platform in question, the software will still run, thinking that it's operating on an Intel 486 computer! Of course, software emulation is always slower than the real thing on silicon, but it does work.

DEC is working on a more advanced Intel instruction execution scheme, which will examine Intel code and convert it to native code on the fly. The next time the code needs to be run, the converted, native code is run instead, so that the translation occurs only once. In effect, this new technology will recompile Intel code into native code and then store the native version on the hard disk, running it whenever it recognizes the need. This minimizes the amount of emulated code that needs to run.

With RISC chip performance being what it is, these emulation and translation schemes generally work out well. However, if for some reason you need to run lots of old Intel code on your server, consider the Intel systems for best performance and compatibility.

The take-home lesson from software 486 emulation and translation is that the RISC systems are not show stoppers, and they deserve consideration.

The Bottom Line: CPU Architecture

High-end Pentium and Pentium Pro systems are a solid bet, with the DEC Alpha 21164 systems leading in the performance race. Alpha 21064 systems offer a price-to-performance ratio that can't be beat right now. But this may all change. If you are concerned about performance, your best bet is to read the trade magazines and see what the tests say. Things change very quickly in the computer world.

How Many CPUs?

Up to a point, you can realize great benefits by adding CPUs to servers that support multiprocessing. You won't get twice the performance out of two processors that you get out of one, but you should see a significant performance difference. However, don't spend all your money on a quad-processor server and then end up skimping on the memory and network interface—you'll have done yourself no good.

We recommend purchasing a server system that can hold at least two, and preferably four, processors up front. If you don't anticipate a real CPU crunch, and it makes economic sense, just get the server with one CPU installed. If you find a need for more CPUs, you'll have the option of adding them later. Adding CPUs should be a relatively simple task. See Skill 7 for a discussion of when to add more CPU power.

 NOTE   You'll need to reinstall NT to take advantage of multiple CPUs after adding a CPU to a single-CPU system. As you recall from Skill 3, NT uses a different HAL for multiprocessing than for single-processor systems.

What Kind of System Bus?

The choices of system bus have gotten more and more diverse over the years. You now have a choice between ISA (Industry Standard Architecture), EISA (Extended Industry Standard Architecture), VLB (Video Local Bus), and PCI (Peripheral Component Interconnect). Oh, and don't forget IBM's MCA (Micro-Channel Architecture) used by IBM, NCR, and some other companies. These various bus architectures represent an evolution toward ever faster computer systems. See how they compare in Table 4.2.

TABLE 4.2 : System Bus Bandwidth

Bus Type	Bandwidth (MB/sec)	Comments
ISA	2.5	Lowest-common denominator
MCA	40	Proprietary, limited hardware availability
EISA	32	More standard than MCA, faster than ISA, not as fast as PCI
VLB	132	Good for video, bad for anything else
PCI	132	Fastest available

For the cards that count—network and disk controllers—PCI makes a great deal of sense. But the number of PCI slots is typically limited to three or four, and PCI is overkill for a serial port. This is why motherboard manufacturers build hybrid systems, typically ISA/PCI, so that there are a number of ISA slots and a few PCI slots.

Get a system with as many PCI slots as possible, with the rest of the slots as EISA, and you'll not go far wrong. Stay away from ISA/VLB motherboards for servers.

 WARNING Stay away from ISA systems in general, because you'll run into problems with them when you put more than 16 MB of RAM in them. And you're going to put a lot more memory than that in them!

How Much RAM?

The answer to this question is lots and lots and lots. NT will love you for it. Get lots of RAM. We deployed systems with 80 MB of RAM, and they could use more if we gave it to them. Get lots of RAM! It will pay off, as you'll see after you fill out Worksheet 4.2.

As an example, I hooked up 250 people to one of my NT servers. I thought that I would get 250 people hitting my server all the time, but when I measured it, I found that I had a maximum of 80 concurrent users, and typically only 75. I still haven't figured that one out, but there it is. Now, I'm running a SQL Server database on this machine, which I connected to Microsoft's Web server, the Internet Information Server. This is a DEC Alpha computer. What's a good, healthy figure for the RAM on this server? Take a look at the worked example in Worksheet 4.3 to see the numbers I came up with.

WORKSHEET 4.2   RAM Worksheet

Line	What	RAM Needed
1	Starting Point	64 MB
	User Requirements	
2	Number of concurrent users	
3	Total User RAM (512 KB × line 2)	MB
	BackOffice Requirements	
4	Internet Information Server: 16 MB	
5	SNA Server: 8 MB	
6	SMS: 20 MB	
7	Exchange: 16 MB	
8	SQL Server: 8 MB	
9	Total BackOffice RAM	MB
	Other Application Requirements	
10	Average RAM needed per application	
11	Number of other applications running	
12	Total Other Application RAM (line 10 × line 11)	MB
13	Subtotal (add lines 1, 3, 9, and 12)	MB
14	If RISC add 20%	
15	ESTIMATED TOTAL RAM NEEDED	MB

Skill 4

 TIP   Don't believe Microsoft's recommendations on sufficient NT Server RAM. Use at least 64 MB as a starting point and work upward from there, using the RAM worksheet (Worksheet 4.2).

W O R K S H E E T   4 . 3   RAM Worksheet Example

Line	What	RAM Needed
1	Starting Point	64 MB
	User Requirements	
2	Number of concurrent users	75 users
3	Total User RAM (512 KB × line 2)	37.5 MB
	BackOffice Requirements	
4	Internet Information Server: 16 MB	16 MB
5	SNA Server: 8 MB	
6	SMS: 20 MB	
7	Exchange: 16 MB	
8	SQL Server: 8 MB	8 MB
9	Total BackOffice RAM	24 MB
	Other Application Requirements	
10	Average RAM needed per application	1 MB
11	Number of other applications running	3
12	Total Other Application RAM (line 10 × line 11)	3 MB
13	Subtotal (add lines 1, 3, 9, and 12)	128.5 MB
14	If RISC add 20%	25.7 MB
15	ESTIMATED TOTAL RAM NEEDED	154 MB

This worksheet shows that I should ideally have 154 MB of RAM on the server! I would probably install ten 16 MB SIMMs, for a 160 MB total, keeping the numbers even.

The worksheet illustrates that you won't go wrong putting lots and lots of RAM in your server. At the other end of the scale, consider my test server, which typically has one or two concurrent users and 32 MB of RAM, which is plenty enough—if you believe Microsoft. Don't! Using Performance Monitor, I see that my server often starts to thrash, especially when I start routing networks with the routing software built into NT. It often spends all of its time swapping memory pages, for hundreds of thousand of milliseconds at a time.

You don't want your server to swap too much. Your best bet is to measure your server, and keep an eye on memory utilization. Properly populated with sufficient RAM, your memory subsystem will account for about half the total system price of your server.

What Kind of RAM?

There was a time when you had plenty of choices in memory for your server—as long as you chose SIMMs (Single In-line Memory Modules) with DRAM (Dynamic RAM) on them. Recently, there has been a proliferation of different memory technologies, as manufacturers continually push the outside of the envelope. In some instances, the envelope that's being pushed is the performance one, which is a good thing. Some memory ideas haven't worked out so well, however, and sometimes the only increase you'll see is in the amount of marketing hype. Scan this section for a rundown on your memory choices and avoid the pitfalls!

30-pin SIMMs

This is the oldest type of SIMM, most common in pre-Pentium computer systems. 30-pin SIMMs each provide 16 data lines and 12 address lines, for a maximum of 4 MB on a single SIMM. These SIMMs need to be installed in groups, or "banks," of four, which can cause confusion for the uninitiated. Every SIMM in a bank of four must be of the same size, and upgrading memory must be done a bank at a time. If you have a server with 16 SIMM slots on the motherboard, with all slots full of 2 MB SIMMs (for a total of 32 MB), you'll need to toss four of those (throwing away 8 MB) when you upgrade a bank with 4 MB SIMMs (adding 16 MB), for a net increase of 8 MB.

If someone gives you a server for free and it has 30-pin SIMMs, well and good. But these days, 30-pin SIMMs are obsolete. In general, you should steer clear of servers with this old memory technology.

72-pin SIMMs

This expanded SIMM is the successor to the first-generation 30-pin SIMMs. With 72 pins, the SIMM provides a full 32 address lines and 32 data lines to the RAM, so 72-pin SIMMs can be larger and faster than 30-pin SIMMs. 72-pin SIMMs are typical in Pentium computers, where the larger SIMMs provide a good match for the Pentium CPU 64-bit data bus.

Skill 4

Pentium-based servers typically have a 64-bit or 128-bit system data bus—check the documentation that came with your computer. For a 64-bit bus system, you install 72-pin SIMMs in same-size pairs. For 128-bit systems, you need to install the SIMMs four at a time, just like the SIMM banks on the 30-pin SIMM systems.

DIMMs

The word *Single* in the term *Single In-line Memory Module* implies that there's something bigger and better waiting around that next technology corner—and so it is: Dual In-line Memory Modules (DIMMs) are 168-pin packages that provide 64 address lines and 64 data lines. DIMMs currently provide the state of the art in convenient memory packaging.

Servers with a 64-bit system bus will let you install DIMMs one at a time, for maximum simplicity and flexibility. Servers with a 128-bit bus usually require DIMMs to be installed in pairs. Many systems allow the installation of single DIMMs but prefer DIMM pairs, because with two DIMMs they can perform memory interleaving (reading memory from one DIMM while the other is being strobed in its refresh cycle), which effectively doubles the speed of the RAM in the best case.

Servers with large system busses may greatly benefit from using DIMMs for their memory packaging. If you're looking to maximize your performance, DIMM is the memory configuration of choice.

 TIP Check with your server documentation to find out if your server requires memory modules to be installed in banks, pairs, or singles, or if memory modules can be interleaved.

Memory Speed

Memory modules come with a speed rating, which is the time that the memory requires for data access. Fast computers may well require memory with 60 ns (nanosecond) times or faster. A RAM speed of 70 ns is typical. Although 80 ns RAM is still available, it is typically too slow for use in modern systems.

 **WARNING** Avoid slow RAM (80 ns or slower). Check your system specifications for the recommended RAM speed.

Memory Quality

The best memory modules have gold-plated connectors, which optimize the electrical connection between the pins and the socket. Go for the gold. It's actually worth the reliability.

If your modules have the more common tin-plated connectors, inspect the modules before installing them and remove any corrosion by firmly rubbing the pins on the SIMM with a pencil eraser (the tech tool of choice). Anything more abrasive, like a wire brush or sandpaper, will strip the tin off those pins, and boy, won't you look dumb holding a $700 DIMM with no pins? Oh, and be sure to wipe the rubber from the eraser off the pins before inserting them.

Some memory manufacturers were making high-capacity SIMMs for a while by cramming a whole bunch of medium-density RAM chips on a single SIMM. Typically, a memory module might hold anywhere from two to nine memory chips. Anything over nine chips is considered a "composite" SIMM, and gangs the chips with on-SIMM electronics to simulate higher-density chips. In some installations, these composite SIMMs exhibit timing problems, since their electrical characteristics differ from normal SIMMs. Avoid composite SIMMs. I asked my vendor if the SIMMs he was selling me were composite, and he said "No," while handing me this thing that had 36 chips all over it. Just say "No" back.

 WARNING   Avoid composite SIMMs or DIMMs. They might exhibit timing problems.

EDO RAM

EDO stands for Extended Data Out, and it is a recent RAM innovation that aims to simplify system design by making the level 2 cache unnecessary. However, industry benchmarks have indicated that EDO systems without the level 2 cache are significantly slower than systems with "normal" DRAM and SRAM cache combinations. Adding a level 2 cache to a system with EDO RAM will boost performance to about five percent above a non-EDO system. Since EDO RAM costs more than five percent more than normal RAM, it's probably not worth it.

While EDO might make sense in a portable computer, where fewer chips mean longer battery life, it's not yet appropriate for servers. You should always use a level 2 cache in your server.

Parity and Error Correction

For ever and ever, PCs shipped with parity-checking RAM systems, and required RAM to provide nine bits to the byte. The ninth bit was for the parity bit, which indicated whether the number of ones stored in that byte was even or odd. If the parity bit indicated an odd number of ones, but the number in the byte contained an even number of ones, a parity error was generated, because the system knew that one of the nine bits was messed up somehow.

Parity RAM is slowly fading from the scene. Many modern Intel systems will accept parity RAM but ignore the parity bit. This is because modern RAM is fairly reliable and tends to work when it's first installed. Chuckle, chuckle—of course, the grizzled veteran system administrators are saying, "Suuure, it does..." But PCs are a commodity market, and cutting out the parity-checking system reduces cost somewhat. RAM problems just aren't that common.

For servers, many vendors offer systems with Error Checking and Correction (ECC) RAM, which can not only detect single-bit errors, but can identify the error and correct it on the fly. If you're worried about maximum reliability, this is the way to go. All parity will get you is a halted system, which is preferable to corrupted data, but otherwise doesn't make your users very happy. ECC RAM systems provide that extra layer of robustness, at a price premium.

The Bottom Line: Memory Type

Properly populated with sufficient RAM, your memory subsystem is going to be at least half the total system price of your server. So you might not have all the money in the world to play with—where do you make the hard choices?

I would opt for DIMM systems, because this memory configuration is becoming common in servers and provides a good performance match for advanced systems. EDO is not worth the price.

Parity checking on the RAM is desired. ECC is better. Your best bet for maximum reliability and performance is ECC DIMMs. However, memory systems don't fail that often, relative to other system components, so this might be an area to do some cost-cutting. It depends on your installation, but I would at least go with parity checking.

System Cache RAM

RAM is very fast, but these days RAM can't keep up with a fast CPU without some help. Because you never want the CPU to be waiting around, system manufacturers buffer the system RAM with some special, more expensive, very fast cache

RAM, which does a better job of keeping the CPU busy. This is the level 2 cache we've been talking about. It's called level 2 because the CPU chip has a bit of memory right on the chip, which is the level 1 cache.

Because the level 2 cache simply buffers the main system RAM, you don't need too much of it. Exactly how much you need is highly dependent upon the overall system design, so your server vendor will probably ship the system with an appropriate amount already installed. If you are installing the level 2 cache yourself, or upgrading an existing system, refer to Table 4.3 for a good rule of thumb. The guidelines in Table 4.3 tend to give you the right amount of cache RAM because the primary factor affecting the cache RAM requirement is the amount of system RAM.

T A B L E   4 . 3 : Cache RAM Requirements

Amount of System RAM	Cache RAM Size
Less than 32 MB	256 KB
32 MB to 64 MB	512 KB
More than 64 MB	1 MB

What Kind of Disk Controller?

For Intel systems, you typically have two choices of disk subsystem type, but really you have just one: SCSI. Use a SCSI controller and SCSI disks for your server. Don't use IDE or its variations. Period.

From the NT hardware compatibility list, select a PCI bus SCSI controller that can handle RAID 0 and RAID 5 disk arrays in hardware, without server software intervention.

NT supports only eight devices per SCSI disk controller, including the controller itself, so really seven devices. Some high-end controllers can support fifteen SCSI disks hanging off of them, but NT won't be able to see beyond the first seven disks. NT does support some dual-channel SCSI controllers, which are simply two SCSI controllers on one card—that's not the same thing. Make sure you refer to the hardware compatibility list!

Caching controllers can cause some problems with NT. SCSI controllers that support hardware RAID typically have some RAM on them to support the disk-array operations, but you don't want a whole lot of cache RAM, believe it or not. For lots more information about disk controllers and disk subsystems, see Skill 10.

What Kind of Hard Disks?

Use SCSI drives, as explained in the previous section. These days, it doesn't make much sense to purchase drives smaller than 4.3 GB for servers. Get 4.3 GB (or larger drives). Get at least three of them.

Some disks are rated as AV, which stands for Audio-Visual and indicates that these drives perform well in digital media applications, where sustained, high-bandwidth input and output are critical over extended periods of time. These disks make great server drives.

You can really perceive a difference between a drive with a 12 ms (millisecond) access time rating and a drive with an 8 ms access time. Get fast drives, at least 10 ms access or faster. Skill 10 is where we go into detail about disk controllers and disk subsystems.

How Much Hard Disk Storage?

Your hard disk storage is going to hold four types of data:

- NT system files
- NT virtual memory swap space
- Application files and storage
- User data

You'll need to count on enough storage for each of these. Fortunately, it's pretty easy these days to provide enough disk storage. Fill out Worksheet 4.4 to get a handle on how much storage you'll need.

Let's take a look at my DEC Alpha server, which will run NT, Internet Information Server, and SQL Server. You can see my numbers for disk storage requirements in Worksheet 4.5.

Per the Disk Storage worksheet, I will fill up at least 13873 MB—call it 13 GB—of storage, just getting started. I feel like my estimate of the SQL Server databases is a bit high, and I've added in a fudge factor, so I think I'll be okay. And of course, my users won't start out with 30 MB each of storage. All in all, I feel good about this number.

WORKSHEET 4.4   Disk Storage Worksheet

Line	What	Disk Space
1	**NT System Files**	**250 MB**
	Virtual Memory Swap	
2	RAM installed	MB
3	**Recommended Page File Size (line 2 × 1.5)**	**MB**
	BackOffice Requirements	
4	Internet Information Server: 50 MB	
5	Total projected size of Web site files	
6	SNA Server: 30 MB	
7	SMS: 100 MB	
8	Exchange: 500 MB	
9	SQL Server: 60 MB	
10	Total size of SQL Server databases	
11	**Total BackOffice Disk Storage (add lines 4–10)**	**MB**
	Other Application Requirements	
12	Total required storage for other applications	MB
13	**Total Application Disk Storage (line 11 + line 12)**	**MB**
	User Storage Files	
14	Number of users on this server	users
15	Average storage required per user	MB
16	**Total User Disk Storage (line 14 × line 15)**	**MB**
17	**Total Disk Storage (add lines 1, 3, 13, and 16)**	**MB**
18	Fudge factor (add 15% to line 17)	MB
19	Subtotal (line 17 + line 18)	MB
20	RISC-based computers (add 25% to line 19)	MB
21	**TOTAL DISK STORAGE NEEDED (line 19 + line 20)**	**MB**

Skill 4

WORKSHEET 4.5   Disk Storage Worksheet Example

Line	What	Disk Space
1	NT System Files	250 MB
	Virtual Memory Swap	
2	RAM installed	160 MB
3	Recommended Page File Size (line 2 × 1.5)	240 MB
	BackOffice Requirements	
4	Internet Information Server: 50 MB	50 MB
5	Total projected size of Web site files	50 MB
6	SNA Server: 30 MB	
7	SMS: 100 MB	
8	Exchange: 500 MB	
9	SQL Server: 60 MB	60 MB
10	Total size of SQL Server databases	1500 MB
11	Total BackOffice Disk Storage (add lines 4–10)	1660 MB
	Other Application Requirements	
12	Total required storage for other applications	-- MB
13	Total Application Disk Storage (line 11 + line 12)	1660 MB
	User Storage Files	
14	Number of users on this server	250 users
15	Average storage required per user	30 MB
16	Total User Disk Storage (line 14 × line 15)	7500 MB
17	Total Disk Storage (add lines 1, 3, 13, and 16)	9650 MB
18	Fudge factor (add 15% to line 17)	1448 MB
19	Subtotal (line 17 + line 18)	11098 MB
20	RISC-based computers (add 25% to line 19)	2775 MB
21	TOTAL DISK STORAGE NEEDED (line 19 + line 20)	13873 MB

How Many Hard Disks?

After you've figured out how much storage you need, figuring out how many hard disks you'll need seems like a straightforward task. Decide on the hard disk sizes, get enough of them to accommodate your storage needs, and you're finished. But if you want to use fault-tolerant disk arrays, you'll need to figure for the storage overhead.

For disk mirroring, you'll need twice as much disk storage as your storage requirements indicate. So, according to my calculations in the previous section, I'll need 26 GB of disk storage to do disk mirroring. If I used 9 GB drives, I could use two disks for my storage, and mirror that—an 18 GB mirrored volume, using a total of four disks. If a 9 GB drive costs $3,000, my disk storage cost will be $12,000.

For RAID 5 arrays, the storage overhead goes down with the number of drives installed. I could use 4.3 GB drives, and with five of them in a RAID 5 configuration, I would have a 17.2 GB volume across the five disks (20 percent RAID overhead). If a 4.3 GB drive costs $1,000, my disk storage cost will be $5,000.

Note that the cost of my RAID 5 array is less than half that of the disk mirror array, but the disk mirror provides faster performance. Because I'm running a SQL Server database on my server, I'll need to think about that. Probably, what I would want to go with the RAID 5 solution for now, and then eventually get another server with a mirror array, dedicated to the SQL Server application. It's a good idea to keep user file and print servers separate from applications servers like my SQL/Web server. But I can't afford two servers right now, so the RAID 5 system will do—five disks it is!

Do I Need a CD-ROM Drive?

You'll need a CD-ROM for installation of NT Server 4.0. Floppy installation support was dropped in the step up from NT 3.51 to 4.0 (a good thing, too, with 60-plus floppy disks to fiddle with for an installation).

NT supports IDE (ATAPI), SCSI, and a handful of proprietary interface CD-ROM drives. Multiple CD-ROM drives are okay, but when installing NT for the first time, be sure to indicate the CD-ROM drive that contains the software distribution media.

 **WARNING**   The Windows NT Setup program might select the incorrect CD-ROM when you're installing. See Skill 5 for more details.

What about CD-ROM changers? You may not notice many of them on the hardware compatibility list, but the CD-ROM changer that I've been using, and similar devices used by others, seem to work under NT 4.0. However, I would not recommend these mechanical changers in a production environment with NT Server 4.0, because the NT Explorer often "walks" the entire changer, shuffling in each of the CD-ROMs in turn, taking about two minutes to complete the process. Presumably, the Explorer needs to poll the CD-ROMs to get disk icon information and such. But the CDs often swap in and out for no obvious reason, and it takes a long time for such a swap to complete; this is a mechanical operation, similar to a jukebox. The adverse effect on system performance is difficult to predict or control. I love having all those CD-ROMs online, but I don't think that it's a good idea on a real server.

What Kind of Network Interface?

The fastest disk system in the world won't help very much if users can't get to your data through the network. Most installations are using Ethernet these days, but Fast Ethernet is a viable option, and stay tuned—ATM may soon be coming to a server near you.

To get started, choose a good network interface card that corresponds to your network (Ethernet? Token Ring?) and cabling type (10BaseT? Coaxial cable?) from the hardware compatibility list.

Don't use 8-bit ISA controllers. The bus can't take the network bandwidth. Use a 32-bit bus-mastering controller.

You can't make a good decision about the kind of network interface without thinking about your network design. We do that in Skill 8.

What Kind of Video System?

You might not think that the video system on a server is very important. Relative to other things you could spend money on, I would provisionally agree with you. But don't ignore the need for a reasonable color display. If you're used to a Unix or Banyan box, where a 12-inch amber monochrome monitor was the height of server fashion, think again. As you saw in Skill 2, the user interface is something that you can't run away from, and it pretty much requires a mid-size color monitor to get any work done.

Make sure that your video system can support SVGA—8-bit, 256 color at 800x600 resolution with a reasonable refresh rate (43 MHz interlaced is unreasonable, for example); 72 MHz and higher are comfortable refresh rates.

> **TIP**
>
> Where we have multiple servers in a data closet, we have one monitor, keyboard, and mouse, and we use a Cybex switch box to switch between the servers. In practice, this has worked out fine, but I can anticipate situations where you would want to see more than one server at a time. Our switch box works great, though, and I would recommend this alternative to those of you with constrained space and money. Just make sure that the video switch box can handle the SVGA bandwidth of 800x600, 256-color, at 72 MHz or better.

What about the Keyboard and Mouse?

There's not much to say about the keyboard hardware. Your server probably already comes with one. You'll need a keyboard that's compatible with the IBM 101-key or 84-key standard, preferably the 101-key version. NT supports various keyboard layouts, and you'll indicate the layout when you install NT.

As for the mouse, you need one. Because NT is a graphical environment, it's not realistic to do without the mouse. While Windows generally has a keyboard equivalent for just about everything, you'll find that certain operations with the new shell in NT 4.0 just scream for a mouse.

> **WARNING**
>
> Intel platforms generally won't boot without a keyboard attached. If you do so, you'll get a keyboard error at boot time, because the BIOS on the motherboard strobes the keyboard to make sure that one exists. Yeah, I think this is dumb, too. You might not want a keyboard or monitor on a server that you keep in the closet. But again, remember that with NT, there are things that you're going to have to do from the console. You'll need that monitor, keyboard, and mouse.

For Intel platforms, if you have a choice for the mouse, a Logitec-compatible bus mouse may be preferable to a serial mouse. That way, you won't need to sacrifice a serial port for the mouse. You'll need the serial ports to talk to the UPS (uninterruptible power supply) and the modem.

What Kind of Serial Ports?

You want at least two serial ports free on your server, after you hook up the serial mouse (if any). One of the serial ports will attach to the UPS, and one will attach to the El Cheapo 2400-baud modem that you dug out of the bottom of your desk.

Why is that? Well, you'll definitely want the UPS connection, so that your server will know about power failures and shut down gracefully when one occurs. You'll want the modem to be a phone dialer, so that you can get paged when the server has problems. Some server hardware platforms will handle this function in the hardware, or you can write a batch file to page you in the event of a terrible failure.

Here is a crude whack at a batch file that can send a page if you've got a modem hooked up to the COM2 serial port. This is for illustration purposes only; it doesn't really work that well. I'm sure you can come up with something better!

```
PAGER.BAT:
qbasic /run pager.bas

PAGER.BAS:
OPEN "COM2:2400,n,8,1" FOR RANDOM AS #1
    PRINT #1, "atdt 9,555-1234,,,,,,,5551212#"
    ' wait for 20 seconds
    triggerTime = TIMER + 20
    WHILE (triggerTime > TIMER)
    WEND
CLOSE #1
```

WARNING   Because NT provides sophisticated remote network access capabilities with its Remote Access Service (RAS), you may not want a modem hooked up to your server if the line can be accessed from outside your company. Ideally, the line should be dial-out only, or you can disable RAS on the server. This is because you want to limit dial-in network services to only those systems that you carefully manage as your network entry points. Consider limiting modem devices to only the remote access servers.

You can also install multiport serial boards, such as those made by DigiBoard or ConSynsys, into your NT server. These make a lot of sense if you're going to use the Remote Access Service (RAS) with NT to create a dial-in server system for remote access to your network.

What Other Components?

The other components you'll need are a UPS and a tape backup unit. You may also want to get a second SCSI controller.

UPS

You definitely want a UPS to protect your server from fluctuations in the line power. While the concept of a UPS is rather straightforward, actually getting one to work exactly right in practice can be a little tricky. For details, see Skill 9.

SCSI Tape Backup Unit

You'll want a tape drive on the server to perform routine server backups. You can go two routes:

- A tape drive on each server

- Centralized backup of NT servers to one dedicated tape backup system

In my experience, the more complex your backup system, the more likely it is to fail.

There are a few different types of SCSI tape backup systems: minicartridge tape, exabyte, 4 millimeter DAT, and DLT. You can just use whichever tape mechanism that you're already using on your other servers. If you don't have an existing system, consider DLT for large servers, and use DAT drives elsewhere. Check the SCSI tape backup units in the hardware compatibility list. Tape backup systems and backup procedures are discussed in detail in Skill 11.

Second SCSI Controller?

It might make some sense for you to consider a SCSI controller dedicated to the CD-ROM and tape backup unit, independent of the hefty controller that may be running your RAID disk array. This may add some complexity to your server design, but it may streamline troubleshooting later. With this setup, you'll isolate the SCSI buses on the RAID system, so that it is relatively unaffected by whatever happens with your CD-ROM or tape drive.

Think of the RAID system, your hard disk storage, as your "production" side of the server storage equation. This is the part upon which the minute-by-minute operation of your server relies. You generally use the CD-ROM only for installation of software, and the tape drive for after-hours backup. You may want to treat your production storage system differently.

The downsides to a second SCSI controller are the complexities of getting the two controllers to coexist and keeping straight which device is on which controller. Depending on your needs and your hardware configuration, this may or may not be a big deal, but you should know that you have the option.

Skill 4

Hardware Compatibility Issues

The Ugly Truth is that many LAN servers share hardware design legacy with the IBM PC. Almost all of the equipment on the NT hardware compatibility list requires you to set IRQ levels, DMA request channels, and I/O port settings. If you don't know what all this stuff is, now is the time to at least become passingly familiar with the concepts and vocabulary—at least until Plug and Pray (sorry, Plug and *Play*) is available for NT.

Interrupt Requests Explained

On a PC system, various hardware components grab the CPU's attention by means of an interrupt mechanism; a signal is applied to a control line on the system bus when the hardware component needs to do something. The system is responsible for coordinating the bus so that only one subunit can signal on the bus at a time. Each of the components gets to signal the bus, in turn, based on the level or its interrupt request (IRQ).

On the original IBM PC, the IRQ coordination was handled by an Intel 8259 chip, which could support up to eight different IRQ levels. By the advent of the IBM PC/AT, there were so many add-in cards and multifunction adapters that it was clear that the system needed more interrupt levels. IBM slipped in another 8259, but to maintain compatibility with the original PC, the designers added the unit by "piggybacking" it to the original interrupt controller, hard-wiring the original controller's IRQ 2 to the new controller's IRQ 9 (see Figure 4.2). When any of the second interrupt controller's interrupts are triggered, that triggers the original controller's IRQ 2 line. It's up to the system BIOS to figure out what's really going on.

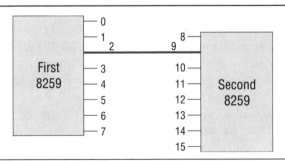

FIGURE 4 . 2 : Cascaded interrupt controllers on the PC

Here are the cogent facts that come out of all this:

- The system services the interrupt requests based on the IRQ level. The lower the IRQ level, the more priority an interrupt has.

- Since the second controller's IRQs are wired in through the first one's IRQ 2, IRQs 8 through 15 have a higher priority than IRQs 3 through 7.

- Put faster devices on IRQs 8 through 15, and slower devices on IRQs 3 through 7.

- COM2 is slightly better-suited to high-speed serial connections (like a modem), and COM1 is better relegated to slower connections (like a UPS or a serial mouse), since COM2's IRQ is at a higher priority than COM1's.

- You can't use IRQ 2 or 9.

- In general, each device on your system should have its own IRQ level; otherwise, an interrupt conflict is likely to occur, and your system will act really, really weird.

- Eight-bit devices (some old sound cards, for example) can't use IRQs on the second IRQ controller and must be set to an IRQ between 3 and 7. (Don't use such old stuff on your cool server.)

Choosing a Card's IRQ Level

Some IRQ levels are defined by the core system hardware and cannot be changed. Over time it has become customary to use the remaining IRQs for specific tasks. Table 4.4 lists the IRQs in order of priority, noting their common use and whether they are available.

Here are the steps for choosing a card's IRQ level:

1. In order to get the best performance and avoid interrupt conflicts, refer to Table 4.4 to find an available IRQ level. You can use any IRQ level except the ones already taken by the system, which are marked "don't use" in the table.

2. Refer to the manufacturer's documentation that came with your card. Typically, there is a choice of two or three IRQs that you can use for that card.

3. Prioritize your cards. Place devices with the highest priority toward the top of the list, within the constraints set by the IRQ choices available for the card. Don't agonize over this, because there are other things that will affect system performance far more significantly. But be aware.

Skill 4

4. Once you've chosen the card's IRQ level, write it down in the IRQ System record (Worksheet 4.8, at the end of the chapter), and tattoo the worksheet on your forehead, backwards, so you see it every time you look in the mirror. Seriously, though, it's a fantastic idea to plaster a copy of the IRQ record to the side of the server's case, and keep a copy where every administrator can get to it.

5. Set the card's IRQ level using the procedures that came with the card. This will vary from card to card. Some cards have jumpers on the board that you set (ugh!), some have proprietary software that only works from DOS (ugh! ugh! ugh!), EISA boards will use the EISA Config utility that comes with your server (that usually only works from DOS), and PCI cards are generally self-configuring. Check your card's documentation.

T A B L E 4 . 4 : IRQs in Order of Priority

IRQ Level	Common Use	Comments
0	System timer	Don't use
1	Keyboard	Don't use—can't change
2	Hard-wired to IRQ 9	Don't use
9	Hard-wired to IRQ 2	Don't use
10	LAN interface	
11	SCSI controller	Adaptec SCSI controller default IRQ
12	Bus mouse Logitec mouse	Also called PS/2 mouse or
13	Math coprocessor	Don't use
14	IDE controller IDE disk drives	Might be available if you don't use
15		Available
3	COM2 or COM4	
4	COM1 or COM3	
5	LPT2	Few systems have two parallel ports, so may be available
6	Floppy controller	Don't use
7	LPT1	Primary parallel port—don't use
8	Real-time clock	Don't use

DMA Channels Explained

DMA stands for Direct Memory Access. It's a way for a peripheral card to transfer data to and from system memory directly, without the intervention of the CPU. Cards that are capable of DMA are typically referred to as *bus-mastering* cards, which refers to the fact that a card initiating a direct memory access must first take control of the system data bus.

Since DMA bypasses the central CPU when it moves data, memory transfers can happen even while the CPU is busy with other tasks, and overall system performance is enhanced. Good candidates for bus-mastering are those peripheral controllers that deal primarily with the movement of data into and out of the computer: SCSI disk controllers and network interface cards.

Like IRQs, DMAs take place through DMA *channels*, which must be uniquely assigned. In general, no two devices can share a DMA channel. So the procedure for allocating DMA channels to your cards is essentially the same as with IRQs. Refer to the device's documentation for the default and allowed DMA settings, and adjust the DMA settings for the device if necessary. You'll log the DMA settings for each device in the worksheet coming up in the next section.

I/O Ports Explained

The original PC used certain memory addresses for accessing input/output devices such as serial and parallel ports. Low-level software transfers data to these memory locations in order to move data out of the port, and reads these memory locations to read data from the port. To the software, the transfer of data looks exactly like a memory transfer, but it really has nothing to do with RAM at all; the hardware transfers the data to an I/O device instead. These magic memory locations are called *I/O ports*.

I/O ports are uniquely assigned one or two bytes at a time. Typically, I/O ports won't be something that you'll run into conflicts with, but when you do, you'll really want to be able to figure out what's going on. You'll log the I/O port settings for each device in the Hardware Design worksheet.

Hardware Design: The Final Worksheet

Now that you're ready to make some informed hardware design and purchasing decisions, it's time to bring all the information together in one place. You can use the worksheets included in this chapter as guides.

RAM System

Filling out the RAM worksheet in Worksheet 4.2 allows you to determine the amount of RAM you'll need for your system. We worked through an example in Worksheet 4.3. Once you've got an idea of the requirements for system RAM, you can estimate the amount of level 2 cache RAM your system will require by referring to Table 4.3. Note that some CPU chips (for example, most Pentium Pro chips and Alpha 21164 chips) have level 2 caches on the chip, so you won't use Table 4.3 for these systems.

Disk Storage

The Disk Storage worksheet is Worksheet 4.4, and we worked through an example in Worksheet 4.5. Complete this worksheet and then enter the total storage requirements in line 18 of the worksheet in Worksheet 4.7, the Hardware Design worksheet.

System Device Record

The System Device record in Worksheet 4.6 is for recording the critical information about each system component installed in your server. You'll want to complete a copy of this table for each card that you install in your system.

WORKSHEET 4.6   System Device Record

Device Name:	
Expansion Slot Number:	
Manufacturer:	
Model:	
Version:	
Serial Number:	
Purchase Date:	
Replacement Part Number:	
Software Versions (if any):	
IRQ Level:	
DMA Channel:	
I/O Port Range(s):	

WORKSHEET 4.7   Hardware Design Worksheet

Line	See Skill	System	Requirements
		CPU	
1	1	Number of CPUs possible	
2	1, 7	Number of CPUs installed	
3		CPU chip manufacturer	
4		CPU chip model	
5		CPU chip clock speed	
		System Bus	
6	1	CPU chip system bus speed	
7	1	Bus types (circle all that apply)	ISA EISA VLB PCI
		System RAM	
8	1, 7	Amount of RAM installed (line 15 from the RAM worksheet, Worksheet 4.2)	
9	1	RAM configuration (circle one)	30-pin SIMM 2-pin SIMM DIMM
10	1	RAM type (circle all that apply)	Parity-checking ECC EDO
11	1	Amount of cache RAM installed	
		Disk System Controller	
12	1, 10	Disk controller manufacturer	
13	1, 10	Disk controller model	
14		Installed in server slot number	
15		*Fill out a System Device record for the disk controller.*	
16	10	Hardware RAID?	Yes No
17	1, 10	Bus mastering?	

Skill 4

WORKSHEET 4.7   Hardware Design Worksheet (continued)

Line	See Skill	System	Requirements
		Disk Drives	
18	4	Total disk storage needed line 21 from the Disk Storage worksheet, Worksheet 4.4)	
19	1, 10	Number of drives	
20	1, 10	Drive size	
		CD-ROM Drives	
21	1, 10	CD-ROM type	SCSI ATAPI Other
22		CD-ROM manufacturer	
23		CD-ROM model	
24		*Indicate the above information for each CD-ROM drive in your system.*	
		Network Interface (NIC)	
25	8	NIC manufacturer	
26	8	NIC model	
27		Installed in server slot number	
28		*Fill out a System Device record for the NIC.*	
		Video System	
29		Video card manufacturer	
30		Video card model	
31		Installed in server slot number	
32		*Fill out a System Device record for the video card.*	
33		Monitor manufacturer	
34		Monitor model	
		Input Devices	
35	1	Keyboard type (circle one)	101-key 84-key
36	1	Mouse type (circle one)	Serial Bus
37	1	For serial mouse: COM port	
38		*For bus mouse, fill out a System Device record.*	

WORKSHEET 4.7   Hardware Design Worksheet (continued)

Line	See Skill	System	Requirements
		I/O Devices (Serial Ports, etc.)	
39		*Fill out a System Device record for each installed I/O interface.*	
		UPS System	
40		UPS manufacturer	
41	9	UPS model	
42	9	UPS volt-amp rating	
43	9	Requires serial port signaling?	
44		Part number for the signaling cable	
		Tape Backup Unit	
45	11	Tape backup type	
46		Tape backup manufacturer	
47	11	Tape backup model	
48		Tape backup SCSI ID	

Completing the Hardware Design Worksheet

The Hardware Design worksheet, Worksheet 4.7, brings together all the information you need to build your server hardware system. Before you fill out this worksheet:

1. Complete the RAM worksheet in Worksheet 4.2.

2. Take a look at the Cache RAM numbers in Table 4.3.

3. Complete the Disk Storage worksheet in Worksheet 4.4.

4. Make sure you understand the System Device record in Worksheet 4.6.

Use the Hardware Design worksheet as a table of contents for the rest of the book. At each step, we've indicated the skill that discusses the information you need to answer the question at hand.

System IRQ Record

Once you've filled out the Hardware Design worksheet, fill in the System IRQ record in Worksheet 4.8. Keep a copy of this information with the server, and make sure to keep it up to date!

WORKSHEET 4.8   IIRQ System Record

IRQ Level	Common Use	Comments
0	System timer	Don't use
1	Keyboard	Don't use; can't change
2	"Hard-wired" to IRQ 9	Don't use
9	"Hard-wired" to IRQ 2	Don't use
10		
11		
12		
13	Math coprocessor	Don't use
14		
15		
3	COM2 or COM4	
4	COM1 or COM3	
5		
6	Floppy controller	Don't use
7	LPT1	Don't use; primary parallel port
8	Real-time clock	Don't use

Are You Experienced?

Now you can...

- ☑ decide whether to purchase Per Server or Per Seat client licenses for your NT Server system

- ☑ determine which server software components your system requires

- ☑ pick the type and number of CPUs for your server

- ☑ choose the appropriate type of system bus for your server

- ☑ decide how much RAM and what type of RAM your server requires

- ☑ make decisions about your hard disk type and storage

- ☑ choose other hardware components, such as the network interface, video system, and serial ports

Skill 4

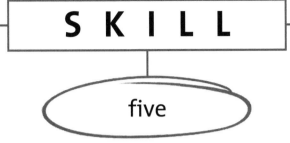

SKILL

five

5

Installing
NT Server

❑ **Installation procedures for Intel and RISC-based systems**

❑ **Disk partitions and file systems**

❑ **NT Server installation from the CD-ROM**

❑ **NT installation repair**

Now that you've built your server, there it sits in all its glory, waiting for you to unleash its potential. Well, the waiting is over. You've done your homework, and now it's time to get your hands dirty!

In this skill, we'll walk through the installation of NT Server from a supported CD-ROM onto a "raw" (no previous operating system) server, the most common form of server setup. Where appropriate, procedural differences between the Intel and RISC platforms are indicated. If you have a RISC computer, you may need to refer to your server documentation for some of the specifics, but the information here should get you going.

Even if you are lucky enough to own a server that has a turnkey NT installation, you should take a look at this information. At some point, the installation programs will ask you about disk partitions and domain controllers. You'll be able to proceed with confidence after reading through this skill.

If you haven't worked through Skill 4, which covers NT Server design, you need to do that before installing NT. If you're like me, you'll want to jump right in. I did that, and ended up installing NT about three or four times on my server before I got it right. This was not NT's fault; it's just that I insisted on learning some network and server concepts the hard way. I urge you to learn from my mistakes (that's why you're reading the book, right?). Don't treat the design instructions in the same way that you treat all those software registration cards. The splash screen that will tell you that "Now would be a good time to fill out Worksheet 4.1 of the Design Review" is going to read more like "Reinstall your NT software to proceed." With that warning out of the way, let's get to it!

Preparing Your Server for Installation

To get all the hardware put together and configured, you'll most likely need to run some configuration software. If you purchased a name-brand server, configuration software came with the server. Most Intel-based servers simply have a DOS partition that contains all the configuration utilities. RISC-based systems typically have setup routines built into the firmware. Refer to your server's documentation for the specifics.

 WARNING   If there is data on your server that you want to keep, be sure to back it up before proceeding with the installation process!

Setting Up Disk Partitions

Before you install NT Server, consider your disk partitions. If your server has a system partition containing the server setup utilities, you should back it up before installing NT. At least make copies of the system utilities and your server's configuration files. As a rule, I like to make backup floppy disks for my server's utilities. On Compaq servers that I configured, the system partition was hidden from normal operation by the hardware setup, but your situation will probably be different. Just be sure to back up any important information.

If you are going to use fault-tolerant disk arrays, read Skill 10 now. As you'll see, server disk arrays are best left up to the server hardware. If you use the controller hardware to manage your disk arrays, you'll need to set up the arrays before installing NT, using your server's configuration utilities. Fault-tolerant arrays are a really good idea, and doing it in hardware is an even better idea. If you're going this route, you'll have already set up your array and created a partition on it before proceeding with installation.

 TIP   It's a good idea to run a full-surface analysis on the hard disks at this stage. This will take hours, but it will identify and lock out any low-level bad sectors on the hard disks. You can usually perform a surface analysis with utility software that comes with your disk controller.

Setting Up Your File Systems

You'll want to use NTFS for the reliability and security it provides. Many server applications require NTFS. Remember that NT Server supports only FAT or NTFS. Because you don't get to set file-level security with FAT, your only choice left is NTFS. Use it.

RISC-based systems must boot from a FAT file system, but that doesn't mean that you can't put NT on the more secure NTFS file system. Simply maintain a small FAT partition on the server that contains all the server utilities and the NT loader. When you boot the server, the FAT partition will be active and will load the NT loader, which will point to the NTFS partition that contains your NT system. This is a good plan for Intel-based computers, as well. You know that if anything happens to your NT system, you can still run many utilities off the FAT partition. Figure 5.1 illustrates an example of a file system setup that uses fault tolerance and the various file systems. We'll discuss this in detail in Skill 10.

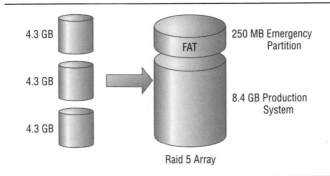

FIGURE 5.1 : A possible file system setup for a fault-tolerant server

We recommend that you start the Windows NT setup process on a server that has a small FAT partition already formatted as the first primary partition of the main volume, which is a large disk array of some kind. You'll get a chance to carve up the rest of the main volume into NTFS partitions during the setup process.

 WARNING If you run NT Setup against a completely "raw" volume (one that's never been formatted) or a disk volume that has been formatted with a file system other than FAT, NTFS, or HPFS, the Setup program may not recognize the volume's boot sector. It may halt, complaining about boot sector viruses. Since the boot sector is a very popular place for DOS viruses to live, the Setup program will refuse to continue if it can't understand the boot sector. To fix this problem, format the drive with the FAT file system. Intel computers can usually do this by simply booting DOS and running FDISK against the offending drive, and most RISC computers can do this from the boot firmware menu. If the problem persists, you might actually have an infected disk, remove the hard drive, install it in a DOS computer, and run a virus scanner against it.

Preparing Yourself for Installation

Now that your server is prepared for NT installation, make sure you are, too, before you begin. You should have the required information and materials at hand.

Gathering Required Information

Before starting the installation process, make sure you have the following information close at hand:

- The Server Software Design worksheet from Skill 4 (Worksheet 4.1)
- The name of the server
- The name of the domain to which you'll add the server (or the name of the new domain, if your server is going to be a primary domain controller)
- The user name and password for an account that has permission to add a server to the domain (for stand-alone servers)
- For TCP/IP networks, the TCP/IP network information (see Skills 8 and 14)

Gathering Required Materials

Once you've got all your information handy, you'll need to gather the following materials that you'll use during installation:

- The NT 4.0 Server distribution CD-ROM
- For Intel systems only, the three setup boot floppies that came with the NT Server distribution CD-ROM
- A 3.5, high-density, blank floppy disk, labeled "Emergency Repair Disk for <servername>" (replace <servername> with the name of your server)
- Any required hardware support disks from your hardware vendors

Installing from CD-ROM

Now we will walk through the NT Setup program, step by step. Get your Software Design worksheet—the one from Skill 4 (Worksheet 4.1)—and the materials listed in the previous section, and then get comfortable.

Starting the Server Setup

Getting the setup process going is different for Intel and RISC computers, but after the ball is rolling, things are generally the same. In this phase of the installation, you'll boot up the computer and run the server setup from the CD-ROM.

1. **Insert the Windows NT Server distribution CD-ROM in the CD-ROM drive.**

If you have more than one CD-ROM drive in your server, you should generally use the one with the lowest SCSI ID. I use an external SCSI CD-ROM changer and an internal ATAPI (EIDE) CD-ROM drive on my Intel system. I used the ATAPI drive for the installation, and the Setup program found it without any problems. I don't recommend that you use either a CD-ROM changer or an ATAPI CD-ROM drive for a production server. Refer to your server's documentation to be sure of which CD-ROM to use.

2. **For Intel systems only, insert the distribution floppy disk labeled "Setup Boot Disk" into the floppy drive.**

Only Intel computers use the boot floppies. RISC machines will use the CD-ROM exclusively. Make sure your Intel computer is set up to boot from the floppy drive. You may need to edit the CMOS setup to make this happen. You don't want the server to boot from the hard disk for this setup. If necessary, you can change the CMOS settings back after you get NT set up (but I don't recommend it, because you might need to boot from a floppy if something happens to your hard disk). See your server documentation for more information about CMOS.

3. **Restart the computer.**

The computer will boot up, with the CD-ROM and (Intel only) boot floppy.

4. **For RISC systems only, at the Boot menu, choose Run a Program.**

The wording varies from computer to computer, but you want to tell the RISC boot firmware to run the SETUPLDR.EXE program, which will set up the NT Boot Loader on your server's boot FAT partition, and set up the server installation.

When you tell the boot firmware to run a program, it will prompt you for a path to the program that you want to run. Type the following at the prompt:

```
<CD drive>:\<platform type>\SETUPLDR
```

where *<platform type>* is one of MIPS, ALPHA, or PPC for the MIPS, DEC Alpha, or PowerPC systems; and *<CD drive>* is the drive specification for the CD-ROM drive containing the NT distribution CD.

Most RISC computers recognize the *CD* for the CD-ROM drive. If your computer does not use *CD* for the CD-ROM drive, you'll need to use the fully qualified ARC name, which specifies the controller, disk, and partition containing the desired file. For example, for a CD-ROM drive with SCSI ID 1 attached to the second SCSI controller, enter:

```
scsi(1)disk(1)rdisk(0)partition(0)\PPC\SETUPLDR
```

ARC drive specifications are discussed in Skill 10. Refer to your server's documentation to be sure.

5. **When the NT Setup program starts up, press Enter to proceed.**

The blue-screen NT Setup program will load and ask if you want more information about Windows NT setup. No, you don't. Then the Setup program will ask if you want to repair a damaged NT installation or start from scratch. Take the default of installing fresh by hitting Enter.

6. **For Intel systems only, Setup will ask for Disk 2. Eject Disk 1, insert Disk 2, and press Enter.**

Different pieces of NT live on the different setup boot disks. At this point, you're actually running a scaled-down version of NT Server. The basic HAL and kernel have been loaded, along with enough device-driver stuff to run your keyboard and talk to the character-mode screen. You can monitor all the cool stuff that's getting loaded by watching the lower-right corner of the screen; the name of the currently loading file is displayed there.

7. **If you have a choice between Express and Custom setup, hit C for Custom.**

You really don't want NT to make its best guess about everything. It will do a good job, but with the Express setup you won't be able to specify any device drivers for your hardware, and you won't be able to specify the installation partition. Choose Custom setup for maximum control.

Discovery of SCSI Disk and CD-ROM

Now that the Setup program is running in earnest, you'll hit your first hurdle when you get to the discovery of storage devices. If you're using supported hardware that is properly configured, things should go smoothly.

8. **You want automatic detection of storage devices. Hit Enter to scan.**

It's always a good idea when you first set up NT to try the automatic detection; it will be significant if the Setup program can't find your hardware. Sometimes, you may just need to specify a device driver for things to work. Other times, the detection failure is indicative of improperly configured hardware.

Setup may hang at this point, if it gets really confused and attempts to load a gonzo driver for some bozo hardware. If you get really stuck, hit F3 to exit the Setup program, or hard reset your computer and start the Setup process over. When you get to this step again, hit S for Skip the automatic detection, and go to step 10 to specify a driver.

9.   **For Intel systems only, Setup will ask for Floppy Disk 3. Eject Disk 2, insert Disk 3, and press Enter.**

Most of NT that can fit on the floppies has been loaded. All the basic device drivers are on Disks 2 and 3. The hardware compatibility list indicates drivers that come with the distribution but are not in the normal NT setup. These drivers are on the CD in the \DRVLIB directory.

Setup will scan for storage devices in your system, based on the device drivers that are on the standard floppies. This can take some time.

10.   **When Setup completes scanning, it will enumerate all found devices. If it finds all your SCSI adapters, hit Enter to continue with step 12. To specify other SCSI adapters, press S.**

NT will not have found non-SCSI storage devices at this point, but not to worry—there are only a couple of basic IDE device drivers, Setup will load them after it gets done playing with this SCSI stuff, so it will detect those devices soon.

11.   **If necessary, highlight the required driver from the list by using the arrow keys and press Enter.**

If your device is not in the list of possible drivers, select Other and press Enter. When Setup asks for the hardware support disk, eject the Setup Disk 3 from the floppy drive (Intel only), insert the disk from the device's manufacturer, and press Enter.

Setup will scan for the hardware device specified on the support floppy and should load the device driver. If so, the name of the new device will appear in the list. If you have other devices to add, hit S again to repeat this step. Otherwise, press Enter to continue with installation.

If you need to cancel the process of specifying custom drivers, press Escape.

For Intel systems only, Setup may ask you to reinsert setup Disk 3. If so, eject any hardware support disk that's in the drive, insert the setup Disk 3, and hit Enter.

NOTE I had a lot of trouble at this stage with an Intel desktop that I was setting up as a Windows NT 4.0 Server. It was not going to be a "production" server, but rather my desktop administration station, from which I could administer all my network servers. I could not get it to find the PCI SCSI card. I tried everything I could think of. Finally, I realized that since I was not booting off the SCSI chain (I used the internal EIDE drive as the boot drive), the BIOS on the SCSI adapter should be disabled. Boy, *that* only took a day of head-scratching! Simple, unless you've never seen it before. Often, problems at this stage indicate hardware that is not configured correctly, rather than any problem with the device driver.

Core Hardware Configuration

Your "core" hardware configuration includes the PC type, video display, mouse, keyboard, and keyboard layout.

12. **Setup will display its best guess about your core hardware. This is almost always correct. Press Enter to continue.**

The only thing here that may obviously deviate from your system setup is the video display. If you have a high-resolution video display, don't worry. You'll have a chance to set that up later. VGA is almost always the correct choice for standard color adapters.

You may want to change your keyboard layout, if you're using a non-U.S. keyboard.

To change any of the settings, use the arrow keys to highlight the offending item and press Enter. A list of alternative types will appear, and you can select among the options by using the arrow keys and the Enter key.

Once you have all the options the way you want them, use the arrow keys to select the options that says "The above list matches my computer" and press Enter.

Specifying the Installation Partition

Here is where it gets interesting. You'll want to make sure that Setup installs NT into the correct partition. If you're setting up a "raw" server, you most likely don't have an NTFS partition set up yet. In this phase of the installation process, you'll be able to create and format new partitions, and then tell Setup to install the bulk of NT there.

Be very careful here. It's really easy to nuke a partition in this section of the installation. You'll see lots of text on that blue screen that you really need to read carefully. A wrong selection can erase a partition (and really cramp your style). All it takes is two taps on the keyboard. Proceed with caution.

Drive-letter assignments in this section will not necessarily match any DOS drive letters, if you can boot your computer under DOS. Don't worry—that's a side effect of DOS not being able to recognize the NTFS partitions. You'll have a chance to reassign drive letters later.

13. If Setup asks if you want to specify the installation partition, answer yes.

If you don't specify the installation partition, Setup will install into the first partition that's large enough. If you've set up your system with a large FAT partition, Setup might just install stuff there. Unless you know what you're doing, always explicitly specify the installation partition.

14. Setup will list all the partitions and unassigned space on the hard disks. If your desired installation partition exists, proceed to step 15. Otherwise, you'll want to create a new partition from unassigned space.

Unassigned space is listed as "unpartitioned." Partitions that have not yet been formatted may be listed as "damaged," but not to worry; that just means that NT does not understand them.

To create a new partition out of unpartitioned space, use the arrow keys to highlight the unpartitioned space and then press C for Create. Enter the size for the partition and press Enter.

If there are unwanted partitions in your way, you can delete them by highlighting them and pressing D for Delete. Setup will ask you to verify this operation, because partition deletion from setup is permanent, meaning that you will lose data. If you are installing to a fresh server, you probably will not need to delete any partitions.

15. Select the installation partition with the arrow keys, then press Enter.

Setup will give you some options for formatting the partition:

- Leave the Current System Intact: If the partition has already been formatted, Setup will give you a chance to leave the partition as it is.

- Convert to NTFS: FAT partitions can be converted to NTFS, changing the file system while preserving the data.

- FAT: This option formats the partition with the FAT file system. *Any previous data on the partition is erased forever.*

- NTFS: This option formats the partition with the NTFS file system. *Any previous data on the partition is erased forever.* (Actually, the partition is formatted with FAT and will be converted when NT reboots.)

16. **Setup will suggest a destination directory for the NT system directory. By default, the system directory name is \WINNT. If you have no problems with this, accept it by pressing Enter.**

The only reason you might want to deviate from this default is if you are trying to maintain different versions of NT on a single partition. This is probably not a good idea for a production server. Whatever you decide, make sure that every administrator that will ever maintain this server knows what the system directory is. It's not a good idea to use \WINDOWS, since most administrators will think of Windows 95 when they see that. Don't confuse the issue.

Finalizing the Blue-Screen Installation

In this phase of installation, Setup will verify the integrity of your hard disks and copy all the required setup files from the CD-ROM to the hard disk. This stage is time-consuming, but easy. The computer does all the work, asking for almost no input. It's coffee-break time!

17. **Setup will ask to perform an exhaustive scan of the hard disks. Press Enter to begin the scan.**

In my experience, this doesn't take that long, despite the words "exhaustive scan." Setup will look only at the partitions that it actually uses. If your first primary partition is large enough, and formatted FAT or NTFS, it will use that partition to temporarily hold the installation files, so it scans that. It will scan the installation partition you specified in step 15.

You shouldn't worry too much if the disk scan cannot be completed. You've already performed a surface analysis on these drives anyway, right? The only cause for concern is when the scan explicitly reports disk errors.

18. **Setup will copy installation files from CD-ROM to your hard disk.**

These files get enough of the rest of NT onto your computer to enable the graphical portion of the setup. It takes a lot to get the graphical interface going, so if this step is successful, you're halfway there.

Skill 5

If Setup cannot copy a file, you might be best off by starting the whole setup process again (yes, painful). You can try to continue the installation, and manually copy the file over later, and you just might get away with it, but there are no guarantees. Because NT is such a complex collection of files, you could go for a while before running into that missing file. It's best to repeat the installation process until you get a smooth installation.

19. **Setup will complete the file transfer. Press Enter to reboot your computer into graphical NT setup.**

I always forget to remove any floppies from the floppy drive at this point, and grumble when the computer fails to boot from the setup Disk 3 or the hardware vendor's disk. Brain damage from my Macintosh days, no doubt.

 WARNING   Be sure to remove any floppies from the disk drive before hitting Enter. Otherwise you'll waste time rebooting again, after removing the offending floppy.

Graphical NT Setup: The NT Setup Wizard

Great! You've made it this far. From here on out, things go quickly. You've got almost all the low-level hardware setup behind you, and now it's time to play server administrator. You have the benefit of the graphical Setup Wizard, which will prompt you with forms to fill out on the screen. For now, the graphic display is limited to VGA mode, but you'll set up your display in a moment.

You'll need your Server Software Design worksheet from Skill 4. See Worksheet 4.1 for a copy of this worksheet.

20. **Welcome to the Wizard. Click on Next or press Enter.**

You can use the mouse and the keyboard for this setup phase:

- You can proceed to the next screen by clicking on the Next button, or hitting the Enter key.

- You can hit the Tab key to move between fields on a form, or click in a specific field with the mouse.

- In most cases, you can repeat a previous step by clicking on the Back button in the Wizard.

21. **Enter a name and organization, then click on Next.**

We standardized the entries at my company. The name we used was the name of the group performing the installation (LAN Production Team), and the organization name we used was the name of our company. The organization name is optional. You might consider having people enter their personal name in the Name field, so you know who to blame for a messed-up installation. But keep in mind that anyone so named will be immortalized in the NT server information.

22. **Select the licensing mode for the server, then click on Next.**

Use your Server Software Design worksheet, line 1. For more information, see Skill 4.

23. **Enter the name of the computer, then click on Next.**

Server names can be no more than 15 characters. Keep your server name simple, and avoid any special characters. Some characters, such as \ and %, are illegal for NT server names, and the Setup Wizard will reject any name containing such characters. But other characters are valid in NT server names, but cause problems just the same. In addition to the illegal characters, avoid the dash (-) and the underscore (_). The dash character is valid in NT and in DNS host names, but is not allowed for NT servers running SQL Server. Any attempt to load SQL Server on a Windows NT computer with a dash in its name will fail. The underscore character may confuse networks that use DNS and TCP/IP host names.

24. **Setup asks you to specify the network role for this server: Primary Domain Controller (PDC), Backup Domain Controller (BDC), or Stand-Alone Server. Select the appropriate role, then click on Next.**

Refer to line 2 of your Server Software Design worksheet. For more information, see Skill 13.

If this is the only NT computer on your network, the default choice of PDC is acceptable. Otherwise, you're much better off with the Stand-Alone Server choice if you don't know exactly what you're doing.

25. **Specify a password for the local administrator account for this server, then click on Next.**

You'll need to type the password, then hit Tab, and type it again. The password should be between 5 and 14 characters long.

We strongly recommend that you standardize on the password for the local administrator account. Let every server have the same administrator password, and make sure the senior administrators know what the password is. Be sure to change the password every so often. For more information, see Skill 13.

26. **Click on Yes to indicate that you want to create an Emergency Repair Disk.**

You really want to do this. Setup will create the disk at the end of the setup process, when all the settings have been recorded.

27. **Select optional software components for installation, then click on Next.**

Refer to your Server Software Design worksheet. If you skip installation of these components right now, you can install them later.

To install only a few select components, click on the Details button to get more specific.

Basic Network Configuration

In this phase of the installation process, you'll be setting up the network portions of NT Server. At this stage, it's best to set up the basic network services only. After you have those working on a fully operational server, you can add network components with a high degree of control.

28. **Setup indicates the start of the network configuration phase of the installation process. Click on Next.**

You'll need information about your network configuration to complete this section. Refer to Skill 17 for your network information.

29. **Your server is wired to the network, not dialing up through an asynchronous connection. Click on Wired to Network, then on OK.**

Even if you're connected to the main office via an X.25 line, you almost certainly won't do that via Remote Access Service (RAS); you'll have an Ethernet LAN that has X.25 equipment and routers hiding that fact from your server. Virtually every installation will be "wired to network."

30. **Click on Start Search to scan for network interface cards (NICs).**

Your computer might hang here, just as it might hang when it searched for SCSI adapters. If this is so, restart the computer, and then repeat the setup starting with the graphical setup portion in step 20.

Setup might find your adapter, but call it by a slightly different name than you're expecting. I have a Farallon EtherWave controller, which is a modified 3Com 3C509 Etherlink III adapter, and sure enough, NT calls it a 3C509. My adapter doesn't seem to mind at all.

31. If you have multiple network interfaces, click on Find Next to continue the scan.

Installing multiple network interfaces enables your server to act as a router and might increase the available network bandwidth to the server. See Skill 8 for more information.

32. If Setup does not find your NIC, and you have a device driver floppy, insert the floppy, click on Have Disk, and specify the path to the driver files.

If the driver files came on a vendor-supplied floppy, insert the floppy drive and hit Enter.

Many of the device drivers are available on the CD-ROM in the \DRVLIB directory, the Windows driver library. Too bad you can't browse the file system at this point. Unfortunately, the Network Control Panel's Have Disk setup forces you to type a full path to the distribution files. But it's good to know that if you get completely stuck here, you can go back and add network devices later, once you've got a functional NT server with a browsable file system.

33. Repeat from step 31 until all the installed NICs appear in the list.

34. Select the network protocols to install: NetBEUI, TCP/IP, and IPX.

Unless there is a compelling reason to do so, you'll want to install the minimum of network protocols at this stage. You can go back and install the other protocols later.

If you have TCP/IP information available, and you want to set up the Internet Information Server (Web server) now, you'll want to install TCP/IP at this point. See Skill 8 for TCP/IP configuration information.

If you are running TCP/IP as the native transport for your NT network, you'll need to install it at this point, because you'll need that transport in order to add your server to a domain. See Skill 13 for more information.

35. Indicate other optional network services you want to install, then click on Next to set up all the network components.

Your choices are RAS and IIS. The Remote Access Service lets remote users call up your server via a modem and connect to the network as if they were on the LAN (just like what Internet service providers do). See Skill 8 for more information about RAS.

The Internet Information Server (IIS) is a Web, FTP, and Gopher server system that is now integrated into NT. For more information about these services, see Skill 19.

Skill 5

I usually install IIS here, if I'm going to install it at all. I don't generally install RAS at this point. See Skill 8 for more information.

36. If you need to specify NIC configuration information, Setup will ask for it.

You might need to refer to your System Device record for your NIC. Refer to the hardware design work that you did in Skill 4.

37. Setup will ask for the name of the domain or workgroup for this server. Enter the domain name in the Domain Name field.

For a PDC, your computer will define the domain. Enter a new domain name. For all other roles, your computer will join an existing domain. You will need to supply the name and password of an administrator account on the domain that you're trying to join.

 WARNING

In previous versions of NT, the Setup program on the Compaq servers was such that the server attempted to join a domain before the TCP/IP configuration was set. Because we run TCP/IP as our native transport, the new server couldn't yet talk to its domain controller, and Setup would get stuck at this point. It seems that the Setup Wizard for 4.0 presents the order of network configuration operations in a manner that will alleviate this problem, but if you have trouble joining a domain at this step, just bag it and join the WORKGROUP workgroup instead. In Skill 14, you'll join a domain after the server is running.

The Home Stretch

We're almost finished. At this point, Setup teases you with a tantalizing Finish button, but a few things still remain.

38. Verify the time zone, date, and time.

The Date and Time information can be way off, so be sure to check. The time might be off on Intel systems because DOS time is absolute; you enter the time, and that's what is set in the CMOS clock. NT keeps track of time using GMT internally. GMT time is kept in the CMOS clock. Be aware.

 TIP

I find it difficult to select my time zone from the drop-down list—the thing scrolls too quickly. And you can't just click on the map as you can in Windows 95 (as of this writing). It's easiest for me to look for my time zone in GMT-relative nomenclature in the drop-down box, as opposed to looking for the name of a city or time zone. This helps because I know that GMT -7 comes after GMT -6.

39. **Setup will scan for your video hardware and select a driver.**

As with the NICs, Setup will sometimes choose a driver that works but has a different name from your video card. Generally, the generic driver works great. You can refer to your video card's documentation for more details.

40. **Adjust the video display resolution, color depth, and refresh rate. When they are satisfactory, click on OK to accept the settings.**

You can adjust the display parameters by modifying the controls in the Display Properties Control Panel, shown in Figure 5.2.

It's quite possible that the Control Panel will select a Refresh Rate that's less than what your system can handle. To get a listing of all the display modes available, click on the List All Modes button in the lower-left corner of the Control Panel. This will bring up the listing of display modes shown in Figure 5.3.

You can double-click on one of the display modes to select it. Try for a display mode that's the best resolution for your monitor, with the highest possible refresh rate. Color depth ideally should be set to 256 colors (it's usually not necessary for a server to have more colors).

When you make changes to the display settings, NT Setup will test the settings for you. If you get a blank screen, or things look strange, don't accept the settings.

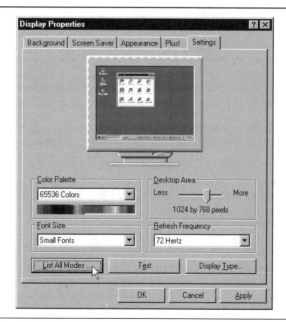

FIGURE 5.2: Use the Display Properties Control Panel to adjust display parameters.

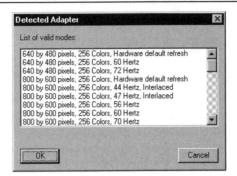

FIGURE 5.3 : Click on the List All Modes button in the Display Properties Control Panel to see this list.

It's possible that some settings will work fine with your multi-synch monitor if you set the monitor image size, geometry, and centering correctly. The image should fit nicely on the screen, almost filling the display area, and should not be pulled to one side or the other.

 WARNING Don't drive a multi-synch monitor for extended periods with a wacked-out screen image that's all the way over to one side. If the CRT is over-scanning, severe damage to your monitor may result.

41. **To create the Emergency Repair Disk, insert your blank floppy labeled "Emergency Repair Disk for <*servername*>" into the floppy drive.**

Setup will format the drive and then copy critical system information files to the drive. You'll need this disk if you ever have to repair an NT installation on this computer.

This step takes a while because the Setup program formats the floppy (even if the floppy is blank and ready to go). But you really shouldn't skip this step!

 WARNING Because the Emergency Repair Disk contains system setup information that's particular to the server, you can't exchange Emergency Repair Disks between servers, or even between the same server with different versions of Windows NT. Make sure that you have an Emergency Repair Disk for each server!

42. Setup is complete! Restart your computer.

When NT restarts, it will take a while, as it converts any NTFS partitions from their temporary FAT status. NT will reboot again after this process is complete. This is normal operation.

Congratulations! You're ready to move on, with a real live server.

Repairing an NT Installation

Sometimes bad things happen to good people. If your NT system gets to a point where it can't boot without displaying the dreaded "Blue Screen of Death," there's probably something seriously wrong with an NT system file somewhere. Or maybe you just added a device driver that you wish you hadn't. Windows NT has some thoughtfully designed features that really come in handy in these cases.

Compared to most advanced operating systems, the installation procedures for NT Server are a breeze. (If you think I'm joking, try to install one of the commercial Unix systems on your server.)

You have five things you can try to fix a wacko NT system. Refer to Table 5.1 as a troubleshooting guide.

T A B L E   5 . 1 :   Repair Methods for NT Server Installation

Problem	Possible Cause	Repair Method
Blank screen, messed up screen	Video driver	VGA mode (Intel only)
Crash, freeze after configuration change	Device driver	Last known good menu
NT can't boot	Missing or corrupted system file or setting	Boot floppy (Intel only)
NT can't boot	Missing or corrupted system file or setting	Emergency Repair Disk
NT can't boot	Missing or corrupted system file or setting	Reinstall (last resort!)

VGA Mode (Intel Only)

At boot time, you'll see the NT Loader Boot menu, with at least two entries: one for your server and one for VGA Mode. What's that? A quick look at the BOOT.INI file reveals the single difference: a \BASEVIDEO switch on the NT command, which forces NT to use the lowest-common-denominator video driver, the same one that was used during the graphical Setup Wizard phase of the NT installation.

VGA mode can save you if you manage to set a resolution that the monitor can't handle. With all the testing built into the Display Settings Control Panel, you might wonder how this could occur. But what if someone sees that nice Sony 15-inch, multi-synch hooked up to a server in the phone closet, turned off, free for the taking? I'll just hook up this here Samsung amber monitor, very nice for server applications. No one will mind...yeah. It can get challenging to manage NT when the monitor has been swapped out.

Simply reboot the server and select the VGA Mode option from the Boot menu.

NOTE   I think I really started to like NT at about Day 2, when I was trying to install using various SCSI controller cards (I had one controller that I suspected was flaky), and I had succeeded somehow in getting my system into Perma-Crash mode, after loading the custom device driver for my (only) disk controller. With the Unix system I had been trying to install, I had to wait 15 minutes while the file system was completely checked, to be rewarded with another spectacular crash as soon as the device driver got loaded. With NT, the NTFS file system came back in two seconds, and I could back out of my driver install by selecting the Last Known Good Configuration at boot time. Boy, did that save my butt!

Last Known Good Menu

If your computer won't load or work properly, after the addition of a device driver or other system component, try the last-known good configuration.

Simply reboot the server and select the NT system from the Boot menu as usual. When the screen blanks and the OS Loader appears, it should prompt you to "Hit the SPACEBAR now for the Last Known Good Menu"—so hit the space-bar! Select the Last Known Good Configuration from the menu, and see how far you get with that.

NT Boot Floppy (Intel Only)

Sometimes, your system will hang at boot time, and you happen to know (or strongly suspect) the file(s) responsible. Perhaps the BOOT.INI file, or another file critical to the startup phase, has been trashed. You know that the NT system files on the primary partition are pretty much okay. If only you could boot the system somehow, you could just copy over that one file. With a boot floppy, you can!

1. From NT, format a blank floppy. This must be from NT, because the boot sector must be written by NT.

2. From the NT Explorer, under the View menu, select Options, select the View tab, and click on Show All Files. Then click on the OK button.

3. Copy the following files to the floppy:

   - NTLDR
   - NTDETECT.COM
   - BOOT.INI
   - NTBOOTDD.SYS (for NT installations on SCSI disks only)

Label the disk "Windows NT Boot Floppy for <servername>" and store it with your other critical tools. If you ever change the partition geometry of your system that involves a change to the BOOT.INI, you'll need to update your boot floppy.

Emergency Repair Disk

You created an Emergency Repair Disk during system setup. The Emergency Repair Disk contains compressed copies of the system Registry, which encapsulates most of the configuration information specific to your server; it's what makes your Windows NT server different from a standard distribution. So the theory goes, if your server ever gets really, really sick, you can restore system files from the standard distribution, then mix in your server's particular configuration information from the Emergency Repair Disk, and get your server back.

So it's critical that you make a new Emergency Repair Disk almost as often as you back up the server. Make a new Emergency Repair Disk whenever you add users, applications, devices, or system services, or modify the disk partition scheme.

NOTE   I find that once my NT file servers are in production, they're pretty stable. I might be able to get away with updating the Emergency Repair Disk once a week. My application servers might be another story, and my PDCs take some special care.

Repairing NT with the Emergency Repair Disk

To use the Emergency Repair Disk, follow these steps:

1. Follow the first four steps of the NT installation in this chapter.

2. Hit R for Repair at the blue screen to tell NT Setup that you want to attempt a repair.

3. Setup will list all the repair options. Press Enter to proceed. This will provide the most comprehensive repair. You can disable certain options by using the arrow keys to highlight them and pressing Enter. But for now, try all the options. Windows NT Setup/Repair will verify and optionally restore the following:

   - **System Registry files:** If the Registry is corrupt, you can restore it from the Emergency Repair Disk.

   - **System files:** If any files are corrupt or missing, NT Setup/Repair will restore them from the distribution CD-ROM. Make sure that the NT Server distribution CD is in the same CD-ROM drive that was used to originally set up NT. Then the file transfers can happen automatically.

   - **Hard disk boot sector:** NT Setup/Repair can fix the boot sector so that the drive will boot properly.

WARNING   With all options enabled, Setup/Repair will remove all security settings on the system files, in case that was what was causing the problem—maybe a file is fine but is set so that no one (including the system) can read it! Make sure to go back and verify proper security on system files after an attempted repair. In particular, with NT 4.0 you'll want to restore user permissions on the \WINNT\profiles\tree.

4. NT Setup/Repair will scan for the CD-ROM, per steps 8 through 11 of the usual NT Server Setup. NT Setup/Repair needs to find the distribution CD-ROM in order to restore files from the distribution, if any system files are found to be corrupt or an incorrect version.

5. Setup will ask for the Emergency Repair Disk. Remove any floppy in the drive and insert the Emergency Repair Disk. Press Enter. You should have a recent Emergency Repair Disk! If you don't, you can hit Escape at this point and have Setup/Repair attempt to "fake it." NT Setup/Repair can still verify system files against the CD-ROM distribution, but it won't be able to restore corrupted Registry hives effectively. Use the Emergency Repair Disk!

6. NT Setup/Repair will prompt you for which Registry hives you wish to restore from the Emergency Repair Disk. Select each of the hives you would like to fix by highlighting them with the arrow keys and pressing the Enter key. Once you've selected all your hives, select Continue and press Enter. NT Setup/Repair will verify the Registry and restore any hives that it finds to be corrupt if you have told it to do so. There are four components to the Registry that may be restored from the Emergency Repair Disk:

    • **System:** Restore this part if your system is distraught over an errant device driver. All system configuration settings are kept here.

    • **Software:** If your high-level software (like SQL Server) is completely messed up, you might try restoring this hive. Note that applications tend to update the Registry rather frequently, so you might want to defer this restoration and see if the other stuff helps. If you can get a somewhat working system out of the other fixes, you might be able to save out your data enough to protect it from the effects of a Software Registry hive restoration, or you may opt to reinstall the software system altogether.

    • **Default:** You should usually check this hive and restore it.

    • **Security/SAM:** This is where the user account information is kept. If your computer is a stand-alone server, this hive can be fairly benign; depending on your domain model, you might have only a few users on such a server.

Skill 5

WARNING   Restoration of the Security/SAM database on a PDC should be performed with the PDC disconnected from the network. Since this server is off-line (you're repairing it, right?), a BDC has presumably been promoted to PDC status. When you restore the Security/SAM hive on the (old) PDC, it will once again think it's the PDC of the domain, and you'll have dueling PDCs. Before restoring the (old) PDC's network connection, you'll need to manually demote it. See Skill 13 for more details.

NT Setup/Repair will scan the Windows NT system files for problems. Once the Registry has been verified and restored, NT Setup/Repair will walk through the \WINNT directory, comparing the system files on the hard disk with those on the standard distribution. You will be alerted about any differences and asked if you wish to restore from the CD-ROM.

In this day of Internet system software *du jour*, it's very likely that some of the files are fine, and are simply more recent than the CD-ROM standard distribution. If you wish to keep a more recent file, press Escape. Otherwise, it will be overwritten with the version from the CD-ROM, and it will be gone.

If you get tired of NT Setup/Repair complaining at you about hundreds of newer files, you can hit A for All, and Setup/Repair will *replace all differing system files* with files from the standard distribution (but be warned: I think this is dangerous).

WARNING   Be careful when "repairing" system files. Make sure you have a backup or some way of restoring the newer files if you accidentally replace one with the standard file from the CD-ROM!

Once the restore procedure is complete, eject any floppies and press Enter to reboot your system. With luck, you will have fixed your problem.

Reinstalling NT

As a last resort, you may need to reinstall NT from scratch. This is harsh, but so is life.

If you are reinstalling NT in an attempt to fix a severe configuration problem, make sure that you keep the same computer name and network role (PDC, BDC, or stand-alone server). Reinstalling NT in order to change network roles is discussed in Skill 13. There are extra administrative steps that you need to perform on the domain to make this happen.

Are You Experienced?

Now you can...

- ☑ run the Setup program and have it detect your storage devices and core hardware configuration
- ☑ specify the correct installation partition for NT Server
- ☑ use the graphical Setup Wizard to complete NT Server installation
- ☑ create an Emergency Repair Disk
- ☑ repair an NT installation if NT Server won't boot properly

Skill 5

PART II

Components of a Solid
NT Server System

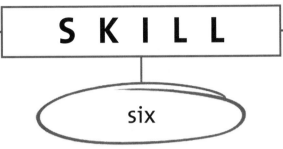

S K I L L

six

6

Building a
Solid Server System

- ❑ System reliability defined

- ❑ How to build a highly available server

- ❑ Elements of hardware and software reliability

Many people are going to rely upon your NT server, so you'll do what it takes to make it as solid and reliable as possible. NT Server 4.0 has many features to support the creation of a high-availability system with secure data. In this chapter, we'll discuss reliable systems and take a look at the options that NT provides. Use this skill as a road map to the information presented in this part of the book. Once you understand the concepts presented in this part, you'll be well on your way to designing a world-class NT system!

Solid Systems Explained

What does it mean to say that a system is *reliable*? Think about what you want in a computer system: You reach over to get some information, and there it is at your fingertips, waiting for you. You have it right when you want it, and it is the correct information. You didn't hesitate to use the system, because it has always worked when you needed it—you've come to rely upon it. Your system is really solid, and you don't need to think about it.

This example illustrates two aspects of reliable computer systems:

- **Availability:** The system is up and running when you need it, no matter when you need it.

- **Integrity:** The data that the system provides is the correct data, and that data is secure from unauthorized access.

If ever there was a system designed to provide highly available, high-integrity data to a LAN environment, NT is it!

We talk about security issues in Skill 13. Here, we'll spend most of the time talking about availability issues.

Server availability has two aspects: responsiveness and physical integrity. Let's explore these concepts in more detail and see where NT features help out.

Achieving Responsiveness

Your system is *responsive* when it handles your requests when you need it to. You get responsiveness by building a scalable, high-performance, tuned system. Let's take a closer look at each of these requirements for building a responsive system.

Scalability Defined

Scalability means that you can double the server's CPU power to double the amount of work it can perform, simply by doubling the amount of hardware. To say a system is *scalable* is to say that the graph of CPU performance versus CPU hardware is a straight line: To double the power, add another CPU; to triple the power, use three CPUs. This ideal of *linear scalability* is approached by NT Server's support of symmetric multiprocessing and its multithreaded architecture.

It's important to note that linear scalability does not necessarily guarantee double the throughput from two CPUs. Unfortunately, server scalability is not usually a simple formula like 2 times x equals $2x$. If you have a server that can take more than one processor, adding a second processor usually will not double the performance of the machine. A linearly scalable system that gets a 30 percent performance boost from a second CPU will get a 60 percent performance boost by going to that third processor, and so on. The graph of CPU performance versus CPU hardware is a straight line, but the slope of that line is almost always less than 1.

Why don't you get a 100 percent performance boost from that second CPU? For one thing, there's processing overhead at the hardware level, keeping the multiple processors synchronized. Scalability is somewhat software-dependent. If you're running a database application on your NT server, and that's all, the major database systems are fairly scalable. For file and print services, however, your mileage may vary. Generally, the software isn't multithreaded enough to get full linear scalability; some sections of code depend on the completion of other threads.

NT Server scalability issues are discussed in detail in Skill 7.

Bandwidth and High Performance

You might think you've achieved system responsiveness with a scalable CPU architecture, only to find that the network or some other subsystem can't keep up. That's where bandwidth and tuning come into play.

When we speak of *bandwidth*, we're talking about the quality of the connection to your network. Your server might be the fastest screamer in the world, but it won't do anyone much good if it's sitting behind a slow serial line. It will spend most of its time waiting on the network, sitting idle.

The amount of bandwidth your system has available depends on your network connection and your network topology.

The network connection must provide enough bits per second (bps) to move the data out of the server. In order to achieve this, the network controllers should support high data rates. You've got plenty of options of network interfaces. NT supports 10 megabits per second (Mbps) and 100 Mbps Ethernet controllers, as well as Token Ring, ATM, and FDDI.

The network topology, or structure of the network, should optimize the server's available bandwidth. You might install a very fast fiber-optic cable link to your server, only to find that your server's packets must duke it out along a saturated Ethernet network before making it to your clients. Getting a faster connection from your server to the network won't do much good if the network topology is poorly planned.

NT provides some sophisticated network services that will help you clean up your network design. It supports multi-homing, so that you can put multiple network interface cards (NICs) into a single server, and have each of the NICs on a different network segment. Or you could put that FDDI NIC in your server, and hang a fast switch off of it. Either way, the result is multiple, independent pipes into your box.

NT also supports multiple-protocol routing, so that you can use an NT server to apply some shape to your network, if necessary. In practice, it's best to just use a real router.

We'll discuss bandwidth and network topology issues in Skill 8.

Tuning: Removing System Bottlenecks

The server's various subsystems must be balanced so there are no gross bottlenecks in the system. It does no good to hook up a fast-wide ultraSCSI disk drive to an ISA-based SCSI controller, because the ISA bus can't handle the data-transfer rates. Of course, you would never do that anyway. And don't put your $20,000 super server behind a 56 kilobit per second (Kbps) serial line (as we talked about in the previous section). Of course, you would never do that, either.

In the Bad Old Days, you needed to worry about stuff like, "How much disk cache do I need?" and, "Which priority level should I give this process?" NT was designed to be self-tuning in this regard: Disk caching is managed for you, based on disk utilization. Task prioritization is a pretty complex game, too. In practice, there are few knobs to tweak.

You'll want to set task prioritization differently for a SQL horse than for a file-and-print monkey or for a compute server. In Skill 7, you"ll learn how to modify (a bit) the task prioritization of NT, given that that is one of the knobs you can tweak.

There are many other things to think about when you're trying to build a tuned, high-performance network system. We'll pull all of it together for you in the solid system design review presented in Skill 12.

Achieving Physical Integrity: Fault-Tolerant Systems

A system with *physical integrity* is one that remains operational despite adverse physical conditions. You get physical integrity by using the fault-tolerance features of NT Server. These features include UPS, RAID disk array, disk duplexing, and tape backup support.

Dealing with Power Failures

NT has built-in support for responding to UPS (uninterruptible power supply) system messages. An NT system can shut down gracefully if the UPS signals that only a few minutes of power remain. "Graceful" shutdown notifies users and closes files to preserve file system integrity before powering-down the system. We'll discuss UPS systems in Skill 9.

Dealing with Server Component Failures

Your computer is mortal, and its life is only as long as the life of the most ephemeral part. Hardware will fail, and you need to plan for it. Of the components that are most likely to fail, the hard disk system ranks first, because it has a lot of moving parts.

Disk Arrays for Redundancy in Storage Systems

NT has built-in support for RAID disk arrays. Note that NT's RAID is independent of any hardware-based RAID systems, such as those supported on the Compaq SmartDrive Array Controller. NT's RAID can run with pretty much any SCSI controller.

 NOTE   RAID stands for redundant arrays of inexpensive disks. And when RAID was first proposed, disks were anything but inexpensive. How nice that the hardware vendors have delivered the $899 4.3 GB drive!

You can do disk mirroring with two IDE drives, of course, but to get more RAID levels beyond mirroring or striping, you should use SCSI. We'll talk about why in Skill 10.

Skill 6

Other Fault-Tolerance Features

Most other component failures are best dealt with in hardware, but NT provides some related features worth mentioning here:

- **Automatic reboot:** NT can be configured to automatically reboot itself in the event of a system crash.

- **Self-correcting file system:** The NT file system, NTFS, logs all transactions to the disk, so that in the event of a system crash, the NTFS system will only need to restore its state from the last logged event that did not complete correctly. It can typically do this in a few seconds. This is in contrast to file systems common in the Unix world, where a system crash might result in lengthy file-system checks when you reboot.

- **Disk duplexing:** When you add duplicate disk controllers to your system, if one of the disk controllers fails, the other one takes over. NT lets you put multiple disk controllers in your server. You can create a mirror pair on disks that are on separate disk controllers, thus protecting the system from disk-controller failure. We'll go into detail about disk duplexing in Skill 10.

- **Fault-tolerant SMP:** NT's support for multiprocessor CPUs is not intended to provide fault-tolerance. If one of your CPUs goes out, the system will halt; it won't simply switch over to a remaining, working CPU. It's likely that data will be lost. However, you can limp along on an SMP server with a failed processor. When you reboot the server, the NT HAL will recognize the remaining, operational CPUs and use them.

NOTE   Some vendors' systems might have different features. Contact your server vendor for information particular to your server.

Preserving Your Data: Backing Up Your Server

The best-built system in the world can't protect your data from operator or user error. At some point, someone will call and ask you for that file that he or she tossed out by mistake last week. Your backup procedures will save you.

NT comes with support for the most popular tape backup systems and includes a full-featured backup program. We'll talk about the proper backup methodologies, including use of the NT Backup program, in Skill 11.

TIP   To make sure that you keep it all straight, fill out the worksheets in Skill 12. You can use the Server Performance worksheet to help you design your system before you build it, or to help identify weaknesses in your current implementation. Either way, filling out the worksheet can help you avoid the most common problems and to fix them quickly when they do arise.

Are You Experienced?

Now you know...

- ☑ solid systems provide the needed data in a timely fashion, or *high availability*

- ☑ solid systems protect the data stored on the system in order to provide *data integrity*

- ☑ a *responsive* system handles your requests when you need it to

- ☑ *scalability* implies that you can continually increase your system's performance by adding more CPU hardware

- ☑ *tuned* computer systems can move data around the various parts of the computer at roughly the same speed throughout

- ☑ NT Server provides many fault-tolerance features, including support for UPS, RAID, and tape backup systems

Skill 6

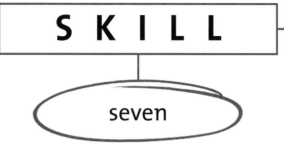

SKILL

seven

7

Scaling Up Your NT System

❑ The "back-of-the-envelope" technique for identifying performance bottlenecks

❑ How to use NT's Performance Monitor

❑ How to deal with system performance bottlenecks

❑ Methods for scaling up server hardware

One of the goals of NT's designers was to create an operating system that scales well—from the desktop workstations to the large, almost mainframe enterprise applications servers.

When you're faced with a task that can't be handled by your current tools, what's the next step? How can you tell which pieces of your system need the most work? How do you build a really huge server? Can you replace the "glass house" of centralized computing facilities with a scaled-up NT Server implementation? And do you want to?

In this skill, we'll take a look at NT system scalability. We'll examine the features of NT that enable scalability, so you have an idea of where you can build up your system. And we'll take a look at the tools you can use to determine where your system might benefit most from a scaled-up implementation.

When you're finished with this skill, you should have an idea of how to choose the best server implementation for your immediate needs, while keeping your options open for the future.

Scalability Explained

What is meant by a *scalable* system? The general idea behind computer system scalability is that for every unit of computational resources that you throw at a problem, you should get a unit of work back out.

Figure 7.1 illustrates this ideal of *linear scalability*. It shows a graph of database transactions per second going up in direct relation to the size of the hardware. Figure 7.2 shows the more common reality: After a certain point, you get less and less of a performance improvement with increased computational power. Such a process is not scalable.

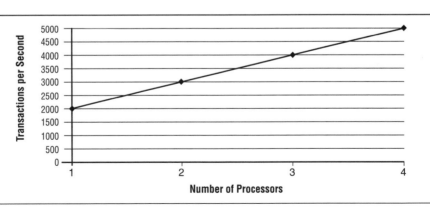

FIGURE 7.1: A scalable process's performance varies linearly with computational resources.

You need to know if your tasks are scalable before throwing lots of money at your server vendor. Fortunately, NT provides a number of process-measuring tools to help you monitor the situation and determine how to get the most bang for your buck.

You can't really talk about scalability without talking about performance optimization and tuning. You need to know what the bottlenecks are in your current system before you can tell where to spend the money on the bigger system. If your hard disks are too slow, adding more CPUs to the server is not going to help matters much.

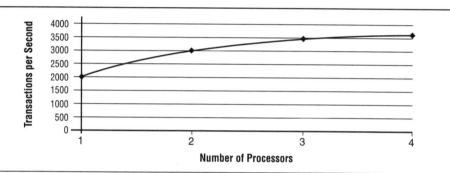

FIGURE 7.2: A process that is not scalable will level off in performance, regardless of increased computational resources.

There are two ways to tune your NT Server system:

- Modify some run-time parameters of NT to change the way the software behaves.

- Identify and correct bottlenecks in the system, which are most often a result of hardware design.

You'll need to know how to do both of these things in order to identify areas of scalability.

Tuning—Removing Performance Bottlenecks

We all know what a "performance bottleneck" is. The phrase invokes the image of trying to empty a bottle with a narrow mouth; the water can't come out as fast as it might because it all has to flow through that constricted area. It would do little good to increase the pressure by turning the bottle completely upside-down—the water still won't flow out very easily.

Skill 7

We hit this problem all the time with computer systems. There are many pieces through which our data must flow from the server, across the network, to our workstations. Within the server, there are multiple subsystems which may be the cause of the hold-up: the disk, the server system bus, the processors, or the memory.

The important thing to remember about performance tuning is that it's an interactive process. You'll succeed in moving the bottleneck around your system until you reach a good compromise. Maybe you'll achieve that compromise with a fast SCSI disk array, local bus, 100 MB fast Ethernet connection to a switch, and dual Pentium Pro processors. You need to look at all the major systems:

- Disk I/O

- Network I/O

- Processor

Once you have these three systems fairly even, you've won: your system is a well-balanced piece of work. By identifying and correcting the performance bottlenecks, you've achieved a *tuned* system.

Until you identify the cause of the problem, you won't be able to appropriately apply a solution. Let's take a look at two methods of identifying performance bottlenecks:

- The "back-of-the-envelope" method, which utilizes your knowlege of theoretical maximum performance on the various subsystems.

- The empirical method, which utilizes performance counters to measure and analyze the "real-world" operation of your server system.

Identifying Performance Bottlenecks with Pencil and Paper

As good as these hard-core performance-monitoring tools are, you can get swamped by too much raw information. It really pays to step back and think about some basics before diving into the hard-core stuff. A little thought up front can save you a great deal of money and time down the road.

Consider the case of a server with a DEC Alpha CPU, dual EISA/PCI bus, and lots and lots of RAM. We install a reasonably good SCSI-2 hard disk on the system and an ISA SCSI controller. Users complain that the system is too slow. Do we add more RAM? Get another hard disk? Replace the controller? Fire the system administrator?

Let's take a look at our options. We won't be able to pull data off the disk any faster if we increase the speed of the drive, because the performance bottleneck is in the disk controller:

Subsystem	Bandwidth (MB/sec)
ISA SCSI controller	2.5
SCSI-2 bus	10
Hard disk	5

Because of the limitations of the ISA bus, we won't be able to pull data off the hard disk any faster than 2.5 MB/second, no matter how fast the hard disk is.

So after realizing our mistake, we give the old ISA SCSI adapter back to the guy in the next cube (he pulled it out of his junk computer), and order a fire-breathing, PCI dual-channel controller with all sorts of features. And for a while, people are happy. And then the phone rings—yeah, it's still too slow. Fix it again:

Subsystem	Bandwidth (MB/sec)
PCI SCSI controller	32
SCSI-2 bus	10
Hard disk	5

Now we've got a bottleneck at the hard disk. But that's easy to fix; our shiny new SCSI controller supports disk striping, so we can create a hard disk volume using multiple hard disk drives, which can be operated in parallel:

Subsystem	Bandwidth (MB/sec)
PCI SCSI controller	32
SCSI-2 bus	10
Hard disk A	5
Hard disk B	5
Hard disk C	5
Total hard disk bandwidth (all operations in parallel)	15

So we've succeeded in moving the bottleneck off the hard disks and onto the SCSI bus itself. If we want to go any faster, we'll need to switch to fast-wide SCSI disks and controllers.

Then the problem will probably be in our Ethernet connection, because the maximum we can get out of our Ethernet is 10 MB/sec. In fact, we probably would look at the network connection right off, to see if there are any obvious pathologies there that can be addressed. We'll discuss network performance optimization in Skill 8.

Identifying Performance Bottlenecks with Performance Monitor

You may remember from the discussion in Skill 3 that NT keeps track of its state and logs critical events as they occur. You can take a peek into the run-time state of NT with two NT Server tools: the Task Manager and Performance Monitor.

As you learned in Skill 2, the Task Manager shows a list of running applications and processes. You can use the Task Manager as you're sitting at the server console to get a quick-and-dirty look at the state of the processor and memory utilization. But to identify performance problems from a remote location or over a long period of time, you'll need a far more powerful tool: the Performance Monitor.

I love the Performance Monitor, and you will, too. You can get all kinds of information about the state of your system just by playing around with it. You can set it up on your NT workstation on your desk and keep track of the performance of every server on your network in real time. This thing comes for free with NT Server, and it's great.

You don't have to be an NT expert to get really smart with the Performance Monitor. Just play around with it. Your best ideas will come as you start to correlate the performance counters with real-world situations.

Using Performance Monitor

You can find Performance Monitor where you find all the important tools: in the Start menu, under Programs, in the Administrative Tools menu. Fire up the Performance Monitor, and it will appear on your screen, waiting for you to tell it what to start counting, as shown in Figure 7.3.

Click on the + button on the toolbar. This is the Add to Chart command, which you can also find in the Edit menu. Once you've clicked on that button, you'll see the dialog box shown in Figure 7.4, which lists all of the possible counters that you can look at.

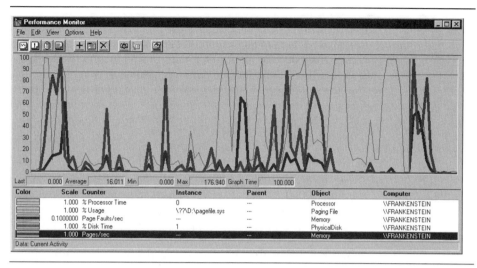

FIGURE 7.3: NT's Performance Monitor lets you view the performance characteristics of various computer systems in real time.

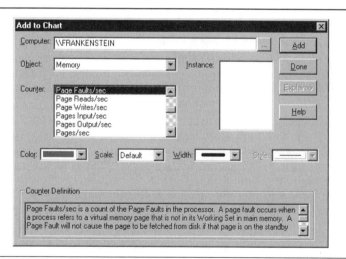

FIGURE 7.4: The Add to Chart dialog box lists all the available performance counters.

On my system, it takes a while for the Add to Chart dialog box to appear, because NT is thinking about all the things that can possibly be monitored (in previous versions of NT, I didn't need to wait for this dialog box). So don't worry if you must wait a bit for the Add to Chart dialog box.

Here are your counter choices in the dialog box:

- **Computer:** By default, you'll be monitoring the performance of the local machine. By clicking on the … button to the right of the Computer Name text box, you'll get a network browser, which will let you choose an NT computer from the network to look at. If you know the name of the computer you want to monitor, you can just enter its UNC (its name prepended with the double-slash) in the Computer Name text box.

- **Object:** There are a number of classes of performance counters that you might want to look at. To keep them all straight, the Performance Monitor classifies them by Object. This refers to the internal, NT operating-system "objects" that were discussed in Skill 3. But here, just think of it as a classification scheme for the performance counters. You can look at Memory, Physical Disk, Processor, and so on.

- **Counter:** For each object or counter classification, there are a number of actual counters that you may add to the chart. If you need an explanation of the significance of a particular counter, choose that counter and click on the Explain button.

Feel free to make liberal use of the Explain option. There's a wealth of tasty information in some of the explanations of the performance counters!

- **Instance:** Some counters might make sense by themselves, and some, like the % Processor Time counter, will be tied to a particular processor—a particular instance of the processor class. For example, I have only one processor in my server, so there's only a 0 in the Instance list for the % Processor Time counter. When I choose the Physical Disk counter, I get five instances: one for each of my disk drives. I would need to choose which disk I wanted to monitor from the Instance list.

The rest of the controls in this dialog box relate to the appearance of the line in the chart. You can select the line color, width, scale, and style. Your choices will depend on your preferences and your system. For example, I find that it's sometimes useful to change the scale, because we get more AppleTalk timeouts on our network than can be accommodated by the default scale for that counter.

Capturing Data for Further Analysis

Although the real-time graphing of the Performance Monitor gives you an immediate feel for the status of your NT systems, there are times when you'll want to capture data over long periods of time for analysis later. The Performance Monitor lets you log performance counters to a log file.

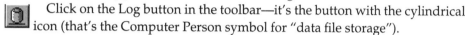 Click on the Log button in the toolbar—it's the button with the cylindrical icon (that's the Computer Person symbol for "data file storage").

Or you can choose the Log command from the View menu. Either route puts the Performance Monitor into logging mode. The top portion of the screen will show you the name of the current log file, which should be blank if this is your first time using the logging mode.

Here are the steps for creating and storing information in a log file:

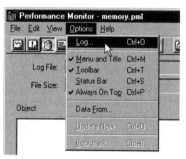

1. Create a new log file by choosing Log from the Options menu.

2. The Log Options dialog box will appear, as shown in Figure 7.5. Much of it looks like a standard file box. Find a good place for the log file. Keep in mind that log files can get large, so put your file in a place where you can afford the disk space.

3. Set the Update Time (Interval) for this log file. The default of 15 seconds will give you a fairly large data file over a few hours: 240 data points for every performance counter per hour. Think about how long you're going to track the data, and think about what you're going to do with it. Over a period of hours or days, a logging interval of 600 seconds (10 minutes) makes sense.

4. Click on the Save button to save the log, then click on Start Log to start logging the data to the file.

5. Come back in a few hours and take a look at your log file size to make sure the log is being generated.

6. When you're finished capturing the data, choose Log from the Options menu and click on Stop Log (it's the same button that you used to start the logging in the first place).

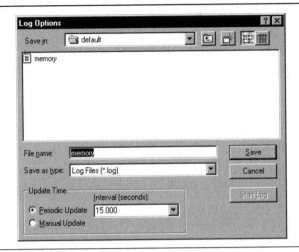

FIGURE 7.5:   The Log Options dialog box lets you specify a place to store your log file.

Looking at the Log File Data

Now that you've got your data, what are you going to do with it? How are you going to look at it? There are two ways: You can examine the data from within the Performance Monitor or you can export the data to a program like Microsoft Excel.

To chart the data in the Performance Monitor, go back to the chart view, and select Data From in the Options menu. Type in the name of your log file, or click on the ... button to bring up a standard file dialog box so you can find your log file.

To examine your data in another program, stay in logging mode, and choose Export Log from the File menu. You can save the data as comma-separated values (CSV) or as tab-delimited text fields.

Things to Look for in Your Performance Data

When you look at your performance data, you can check for two main problem areas: memory and processes.

Monitoring for Memory

To see how NT is handling memory, monitor the Pages/Sec and Page Faults/Sec under the Memory Object, and % Usage and % Usage Peak under the Paging File Object.

Is your computer spending lots of time swapping virtual memory? Is your paging file being used, or is most of it empty? Is your paging file growing over time? Does it reach a steady state?

You usually want your paging file to be between 150 and 200 percent of physical RAM—no more than that.

Monitoring for Processes

Is your computer bogged down under too many simultaneous processes? How many threads are there running on the system over time?

Monitor the Process–Thread Count–Total counter to keep an eye on the number of threads in your system. More than a few hundred threads on your system might indicate that your computer could benefit from multiple processors, especially if the % processor time stays high.

You can get some indication of how well your processes will respond to multiple CPUs by keeping an eye on the System–Processor Queue Length counter, which you'll need to monitor in conjunction with a counter from the Thread category. Your system will be able to distribute threads among multiple processors if the processor queue length remains high.

Where to Go from Here with the Performance Monitor

You can go a long way with the Performance Monitor by simply playing around. One of the best tools in NT is the built-in performance counters, and it's great that the Performance Monitor comes free.

You'll be able to get a great deal out of watching those little squiggles on your screen and playing around in an intuitive fashion. But to really get all you can out of the Performance Monitor, you'll need some hard-core help.

TIP   One could write a whole book about the Performance Monitor. Fortunately, someone did—Russ Blake wrote a book called *Optimizing Windows NT*, which is a fantastic in-depth course in the use of the Performance Monitor and other NT tools. The book is available from Microsoft Press, and is commonly sold as volume three of the Windows NT 3.51 Resource Kit.

Modifying NT Run-Time Parameters

Once you've identified some of your performance bottlenecks, you'll want to do something about them. One option is to run out and purchase all new hardware, tear down your system, work all weekend, and frantically get it all put back together before people start showing up at seven on Monday morning. Ah, yes, we live for those moments of glory and terror, but how long is it going to take to get permission for a weekend outage?

Fortunately, there are things you can do in software, with some of NT Server's operational parameters, which might alleviate some performance issues. You'll need to reboot your server to have these changes take effect, but you'll be able to do it in a few minutes (with an hour of testing afterwards, of course), so you can play with things and not have to wait for the weekend.

In the old days of computer systems, there were many parameters in the operating system software that could be modified to fit a particular task: the amount of memory used for file cache, the amount of memory to keep for network buffers, and so on. One of the design goals of NT was to provide a *dynamically self-tuning* system—one that monitors current conditions and reacts accordingly. NT decides on the fly how much of the system should be devoted to file cache or network buffers. You generally don't touch a thing.

However, there are two big system parameters that you can change in NT Server:

- The minimum and maximum sizes of the virtual memory page file, and the page file(s) location(s)

- The amount of performance priority given to tasks that are running in the foreground

Managing the Virtual Memory Page File

The first parameter, the size of the page file, is still controlled by NT during runtime. You simply tell NT what the minimum and maximum values are. NT still decides dynamically how large the virtual pool is.

You determine the size of NT's page file through the Performance tab of the System Properties dialog box, shown in Figure 7.6. Click on the Change button in the Virtual Memory section to bring up a dialog box that lists all of the hard disk volumes on your system and indicates which of these volumes currently host a page file, as shown in Figure 7.7.

You can create or delete a page file on a volume as follows:

- To create a page file, select the volume from the list. Enter a minimum size in the Initial Size field and a maximum size in the Maximum Size field, and then click on the Set button.

- To delete a page file, set its maximum size to zero, or simply clear out the size information, leaving it blank. Then click on the Set button.

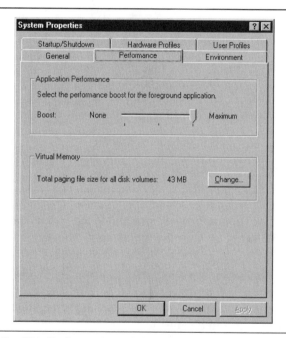

FIGURE 7.6: The Performance tab in the System Control Panel

TIP   On systems with SCSI hard drives (you *do* use SCSI, right?), you can increase the performance of your system by distributing the page file across multiple volumes, so that the hard disks involved can perform disk operations (reads and writes) in parallel. You'll trade some reliability: If one of the volumes goes off-line, your system will halt. However, upon reboot, the system will work fine (complaining about the missing page file). Just make sure that no one page file is smaller than the recommended amount indicated in the Virtual Memory dialog box.

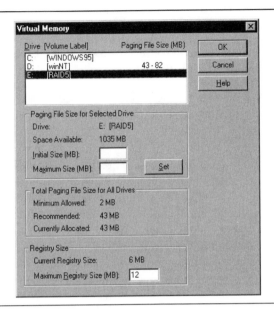

FIGURE 7.7 : The Virtual Memory dialog box

Once you're finished modifying the virtual memory page file sizes, click on the OK button to commit your changes. The server will ask you to reboot it in order for your changes to be made. Your changes to the size of the page file, including adding page files to other volumes, will not take effect until you reboot the server. You can defer the reboot of the server, and your changes will be in place the next time the server boots (unless some other administrator changes these parameters in the meantime).

Managing Foreground Process Priority

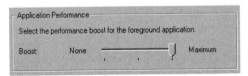

The Performance tab in the System Properties dialog box also has a slider that you can use to modify the amount by which NT boosts the priority of the front-most task.

Normally, NT gives the front task the higher-than-usual priority. It assumes that the front-most task must respond to user events, such as a mouse click or a key press, and that these user events are time-critical. For a workstation, this might make a lot of sense, but for a computer that's mostly used as a file server, there are almost never any foreground tasks except the backup program, which should be run when the server is not in use anyway. For a file server, you can move the slider to indicate that NT not give any priority to foreground tasks.

When might you want to give priority to foreground tasks? If your server is running applications such a Microsoft Excel under remote Visual Basic control, as a compute server, for example, you might want NT to boost the foreground execution priority.

Boosting the foreground task's priority does not necessarily mean that this front-most task has the *highest* priority on the system. Critical system tasks will still get priority, and will still bump any foreground task if necessary.

Scaling Up Your Hardware

Tweaking run-time parameters is fun, but what you really want to do is to put together a system that will take care of your needs for now and in the future. How big does your server have to be, and how will you build it?

There are two ways to scale up your server hardware environment:

- Build really huge servers that will be able to take care of large loads with ease, and will scale well by adding even more processing power in the future. This solution can work well for NT applications servers, where the CPU is being worked hard.

- Build lots of relatively modest servers that are adequate for up to 150 users, and place these servers on the network as close to the users as possible. This solution works well for file and print servers, where the load on the server is bound by network bandwidth. Multiple servers provide options for load-balancing as users move from building to building.

Some solutions for *clustering* a group of NT servers together, making them appear as one larger server, are becoming available. This method of aggregating computational resources is common in the mini-computer world, in which a computer cluster serves as an applications server, providing database and number-crunching power to remote users throughout the company. So we'll likely see some convergence of these two methods of scaling up: the distributed servers will grow out of their file-and-print origins as we increase their capacity, and the applications servers in the data center will split up into clusters of less-expensive servers as the cost benefits of NT clustering technology appear.

Skill 7

An Example: Scaling Up File and Print Servers

For the file and print servers at my company, the way we went about it was to deploy NT-based servers of about the same power as the departmental LAN servers already in operation, and then measure the performance response of those servers. Here's what we found for our NT-based file and print servers:

- For our network situation, modest servers (single-processor Pentium systems with hardware RAID disk controllers) were able to handle the performance load if they were on the same subnet as most of that server's users.

- Once we started putting more widely distributed users on a server, complaints about response time went up. This performance bottleneck was attributed to the network bandwidth between the subnets.

We solved our problem in two ways: deploying more of these smaller-scale servers and optimizing the network connections on some of the servers by adding more Ethernet interfaces, and segmenting our network appropriately.

We learned that because our network was the problem, our performance problems would not have been solved by consolidating network services onto one huge super-server. We are moving in that direction, but it will take network reengineering.

We were able to measure the servers using the Performance Monitor, and we found that the CPUs were pretty bored most of the time. For file and print servers, this is likely to be the case: The bottlenecks will occur in disk and network I/O. However, if you're planning on downsizing your corporate database onto NT servers, using BackOffice or another commercial database product, you'll definitely want to consider a larger server system.

Where to Focus

Focus on the following systems:

- Disk I/O

- Network I/O

- Memory

- Processors

- Bus architecture

Disk I/O

Consider moving up to a fast SCSI array to increase performance. Measure the performance using the "back-of-the-envelope" technique presented at the beginning of the skill to ensure that your disk system is optimal.

Interface	Approximate Maximum Bus Transfer Speed (MB/sec)
SCSI-1 (obsolete)	5
Fast SCSI-2	10
Wide SCSI-2	20
Fast-Wide SCSI-2	40
UltraSCSI (Wide)	40

Network I/O

NT Server 4.0 provides many options for optimizing network performance. Read Skill 8 for details.

Memory

Make sure that your system can accommodate large amounts of RAM. Systems that can handle 128-bit interleaved DIMMs are doing very well in memory subsystem benchmarks these days. Don't ignore the need for more level 2 cache as you increase primary physical RAM. Check with your server vendor to make sure.

Processors

In general, the RISC-based systems are faster processors than the Intel-based systems of the same generation; however, it depends on your application. Many server vendors are offering systems with up to four processors in them, and these systems may be appropriate for your application. Companies such as Tandem and NCR (AT&T) have been producing systems with even more processors in them, and they have been getting good reviews. These systems might be appropriate for data-intensive applications, but check with the vendors first. Some applications don't scale very well after about four processors.

Skill 7

Bus Architecture

These days, PCI is the way to go. For maximum flexibility, you'll want an EISA/PCI computer, which can handle all the different kinds of add-on cards.

Bus Architecture	Bandwidth (MB/sec)
ISA	2.5 to 3
EISA	5 to 12
PCI	32 to 132

Note that the actual bandwidth depends on your system clock speed.

Are You Experienced?

Now you can...

- ☑ identify performance bottlenecks by comparing the maximum theoretical performance of each component of your system

- ☑ measure the performance of your server with NT's Performance Monitor tool

- ☑ optimize the amount of virtual memory made available to your system

- ☑ modify the priorities of foreground tasks

- ☑ determine whether a setup with multiple, smaller servers or one large server is the best for your situation

356-555-3398.

PROGRAMMERS
C, C, VB, Cobol, exp. Call 534-555-6543 or fax 534-555-6544.

PROGRAMMING
MRFS Inc. is looking for a Sr. Windows NT developer. Reqs. 3-5 yrs. Exp. In C under Windows, Win95 & NT, using Visual C. Excl. OO design & implementation skills a must. OLE2 & ODBC are a plus. Excl. Salary & bnfts. Resume & salary history to HR, 8779 HighTech Way, Computer City, AR

PROGRAMMERS
Contractors Wanted for short & long term assignments: Visual C, MFC Unix C/C, SQL Oracle Dev elop ers PC Help Desk Support Windows NT & NetWareTelecommunications Visual Basic, Access, HTMT, CGI, Perl MMI & Co., 885-555-9933

PROGRAMMER World Wide Web Links wants your HTML & Photoshop skills. Develop great WWW sites. Local & global customers. Send samples & resume to WWWL, 2000 Apple Road, Santa Rosa, CA.

TECHNICAL WRITER Software firm seeks writer/editor for manuals, research notes, project mgmt. Min 2 years tech. writing, DTP & programming experience. Send resume & writing samples to: Software Systems, Dallas, TX.

TECHNICAL Software development firm looking for Tech Trainers, Ideal candidates have programming experience in Visual C, HTML & JAVA. Need quick self starter. Call (443) 555-6868 for interview.

TECHNICAL WRITER/ Premier Computer Corp is seeking a combination of technical skills, knowledge and experience in the following areas: UNIX, Windows 95/NT, Visual Basic, on-line help & documentation, and the internet. Candidates must possess excellent writing skills, and be comfortable working in a quality vs. deadline driven environment. Competitive salary. Fax resume & samples to Karen Fields, Premier Computer Corp., 444 Industrial Blvd. Concord, CA. Or send to our website at www.premier.com.

WEB DESIGNER
BA/BS or equivalent programming/multimedia production. 3 years of experience in use and design of WWW services streaming audio and video HTML, PERL, CGI, GIF, JPEG. Demonstrated interpersonal, organization, communication, multi-tasking skills. Send resume to The Learning People at www.learning.com.

WEBMASTER-TECHNICAL
BSCS or equivalent, 2 years of experience in CGI, Windows 95/NT, UNIX, C, Java, Perl. Demonstrated ability to design, code, debug and test on-line services. Send resume to The Learning People at www.learning.com.

PROGRAMMER World Wide Web Links wants your HTML & Photoshop skills. Develop great WWW sites. Local & global customers. Send sam-

ing tools. Experienced in documentation preparation & programming languages (Access, C, FoxPro) are a plus. Financial or banking customer service support is required along with excellent verbal & written communication skills with multi levels of end-users. Send resume to KKUP Enterprises, 45 Orange Blvd., Orange, CA.

COMPUTERS Small Web Design Firm seeks indiv. w/NT, Webserver & Database management exp. Fax resume to 556-555-4221.

COMPUTER/ Visual C/C, Visual Basic Exp'd Systems Analysts/ Programmers for growing software dev. team in Roseburg. Computer Science or related degree preferred. Develop adv. Engineering applications for engineering firm. Fax resume to 707-555-8744.

COMPUTER Web Master for dynamic SF Internet co. Site. Dev., test, coord., train, 2 yrs prog. Exp. C C, Web C, FTP. Fax resume to Best Staffing 845-555-7722.

COMPUTER PROGRAMMER
Ad agency seeks programmer w/exp. in UNIX/NT Platforms, Web Server, CGI/Perl. Programmer Position avail. on a project basis with the possibility to move into F/T. Fax resume & salary req. to R. Jones 334-555-8332.

COMPUTERS Programmer/Analyst Design and maintain C based SQL database applications. Required skills: Visual Basic, C, SQL, ODBC. Document existing and new applications. Novell or NT exp. a plus. Fax resume & salary history to 235-555-9935.

GRAPHIC DESIGNER
Webmaster's Weekly is seeking a creative Graphic Designer to design high impact marketing collateral, including direct mail promo's, CD-ROM packages, ads and WWW pages. Must be able to juggle multiple projects and learn new skills on the job very rapidly. Web design experience a big plus, technical troubleshooting also a plus. Call 435-555-1235.

GRAPHICS - ART DIRECTOR - WEB-MULTIMEDIA
Leading internet development company has an outstanding opportunity for a talented, high-end Web Experienced Art Director. In addition to a great portfolio and fresh ideas, the ideal candidate has excellent communication and presentation skills. Working as a team with innovative producers and programmers, you will create dynamic, interactive web sites and application interfaces. Some programming experience required. Send samples and resume to: SuperSites, 333 Main, Seattle, WA.

MARKETING
Fast paced software and services provider looking for MARKETING COMMUNICATIONS SPECIALIST to be responsible for its webpage, seminar coordination, and ad place-

PROGRAMMERS Multiple short term assignments available: Visual C, 3 positions SQL ServerNT Server, 2 positions JAVA & HTML, long term NetWare Various locations. Call for more info. 356-555-3398.

PROGRAMMERS
C, C, VB, Cobol, exp. Call 534-555-6543 or fax 534-555-6544.

PROGRAMMING
MRFS Inc. is looking for a Sr. Windows NT developer. Reqs. 3-5 yrs. Exp. In C under Windows, Win95 & NT, using Visual C. Excl. OO design & implementation skills a must. OLE2 & ODBC are a plus. Excl. Salary & bnfts. Resume & salary history to HR, 8779 HighTech Way, Computer City, AR

PROGRAMMERS/ Contractors Wanted for short & long term assignments: Visual C, MFC Unix C/C, SQL Oracle Developers PC Help Desk Support Windows NT & NetWareTelecommunications Visual Basic, Access, HTMT, CGI, Perl MMI & Co., 885-555-9933

PROGRAMMER World Wide Web Links wants your HTML & Photoshop skills. Develop great WWW sites. Local & global customers. Send samples & resume to WWWL, 2000 Apple Road, Santa Rosa, CA.

TECHNICAL WRITER Software firm seeks writer/editor for manuals, research notes, project mgmt. Min 2 years tech. writing, DTP & programming experience. Send resume & writing samples to: Software Systems, Dallas, TX.

COMPUTER PROGRAMMER
Ad agency seeks programmer w/exp. in UNIX/NT Platforms, Web Server, CGI/Perl. Programmer Position avail. on a project basis with the possibility to move into F/T. Fax resume & salary req. to R. Jones 334-555-8332.

TECHNICAL WRITER Premier Computer Corp is seeking a combination of technical skills, knowledge and experience in the following areas: UNIX, Windows 95/NT, Visual Basic, on-line help & documentation, and the internet. Candidates must possess excellent writing skills, and be comfortable working in a quality vs. deadline driven environment. Competitive salary. Fax resume & samples to Karen Fields, Premier Computer Corp., 444 Industrial Blvd. Concord, CA. Or send to our website at www.premier.com.

WEB DESIGNER
BA/BS or equivalent programming/multimedia production. 3 years of experience in use and design of WWW services streaming audio and video HTML, PERL, CGI, GIF, JPEG. Demonstrated interpersonal, organization, communication, multi-tasking skills. Send resume to The Learning People at www.learning.com.

WEBMASTER-TECHNICAL
BSCS or equivalent, 2 years of experience in CGI, Windows 95/NT, UNIX, C, Java, Perl. Demonstrated

COMPUTERS Small Web Design Firm seeks indiv. w/NT, Webserver & Database management exp. Fax resume to 556-555-4221.

COMPUTER Visual C/C, Visual Basic Exp'd Systems Analysts/ Programmers for growing software dev. team in Roseburg. Computer Science or related degree preferred. Develop adv. Engineering applications for engineering firm. Fax resume to 707-555-8744.

COMPUTER Web Master for dynamic SF Internet co. Site. Dev., test, coord., train, 2 yrs prog. Exp. C C, Web C, FTP. Fax resume to Best Staffing 845-555-7722.

COMPUTERS/ QA SOFTWARE TESTERS Qualified candidates should have 2 yrs exp. performing integration & system testing using automated testing tools. Experienced in documentation preparation & programming languages (Access, C, FoxPro) are a plus. Financial or banking customer service support is required along with excellent verbal & written communication skills with multi levels of end-users. Send resume to KKUP Enterprises, 45 Orange Blvd., Orange, CA.

COMPUTERS Programmer/Analyst Design and maintain C based SQL database applications. Required skills: Visual Basic, C, SQL, ODBC. Document existing and new applications. Novell or NT exp. a plus. Fax resume & salary history to 235-555-9935.

GRAPHIC DESIGNER
Webmaster's Weekly is seeking a creative Graphic Designer to design high impact marketing collateral, including direct mail promo's, CD-ROM packages, ads and WWW pages. Must be able to juggle multiple projects and learn new skills on the job very rapidly. Web design experience a big plus, technical troubleshooting also a plus. Call 435-555-1235.

GRAPHICS - ART DIRECTOR - WEB-MULTIMEDIA
Leading internet development company has an outstanding opportunity for a talented, high-end Web Experienced Art Director. In addition to a great portfolio and fresh ideas, the ideal candidate has excellent communication and presentation skills. Working as a team with innovative producers and programmers, you will create dynamic, interactive web sites and application interfaces. Some programming experience required. Send samples and resume to: SuperSites, 333 Main, Seattle, WA.

COMPUTER PROGRAMMER
Ad agency seeks programmer w/exp. in UNIX/NT Platforms, Web Server, CGI/Perl. Programmer Position avail. on a project basis with the possibility to move into F/T. Fax resume & salary req. to R. Jones 334-555-8332.

PROGRAMMERS / Established software company seeks programmers with extensive Windows NT

ment. Must be a self-starter, energetic, organized. Must have 2 years web experience. Programming a plus. Call 985-555-9854.

PROGRAMMERS Multiple short term assignments available: Visual C, 3 positions SQL ServerNT Server, 2 positions JAVA & HTML, long term NetWare Various locations. Call for more info. 356-555-3398.

PROGRAMMERS
C, C, VB, Cobol, exp. Call 534-555-6543 or fax 534-555-6544.

PROGRAMMING
MRFS Inc. is looking for a Sr. Windows NT developer. Reqs. 3-5 yrs. Exp. In C under Windows, Win95 & NT, using Visual C. Excl. OO design & implementation skills a must. OLE2 & ODBC are a plus. Excl. Salary & bnfts. Resume & salary history to HR, 8779 HighTech Way, Computer City, AR

PROGRAMMERS/ Contractors Wanted for short & long term assignments: Visual C, MFCUnix C/C, SQL Oracle Developers PC Help Desk Support Windows NT & NetWare Telecommunications Visual Basic, Access, HTMT, CGI, Perl MMI & Co. 885-555-9933

PROGRAMMER World Wide Web Links wants your HTML & Photoshop skills. Develop great WWW sites. Local & global customers. Send samples & resume to WWWL, 2000 Apple Road, Santa Rosa, CA.

TECHNICAL WRITER Software firm seeks writer/editor for manuals, research notes, project mgmt. Min 2 years tech. writing, DTP & programming experience. Send resume & writing samples to: Software Systems, Dallas, TX.

TECHNICAL Software development firm looking for Tech Trainers, Ideal candidates have programming experience in Visual C, HTML & JAVA. Need quick self starter. Call (443) 555-6868 for interview.

TECHNICAL WRITER Premier Computer Corp is seeking a combination of technical skills, knowledge and experience in the following areas: UNIX, Windows 95/NT, Visual Basic, on-line help & documentation, and the internet. Candidates must possess excellent writing skills, and be comfortable working in a quality vs. deadline driven environment. Competitive salary. Fax resume & samples to Karen Fields, Premier Computer Corp., 444 Industrial Blvd. Concord, CA. Or send to our website at www.premier.com.

WEB DESIGNER
BA/BS or equivalent programming/multimedia production. 3 years of experience in use and design of WWW services streaming audio and video HTML, PERL, CGI, GIF, JPEG. Demonstrated interpersonal, organization, communication, multi-tasking skills. Send resume to The Learning People at www.learning.com.

WEBMASTER-TECHNICAL

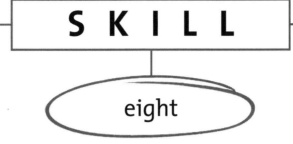

SKILL

eight

8

Optimizing Your Network Design

❑ Methods for identifying network bottlenecks

❑ How to maximize server network bandwidth

❑ Network segmentation strategies

❑ Network transport protocol options

In the previous chapters, we described how to identify and rectify some of the performance bottlenecks in your NT server. But the fastest, most highly tuned server in the world will not be of much use if you have it connected to your users with a slow serial connection. No one comes up with a poor network design intentionally, but we all know how common unanticipated network bottlenecks can be.

This Skill is not meant to teach you about network bottlenecks in general, but rather to point out the NT Server 4.0 features that can help you tune your network performance. Familiarity with basic networking concepts is assumed. We will discuss some basics, showing you how to set up an NT server with DNS, for example, but there won't be a huge discussion of what DNS is and how it came to be. We'll illustrate most of the networking concepts by using the TCP/IP protocol.

With the NT configuration options presented in this chapter, you'll be able to scale up the network connection of your highly tuned NT server to get the most performance out of it. Your network clients will be able to keep your server busy, so you'll get the computing power that you paid for. Let's see how it's done.

The Network Bottleneck Explained

These days, the typical corporate LAN is running on 10 MB/sec Ethernet. Plug a figure like 10 MB/sec into your "back-of-the-envelope" performance analysis from Skill 7, and it's easy to see that your server could keep that network saturated with data if it wanted to—a workstation with a SCSI disk could dump data at 5 MB/sec easily. With the performance tuning that we worked through in Skill 7, we simply succeeded in pushing the bottleneck out to the network wire. We need to keep pushing before our job is done. We want that bottleneck to live somewhere on the outlying borders of our network. Until the problem retreats over the horizon, we'll keep shooting at it.

Typical Ethernet causes a bottleneck with your server, simply by being there. There isn't enough bandwidth to keep a modern server completely busy. This may not necessarily be a problem with your server, of course. It could be that your server is performing some data manipulation that is CPU-bound, and it won't be able to keep a 10 MB/sec stream in any case. But for file servers and database engines, the network bandwidth is the limiting factor.

 TIP   **File servers are typically limited by the speed of their network connection. Network improvements tend to scale linearly for servers with saturated network connections, so improving the network connection is very cost-effective.**

There's another aspect to the network bottleneck problem, however: The more computers we have on the network, the slower the network becomes. Let's see how that can happen, and what we can do about it.

Eliminating the Bandwidth Bottleneck

Here we've got a problem: a flat network with 300 clients on it. Figure 8.1 illustrates the setup; each computer icon in the diagram represents 100 client PCs. A flat network is one that has no routing going on.

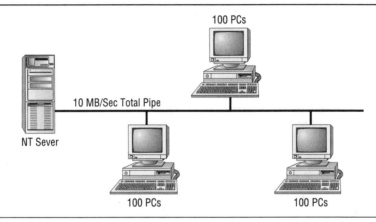

FIGURE 8.1: A flat 10 MB/sec Ethernet network with 300 clients (each PC icon represents 100 client PCs) and your NT server. All the computers on the network share the 10 MB/sec total bandwidth, so that in practice, each computer realizes only a fraction of a 10 MB/sec throughput.

NOTE   A network can be flat with respect to one protocol and segmented with respect to others. If you're routing only TCP/IP, and your NT server and PC clients are using NetBEUI (which isn't routable), you have this flat-network situation, no matter how many routers you've spent money on!

What's the throughput going to be if everyone lights up the net at the same time? That 10 MB/sec divided among 300 clients gives us about 33 KB/sec—about what my modem can do on a good day. Sure, it's not that straightforward, since not all 300 computers will stay lit up for long periods of time. But what if each machine tried to talk 7 percent of the time? Out of 100 milliseconds, the network would be talking for 7 of them. Then we would still be able to sustain only about 480 KB/sec out of the network pipe. You might as well not spend any more money on that hard disk controller than you have to—a cheap IDE controller should be able to give you enough bandwidth!

Routing

The first obvious solution is to reduce the number of clients that are hitting the network at the same time. You could fire half the employees ("Gee, my net would work great if there were no users"), but that's probably not realistic or desirable. Ultimately, it would just mean more work for you, somehow. It always does.

What most people do is split up the network into a bunch of subnetworks, as illustrated in Figure 8.2. Each subnetwork still runs on a 10 MB/sec Ethernet pipe, but you put only 100 computers on each subnet. Now instead of 480 KB/sec, you find that you're getting 1.5 MB/sec, which is pretty good. As far as your client computers are concerned, you're a hero!

 NOTE   When routing is used to partition networks for performance reasons, you'll most certainly want to use a dedicated router, not a server running NT. The routing capabilities built into NT are more appropriate for the flexible network scenario we'll talk about soon.

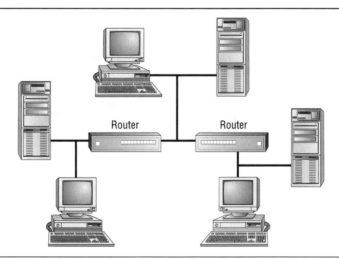

FIGURE 8.2: Segmenting a network with routers can increase the effective bandwidth available to each computer.

Multiple NICs: Getting More Pipes

But that $30,000 server still has a couple of problems. To realize the server-side benefits of subnetting, you can put one server on each subnet. But that's a really expensive way to provide 1.5 MB/sec data streams to folks. The network is still a major bottleneck for these file servers. Sure, you're better off now, because if you keep the server on a "central" subnet and have everyone hit it, then you're back to square one—you just move the bottleneck upstream.

Fortunately, you can put lots of NICs (network interface cards) in your server and configure each one to act as an independent network. NICs are cheap—cheaper than another server. The conceptual view is shown in Figure 8.3. For a typical implementation, see Figure 8.4. We still have routers and network segments in there; we simply put one server on multiple networks by adding a separate network interface for each net segment. As indicated by the conceptual view in Figure 8.3, what we've done here is given our server a 30 MB/sec pipe to the network.

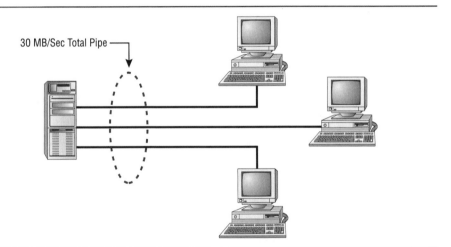

30 MB/Sec Total Pipe

FIGURE 8.3: An easy way to increase the bandwidth of the server's network connection is to add more network cards. Each network interface can act as if it's on a different network.

Network folks refer to this idea as *multihoming*. The server sits on multiple "home" networks. In the next section, we'll see how to set up a multiple-NIC, multihomed NT server.

Skill 8

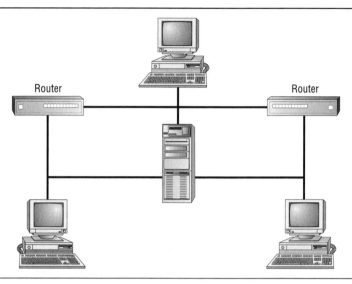

FIGURE 8.4: You usually still use routers and network segments when you have multiple NICs. Generally, you won't use NT as a router (but you can).

 **WARNING**   Network adapters typically come from the hardware vendor preconfigured for a particular IRQ level and I/O port range, and (where applicable) DMA channel. If you are setting up a server with multiple NICs, make sure you set them up so that each of them has unique settings!

Multihoming with High-Speed Server NICs

A larger network pipe for your server is a great idea, but you would be hard-pressed to manage more than a few NICs per server. So why not simply put in a faster network connection? Fast Ethernet (100 MB/sec) cards are common now, and NT provides drivers for many different kinds. You'll connect your fast network segment to the rest of your "normal," 10 MB/sec Ethernet LAN by breaking out the fast segment's bandwidth with an Ethernet switch. Figure 8.5 shows an NT server with a Fast Ethernet connection to a ten-port Ethernet switch.

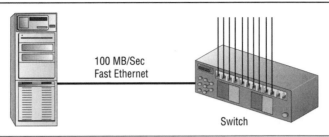

FIGURE 8.5: With a Fast Ethernet NIC on a short run to an Ethernet switch, you can break out multiple network connections to your server while actually installing only a single, fast NIC.

Each port of the switch is a separate network segment. NT supports multiple network segments on a single network interface, so we have all the benefits of multihoming with the simplified server configuration of a single network interface. With the switch and the multihomed single NIC, each network segment thinks it has a dedicated line to the server—the server appears to be in each segment's network. The conceptual view of a multihomed server is depicted in Figure 8.6.

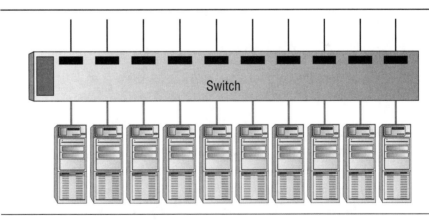

FIGURE 8.6: A conceptual view of the multihomed server shown in Figure 8.5. With a multihomed, switched server, each network segment thinks it has its own pipe to the server.

Skill 8

The same general network geometry applies to NT servers with FDDI interfaces. The FDDI ring would connect the server to some kind of network switch, which would then break out the bandwidth to the LAN clients downstream.

Networking Protocols

In this discussion about network protocols, we use the terms network transport protocol and native transport.

We define *network transport protocol* as a method of moving data across the network. Examples of network transport protocols are TCP/IP, NetBEUI, and IPX. We call these "transport" protocols because they are primarily concerned with the transport of data. Other, higher-level network protocols exist (like HTTP and FTP), so it's not just a "network protocol"—it's a *transport* protocol.

Native transport refers to a transport protocol that can be used by a server to provide all the necessary server functions, without any additional transport. For example, TCP/IP can be used as a native transport for NT, because an NT server can offer the full range of core server services, including file, print, and administrative services, using TCP/IP exclusively. AppleTalk is not a native transport, because you need another protocol on the server to provide administration, network authentication, and other services that are not provided by AppleTalk.

Three Native Network Transports

NT supports three native network transports "out of the box": NetBEUI, TCP/IP, and IPX/SPX. Let's take a look at each of these.

NetBEUI

NetBEUI stands for NetBIOS Extended User Interface, developed by IBM in 1985. Why they call a low-level network interface a "user interface" is beyond me. NetBIOS is the Network Basic Input/Output System, developed by IBM, which defines a method of communication between two computers via a virtual connection—a *session*—across a network. Each computer on a NetBIOS network is identified by a unique NetBIOS name, which is a human-readable (generally) name for the computer.

NT uses NetBIOS for its Windows file and print services and for all the administration tools. The default transport protocol for the NetBIOS information is the NetBEUI transport, perhaps for historical reasons. NetBEUI works as an efficient network transport for small networks of up to 100 nodes, but as you add more nodes, its limitations become manifest. NetBEUI was invented before network routing was common, and it lacks sufficient information to be a routable transport. There is no network topology information encapsulated in the computer names, so there is no way to tell a router how to route the data. Despite this limitation, NT will insist on using NetBEUI if it is installed.

> **TIP**
>
> NT likes to use NetBEUI for remote administration and other server functions, but NetBEUI is not routable. For large (or soon-to-be-large) networks, consider using TCP/IP as your transport instead.

TCP/IP

TCP/IP stands for Transmission Control Protocol/Internet Protocol, and it is now ubiquitous. TCP/IP is familiar to us all, given the popularity of the Internet. TCP/IP is a scalable, routable protocol that is common on many computer platforms. As such, it is fast becoming a standard network protocol, not only for academic and Internet networks, but for corporate LANs as well.

Computers on a TCP/IP network are uniquely identified by their TCP/IP network address. This address is a 32-bit number, typically written as a series of four octets, or eight bits, as a decimal (base ten) number (for example, 9D160107, written as 157.22.1.7).

The most significant bits of the number are used to specify a *network number*, with the remaining bits left to distinguish the individual computers within the network—the *node number*. Network numbers provide a way to aggregate computers into logical groups. Since network numbers are implicit in a computer's network address, every packet of information addressed to a computer identifies the destination network. For this reason, TCP/IP is a routable protocol, which allows network administrators to build large networks of optimal shape. We'll talk a lot more about this in the next section.

TCP/IP Subnet Masks

Exactly which bits are used for the network number is specified by the *subnet mask*, a 32-bit number that contains ones for digits that are to be used for the network address, and zeros for the digits that are to be used for the node numbers. To obtain the network number from the network address, the computer computes the result of:

```
network address AND network subnet mask
```

which is the bitwise AND operation. Remember that a bitwise AND examines each of the bits of the arguments. If *both* of the bits are a one, the result will be a one. Otherwise, the bit is cleared; it's *masked off*.

To figure out an appropriate subnet mask, take the maximum number of nodes desired on a subnet, and take the log base two of that number. The result is the number of digits you'll need (at least) in your node number.

If you have a maximum of 120 computers per subnet, you need a seven-digit node number, because $\log_2(120) = 6.9$. To get a network node number that has seven binary digits, you need a subnet mask with all ones except for seven zeros at the end. Start with all ones: each octet of the subnet mask set to 255 (binary 11111111), for a subnet mask of 255.255.255.255. Now zero out the last seven binary digits: Change the last octet from 255 (binary 11111111) to 128 (binary 10000000), for a subnet mask of 255.255.255.128.

 NOTE   NT can use TCP/IP as a native transport protocol, encapsulating NetBIOS information as TCP/IP datagrams (UDP). However, because much of NT networking is, at its core, reliant upon NetBIOS names for network session establishment and maintenance, some way of resolving NetBIOS names into TCP/IP addresses is necessary. Microsoft developed the Windows Name Service, or WINS, to provide this NetBIOS name resolution.

IPX/SPX

IPX/SPX is the transport protocol used by Novell NetWare networks. Microsoft's implementation of this protocol is called NWLink IPX/SPX, the NetWare Link protocol. As the native transport for NetWare, IPX was well on the way to taking over the world until the Internet mania started.

A big advantage of IPX is that it's largely self-configuring. The ease of IPX network administration, coupled with IPX/SPX routability and efficient packet transport, make this a protocol of choice for many corporate LANs.

NT Server supports IPX/SPX client services with the Gateway Services for NetWare, and through the NetWare File and Print Services (an add-on product). An NT server can provide IPX network information via the RIP Service for NetWare and can maintain NetWare network browsing information through the SAP Agent. We talk about NT and NetWare in detail in Skill 16.

AppleTalk

AppleTalk is a routable network protocol that's the native transport for Macintosh computers. AppleTalk was designed to be completely self-configuring; there is virtually no network address configuration of the Macintosh client.

NT cannot use AppleTalk as a native transport, but can provide AppleTalk network information ("seeding" the network) and routing. We talk about AppleTalk networking and routing in detail in Skill 15.

What Network Transport Protocols Are Needed for What Services?

In many cases, your choice of which network protocol to use will be dictated by the applications and network services that you need to provide with your server. See Table 8.1 for a listing of required network transport protocols for some selected network services.

T A B L E 8 . 1 : Network Transport Protocols Required for Selected Network Services

Service	Protocol	Transport
File Transfer Protocol	FTP	TCP/IP
WAIS text searching	Gopher	TCP/IP
Web servers	HTTP	TCP/IP
Microsoft networks	SMB, NetBIOS	TCP/IP, NetBEUI, IPX
NetWare browsing	SAP	IPX
NetWare routing	RIP	IPX
File service for Mac servers	AFP	AppleTalk
Print services for Macs	PAP	AppleTalk

NT Server Network Configuration

At the beginning of this skill, we talked about the various methods of increasing the bandwidth of your server's network connection by means of routing, multiple NICs, and multihoming on a single, fast network interface. The concepts should probably become clearer once you've seen a practical example. Let's take a look at how we might configure one of the transport protocols, TCP/IP, to implement our network optimization strategy. We discuss the configuration of other protocols later in the book (AppleTalk for Mac clients in Skill 15, and NetWare's IPX/SPX in Skill 16).

Configuring TCP/IP Addresses

You configure TCP/IP through the Network Control Panel. Open the Network Control Panel and click on the Protocols tab. You'll see the list of installed protocols at the top of the dialog box, as shown in Figure 8.7.

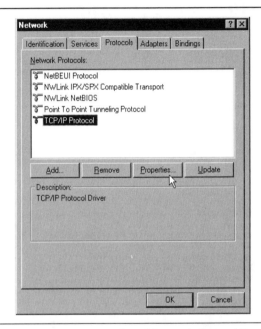

FIGURE 8.7: The Protocols tab of the Network Control Panel lists the currently installed transport protocols. You can configure a protocol by selecting it and clicking on the Properties button.

You can select a protocol from the list by clicking on it. Double-clicking on a protocol in the list is the same as selecting it and then clicking on the Properties button; either way, you'll open the Properties sheet for the selected protocol.

The first tab in the TCP/IP Properties sheet is the IP Address tab, shown in Figure 8.8. Notice the Adapter drop-down list in the middle of the screen. NT supports multiple NICs. You determine which of the interface cards you're configuring by selecting it from the drop-down list. Of course, if you only have one NIC, it will be the only one in the list.

 NOTE   Here, we discuss manual TCP/IP configuration. Your NT server can also act as a DHCP (Dynamic Host Configuration Protocol) client, requesting TCP/IP address configuration information from a centralized DHCP server.

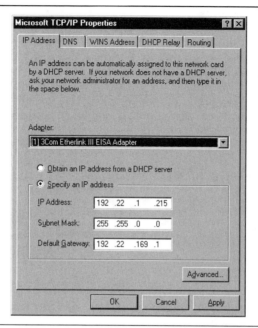

FIGURE 8.8: The IP Address tab of the TCP/IP Properties sheet

There are three aspects to the TCP/IP address configuration:

- **IP Address:** The TCP/IP network address for the specified network interface. This address must be unique.

- **Subnet Mask:** The subnet mask determines which of the bits in the TCP/IP address are used for the network number.

- **Default Gateway:** This is the TCP/IP address of a router that connects the network segment attached to this network interface to the rest of your net. Refer back to Figure 8.2—the routers in that diagram are acting as gateways between the network segments. In order for a computer on one segment to see computers on other segments, it needs to be told to go through the gateway router.

Enter the TCP/IP address information in the appropriate fields. Pressing the period or dot (.) key will move you to the next octet of a TCP/IP address. Double-clicking on an octet will select that octet for editing. Pressing the Tab key moves between the entry fields.

WARNING   In previous versions of NT, the system would make assumptions about your subnet mask based on your TCP/IP address. If you are subnetting at a fine degree of granularity (say, only 128 nodes on a network, for a subnet mask of 255.255.255.128), the system might complain that your subnet mask does not jibe with your TCP/IP address. As long as you've got the straight dope from your network gurus, you can ignore this message. But make *sure* that the subnet mask is correct before you apply the changes. NT may attempt to "help" you by supplying a subnet mask that it thinks is correct!

Configuring Multiple NICs

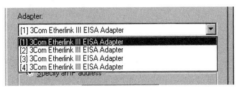

When you're using multiple NICs, the scenario is fairly straightforward. Simply select the network interface you would like to configure in the Adapter drop-down list.

Go through the list of adapters and enter the network address information for each one. Remember, the TCP/IP address must be unique for each adapter.

Obtain the appropriate network information from your network gurus. If they give you a range of TCP/IP addresses that are all in the same subnet, then tell them what you're trying to do: You want each of the network interfaces to be in a separate network segment. The TCP/IP addresses for the different network interfaces do not need to have any other relation to one another (besides uniqueness)—they don't need to fall inside a contiguous range of network numbers or anything like that.

 WARNING   If you configure more than one NIC on the same network segment, those NICs will be competing with one another for the same network bandwidth, which will defeat the purpose of installing the multiple NICs in the first place! Make sure that each of your server's NICs is on a separate network segment.

Routing between NICs

If you have more than one network interface installed, your server can move data between them, acting as a TCP/IP router. If you enable routing, your server takes the place in the network of one of the routers shown earlier in Figure 8.2. You enable routing through the Routing tab in the TCP/IP Properties sheet, as shown in Figure 8.9. There is CPU and I/O overhead associated with routing, and for the best performance, you may wish to avoid routing TCP/IP traffic between your LAN segments with your server, and use a dedicated network router (such as devices made by Cisco or Bay Networks) instead.

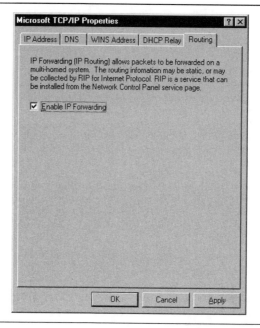

FIGURE 8.9: If you have more than one network interface installed, your server can act as a TCP/IP router.

Multihoming on a Single Network Interface

The other method of eliminating the network bottleneck we discussed involved the use of a single, fast network interface, such as a Fast Ethernet or FDDI connection, and breaking out that connection to the slower, more common Ethernet LAN connections downstream. To make this work across subnet boundaries, you'll want to configure the network interface so that it can exist in multiple subnets simultaneously. For this configuration, click on the Advanced button in the IP Address tab of the TCP/IP Properties sheet, located at the lower-right corner of the dialog box.

RAS AND PPTP—BUILDING WAN CONNECTIONS

Routing on your server might make sense if you're using your server as a dial-up server, with the Remote Access Service (RAS). RAS was originally intended to provide mobile users with a network connection while they were on the road. Configuring RAS as a PPP server lets your mobile users access your server, and possibly the rest of your corporate network, just as if they were plugged into the LAN—just as dial-up Internet access providers can provide home users access to the Internet via their modem.

Coupling RAS with TCP/IP routing will enable your server to maintain an asynchronous connection to a remote location as if that connection were on your LAN. You can build a WAN connection, using your NT Server and some dial-up equipment to hold up your end of the connection, like this:

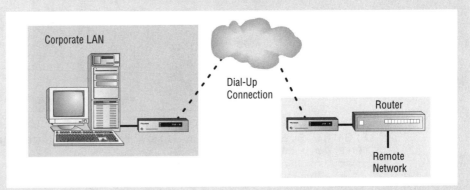

In essence, RAS provides an alternate network interface "card"—the dial-up adapter—so you're simply routing data between the dial-up network interface and the more usual Ethernet NIC.

When you install RAS, it enables routing by default. This is why when you're installing NT, you usually don't want to install RAS right at the beginning. It's easy to forget to go back and disable routing. It's much better to install RAS after the fact, during a comprehensive network configuration session, so that you can catch things like this.

And how about that WAN connection? Traditionally, network builders have used dedicated leased lines to create WAN connections between their sites. Presumably, the data on a leased-line connection between two trusted locations is somewhat secure. These days, it's compelling to use the Internet for the WAN carrier, since Internet access is so widespread and relatively cheap, but security is a real concern.

Microsoft developed the Point-to-Point Tunneling Protocol (PPTP) to provide a secure, encrypted connection between two points. You can use PPTP as the connection between your main location and a remote site, and the data on that line will be encrypted. Anyone intercepting the data should have a hard time figuring out how to read it. Using PPTP, you could take the cloud in our dial-up connection diagram and make that the Internet—use a common carrier to link up remote sites.

For more information on network routing with your NT server, including using NT to build WAN connections, see the *Windows NT Server Networking Supplement* that came with your NT Server software.

Skill 8

Clicking on the Advanced button brings up the Advanced IP Addressing dialog box, shown in Figure 8.10. Specify the network interface you would like to configure with the drop-down list at the top of the dialog box. You can add a network address—I call them network "identities"—to the specified network interface by clicking on the Add button. You'll be asked to specify a TCP/IP address/subnet mask pair, which together specifies an additional network number and node number for the interface. If you're setting up your server to participate on ten subnets simultaneously (as shown earlier in Figure 8.5), you'll need to configure ten different addresses.

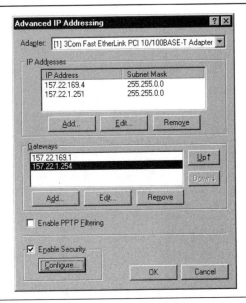

FIGURE 8.10: The Advanced dialog box of the IP Address tab lets you specify multiple network addresses on a single network interface.

Network Monitoring and Troubleshooting

Once you have your network set up, you'll want to monitor the performance of your network interface to ensure that any problems that crop up are quickly identified. We'll say it again—measure, measure, measure, and optimize the right thing. NT provides a number of tools that help you measure the performance of your network interface:

- NT Diagnostics program
- Performance Monitor
- Network Monitor and Agent

These tools are wonderful. Let's see how you can add them to your bag of tricks.

Using the Diagnostics Program for Network Performance Analysis

Before we jump in all the way with the sophisticated performance analysis tools, let's take a look at some "quick-and-dirty" tricks. In Skill 7, we mentioned that you can use the Task Manager from the console of a server to get a snapshot of the CPU utilization. The network counterpart to this local snapshot tool is the Windows NT Diagnostics program, which is accessed from the Administrative Tools submenu, under the Programs menu in the Start menu.

The Windows NT Diagnostics program provides information that can help you monitor the health of a server, without setting up any performance counters. Simply fire up the Windows NT Diagnostics tool and choose the Network tab. You'll see the dialog box shown in Figure 8.11. Click on the Statistics button, and you'll get a quick count of current network statistics.

Stuff you want to look at includes:

- Sessions timed out

- Sessions errored out

- Jobs queued

- Server response time

TIP   The Windows NT Diagnostics program also lets you look at statistics on remote servers. Choose Select Computer from the File menu to bring up a network browser. If you have administrative permissions on the remote server, you'll be able to get quick statistics on the computer from across the network.

Performance Monitor for Network Performance Analysis

The Windows NT Diagnostics program doesn't require any setup, so it's great for those quick peeks at server performance. But it doesn't log data, and it's difficult to visualize network performance over a period of time. To do that, you'll need to fire up the good old Performance Monitor.

We talked a lot about the Performance Monitor in Skill 7. Table 8.2 lists some of the performance counters that you might want to track in order to monitor network performance.

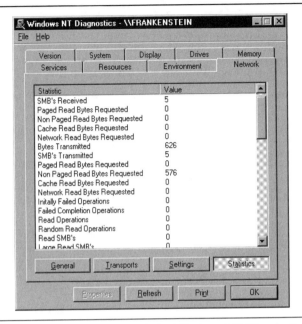

FIGURE 8.11: The Network tab of the Windows NT Diagnostics program can give you a quick look at the network statistics counters if you're at the server's console.

TABLE 8.2: Some Counters to Look at with the Performance Monitor

Object	Counter
Network segment (for each network interface)	% Net Utilization
NetBEUI	Session Timeouts
NetBEUI	Failures Link
NetBEUI	Resource Local
NWLink IPX	Session Timeouts
NWLink IPX	Failures Link
NWLink IPX	Resource Local
Server	Bytes Total/Sec
Server	Sessions Errored Out

Network Monitor Tools and Agent

NT Server 4.0 comes with a sophisticated network protocol analyzer, the Network Monitor, which it inherited from SMS (Systems Management Server). This protocol analyzer alone is comparable to tools costing thousands of dollars—and you get it with NT Server, built right in! With the Network Monitor, you'll be able to capture every packet of data on your network and get detailed descriptions of what's going on with your network.

The version of the Network Monitor that comes with NT Server 4.0 will capture and analyze only those packets flowing into or out of the server. It will not pay attention to other packets not addressed to the server, beyond the general network utilization statistics, which are a function of the total number of packets on the network segment. If you want to use the Network Monitor as a general-purpose network analysis tool, you're better off with the version that comes with SMS. However, this limitation is not as severe as it might seem. When you're trying to troubleshoot a connection to your server, the included Network Monitor does just fine. Figure 8.12 shows an example of a Network Monitor window.

The real power of the Network Monitor tool lies in its ability to capture packets from a remote NT server, which may be on a different subnet. Routers will prevent packets addressed between computers in one subnet from appearing on any other subnet—that's what the router is for. This can hamper your ability to troubleshoot a network login procedure; for example, the login authentication may initiate a dialogue between computers that are not on your subnet, and you would normally not be able to follow that dialogue from your computer.

The Network Monitor can connect to a Network Monitor Agent that's running on other NT computers. You can set up the Network Monitor to collect data from a number of different Network Monitor Agents, which could be on computers all over the place; once you've pulled all the data together, you can use the packet-analysis capabilities of the Network Monitor to figure out what's going on.

Again, you'll probably want the version that comes with SMS for the full functionality. But you'll be able to realize maximum benefit from the built-in Network Monitor and Agent by loading and enabling the Agent on every NT computer. You install the Network Monitor and Agent from the Network Control Panel's Services tab. Simply click on the Add button and select the Network Monitor Tools and Agent for installation, as shown in Figure 8.13.

Skill 8

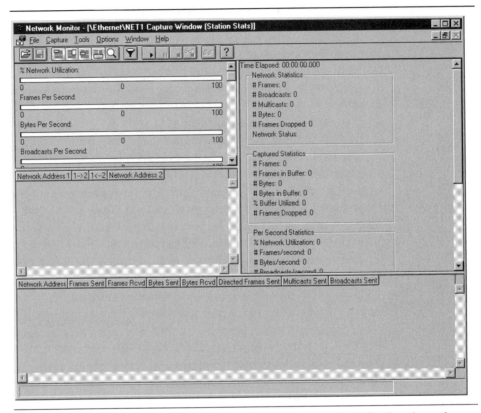

FIGURE 8.12: The Network Monitor can capture packets flowing through your server and provide a detailed analysis of these packets.

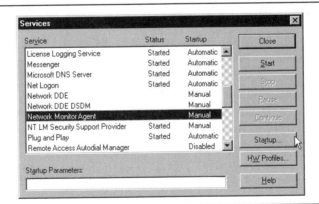

FIGURE 8.13: Manually starting the Network Monitor Agent from the Services Control Panel

You can open the Services Control Panel of a remote NT server from the Server Manager. Select the server, and choose Services from the Computer menu.

Once the Network Monitor Agent service is installed, you need to start it before you can connect to it.

WARNING It's a good idea to leave the Network Monitor Agent service off until you need it. Simply keep it loaded, and ensure that it's set for Manual startup in the Services Control Panel. There are security issues involved in such powerful tools as a packet capture and analysis utility. Keep it around, but turn it on only when you need it.

Are You Experienced?

Now you can...

☑ deal with network bottlenecks by dividing the network into subnetworks, using routers

☑ decide whether to install multiple network interface cards in a single server or "multihome" your server on a single, fast network interface

☑ determine which network transport protocol is necessary to support your network services, and configure the protocol you selected

☑ use the NT Diagnostics program for network performance analysis

☑ use counters in the Performance Monitor to monitor your network's performance

☑ set up the Network Monitor to collect data from Network Monitor Agents to capture and analyze packets

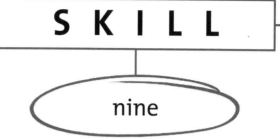

SKILL

nine

9

Protecting Your Server from Power Failures

- ❑ How to determine your UPS load
- ❑ How to estimate UPS run-time
- ❑ Server-to-UPS communications
- ❑ Features of NT UPS services

D o you want an uninterruptible power supply (UPS) in your system? The answer is yes!

The most likely failure point of your computer system is your AC line power. Unless your physical plant has its own generation facilities that *you* control, you *must* assume that the power is going to fail. You don't have control over the power. It will fail. Fortunately, you can avoid disaster by hooking up a UPS to your system.

On the surface, UPS systems are simple. After all, a UPS is just a big battery with some power-conditioning electronics and control circuitry hooked up to it. But having a UPS is not enough. A UPS that is not configured correctly will severely threaten the stability of your system.

In my years as a LAN administrator, the majority of power-related system failures were due to incorrectly configured UPS systems. I've watched team after team try to do this right and fail, because they didn't give the subject enough thought. UPS systems control the power to your computer. No power—no server, no matter what else you've done in the reliability department.

So read through this material, and make sure you understand the UPS requirements before moving on!

How Big Should My UPS Be?

You need two pieces of information to decide how large your UPS should be:

- How much load you'll be carrying on the UPS

- How long you want the system to run on battery power

The next sections will tell you how to figure out the UPS load and battery run-time requirements.

Figuring UPS Load

UPS systems are typically rated in volt-amps, which give some indication of the relative battery size between UPS systems. However, the ratings don't help much when it comes to making the purchase decision.

Your server system is comprised of many components: CPU, monitor, perhaps an external hard disk system. Should you hook all this up to the UPS? Yes!

NOTE   Volt-amps are almost watts (Watts = Volts × Amps). For DC power, the volt-amp rating is the same as watts. But AC voltage varies from a positive to a negative value, so the line voltage is only at the maximum value (120 volts in the U.S.) for a tiny fraction of the total time. There's a "power factor" that you can use to convert watts to and from volt-amps. For the sine-wave voltage of AC power, the power factor is $1/\sqrt{2}$, or 0.71. But keep it simple: As a rule of thumb, use 1 as the power factor, and use watts as the estimate of the volt-amps you need, and you'll be fine.

Some administrators suggest that you do without the monitor hookup to the UPS, thus increasing the battery's run-time. Although this might be indicated for some systems (Unix, perhaps), you'll find that it's difficult to perform emergency surgery on an NT server without a monitor. Depending on the severity of the power outage, you might not be in a position to do everything you need to from a remote computer. Hook that monitor up to your UPS.

There are some instances where you might need more than one server attached to the UPS. Of course, you'll figure in the power requirements for each of them when deciding how much UPS you need. Worksheet 9.1 is a worksheet you can use to figure out your UPS load.

Use the value you obtained in line 9 of the UPS Load worksheet as a minimum working value for your volt-amp requirement.

W O R K S H E E T   9 . 1   UPS Load Worksheet

Line	Load	Watts
1	Server 1 power supply rating	
2	Monitor 1 power requirement	
3	Other equipment power (e.g., a modem for paging in emergencies) for server 1	
4	**Total for Server 1**	
5	Server 2 power supply rating	
6	Monitor 2 power requirement	
7	Other equipment power (e.g., a modem for paging in emergencies) for server 2	
8	**Total for Server 2**	
9	**TOTAL UPS LOAD (line 4 + line 8)**	

Skill 9

NOTE   This method of counting watts to figure volt-amp requirements should be considered a *starting point only*—a way to ensure that you won't buy a UPS that can't handle your load. There's no consensus on a good formula for figuring out what you'll need in practice. You'll need to test your equipment under typical loads.

Figuring UPS Battery Run-Time

Your UPS should be able to supply power to every device hooked up to it, for a sufficiently long time. What's a sufficiently long time? You should allow a reasonable amount of time for the following:

- Notification of network administration personnel
- Contact of help desk or other support personnel
- Notification of affected users
- Graceful shutdown of server connections by users
- Graceful shutdown of all services by the server

That's the ideal. Give yourself enough time! Depending on your application, you might settle for 20 minutes of battery power, or you might need quite a bit more.

Virtually all power "failures" are not complete blackouts, but are sags in the voltage. A UPS can safeguard against these sags very effectively, without really hitting the battery that hard.

My testing gave me 45 minutes of battery run-time for a Compaq ProLiant 1500 server with one processor, three 4.3-GB disks, and a Sony 15-inch color monitor, using an APC SmartUPS 1600. That's a UPS system that's rated at 1600 volt-amps. This amount of time is pretty good, and it's sufficient for my purposes.

UPS-to-Server Communications

If you're building your server, make sure that you have a serial port free for the UPS. A quick scan of the hardware compatibility list shows a whole bunch of

UPS systems provided by two popular vendors, designed to communicate with your server via the serial port, to let it know the AC line status. If your server is properly configured to talk to the UPS, then it can know that the power is out and can shut down gracefully when the UPS battery runs down. Figure 9.1 illustrates how the UPS hooks up to your serial port.

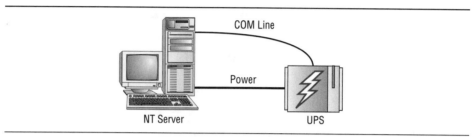

FIGURE 9.1: Connecting your UPS to your serial port

Here are three ways in which you might set up this server-to-UPS communication:

- **Server vendor-specific solutions:** Some popular server vendors have their own sophisticated hardware-monitoring solutions. Compaq Insight Manager is one example. Compaq servers generally install their own UPS services into NT, permitting a LAN administrator to get the status of the UPS from a remote location.

- **UPS vendor-specific solutions:** The UPS vendors bundle UPS-monitoring software with the systems that are designed for servers. The proprietary software talks to the UPS, permitting you to perform analyses on the real-time load and actual battery life, and to optionally monitor other environmental conditions such as ambient temperature. APC's PowerChute software is an example of this sort of system.

- **NT's UPS Control Panel:** Unless the vendor of your server or UPS system specifically states otherwise, you can use the UPS Control Panel that comes with NT Server. This Control Panel is free and provides most of the communications functionality that you really need.

Let's take a look at the functions available in NT's own UPS Control Panel.

Skill 9

Using the UPS Control Panel

When you open NT's UPS Control Panel, you'll see the dialog box shown in Figure 9.2.

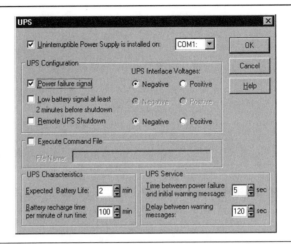

FIGURE 9.2: The UPS Control Panel

The first field, Uninterruptible Power Supply Is Installed On, indicates the serial port to which you've attached the UPS communications cable. The other sections of the Control Panel allow you to choose options regarding your UPS configuration, characteristics, and service.

UPS Configuration

You have the following choices for your UPS configuration:

- **Power Failure Signal:** Check this box to indicate that the UPS can tell the server that the AC line power has gone out. The UPS Interface Voltages choice is almost always negative; you shouldn't need to change it.

- **Low-Battery Signal at Least 2 Minutes Before Shutdown:** Some UPS systems will keep track of battery levels in terms of expected run-time. If your UPS can tell the server when it has only a few minutes left, check this box. If your UPS can't indicate time remaining to the server, NT will use the UPS characteristics that you enter at the bottom of the screen.

- **Remote UPS Shutdown:** Check this box if your UPS will respond to a shutdown command signal from the server. When the UPS receives this signal, it will turn itself off. If this checkbox is enabled, NT Server will send a signal to the UPS to shut down when it shuts down gracefully. Note that the UPS Interface Voltages (negative or positive) are enabled for this item, regardless of the status of the Remote UPS Shutdown checkbox. This is because the UPS will shut down if it receives the proper signal, regardless of whether you want it to or not!

WARNING If you're going to use a communications cable between your server and UPS, you should make sure that the UPS Interface Voltages setting for the Remote UPS Shutdown signal is correct, even *if you're not planning on using this feature*. If the Interface Voltages setting is incorrect, it's possible that the UPS will receive a command to shut down from the server at an unexpected time, immediately cutting off power to the system! Refer to your UPS documentation and verify this setting.

- **Execute Command File:** If you would like the server to run a program or batch file in the event of a power failure, check this box and enter the path to the command file in the File Name text box. An example of a command file might be a program that pages you or sends an e-mail message. The command file should be able to launch and complete its task within two minutes. In the event of a UPS shutdown, NT gives the UPS tasks a high priority, and they are likely to preempt any other processing that could be happening on the server (such as serving up Web pages, for example). Even so, it's good practice to make your command file as simple and clean as possible.

UPS Characteristics: Estimating the Battery Life

In the UPS Characteristics section of the Control Panel, you can enter values for the expected battery life and required recharge times for your UPS. These parameters are used by NT to determine remaining battery run-time, if you haven't enabled the low-battery signal from the UPS, in the following manner:

- When NT first starts up, it assumes that the battery in the UPS is completely empty—the worst-case condition.

Skill 9

- NT looks at the value you've entered for the battery recharge time. Let's say that you left it at the default 100 minutes. After NT has been running for 100 minutes, it will add a minute to the expected battery life.

- If the new value of the expected battery life (after adding another minute) is greater than the value you entered for the expected battery life, it uses your value. The value you enter is the maximum.

WARNING   Unless you use the low-battery signal setting in the UPS Control Panel, NT will use its estimated value for the battery life, which will be very low in the first few hours of server operation. If the *estimated* battery life is less than two minutes, NT will immediately shut down the server upon receiving a power failure signal from the UPS, even if the UPS has hours of run-time available! In the absence of data to the contrary, NT assumes the worst. You should use an "intelligent" UPS that can signal the low-battery status.

UPS Service

The NT UPS Service will send out broadcast messages on the NT network when it receives a power failure signal from the UPS. Everyone using the server from a Microsoft Networking client will receive a pop-up message on their screen indicating the status of the server, warning that the server may shut down soon. (If you're in the Administrators group on the server, logged in to the network, but not using this particular server, you'll still get notification.)

The UPS Service section of the Control Panel lets you determine how often these broadcasts will occur.

UPS Checklist

Here's a checklist for planning and setting up your UPS system:

1. Estimate how large a UPS system you'll need, from your own experiences and by asking the vendors.

2. Fill out the UPS Load worksheet (Worksheet 9.1).

3. Check your estimate against the UPS Load worksheet. Make sure that your estimate is high enough.

4. Check the NT Server hardware compatibility list for a good candidate UPS system.

5. Verify that your server has a spare COM (serial) port available for UPS communications. The COM port doesn't need to support speeds higher than 9600 baud. I've used cheap serial boards on Intel servers for this purpose (and lived to tell about it), but usually this isn't necessary. Usually, your server will have a port available. If necessary, ask your server vendor.

6. Decide if you're going to use the manufacturer's software or the NT built-in UPS Service.

7. Order your UPS and the appropriate communications cable. Order the appropriate software, if you're not using NT's services.

8. Schedule a night of downtime for your server. (Ideally, you haven't deployed the server yet, and you're still setting it up.)

9. Receive all the pieces: UPS, software, and communications cable.

10. Wait until the scheduled night of Fun n' Downtime.

11. Shut down your server.

12. Install the UPS per the manufacturer instructions.

13. Install the communications cable.

14. Power on the server.

15. Install the software, if you're using third-party software.

16. Test your UPS system:

    • Does the UPS charge up?

    • Does the UPS battery kick in when you cut the line power?

    • How long does the UPS last?

    • How long does it take to charge up the UPS?

    • Are the UPS and the server communicating?

    • Do administrators get network notification of UPS events?

    • Does the server shut down gracefully?

Once everything is tested, go home and sleep more soundly, knowing that your server is better protected!

Skill 9

Are You Experienced?

Now you can...

☑ determine the volt-amp requirement for your UPS, by adding up the wattage rating of your server system's components

☑ figure out how much UPS battery run-time you need, allowing enough time for notifications, as well as for a graceful shutdown

☑ allow your UPS to communicate with your server by connecting your UPS system to the server's serial port

☑ use NT's UPS Control Panel to configure your UPS system

☑ test the actual UPS performance, including its battery run-time, battery load, and required recharge time

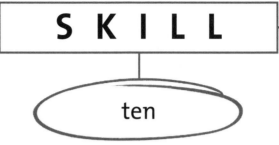

SKILL

ten

10

Building Reliable and Efficient Mass Storage into NT Server

❑ Why you should use SCSI drives for NT servers

❑ SCSI features that affect server performance

❑ SCSI drive and controller setup

❑ How RAID levels 1 and 5 work

❑ How to set up fault-tolerant disk arrays using NT's Disk Administrator

In many respects, your disk system *is* your server. All the "personality" of your server, not to mention your company's data, is stored on the hard disk subsystem. You want to do everything within reason to ensure that the data on your disks is secure.

As we all know, the bad news is that your hard disks are the most likely component in your system to fail, after the AC line power. They operate all the time, they have lots of moving parts, and a typical NT server pushes them pretty hard. Don't listen to the "Mean Time Between Failures" theory—listen to your experience, and to the war stories of the grizzled system administrators around you: your hard disks will die.

Since you *know* they're going to die before the rest of your system, it makes sense to plan for that eventuality. The good news is that these days, hard disks are cheap. Hard disk prices tumbled about two years ago. Advanced features are showing up in mass-market controllers, as well.

And NT makes it easy to use fault-tolerant drives. So now there's no excuse—fault-tolerance is cheap and easy to provide, and it will protect your data from certain doom. In this skill, we'll examine the types of hard disk systems available, the relative merits of each, the best way to configure them, and what to do to prevent disasters as well as recover from them.

Storage Systems Theory and Practice

As you know, hard disks are the heart and soul of your server system. When the power goes down on a computer, what's stored on the server's hard disk defines its configuration. Since hard disks are, in essence, your data, their centrality to your server system can't be underestimated.

Despite the radical improvements to hard disks in the last ten years, and the plummeting prices for huge disk storage, they are still prone to hardware failure. Such a failure could take down all the data central to your mission-critical installation, or at least create a serious inconvenience.

Hardware manufacturers have busied themselves increasing throughput with caching controllers, faster rotational speeds, quicker head positioners, more efficient recording technologies, higher flux media, closer track positioning, decreased seek time, wider data paths (such as wide SCSI), and many other optimizations. At the same time, software developers such as Microsoft have built intelligent, dynamically self-tuning caching into their operating systems. The 32-bit disk-caching algorithms built into NT are complex and intelligent.

There are two primary relevant discussions in the area of hard disks: fault tolerance and performance. NT's disk system was designed to optimize data integrity
and system performance. Consider the illustration in Figure 10.1.

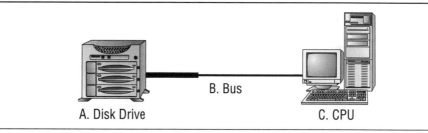

B. Bus

A. Disk Drive   C. CPU

**FIGURE 10.1: A significant bottleneck occurs between the disk drive
and the CPU.**

As system administrator, your first responsibility is to ensure that data is available to your users. In this case, fault tolerance is probably a higher priority. In
mission-critical applications, however, high performance can be equally important. Getting data on and off of the hard disk as fast as possible all the time can be
achieved only by making intelligent system integration decisions. The next sections will discuss which decisions are imperative, and how to best analyze your
needs.

IDE versus SCSI

The first drive-related consideration you'll undoubtedly bump into while shopping for systems concerns a general classification of competing disk drive interface technologies. On Intel platforms, you generally have two choices with your
hard disks: IDE (which stands for Integrated Drive Electronics, but no one
remembers that anymore), which includes the more modern Enhanced IDE
(EIDE), and SCSI (which stands for Small Computer Systems Interface, but no
one remembers that anymore either). Prior to IDE, we all suffered with FM,
MFM, RLL, and ESDI—various incompatible encoding and interfacing standards
abounded.

Once SCSI and IDE arrived on the scene, tying hard disks to PCs became significantly less of a headache. Simply choosing the right disk type in the BIOS setup,
formatting the disk, and booting up were all it took. Prior to that, command-line
codes issued from the Microsoft-DOS debugger were required, the disks failed
more often, and drives were often packaged with hand-tuned or otherwise

proprietary and expensive controllers. Nowadays, your standard IDE disk controller for a vanilla PC costs about $19.95, and even includes a game port, serial port, or parallel port!

 WARNING   Please don't use a $19.95 controller for your NT server! Keep reading, and consider not even using IDE drives for NT Server machines.

Currently the most popular type of adapter/drive combination shipped in today's PCs, IDE owes its existence to predecessor PC hard disk drive technologies, including ST506 (used in the IBM XT) and ESDI (used in the IBM AT).

Technically, IDE is easier to implement than SCSI. The chip count on a typical IDE controller card, for example, is minimal, since the bulk of the electronics are on the drive itself. This keeps controller costs down. The cabling is simple. IDE drives are pretty much plug and play, and they tend not to require fancy, proprietary drivers.

The Case against IDE

But there is a downside to all this ease and low cost of IDE. Standard IDE drives (non-EIDE) are limited to two drives on the same controller. The parallel data cable connecting the drives could be daisy-chained to two drives, designated "master" and "slave." In this arrangement, the two drives can connect to a single IDE adapter, which is convenient. However, due to the way the connection is implemented and how the controller is built, only one of the two drives can be active (receiving commands and dishing out data) at any given time. This limits the throughput of IDE-controlled drives. Moreover, if the master drive fails, the slave drive is dead as well.

Even though the IDE standard lets you include up to four drives in a PC by using two IDE adapters, this too imposes limitations—if not now, then as you expand your network or system. To get anything close to what would be necessary for high-throughput RAID arrays, for example, you would need to tie up precious bus slots in the machine by plugging in additional controllers. Also, in a typical installation, you're likely to need more than four drives at some point.

EIDE is an extension of IDE that supports faster transfer rates, larger disk capacities, and storage devices other than hard disks. Unfortunately, it suffers from the same master/slave serialized drive access as IDE. With this later standard, up to four drives are supported by a single controller. In this arrangement, there are two masters and two slaves. This is an improvement, but still not up to the reliability or flexibility of SCSI.

Any decent NT Server implementation will rely upon at least some of NT Server's fault-tolerance RAID options for data redundancy and improved performance. Therefore, you should seriously reconsider your position if you have been thinking about using IDE or EIDE drives. Remember that IDE is limited to working with one drive at a time (other drives are locked out while a single drive is being accessed), so performance of mirrors and stripe sets plummets using IDE. Even if you're not using RAID features, using multiple IDE or EIDE drives can cause real server performance bottlenecks for this reason. Worse yet, the system drive (the one the system boots from) must be the first IDE drive (drive 0). The system cannot boot off of other drives. So, if your first drive goes down, you're up the creek.

 NOTE   Even though the number of hard disk drives on the NT hardware compatibility list is relatively small, this isn't an issue. Almost all drives (the actual drives themselves, not the controllers) will work fine under NT as long as they're attached to NT-compatible adapters. The reason the list of compatible drives is short is that a few disk manufacturers wanted their devices listed as a possible leg up on the competition. But the bottom line is that there's no technical reason why almost any hard disk drive shouldn't work on NT as long as the drive meets the IDE, SCSI, or PCMCIA (credit-card-sized cards that plug into laptop computers) standard.

Enter SCSI

Your other hard disk technology choice is SCSI. SCSI is great because it overcomes the multiple disk-access problem by allowing independent and concurrent access to each attached drive. One drive can be off seeking some data on its platter while another is writing some data to its platter. Also, SCSI controllers can control up to 15 drives per adapter—a big improvement over 2 or 4 for IDE.

For Intel-based server platforms, you're clearly better off with SCSI. On non-Intel platforms, you're likely not to have the option of anything but SCSI, so it's a no-brainer. If you're on the Intel platform, and thinking about EIDE drives, please consider the following:

- SCSI is better at doing more than one thing at a time, with more than one disk at a time. If there are five disks on your server and three of them need to be written to at the same time, the write can take place in parallel.

- SCSI permits the reordering of disk-access commands for optimal use. For example, suppose that one process is writing to drive A at the same time other processes need to read from drives A, B, and C. The requests to read from the drives that aren't busy (B and C) can happen before the read from the busy drive A.

- A single SCSI controller can usually handle seven devices, and some adapters can support up to fifteen. IDE supports only four and is not presently extensible. With SCSI, you can hook up lots of hard disks with a minimal amount of hassle.

- SCSI supports huge, high-performance hard disks. Most of the super-large, high-performance hard disks are SCSI drives. At the time of this writing, the maximum for hard disks of the IDE variety is around 2.3 GB, with a rotational speed of over 5400 rpm.

- SCSI supports a wide variety of peripheral device types, such as printers, scanners, CD-ROMs, and the like. Although the recent ATAPI (AT Attachment Peripheral Interface) modifications to the IDE specification may give the same abilities to an IDE adapter, the only types of devices currently available are hard disks, CD-ROM drives, and tape drives; and your choices are generally more limited than with SCSI.

- A good SCSI subsystem can do something called *bus mastering*, which significantly speeds up data transfers within the computer and off-loads a significant amount of work from the system CPU, freeing it for other tasks.

In the long run, assuming you will be creating anything close to a serious NT Server network, you'll make out better by moving your IDE equipment into NT Workstation, Windows for Workgroups, or Windows 95 machines, and upgrading your server machines with SCSI drives.

Choosing and Setting Up Your SCSI System

You see a lot of different kinds of SCSI specifications on the market today: SCSI-2, Fast/Wide SCSI-2, SCSI-3, UltraSCSI—what is all this, anyway? Like everything else in the computer industry, the SCSI specification is evolving as new technologies emerge.

About SCSI Data-Transfer Rates

Refer to the SCSI data-transfer rates shown in Table 10.1 to get a quick feel for the advantages related to each type of SCSI. The important things to note here are the connector type and the maximum bus transfer speed. A Fast/Wide SCSI-2 bus will transfer data at four times the rate of standard SCSI, but will a Fast/Wide drive connect to your standard controller? Not without some weird adapter cabling—so beware!

T A B L E   1 0 . 1 :   SCSI Bus Data Transfer Rates

Interface	Max. Bus Transfer Speed (approx.)	Typical Connector (Internal)	Typical Connector (External)
SCSI-1	5 MB/sec	50-pin ribbon	50-pin Centronics (obsolete)
Fast SCSI-2	10 MB/sec	50-pin ribbon	50-pin mini-DIN
Wide SCSI-2	20 MB/sec	68-pin flat	68-pin mini-DIN
Fast/Wide SCSI-2	40 MB/sec	68-pin flat	68-pin mini-DIN
UltraSCSI (Wide)	40 MB/sec	68-pin flat	68-pin mini-DIN

These days, you see drives that are rated AV, for Audio-Visual. These drives are designed for digital audio and video applications, where information absolutely, positively must get off the drive in real time, for a long time (five minutes or so at a time). Most hard disks can't sustain peak transfer rates for very long. As drives warm up, they expand, and the position of the drive heads must handle this gracefully in order to find the information on the drive platter.

Hard disks constantly recalibrate themselves to handle this thermal deformation. AV drives are able to defer the thermal-recalibration cycle if necessary, so they can keep that data coming. They can be a great candidate for server drives. If you have the choice between an AV drive and a non-AV drive with the same transfer specifications for about the same money, the AV drive makes sense.

Comparing performance between drive brands and models can be difficult. The published specs on drives typically refer to only average access time, which is not a reliable measure of real-world performance. Although there are many other performance factors applicable to drives, the most important of them is

Skill 10

transfer rate—how fast data can pass from the drive to the bus. Shortest access time coupled with highest transfer rate will produce the overall highest performance drive. Of course, price considerations will probably figure somewhere in your purchasing equation.

DMA Bus-Mastering Support

There are two basic ways that a SCSI adapter gets data from the hard disk into the computer. One is more efficient than the other. The older method, popularized by the old IBM AT, is called PIO (programmed input/output, sometimes known as processor I/O). The newer and faster one is dubbed bus-mastering DMA.

The bulk of today's popular IDE systems use PIO transfers. In this arrangement, the disk controller places a block of data (from 512 bytes to 64 KB) into a transfer location in low memory, and the processor moves the data to its final destination. This process takes up precious CPU cycles that could be better spent on other tasks.

With bus mastering, the adapter itself takes over the computer's internal bus temporarily, to directly move data into or out of system memory using a process called DMA (direct memory access). In this arrangement, the CPU needs only to set up the operation. The SCSI adapter takes it from there, using its own microprocessor.

When used with a relatively slow SCSI device, such as a CD-ROM drive, the two methods perform about the same. But on complex tasks such as reading, decompressing, and displaying video files on a screen, or servicing SQL database queries, bus mastering is the hands-down winner. As a rule, a bus-mastering controller should be on your shopping list when constructing any serious NT Server machine.

 NOTE   Microsoft warns that you shouldn't use an ISA-based bus-mastering SCSI adapter in a machine containing more than 16 MB of RAM. These adapters will still work, but will greatly reduce potential performance. In machines with more than 16 MB RAM, EISA, PCI, or VLB bus-mastering adapters should be used.

SCSI IDs, Connections, and Termination

To garner your SCSI performance payoff, you need to work a little bit. For starters, you need to keep a couple of things straight: SCSI IDs and termination. There are also some cabling issues to remember.

Setting the SCSI ID Numbers

Let's start with ID numbers. Since SCSI was designed to support multiple devices, each device has a SCSI address, or ID, which is typically a number between 0 and 7. In the case of a seven-device adapter, SCSI address 7 is for the SCSI controller itself. The other drives can be in the 0 to 6 range.

Each device must have its own unique SCSI ID; otherwise, bad things will happen. It won't actually spell the end of civilization as we know it, but it will at least give you a headache. The drives that overlap will perform erratically, seem to disappear, or fail to work altogether. Overlapping drives (or other devices connected to the SCSI chain) certainly won't be visible to the operating system at the same time.

Typically, ID numbers are set by jumpers on each drive's printed-circuit board, or with a nice little switch or thumb-wheel somewhere on the drive. Since SCSI also is used for other types of equipment (such as scanners, some color printers, CD-ROM drives, and the like), you'll want to check all other SCSI devices on a system before assigning ID numbers to your disk drives.

Plug-and-Play Support and SCSI ID Assignments

As you may know, Windows 95 has the ability to recognize and configure a plethora of plug-in cards and other peripherals (such as printers and monitors), taking much of the headache out of systems configuration. Plug-and-Play SCSI controllers coupled with an operating system that does Plug and Play will "automagically" prevent and/or fix a SCSI ID collision problem caused by erroneously setting devices to conflicting addresses. This is called SCAM support, for SCSI Configuration AutoMatically.

With SCAM, the host adapter BIOS and/or the driver software will assign SCSI ID numbers to devices on the SCSI bus automatically, preventing errors. This is great, since without SCAM, you need to manually configure all the SCSI devices' ID numbers so they don't conflict with each other. Since every device uses a different method for setting the ID number, manual configuration can be a big pain. SCAM makes this process completely transparent and hassle-free. Unfortunately, it doesn't work with non-SCAM-compliant devices, and there are not many SCAM-compatible devices or host adapters on the market yet. You might check to see whether a drive or controller you're buying is SCAM-compliant. Ideally, SCSI devices should support SCAM Level 2, although only SCAM Level 1 is required for Windows program compliance.

Unfortunately, NT doesn't support Plug and Play, and thus not SCAM. However, sometime in the near future we'll see it incorporated, just not in the 4.0 version. In the meantime, Microsoft suggests that you plan for the future by

Skill 10

purchasing Plug-and-Play SCSI cards. These cards should have the following minimum requirements:

- Mapping of the base I/O address to a minimum of seven locations
- A minimum of seven IRQ level selections
- A minimum of three DMA channel selections, if DMA is supported
- The ability to disable the card automatically if I/O address or IRQ conflicts cannot be resolved

SCSI Termination

Next, there is the topic of SCSI termination. You can have as many as six drives connected to a standard SCSI controller, and the long line of them is referred to as a SCSI *chain*. Unless the ends of your chain of SCSI devices are plugged up with a *terminator*, data will dribble out the ends and end up in a big puddle on the floor around your server. Well, not actually, but effectively speaking, that's about the gist of it—your drives won't work, and the data appears to get lost. This is similar to trying to use "thin-net" Ethernet coax cable with terminators. The network appears to be down, when really you're just missing a terminator.

There are various schemes for achieving termination of SCSI devices. Internal drives usually have terminator resistors mounted on them, but some of the newer ones have a jumper that can be set to enable or disable termination. External SCSI devices may have a switch that enables termination, or may require a separate SCSI terminator.

If you have only internal drives connected to your server, you put a SCSI terminator on the SCSI controller, since that's on one end of the chain, and then the other SCSI terminator goes on the other end, on the last hard drive in the chain. Note that this has *nothing* to do with SCSI IDs; the drives do not need to be installed in the chain in any order relating to their ID numbers.

This is exceedingly simple, but in practice it can get tedious to remember which drives are the magic, "install only at the end of the chain" drives—the ones with terminators on them.

These days, you have a couple of things going for you. The better-built servers have ways of managing SCSI IDs and termination for you. Usually, you purchase the hard drive from the server vendor at some exorbitant price, and it comes in a proprietary mounting sled that you just pop into the server. Such systems can be worth it, because they save you a lot of hassle in ID and termination issues.

If your server doesn't manage SCSI termination for you, you can invest in a long SCSI ribbon cable that has the terminator on the end of it. You'll have one less thing to worry about.

The better SCSI adapter offerings provide an auto-termination feature. These adapters can determine automatically if they should enable termination on the adapter. If you can find these adapters, they do make SCSI life a lot easier.

Termination is applied to the SCSI bus by an actual voltage that the terminating device supplies. The deal is that at least one device on the bus must provide this termination power. In the best of all worlds, termination power is applied to the SCSI chain at the end of the bus, where it's needed, and not in the middle of the bus. However, this isn't always possible, as in the case where a device such as an external CD-ROM drive or scanner is at the end of the chain: if the scanner isn't powered on, it can't provide the termination power. Powered active SCSI terminators come in handy in these situations. These devices monitor the termination power on the SCSI chain and attempt to keep termination voltage within the appropriate range. Active terminators that have their own power source (usually a nine-volt battery or five-volt power supply) can maintain termination even if an external device is not turned on. I have yet to encounter a SCSI termination problem that has not been resolved by such a device.

Remember, proper SCSI bus termination is absolutely critical to your system, both in terms of performance and reliability. If you've improperly terminated your SCSI bus, your system will behave in ways that will lead to major headaches. Your hard disks will behave very erratically. Sometimes, things may seem to work just fine. At other times, you'll observe a high degree of error rates, disk retries, and so on. In the worst of all cases, the computer won't even be able to see the SCSI devices when it's trying to boot up.

It's really simple. Just make sure that both ends of your SCSI bus are properly terminated, and that no other drives or devices that are *not* at the ends of the chain are terminated.

SCSI Cabling

Remember that data is flying at incredibly high speeds across the SCSI cable, and so the kind of cabling you use can be critical. On a Fast/Wide SCSI, there can be 40 million bits flying along every second! If your cable is cheap, you're asking for trouble. Don't scrimp when it comes to SCSI cable quality. You're going to need tight-fitting, well-shielded cables, with high-quality, nonoxidizing connectors (gold is best).

What can happen with poor-quality cables? Your throughput will mysteriously decrease while your SCSI controller repeatedly retries reads and writes until data is transferred correctly.

 TIP   If, after installing really good cable, you still experience reliability problems, try terminating the SCSI bus with active terminators. Microsoft recommends installing a permanent internal active terminator at the end of the internal SCSI cable. However, internal ribbon cable active terminators are rare and difficult to find at retail outlets. One source is Digi-Key Electronics, at 800-DIGIKEY. This kind of termination is most reliable, and is required for SCSI Plug-and-Play compliance. Any product with the Windows 95 logo on it provides this type of termination.

There are two types of SCSI bus wiring in use today. One is called *single-ended*, which uses a single wire for each signal on the bus. The other, less common, type is called *differential*, which uses two wires for each signal, sending the signal on one wire and its inverse on the other. Differential SCSI is more reliable, because it's less affected by external noise and lets you use longer cables. Even though differential SCSI is a bit hard to find today, it's worth considering if you need to connect lots of devices to your SCSI bus or need long runs of SCSI cable. But don't mix the two types of cabling on the same bus. This can freak out your disk system and possibly cause data loss.

A final bit of advice is that you should avoid using external SCSI devices when possible. It's much easier to put together a solid SCSI subsystem using only internal devices. Flat ribbon cable is extremely reliable, and each wire in the ribbon is separately shielded. Since external SCSI cables are often of shaky quality, if you must use external SCSI, use only a good name-brand external SCSI cable, and keep it as short as possible.

SCSI Drive Summary

To wrap up, when shopping for SCSI drives, remember:

- Make sure the drive connectors match the connectors on your system (50- or 68-pin ribbon cable)!

- Get at least 4 GB drives. These days, anything smaller than this is a waste of money.

- Get lots of them—at least three per server if you're going to do RAID fault tolerance (discussed next), plus a few more for spare parts. Disks are cheap; your data is not.

- What are the sustained and peak transfer rates for the drive? Higher is better. Sustained is generally your more important number.

- What's the seek time of the drive? I used to think that I wouldn't be able to tell the difference between a 12-millisecond and a 9-millisecond seek. I was wrong—it seems to make a big difference.

SCSI Controllers Summary

When shopping for SCSI controllers, keep these questions in mind:

- Is it on the NT hardware compatibility list?

- How many devices does it support?

- Does it support Plug and Play (for future releases of NT)?

- Does it support DMA bus mastering?

- Can the bus architecture (such as EISA or PCI) keep up with your application? Refer to Table 4.2 in Skill 4, and note that only PCI controllers can keep up with Fast/Wide SCSI-2 or UltraSCSI drives. You will also want to take a look at the "Identifying Performance Bottlenecks with a Pencil and Paper" section in Skill 7.

- Does it support fault tolerance in hardware? Does it support RAID 5?

- Does it support Fast/Wide SCSI?

Fault-Tolerant Drive Arrays Explained

The concept behind all the fault-tolerant drive array methods is the same: Since a disk drive is going to fail at some point, make sure that the data lives on at least two drives at a time. When one drive fails, get its data off the other. This concept is referred to as RAID (redundant arrays of inexpensive disks).

Two methods of disk array fault tolerance have emerged: disk mirroring (RAID Level 1), and disk striping with parity (RAID Level 5).

Skill 10

RAID 1: Disk Mirroring

The most basic way to achieve fault tolerance is to have two drives where you would normally have one. Whenever you write to one drive, you copy the data to the other; the drives are exact copies of one another. You can read data from either of the drives.

This method of "mirroring" each drive means that you take a 50 percent hit in storage space—half of your available storage is consumed by your fault-tolerance. But the simplicity of the design makes it one of the faster RAID methods, since it's fairly easy to write the same data to two different disks at the same time. Figure 10.2 illustrates how RAID 1 works.

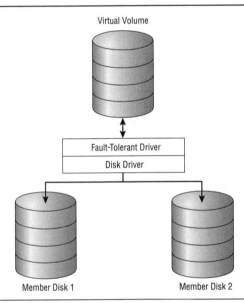

FIGURE 10.2: RAID 1 provides fault tolerance with disk mirroring.

 NOTE   RAID's name comes from the paper that first promulgated these ideas. In that paper, numerous methodologies were discussed, each with an associated "RAID Level." These days, many people refer to the disk array method by simply referring to the RAID level number.

RAID 5: Disk Striping with Parity

RAID 5 also spreads the data across multiple disks, but with a crucial difference: Parity information is also computed and distributed across the disk set. If one disk in the array goes bad, that disk's information can be computed from the data on the remaining disks.

Briefly, here's how it works: Consider the equation A + B = C. If you somehow forget what B is, but know A and C, you can quickly get B back by subtracting A from C (B = C–A). Parity information works much the same way. With three disks, you'll always be able to get your data back in the event of failure of any one of the disks. Figure 10.3 illustrates how RAID 5 works.

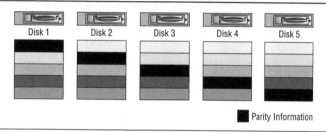

Parity Information

FIGURE 10.3: RAID 5 provides fault tolerance with disk striping and parity.

Storage Overhead of Drive Arrays

You need at least three disks to make a stripe set with parity, and NT can't handle more than 32 disks in a set. Note that the more disks in your RAID 5 stripe set, the lower the parity overhead.

Generally, five disks are used in a RAID 5 array, because after that, the complexity and expense of adding disks to the array outweigh the reduction in parity overhead. Remember, SCSI controllers generally max out at seven devices, and you'll want a SCSI tape drive and CD-ROM. So for most implementations, five disks are it. Figure 10.4 is a graph showing how fault-tolerance overhead grows with the number of disks.

The storage overhead is typically expressed as a percentage of the storage that's sacrificed for the fault tolerance. So a 12 GB array that has 33 percent storage overhead would give you 8 GB of usable drive space.

Skill 10

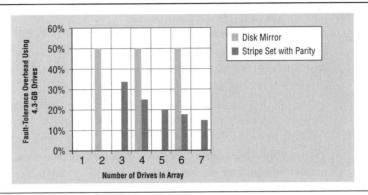

FIGURE 10.4: Overhead of fault-tolerance array implementations

Hardware Fault Tolerance Is Better Than NT Fault Tolerance

For the solid SCSI controllers that appear on the hardware compatibility list, it is generally true that you want the management of your fault-tolerant arrays to happen in the hardware, at the controller level. NT will permit you to create fault-tolerant arrays with the Disk Administrator utility, but this is managed by NT itself. The controller doesn't know anything about it.

As an example, suppose that you want your NT system to be on a RAID 5 array, to get the best trade-off between reliability and performance. But you can't install NT to an array maintained by NT—at least not from the NT installation program. Therefore, generally speaking, if you want your NT system partition on RAID, you'll need to do it in hardware.

Another related issue is that NT supports fault-tolerant arrays only on NTFS partitions. There may be very good reasons for desiring fault tolerance on a FAT partition. If you have a RISC (non-Intel) system, you'll need your boot partition to be FAT, but you'll be dead in the water for sure if anything happens to that boot partition! You'll want all the fault tolerance you can get on that, and you can't do it with NT. You'll need to rely on the SCSI controller.

Not every SCSI controller supports RAID 5. Get one that does.

Caching Controllers

A *caching* controller is one that has some RAM—usually quite a few megabytes—on it, storing the data that is most likely to be needed right there in RAM, so it never has to hit the hard disk. Any time you hit a hard disk, your computer is waiting and waiting for that data to come back; disks are slow. Generally, caching makes sense.

Now the NT architects knew this, so they paid a great deal of attention to NT's use of disk subsystems: when to cache the data, how much, and so on. The file cache in NT takes a significant amount of system RAM. On my old 32 MB server, usually about half the RAM is devoted to file cache at any given moment! This is not a parameter that's easy to tweak. It happens at a low level, and NT is always trying to keep the cache size optimal.

For this purpose, I have not personally seen much of a difference between caching and non-caching controllers. Gasp, it's true—I spent all this money on large caching controllers (no hardware fault tolerance), and couldn't tell the difference! With 15 MB of RAM file cache in NT, this is not so surprising.

Some of the controllers that do hardware RAID usually have some cache in them to facilitate the optimal performance of these hardware-level operations. Since NT never sees these controller-level operations (like figuring parity for a RAID 5 array), NT can't use its cache to help out. The controller benefits from some cache in these cases, and you generally don't need to worry about it.

 **WARNING**   If you have a caching controller, be careful when shutting down your server, because the controller needs some time to flush the cache out to disk. For my servers, I let them sit for a couple of minutes *after* NT has indicated it's okay for me to cut the power, until I'm sure the disks are not doing anything. A couple of minutes should be plenty of time, but refer to your controller documentation to be sure.

Protecting against System File Corruption

The files stored in the NT system directory (usually called \WINNT) are critical to the operation of your server. You may be able to provide for reliability in the face of a hard disk crash with RAID 5 arrays, but such systems will not be of much help if your NT system files somehow become corrupt. While a good backup methodology is the best protection against corrupted system files, you can use file system and disk array configurations to keep your system running even in the face of a damaged drive and corrupted system files. Let's see how this is done.

It's possible to set up multiple NT system installations on the same server and point to each of them independently. Your NT system just needs to know, at boot time, where to find the NT system files. There is a small process that is loaded at boot time: the NT Loader (NTLDR). The NT Loader can be configured to load the NT system from any disk volume on your system. On Intel platforms, all you need to do is tell it the location of the NT files in a configuration file called BOOT.INI. (RISC platforms boot from the system firmware; you'll configure the firmware from the firmware-based configuration menus.) A system so configured is called a *multi-boot system*.

Most multi-boot systems are used in workstation configurations, where system developers or power users switch between Windows 95 and Windows NT Workstation. However, we can use this functionality in our server configurations, too. All we need to do is set up the appropriate volumes and partitions in the hardware, and then install NT Server in each of the places where we will need a functioning NT system. Although this process is time-consuming, the time you spend configuring a multi-boot server in the peace and quiet of your LAN lab can save you hours later in a crisis situation. It really can pay off.

Figure 10.5 shows one possible setup, using fault tolerance and the various file systems. In this setup, we use a SCSI controller to produce a RAID 5 array in hardware, made up from three 4.3 GB SCSI drives. We create a FAT partition as the first primary partition on the array volume, leaving the remainder for NTFS. We install NT on each of the partitions, first the FAT (a basic install, just enough to boot NT and get the network and the SCSI controller working fine), and then the NTFS (the full install).

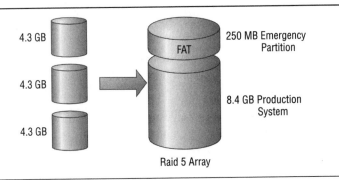

FIGURE 10.5: An example of a multi-boot system setup

Many commercial servers come configured with a scheme that's similar to this: The first partition is a small FAT partition that holds the hardware configuration programs, such as the EISA configuration files, the firmware utility programs (for RISC computers), and the SCSI controller configuration utilities. By booting the system into this partition, you'll get a proprietary server setup procedure.

When something goes wrong with a hard disk drive, we'll just pull it and swap in a new, working drive. Some servers and controllers support hot-swappable drives, and this is a great idea; it means that you don't need to shut down your server in order to plop in a new working hard disk. Since the system is RAID 5, the system will rebuild the data on the missing drive while still maintaining the capability of serving up the data using the working drives. We're completely protected from hard disk failure.

When something goes wrong with our NT system files—say a corrupted file somewhere that's critical to system operation—we simply boot the computer from the backup NT system that we installed on our FAT partition. Why FAT? Well, for RISC-based computers, the first partition needs to be FAT. For most Intel servers, it would be possible to boot from a DOS floppy and see the FAT partition. So FAT remains the lowest common denominator, or the system of last resort.

Since we have a working NT system on our FAT "emergency" partition, we can reboot our server by simply choosing the emergency partition from the boot loader menu. (Since we installed NT on the system in multiple places, the NT setup program created the boot loader information for us, and we're presented with a boot menu on startup.) We can thus choose our emergency FAT partition as the boot partition, instead of trying to boot against the now-corrupted NTFS system. But since we've booted a full NT system, we can now look at the NTFS partition and correct the broken file by dragging a fresh copy of the file over to the appropriate directory.

EDITING BOOT.INI

The BOOT.INI file is a hidden, read-only system file. You can render it editable by typing:

ATTRIB -s -h -r C:\BOOT.INI

You can then edit the file in your favorite editor.

Here is an example BOOT.INI file for the emergency FAT partition scenario:

```
[boot loader]
timeout=30
default=multi(0)disk(0)rdisk(0)partition(2)\WINNT
[operating systems]
multi(0)disk(0)rdisk(0)partition(2)\WINNT="Windows NT Server"
multi(0)disk(0)rdisk(0)partition(1)\WINNT="Emergency FAT"
```

Skill 10

The upside to all this is that, in many cases, it may be easy to fix simple problems. The downside is that this multiple-boot system is almost twice as complex as a standard NT installation, and in some cases the "emergency" version of NT that's kept on the FAT partition might not buy you much. You could run the NT setup program and then choose to repair NT. If the server halts because of a critical error in a system-level file, you can simply run the setup program again, but choose to repair the NT installation. However, this can take a long time, and you may lose configuration data in the process. You may be better off just relying on a solid backup scheme, and simply restore the server back to yesterday's state. Again, you lose today's configuration and data in the process. Maybe having the emergency FAT system isn't so bad!

> **TIP**   On an Intel server, you may be tempted to run your production NT system on a FAT partition, so that you can use commercially available disk repair and recovery utilities to quickly rebuild a corrupted NT system. While compelling, with NT 4.0 even more information is stored in the \WINNT system directory. It includes the Desktop, other profile files for any users who have logged on locally, and the Internet server (default location). You can certainly work around the fact that you can't set NT security on FAT partitions, but you'll need to constantly keep that in mind. Believe me, with NT 4.0 you're much better off with an NTFS system partition!

Performance and Reliability at Any Cost: A Disk-Duplexing Database Server

With time-critical, transaction-processing database systems, any sacrifice in hard disk subsystem performance is too painful, no matter what the benefit. It's possible to add duplicate disk controllers to improve system performance and reliability. Figure 10.6 illustrates this setup.

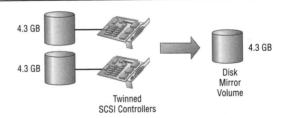

4.3 GB

4.3 GB

Twinned
SCSI Controllers

4.3 GB

Disk
Mirror
Volume

F I G U R E   1 0 . 6 :   Using two SCSI controllers

In this case, we've installed two independent SCSI controllers in the system, each responsible for a 4.3 GB hard disk. These two hard disks are defined in NT as a mirror pair, creating a 4.3 GB volume that is used for a database application. The NT system files are kept on some other hard disk somewhere.

If one of the hard disks or controllers in the mirror pair goes down, we can still use the remaining system. There is a performance advantage to using the two SCSI controllers in parallel like this, as well.

Setting Up Fault-Tolerant Arrays Using Disk Administrator

We've talked about how to use and set up hard disk fault-tolerant arrays in hardware. NT provides a graphical tool for managing hard disks and disk volumes: the Disk Administrator. Once you've created fault-tolerant disk arrays with the Disk Administrator, you can use the fault-tolerant volumes in the same way that you use any other disk volume (drive letter) on your system. To start this tool, choose Programs from the Start menu, choose Administrative Tools, and then select Disk Administrator.

Creating a RAID 5 Array with the Disk Administrator

Although it's best to use hardware controllers to create RAID 5 arrays, in some cases, you may want to let NT handle it. Hardware controllers tend to be very particular. For example, you may need to have every drive in the array be the same model in order to get some controllers to permit a RAID 5 array across the drives. NT has no such restrictions.

Once you fire up the Disk Administrator, you'll get a graphic for each of the drives that is installed on your system. The Disk Administrator will indicate the free space available on each of the hard disks. You can select any partition, including free space, by clicking on it. You can perform certain operations or get more information about a partition by right-clicking on it and choosing the appropriate operation from the pop-up menu.

To create a RAID 5 array in the Disk Administrator, you'll need at least three partitions on different hard disks. Select the partitions by Ctrl-clicking (click with the mouse while holding down the Ctrl key on the keyboard, a Windows method for selecting multiple, noncontiguous objects) on each of the partitions in turn. As

Skill 10

you select each of the target partitions, the Disk Administrator will indicate the current selection by drawing a dark, heavy line around the selected partitions. Once you've selected all the free space you require, choose Create Stripe Set with Parity from the Fault Tolerance menu, as shown in Figure 10.7.

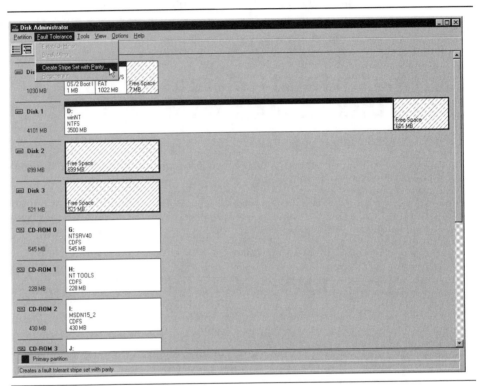

FIGURE 10.7: Creating a stripe set with parity from free space

The Disk Administrator will ask you how large you would like the stripe set volume to be, as shown in Figure 10.8. It's easiest to simply choose the largest available size. This size is related to the size of the largest chunk of free space on a disk that you selected; the RAID 5 array cannot have any pieces on any drive larger than the smallest piece of free space. For example, if you selected the free space on disks with 120, 89, and 72 MB, your stripe set could be at most 144 MB, and would use up 72 MB of free space on each of the selected disks.

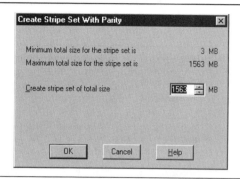

FIGURE 10.8: Specifying the size of the stripe set

WARNING   You will not be able to add hard disks to the stripe set later. There is no way to enlarge a stripe set with parity. You'll need to copy the files on the stripe set to another volume or backup tape, delete the stripe set, and create another new stripe set of a larger size.

The Disk Administrator will create the RAID 5 array. It indicates the presence of the array's components on the hard disks with special shading. Clicking on any of the stripe set's components will select all of them. Once the array volume is created, the Disk Administrator will assign a drive letter to it, as shown in Figure 10.9. Once you've gotten this far, you'll want to tell NT about the new volume by choosing Commit Changes Now from the Partition menu.

This operation updates some low-level data structures that NT uses to keep track of server storage. Some of these structures are critical, and they may be needed in case the server crashes and needs to be repaired. The Disk Administrator will prompt you to create a new Emergency Repair floppy disk, to which it will write the new data.

Skill 10

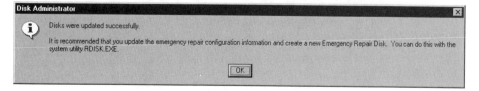

You should go ahead and create such an Emergency Repair disk after you've completed all the changes to the disk partitions.

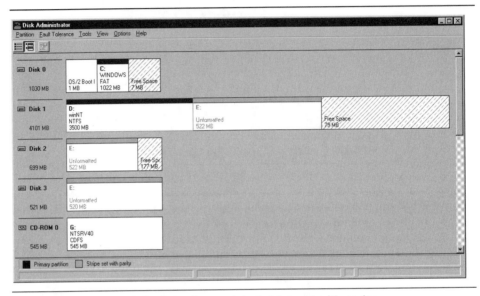

FIGURE 1 0 . 9 : A formatted, completed stripe set with parity

Creating a RAID 1 Disk Mirror with the Disk Administrator

Creating a mirrored set is just as easy as creating a RAID 5 stripe set with parity. All you need to do is select some free space and create a mirrored set out of it.

There's an extra step: You need to create the partitions first. To create a new partition in the Disk Administrator, simply click on a piece of free space to select it, and choose Create from the Partition menu, as shown in Figure 10.10.

Depending on how large your disk drives are, you may get a warning message indicating possible problems with using this partition with DOS.

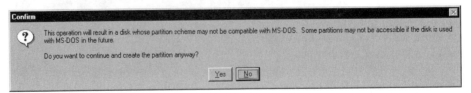

In general, you can ignore these warnings.

The Disk Administrator will ask you how large you would like the partition to be, as shown in Figure 10.11. Note that mirror sets cannot be of different sizes, so you should create a partition that's the size of the smallest partition in the mirror set.

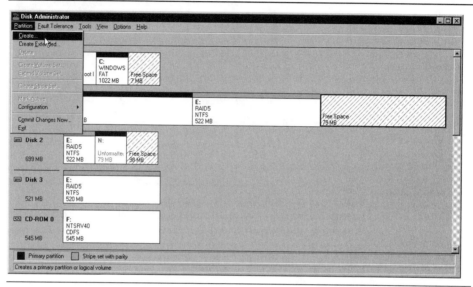

Figure 10.10: Creating a partition

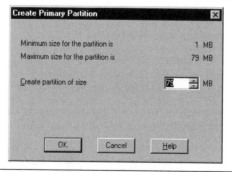

FIGURE 10.11: Specifying the size of the partition

Once you've gotten this far, you'll want to tell NT about the new volume by choosing Commit Changes Now from the Partition menu.

Now that you've created the partitions, you'll need to format them with the NTFS file system by choosing Format from the Tools menu. You'll see the dialog box shown in Figure 10.12.

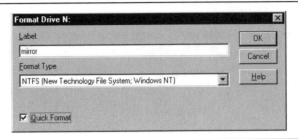

FIGURE 10.12: Formatting your new partition

 WARNING Before you format that drive, remember that formatting a new partition is the easiest way to zap the data that's on the drive. Before you format, make sure that there's nothing in that disk that you care about!

 Now that you have a partition that you want to mirror, select it by clicking on it, and then select some free space on another drive by Ctrl-clicking on the free space. Then choose Establish Mirror from the Fault Tolerance menu.

The Disk Administrator will create the mirror set for you, using the selected partition and the free space from the second drive, as shown in Figure 10.13.

After you've established the mirror set, choose Commit Changes Now from the Partition menu.

Once you're finished working with the Disk Administrator, you'll want to update your Emergency Repair disk. Quit the Disk Administrator program and run RDISK.EXE.

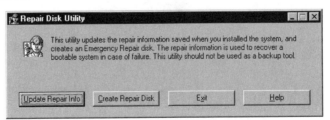

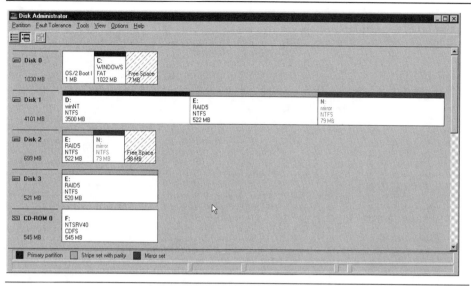

FIGURE 10.13: The completed disk mirror set

Are You Experienced?

Now you can...

- ☑ choose the most suitable disk drive interface technology for your NT Server system

- ☑ set up your SCSI system with SCSI ID numbers, proper termination, and high-quality cables

- ☑ use either disk mirroring (RAID 1) or disk striping with parity (RAID 5) to build a fault-tolerant disk drive array for your server

- ☑ use NT Server's Disk Administrator utility to set up fault-tolerant disk arrays

Backing Up Your NT System

☐ **Strategies for backing up your server**

☐ **Types of backups**

☐ **Tape-rotation schemes**

☐ **How to use the NT backup program**

No discussion of solid systems can be considered complete without talking about backup systems. To protect your data, you must keep copies of it somewhere cool, dry, and fireproof. Period. No amount of fancy disk-array technology will protect you from the most common cause of data loss: human error. People are going to call you in a panic, because they just deleted their only copy of Very Important File. Only your backup system will save you.

Here, we'll talk about backup strategies and the use of the NT Backup program.

Backup Systems Explained

At my company, we have two different backup systems: one for the servers and one for desktop-based data.

We found that the Macintosh users (those deviant weasels) tend to keep really, really important data on the desktop. This is probably because the GUI encourages them to organize their data in a very effective manner, and because our Mac file servers have traditionally been really slow, so the users got used to keeping the data where they could count on it—on their desktop.

The advent of Windows 95, with its compelling GUI system, coupled with the increase in the hard disk size on our standard corporate desktop computers, might encourage the PC users to follow suit and start keeping more data on the desktop. At our company, we're discouraging this with the judicious use of user profiles and training.

Your situation may be different, but we've found that we get the most reliable storage of data by encouraging the use of centralized file servers, which are backed up on a nightly basis. Here is how our system works:

- The servers are maintained by the Information Systems department, which limits changes to the server systems. New software and hardware configurations are completely checked out before going into production. Contrast this to the user-driven desktops at our company, where there's nothing to stop someone from going out to the computer shop down the street and purchasing (and attempting to install) the latest and greatest version of the system software.

- The servers are running 24 hours a day and are available after hours for backup. Although we've trained our desktop folks to leave their computers on for certain nights of the week, we never, ever get everyone to leave their computers on.

- Successful backup of our desktop systems requires the successful operation of the 250 workstations that currently participate in our backup system. How many time-critical systems involving 250 of anything work all the time?

The bottom line: Our servers are a controlled environment; the desktops are a free-for-all. When our users have data they want to protect, they copy it to the server.

The NT Backup program will copy files from remote computers. You could create a batch file that would walk the network of NT workstations, Windows 95 computers, and Windows for Workgroups machines, mounting the drive of each in turn and backing it up. But I don't know how you would make it bullet-proof. Here, we'll be talking primarily about how to create solid backup systems for your servers—that's something we can do.

Server Backup Strategies

The NT Backup program is capable of backing up data from any mapped network drive, so you can envision a system in which you have a master backup server, which backs up all the servers in your enterprise. But I don't like this scenario. I think you should give each server its own, local tape drive. Here's why:

- Tape drives are not that expensive any more. Economics used to make a central tape system a cost-effective situation. These days, you can afford to outfit each server with its own tape drive.

- Backups involve copying a significant amount of data—hundreds or even thousands of megabytes—in a finite amount of time. With state-of-the-art equipment (fast SCSI DLT drives), we're able to keep up on our largest servers. But if you're as successful at scaling up your servers, you'll run up against the "backup window"—the time period during which you can keep the server relatively unused while it takes care of the backup operation. You're not going to fit through the backup window if you're sucking gigabytes of data across the typical corporate LAN. You need local, high-speed backup mechanisms.

- You want to keep the backup operation as simple as possible. A central backup server requires at least two computers—the server being backed up and the backup server itself—to be operational for a backup to occur. This system is twice as likely to fail (at least) as the local backup scheme.

With all that, why would anyone consider a centralized backup system? It all depends on your particular network system. The objections listed here assume

Skill 11

that your servers are small or mid-sized systems, along the lines of a Compaq ProLiant 4500, and also that you haven't spent a million dollars on a FDDI server backbone with a dedicated super DLT (digital linear tape) jukebox. Scaled-up backup systems are nothing new. If you want to apply full-scale enterprise/mainframe technology to your NT environment, you might make a good case for the centralized, "glass house" backup scheme. For the rest of us, one tape/one server is the best way to go.

The Backup Window

Your backup window, as in "window of opportunity," is the amount of time that you have to perform your backup operation. Typically, the backup window is limited.

Backups need to occur when the server is not being heavily used. In particular, you don't want to be backing up files that are in the process of being changed, including active application log files as well as user files that are being edited. In most cases, the NT Backup program will recognize a file lock on a file being edited, and simply save the version of the file that's currently on the hard disk; the file will be backed up as of that moment.

In other cases, backup programs will be locked out of files that are currently in use. This is the biggest reason for performing backups during off-peak hours, preferably when no users at all are hitting the machine.

Another reason to perform backups after regular work hours is that backups involve sustained, huge data transfers. You're basically walking your entire hard disk. You'll want to make sure that people are not expecting anything like snappy performance during the backup period.

 TIP   Saint Bernard Software markets a product called Open File Manager, which claims to enable backup programs to make backup copies of files that would otherwise be locked out because they're in use. This type of product won't alleviate the impact that the large data transfer has on server performance. And adding software components to your backup scheme increases complexity. However, if you're simply not able to fit through your current backup window, a product like Open File Manager might give you more options. For more information, see the Web page at http://www.stbernard.com.

There are two ways to make sure you fit through your backup window:

• Maximize the speed with which your files get backed up. You can do this most easily by keeping the tape drives local to the system being backed up, using fast SCSI tape drives. DLT drives currently offer the greatest through-put of all the tape backup devices, but computer technology is a moving target. Refer to industry sources and the NT hardware compatibility list for your best bet on maximum performance.

- Minimize the amount of data that needs to be transferred. Not every file on your server changes every night. How often do your system DLLs change? Probably not often at all. Backing up every file each time can be a waste of time.

We've talked at length about fast hardware. Fast tapes will get you only so far. Smart backup procedures that minimize the amount of data you need to track every day will get you much further down the road to success (work smarter, not harder—you've heard this before). We'll talk about ways to back up only the data that has changed, which should be a small subset of the entire volume. With this strategy, you're more likely to fit through your backup window.

Types of Backup

The NT Backup program provides for four common types of backup:

- **Full:** These backups are commonly called "normal" backups, and that's how NT's Backup program refers to them. They copy every file from the selected volumes, and mark the files as backed up.

- **Copy:** These backups are normal (full) backups that don't mark the files as backed up. You could perform a Copy backup to make a monthly archive tape of the whole volume, without disrupting the normal backup cycle. We'll give an example in a bit.

- **Incremental:** These backups copy only the files that have changed since the last backup.

- **Differential:** These backups are incremental backups that don't mark the files as backed up.

These backup types work as follows:

	Copies All Files	Copies Only Changed Files
Marks Files as Backed Up	Full	Incremental
Does Not Mark Files	Copy	Differential

Skill 11

Marking a file as backed up means that the file won't be copied by the next incremental or differential backup, unless the file changes before the next such backup occurs. (Technically, the files have their Archive attribute cleared, exactly like performing the DOS command ATTRIB -a on the file.)

Backup Examples

Let's say that you have some period of time during the week that is relatively quiet. For our examples, we'll call that the weekend. At my company, we finally needed to define the servers as "not busy" from 6 pm Saturday to 6 am Sunday—go home, people, go home! (My colleagues on the Right Coast are shocked at this.)

You'll perform your full backups during the weekend, because that's when you have the largest backup window. You'll perform incremental or differential backups at night during the week, because you don't need that extra day as a buffer in case the backup runs over—your window is smaller.

Mixing Full and Differential Backups

Here's an example of a weekly backup schedule with full and differential backups:

Mon	Tues	Wed	Thurs	Fri
				Full
Differential	Differential	Differential	Differential	Full

For example, on Day 1, you perform a full backup of your server—the entire 8 GB volume. On Day 2, you perform a differential backup, which copies all the files that have changed since Day 1, but does *not* mark these files as backed up. On Day 3, you perform another differential backup, which copies all the files that were copied on Day 2 (since those files were not marked as backed up), and also copies files that changed on Day 3. The Day 1 backup is huge, the Day 2 backup is relatively small, and the Day 3 backup is a little bit bigger than the Day 2 backup.

The advantage to mixing full and differential backups in this manner is that you can always restore a file system from just two tapes. You can first load the version off the full tape, and then get the most recent version off the most recent differential tape. The disadvantage is that if you go too long between full backups, the differential backup becomes just about as big as a full backup. And the files are copied multiple times; each file that changes between full backups is copied with every differential.

If this is not a problem, the full/differential backup scheme provides the best compromise between ease of backup and ease of restoring backups. You have relatively small (and thus fast) backups during the week, and a restore operation that takes only two tapes.

Mixing Full and Incremental Backups

You could alternatively mix full backups with incremental backups, as in this example:

Mon	Tues	Wed	Thurs	Fri
				Full
Incremental	Incremental	Incremental	Incremental	Full

On Day 3, the only files that are copied are the files that changed on that day, since on Day 2 you performed an incremental backup. This marked the files that changed that day as backed up, so they don't get backed up a second time.

The advantage here is that the incremental backups stay about the same size (assuming that about the same amount of data changes each day), and generally don't grow as big as the differential backups. The downside is that you'll need to wade through as many as six tapes to restore a file system, including the weekly full backup, as well as each of the daily incremental backups, up to the next full backup.

This limitation aside, you might consider the full/incremental mix if you're having trouble fitting the differential backups through your backup window late in the week.

Using Copy Backups to Make Archive Tapes

Okay, so you're cruising along with your mix of full and incremental or differential backups. Once a month (say, the first Saturday of the month), perform a copy backup after you perform the full backup, and ship that copy backup off to the salt mine (or safety deposit box) for storage.

You'll want to perform a copy backup to make the archive tape, so that when the next differential backup happens, it will copy all the files that changed from your last full backup, as opposed to copying all the files that changed since you made the archive tape. You won't be able to restore files from the archive tape if it has been swapped out of rotation until you can get it back from the salt mine. Since the copy operation is just a full backup that doesn't make any changes to the system (doesn't mark files as backed up), you're safe. You can pretend the archive copy didn't happen, and otherwise stick to your normal backup schedule.

Tape-Rotation Schemes

Here is a popular method of swapping your tapes out:

Mon	Tues	Wed	Thurs	Fri	Sat
1-Differential	2-Differential	3-Differential	4-Differential	5-Full	
6-Differential	7-Differential	8-Differential	9-Differential	10-Full	
1-Differential	2-Differential	3-Differential	4-Differential	11-Full	
6-Differential	7-Differential	8-Differential	9-Differential	12-Full	13-Copy

To implement this scheme, first identify an off-site location that has secure, fireproof, temperature- and humidity-controlled storage for your tapes (we really do send our tapes to a salt mine—in Arizona, somewhere, I think). Then collect 24 new tapes together at the beginning of the cycle. It's easiest for me if I start the cycle in January, but you might have your cycle correspond to your company's fiscal year or some other schedule.

Label the types as follows. Every tape should indicate the server name and location. Every tape should have a label on which you can indicate the date of last use:

- Label tapes 1 through 4 "Monday1, Tuesday1, Wednesday1, Thursday1," respectively. Label tapes 6 through 9 "Monday2, Tuesday2, Wednesday2, Thursday2."

- Label tapes 5, 10, 11, and 12 "Full Backup."

- Label tapes 13 through 24 after the names of the months: "January, February," and so on.

Rotate the tapes following this schedule:

- At the end of week 1, tapes 1 through 4 are shipped off-site.

- At the end of week 2, tapes 5 through 9 are shipped off-site, and tapes 1 through 4 come back.

- At the end of week 3, tapes 1 through 4 and tape 10 are shipped off-site, and tapes 6 through 9 come back.

- At the end of week 4, tapes 5 through 9, tape 11, and tape 13 are shipped off-site, and tapes 1 through 4 come back.

- At the end of week 5, tapes 1 through 4 and tape 12 are shipped off-site, and tapes 5 and 6 come back. And so on…

In this manner, you will have an archive tape for each month, a full backup tape for each week, and the most recent tapes on site. If you lose a server, you can restore the system with two tapes: the one from the previous Friday and today's or yesterday's tape. Then if Tom comes to you because he deleted a file three weeks ago, you can retrieve a version of that file from the full backup for that week. If he needs a file from four months ago, you can get that file from the monthly tape. You've got it covered.

Using NT Backup

You can use NT's Backup program to implement your backup scheme. You can find the Backup program on the Administrative Tools menu in the Start menu's Programs menu. When you fire it up, the Backup program will sniff out your tape drive and will take a look at the tape that you have inserted in the tape drive, if any. I always insert the tape into the drive before starting the Backup program. Figure 11.1 shows this opening screen.

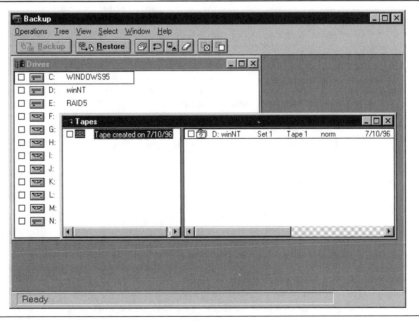

FIGURE 11.1: The NT Backup program finds the tape inserted in your tape drive.

Backing Up Files

Select the disk volumes you want to back up by clicking on the checkboxes in the Drives window. If you wish to select a subset of files on a disk volume, you can double-click on a drive to "drill down" its directory hierarchy.

When you're ready to back up the selected files, make sure the tape is in the tape drive, and click on the Backup button in the toolbar. The Backup Information dialog box will appear, as shown in Figure 11.2.

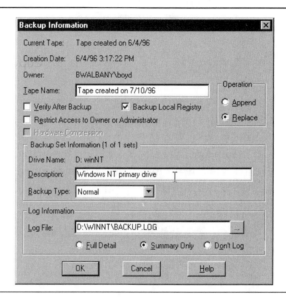

FIGURE 11.2: Specify the information about the backup set in the Backup Information dialog box.

The things that you're most interested in here are:

- **Tape Name:** Enter a name for the backup tape, such as "Monday1 for Server Frankenstein."

- **Backup Local Registry:** You generally want to do this. If you're backing up a file system that does not contain NT system files, this option will be disabled.

- **Verify After Backup:** You generally want to do this, too, unless you're finding that it takes too long or that it generates a lot of spurious errors. If a file changes between the time it has been backed up and the time that it is verified, the verification will fail.

- **Restrict Access to Owner or Administrator:** You also generally want to do this. Enabling restricted access means that only members of your Administrators or Backup Operators groups can restore from the tape. You really want this option checked if you're handing the tape over to someone for off-site storage!

- **Append/Replace:** You generally want to replace the contents of the tape if you're using the tape-rotation scheme that we discussed earlier.

- **Description:** You can type a description of the file set that is being backed up here, such as "Main volume from server Frankenstein, including all system files."

- **Backup Type:** Choose Normal (full), Copy, Incremental, Differential, or Daily. Choosing Daily simply copies any files that changed on that day.

 WARNING   Make sure that the backup type is set correctly! This is very important to ensure that your backup scheme works.

After you've filled in the Backup Information dialog box, click on OK, and the backup will begin.

For more information about the contents of the Backup Information dialog box, take a look at the online help.

Restoring Files with NT Backup

Restoring files is just about as easy as backing up files. Just as you can double-click in the Drives window to drill down through the file system, you can double-click on the tape in the Tapes window to drill down the catalog of files stored on the tape.

I hate the way NT backup stores the listing of files that are on the tape. If you select more than one disk volume to back up, the catalog and data for each volume will be written to the tape in this order:

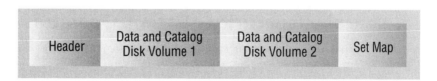

| Header | Data and Catalog Disk Volume 1 | Data and Catalog Disk Volume 2 | Set Map |

So? Well, in order to get the catalog information off of the tape, for all the volumes, NT Backup might need to walk a good distance along the tape. This takes about a bazillion years, as the tape grinds ("shoe-shining," we call it) along. However, once the catalogs are loaded into memory, browsing the tape is a breeze.

Simply find the files you would like to restore and click on the checkbox next to each one in order to select them. Once you're finished selecting the files, click on Restore in the toolbar to start the restore operation.

If the file exists on disk and is more recent than the file on the tape, the file is not restored unless you confirm that you want to replace the newer file with the old one.

 WARNING   If you replace a file on disk with a file from the tape, there's no way to get the disk file back (except by restoring it from tape, of course). Remember, there's no "undelete" feature in NT Server, at least not for NTFS volumes.

Using NT Backup from a Batch File

It would sure be nice if all you had to do was to make sure the proper tape is inserted into the drive, and then hit "Go." This is actually something you can set up with a batch file.

NT Backup can be driven from a command line. Here's a command line that performs a differential backup on my server's main volume, with appropriate labels and access restrictions:

```
ntbackup backup /r /d "Tuesday2 for Frankenstein" /b /hc:on /t differential
```

See the online help and the server documentation for more details on the command-line options.

Generally, you'll want someone to log in to run the batch file, so you will have a record of who ran the file. It's possible to schedule the batch file for periodic operation. The Windows NT Resource Kit, available for previous versions of NT, included an at command, similar to the Unix at command, that could schedule jobs to run at certain times. The at command does not ship with NT Server 4.0 at the time of this writing. Remember, keep your backup system simple, and test it before you rely on it!

A Note about Security—Backup Operators

You can back up only those files to which you have read permission, unless you're a member of the Administrators or Backup Operators group. Administrators have full privileges, of course, to administer the system.

You needn't give people membership to the Administrators group to let them back up or restore files! Give them membership to the Backup Operators group instead. This will allow them to back up all files, even those to which they do not have access. They won't be able to read the files, but they will be able to back them up (and restore them).

TIP   A popular third-party backup system for Windows NT by Arcada Software actually requires an administrator account to run. It adds a dummy administrator account to your NT enterprise network when it's installed. I find this to be an unacceptable security hole—the program should run just fine as a member of the Backup Operators group. But since it's a port from other LAN environments that lack such distinctions, it refuses to run unless it can get administrator access. If this isn't a problem for you, and you like the NT Backup program, you'll love Arcada's product, which is a super-duper version.

Are You Experienced?

Now you can...

- ☑ develop an efficient backup strategy that allows you to perform backups that fit through your "backup window"

- ☑ use Copy backups (full backups that don't mark the files as backed up) to create archive tapes

- ☑ use NT's Backup program to make backup copies and to restore backups from tape

- ☑ set up a batch file to automate your backups

Skill 11

Designing a
Balanced System

- ❑ How to build a highly available server
- ❑ A case for upgrades
- ❑ Server Performance worksheet
- ❑ Fault-Tolerance worksheet

In this skill, we come full circle. We began in Skill 6, where we said that you want to build a highly available computer system, and that the way to achieve this is by providing your system with sufficient power to be highly responsive under expected loads. You need high performance, but high performance isn't enough. You also need to ensure that your computer system remains operational under adverse conditions. You need to build fault tolerance into your computer system.

Fill out the worksheets in this skill. If you have yet to build your server, the worksheets will help you get off to a good start. If you already have NT servers running, you can use the worksheets to identify areas where your server design can be improved. You might be in for a surprise. For example, if you're prepared to spend $3,600 for an upgraded disk storage system, you may discover that a $200 network interface card would make a greater impact on performance. The worksheets can help you set your priorities and, if necessary, make a strong case for the upgrades you really need.

Bringing It All Together in the Server Performance Worksheet

There's a lot to know when it comes to balanced server design. You need to bring together a thorough understanding of hardware and software. You need to know how NT's system requirements will affect system performance and reliability.

Balancing Server Subsystems

The Server Performance worksheet brings together the worksheets from the previous skills, and helps you identify bottlenecks in your server hardware design. You will compute estimated bandwidth of the system bus, disk system, and network interface, and compare these estimates to obtain a balanced system design. To help you think about the balance between these subsystems, take a look at Figure 12.1.

Server Performance Worksheet Instructions

To help you fill in the Server Performance worksheet, presented in Worksheet 12.1, we'll go through it, section by section.

Lines 1–21: Disk Storage Needed

This section of the worksheet helps you estimate the amount of hard disk storage your server will need. Copy these numbers from the Disk Storage worksheet in Skill 4 (Worksheet 4.4).

In our example, our server needs 13 GB of disk storage (Worksheet 4.5).

Lines 22–28: Number of Disk Drives Needed

Once you have an estimate of required disk storage, you can get a good idea of the number of hard disks your server will need. These days, server hard disks are typically 1.2, 2.0, or 4.3 GB devices. The 4.3 GB drives are usually the most economical in terms of price per megabyte, but there are other considerations. As the number of disk drives goes up, the likelihood of component failure may increase somewhat (since there are more devices in your system, more cabling, and so on). However, in the case of a drive failure in a RAID 5 array, 2 GB drives cause half as much recomputation as 4 GB drives. And with more drives in your array, the total array disk bandwidth is increased.

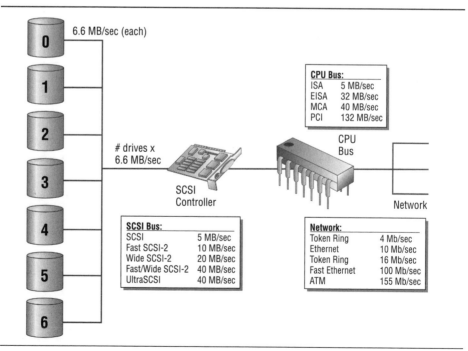

FIGURE 12.1: The storage requirements can determine the storage system bandwidth, which can help you make decisions about the CPU bus and network architecture. Try to match the disk and network subsystem bandwidths.

WORKSHEET 12.1   Server Performance Worksheet

Line	Disk Storage Needed		Requirements
1	NT System Files		250 MB
	Virtual Memory Swap		
2	RAM installed		MB
3	Recommended Page File Size (line 2 × 1.5)		MB
	Applications		
4	Internet Information Server	50 MB	MB
5	Total projected size of Web site files		MB
6	SNA Server	30 MB	
7	Systems Management Server	100 MB	
8	Exchange Server	500 MB	
9	SQL Server	60 MB	MB
10	Total size of SQL Server databases		MB
11	Total BackOffice storage needed: (add lines 4–10)		MB
12	Total required storage for other applications		MB
13	Total Application Storage (line 11 + line 12)		MB
	User Storage Files		
14	Number of users on this server		users
15	Average storage required per user		MB
16	Total user storage (line 14 × line 15)		MB
17	Total storage needed (add lines 1, 3, 13, 16)		MB
18	Fudge factor (add 15% to line 17)		MB
19	Subtotal (line 17 + line 18)		MB
20	RISC-based computers (add 25% to line 19)		MB
21	**Total Disk Storage Needed (line 19 + line 20)**		**MB**

WORKSHEET 12.1   Server Performance Worksheet (continued)

	Number of Disk Drives Needed		
22	Hard disk size (typically, 2 GB or 4.3 GB)		GB
23	Divide line 21 by line 22		
	For RAID 1 Disk-Mirroring Systems		
24	Multiply line 23 by 2		
	For RAID 5 Disk Arrays		
25	Add one to line 23		
26	Hard disks needed for primary array storage (copy line 24 or 25):		
27	Online spare drives?		
28	**Total No. of Hard Disks (line 26 + line 27)**		
	Hard Disk Bandwidth		
29	Typical max bandwidth of a single hard disk		6.6 MB/sec
30	Maximum Disk Array Bandwidth (line 26 × line 29):		MB/sec
31	Fudge Factor		0.83
32	**Disk Array Bandwidth (line 30 × line 31)**		**MB/sec**
	Type of SCSI Controller		
	SCSI	5 MB/sec	
	Fast SCSII-2	10 MB/sec	
	Wide SCSI-2	20 MB/sec	
	Fast/Wide SCSI-2	40 MB/sec	
	UltraSCSI	40 MB/sec	
33	**Selected Controller Bandwidth**		**MB/sec**
	Make line 33 as close to line 32 as possible.		

Skill 12

WORKSHEET 12.1   Server Performance Worksheet (continued)

	Bus Architecture for SCSI Controller		
	ISA	2.5 MB/sec	
	EISA	32 MB/sec	
	MCA	40 MB/sec	
	PCI	132 MB/sec	
34	**Selected CPU Bus Bandwidth**		**MB/sec**
	Make sure line 34 is greater than line 33.		
	Network Bandwidth		
	Token Ring	4 Mb/sec	
	Ethernet	10 Mb/sec	
	Token Ring	16 Mb/sec	
	Fast Ethernet	100 Mb/sec	
	ATM	155 Mb/sec	
35	Network segment bandwidth		Mb/sec
36	Number of independent network segments attached		
37	**Total Server Network Bandwidth (line 35 × line 36 ÷ 8)**		**MB/sec**
	Note that you MUST route your network traffic to achieve independent segments.		
	Server Hardware Balance Analysis		
38	Disk system bandwidth (line 32 or line 33, whichever is less)		MB/sec
39	**Network-to-Disk Ratio (line 37 ÷ line 38)**		

In the final analysis, your drive size, and possibly your array type, will be determined by your storage requirements.

Our sample server needs 13 GB of storage. With disk mirroring, we would need six 4.3 GB drives, which would give us three mirrored 4.3 GB volumes, for a total of 12.9 GB, which is not quite enough. It is unlikely that a single application will require more than 4 GB, but NT will see three discrete volumes, and most RAID controllers can't aggregate the three mirror pairs into a single volume in the hardware. We could, however, use this hardware configuration, and create a 250 MB FAT partition (for emergencies, and for booting the RISC machine) on the first volume, and a 4 GB NTFS partition on the remainder of the first volume. The other two 4.3 GB volumes would be completely NTFS. We could install the NT system and all applications on the 4 GB partition on volume 1, and from the Disk Administrator, create a volume set out of the other two 4.3 GB volumes, to obtain a single 8.6 GB logical drive. But that's a lot of work.

As an alternative, we could use a RAID 5 array on our server. We would enter 3 (13 GB/ 4.3 GB) on line 23, so we would need four drives in the array. The hardware controller could make this array look like a single, monolithic 13 GB volume, so there's less to worry about.

Some RAID controllers support an "online spare" drive. This drive is installed in the server just as the others are, but it is not used in the array. Your controller might not even spin the drive up, so it is not at risk of a head crash or as much component fatigue as the production drives. When a drive in the array fails, the controller can immediately activate the online spare drive and build it into the array on the fly, with no perceived server downtime. This means that there is no need to have someone run over there with a hot-pluggable drive to install. If your controller supports an online spare, enter 1 for the drive on line 27, and add it to the array total in line 28.

For some final considerations, note that your server may not be limited to a single SCSI controller. The Compaq SmartDrive controller card comes in a duplexed version, which has two controllers on a single card. Or you could install a second SCSI controller card to support another array, increasing your server's storage capacity. Most servers require an external storage cabinet for more than six or seven disk drives.

Our sample server will use five 4.3 GB drives: four in a RAID 5 array, with one online spare. We'll order seven drives when we order the server, so that we have two more spares sitting on the shelf.

Lines 29–32: Hard Disk Bandwidth

Once you've decided how many drives to use in your server, you can estimate the aggregate bandwidth of all the drives. The worksheet indicates 6.6 MB/sec for a SCSI drive, which is a solid number for a typical modern SCSI drive. To be more accurate, refer to your drive's specifications and use that for line 29.

Simply multiply the number of drives times the drive bandwidth to get the maximum bandwidth of the array on line 30.

Skill 12

The worksheet indicates a "fudge factor" of 83 percent on line 31. It's unlikely that every drive in the array will be dumping data at the maximum sustained rate all the time. I hand-waved over this, and used a figure of $1/\sqrt{2}$, for which I offer the weak justification that the disk access might be periodic, and the stronger justification of, well, it's better than nothing! It's likely that this fudge factor is very conservative, resulting in a high figure for total bandwidth, but that's a good idea for pencil-and-paper engineering. Use the indicated fudge factor, or enter your own value for line 31.

Simply multiply the fudge factor in line 31 by the maximum array bandwidth to obtain the expected nominal array bandwidth for line 32.

For our sample server, we chose to go with the RAID 5 array of four disks, with one online spare. We use the figure of 6.6 MB/sec in line 29, and enter $4 \times 6.6 = 26.4$ MB/sec for line 30. We'll use the given fudge factor of 83 percent in line 31. We enter $26.4 \times 0.83 = 22$ MB/sec for the total array bandwidth in line 32. Note that we don't figure in the bandwidth of the online spare drive, since it does not participate in the array. At any given time, there are only four drives in the array.

Line 33: Type of SCSI Controller

Compare the bandwidth of your drive array with the SCSI specifications. This is not quite as straightforward as we're making it out to be. Fast/Wide SCSI drives will have a higher bandwidth (on line 29) than standard SCSI drives. So increasing the SCSI specification of the controller in an attempt to catch up to the drive array may not seem like it makes much sense. In practice, however, you can't change the laws of physics: Hard drives must move physical parts faster in order to increase data-transfer rates, and today they max out at about 14 MB/sec sustained transfer, regardless of the interface type.

Still, it's quite likely that your SCSI controller will be the bottleneck, at least on paper. You can eliminate this bottleneck most effectively by duplexing your controllers. Instead of using lots of disks in a large array, use fewer disks in multiple, smaller arrays, each with its own SCSI controller.

Note that there is performance overhead associated with RAID arrays. The controller had better be able to keep up. Refer to your controller specifications to be sure.

For our sample server, the RAID 5 array has four disks in it, for an estimated bandwidth of 22 MB/sec. We could use Wide SCSI drives and a Wide SCSI controller, for a SCSI bandwidth of 20 MB/sec that closely matches our array. (Note that we assume that the estimate for the array bandwidth will still hold if we bump up to Wide SCSI, which is a pretty good assumption.) If we absolutely, positively need the fastest server possible, we could probably get away with a Fast/Wide SCSI-2 controller with Fast/Wide drives. The drives would need to sustain a data-transfer rate of 8.3 MB/sec, all the time, to catch up to the controller—something that might be possible.

If you want to over-engineer the system, you could use two Fast/Wide controllers, each with two 4.3 GB mirror pairs, for a total of eight 4.3 GB drives (plus four online spares). You would triple the amount of hardware with a nominal increase in performance: Disk mirroring is less computationally intensive than RAID 5; the hardware bandwidth is exactly the same (try it and see)! Okay, that doesn't pay off. Instead, how about two controllers, each with a three-disk RAID 5 array? The disks would need to sustain 11 MB/sec to catch up.

For our storage requirements, duplexing controllers doesn't seem to make sense. Plug in your own numbers and see. For our example, we'll go with a single, Fast/Wide SCSI controller with Fast/Wide drives. We enter 40 MB/sec for line 33. (If we had decided to use two controllers, we would have entered 80 MB/sec.)

Line 34: Bus Architecture for SCSI Controller

Compare the CPU bus specifications with your SCSI controller performance. Note that your CPU bus bandwidth is shared among the SCSI controller, network interfaces, and video. Make sure your CPU bus has plenty of bandwidth relative to your controllers!

For our example, we'll use a PCI SCSI controller. We enter a figure of 132 MB/sec on line 34.

Lines 35–37: Network Bandwidth

Enter the bandwidth for your network type on line 35. Note that network bandwidth is measured in mega*bits* per second, not mega*bytes*. For the same numbers, the network is one-eighth the speed of the other components in your system, since there are eight bits in a byte.

It can be challenging to design the network connection so that it can keep up with the rest of the system. Compare the bandwidth specifications of the different network types with line 33. Is your network a good match for the server's storage bandwidth? If not, you will want to consider the multihoming strategies presented in Skill 8. Enter the number of network segments that you'll attach to your server on line 36. Multiply line 35 by line 36 to obtain your server's total network bandwidth, and remember to divide by eight (since there are eight bits to a byte). Enter the result on line 37.

Skill 12

For our example, our client PCs are using standard Ethernet, so we enter 10 Mbit/sec on line 35. That's only 3 percent of the bandwidth of the SCSI controller—not a great match. To make things better, we can add three more network interface cards, and put the server on four independent network segments. It might be easier to install a Fast Ethernet card on the server, and use a network switch to break out the 100 Mbit/sec server connection into the different network segments. If we multihomed the computer to ten Ethernet network segments, our disk array would be three times as fast as the network interface.

We'll go ahead and install the Fast Ethernet card on the PCI bus, and multihome the server onto two network segments to start with. Perhaps we'll expand the network later. We enter 20 Mbit/sec, or 2.5 MB/sec, on line 37.

Lines 38–39: Server Hardware Balance Analysis

Compare the bandwidth of your network and disk subsystems. Is there a good balance between them?

Determine the bandwidth of the disk storage subsystem, which is the minimum of the SCSI controller bandwidth and the disk array bandwidth. Compare line 32 and line 33, and enter the lower of the two on line 38.

Divide line 37 (total network bandwidth) by line 38 (disk system bandwidth) and enter the result on line 39.

For our example, we made sure that the network interface matched the disk subsystem. The RAID 5 array has a bandwidth of 22 MB/sec, and the SCSI controller can handle 40 MB/sec, so the bandwidth of the disk storage subsystem is determined by the array. We enter 22 MB/sec on line 38. Dividing line 37 by line 38, we get 2.5 MB/sec ÷ 22 MB/sec = 11% for our network-to-disk system ratio, which isn't so good.

You want the net-to-disk ratio to be 25 percent or better. We decided to start with a multihomed Fast Ethernet NIC with two independent network segments. We can easily add more segments to the NIC in the Network Control Panel, and configure the network switch attached to the server, so we don't need to add any more hardware. We'll deploy this server, and measure the system carefully, using the Performance Monitor and Network Monitor.

Fault-Tolerance Design Review

Protecting your server's integrity is part system design and part "people" design. The most sophisticated server in the world won't stay up if inappropriate procedures are in place. Fill out the worksheet and checklists in the following sections to test your understanding of fault-tolerance procedures and systems.

UPS System Design Review

You'll recognize the first part of Worksheet 12.2 as the UPS Load worksheet from Skill 9 (Worksheet 9.1), and the second part as the checklist from the end of that skill.

WORKSHEET 12.2   UPS Load Worksheet and Installation Checklist

	UPS Load Worksheet	
1	Server 1 power supply rating	Watts
2	Monitor 1 power requirement	Watts
3	Other equipment power (e.g., a modem for paging in emergencies) for server 1	Watts
4	**Total for Server 1**	**Watts**
5	Server 2 power supply rating	Watts
6	Monitor 2 power requirement	Watts
7	Other equipment power (e.g., a modem for paging in emergencies) for server 2	Watts
8	**Total for Server 2**	**Watts**
9	**Total UPS load (line 4 + line 8)**	**Watts**
	UPS Installation Checklist	
	Estimate how large a UPS system you'll need, from your own experience and by asking the vendors.	
	Fill out the UPS Load worksheet (above).	
	Check your estimate against the UPS Load worksheet. Make sure that your estimate is high enough.	
	Check the hardware compatibility list for a good candidate UPS system.	
	Verify that your server has a spare COM (serial) port available for UPS communications. The COM port doesn't need to support speeds higher than 9600 baud. If necessary, ask your server vendor.	
	Decide if you're going to use the manufacturer's software or the NT built-in services.	
	Order your UPS and the appropriate communications cable. Order the appropriate software, if you're not using NT's services.	
	Schedule a night of downtime for your server.	
	Receive all the pieces: UPS, software, and communications cable.	

Skill 12

WORKSHEET 12.2   UPS Load Worksheet and Installation Checklist (continued)

	UPS Installation Checklist
	Wait until the scheduled night of downtime.
	Shut down your server.
	Install the UPS per the manufacturer's instructions.
	Install the communications cable.
	Power on the server.
	Install the software, if you're using third-party software.

	Test your UPS system:
	    Does the UPS charge up?
	    Does the UPS battery kick in when you cut the line power?
	    How long does the UPS last?
	    How long does it take to charge up the UPS?
	    Are the UPS and the server communicating?
	    Do administrators get network notification of UPS events?
	    Does the server shut down gracefully?

Fault-Tolerant Storage Design Review

We discussed fault-tolerant drive arrays in Skill 10. Work through the following checklist to nail down your storage architecture.

1. Complete the Server Performance worksheet (Worksheet 12.1) to determine your disk system hardware. Refer to the discussions of lines 1 through 34 in the section "Server Performance Worksheet Instructions" for more information, keeping in mind the following questions:

   - RAID 5 (striping with parity) or RAID 1 (disk mirroring)?

   - (RAID 5) How many drives in the RAID 5 array?

   - (RAID 1) How many disk mirror pairs total?

   - Does your controller support online spares? If so, you should use one online spare for each disk mirror pair or RAID 5 array.

   - (RAID 1) Will you use more than one SCSI controller (duplexing)? Note that for maximum fault-tolerance, you'll set up mirror pairs in NT, with each member of the pair on a different SCSI controller.

2. How many disk volumes do you have?

3. For the first volume, define a small (250 MB) FAT partition. Install any hardware-configuration tools (such as EISA configuration or RISC system diagnostics) to that partition. Your server may already have such a partition set up by the vendor.

4. Consider installing a basic NT system to that partition, and using it for emergency troubleshooting. Intel servers only: If you do so, or if you install a DOS system to that partition, edit the BOOT.INI file in that partition to indicate the nature of the emergency systems in the multi-boot menu. See Skill 10 for more details.

5. For the balance of the first volume, and the remainder of the other volumes, set up NTFS partitions using the Disk Administrator or during the NT installation process.

6. After NT is installed, create any volume sets using the Disk Administrator.

7. Create an emergency boot floppy disk using RDISK.EXE and store the disk as a "baseline" configuration.

8. Draw a diagram illustrating your fault-tolerant storage architecture and keep it with the server. See Figure 12.2 for an example.

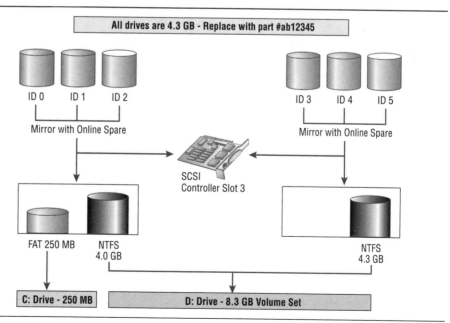

FIGURE 12.2: Draw a diagram illustrating your fault-tolerant storage architecture and keep it with the server.

Skill 12

Backup Procedure Design Review

You need to decide on the backup tape-rotation scheme you intend to use. Here is the recommended tape-rotation scheme, which you'll recognize from Skill 11:

Mon	Tues	Wed	Thurs	Fri	Sat
1 *Differential*	2 *Differential*	3 *Differential*	4 *Differential*	5 *Full*	
6 *Differential*	7 *Differential*	8 *Differential*	9 *Differential*	10 *Full*	
1 *Differential*	2 *Differential*	3 *Differential*	4 *Differential*	11 *Full*	
6 *Differential*	7 *Differential*	8 *Differential*	9 *Differential*	12 *Full*	13 *Copy*

Work through the following checklist for each server every day:

1. Swap the tape according to the tape-rotation scheme.

2. Store the previous night's backup according to the tape-rotation scheme.

3. Make an emergency backup disk for the server, using the RDISK.EXE command. This stores compressed copies of the system registry and security database onto the floppy. Consider scheduling the RDISK.EXE procedure with a batch file or scheduling utility.

4. Store the emergency backup disk according to the tape-rotation schedule.

5. Verify normal server operation (the server is on, is physically connected to the network, UPS is charged up, no obvious warning lights blinking, and so on). What other cursory inspection can be made by backup technicians during a nightly on-site visit?

Are You Experienced?

Now you can...

- ☑ complete the Server Performance worksheet, which will help you to identify bottlenecks in your server hardware design

- ☑ discover which upgrades will makes the most impact on your server system

- ☑ complete the UPS Load worksheet and installation checklist to check the reliability of your UPS system

- ☑ evaluate your disk-storage system for adequate fault tolerance

- ☑ review your backup tape-rotation scheme and schedule to make sure your backup scheme is efficient and effective

Skill 12

PART III

Networking and Security

S K I L L

thirteen

13

Planning and Managing Network Domains

❑ An explanation of NT's domain-based security

❑ How trusts work in NT Server

❑ Types of domain models

❑ Primary and backup domain controllers

❑ Elements of network security

NT uses the domain model of user account management, which may be unfamiliar to most LAN and Unix networking professionals. In this Skill, we'll discuss NT's network domain design. After you understand the concepts presented here, you'll be able to figure out which domain model makes the most sense for your organization, and you'll be able to implement that model.

NT Networking Explained

NT Server is all about networks. The way in which NT servers interoperate on a network introduces the concept of *domain-based security*, which is probably not familiar to folks coming from a LAN background. In this section, we'll develop the concepts of NT networking and see how domains of NT servers interact.

Starting with a Single Server

If you're just starting out, you can set up an NT server as a "stand-alone" server. Each stand-alone server on the network has its own list of user accounts that it keeps to itself.

Stand-alone servers are much like Windows for Workgroups machines. In Windows for Workgroups, each workstation can share items that other workstations in the "workgroup" can see. This peer-to-peer system is scaled up by NT Server. There is no hard-wired limit on the number of users that can be connected to an NT server, even in stand-alone mode. But just the same, a server that's stand-alone will be a member of a Windows networking workgroup. Figure 13.1 illustrates this concept.

Administering a stand-alone NT server is a piece of cake—at first. Adding a user to the server is very straightforward: Just go to the User Manager program, select New User from the File menu, enter the user's name and password, and you're finished! You'll want to give the user membership in any groups that are appropriate. We'll talk about how to do all this in detail later, but you're pretty much off and running.

Stand-alone server user administration is similar in some ways to my experience with AppleShare servers. It's simple to add users, but the problems come up when you start adding servers to your network. For example, Janie in Purchasing calls you, asking to get on the new server. You've set her up already, but that account was on the server in Finance. Now that Purchasing has its own server, you'll need to start over.

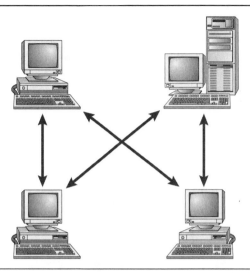

FIGURE 13.1: A stand-alone server works much like peer networking under Windows for Workgroups. Each computer in the workgroup maintains its own user account information.

It gets worse, right? There's no guarantee that a person's user name on one server is going to be the same as her user name on another. And if a password expires or is otherwise changed on one of the servers, there's no relationship between that password and the password of the user's accounts on other servers.

The main point here is that a stand-alone server doesn't share user account information with other servers, and it won't listen to you unless you specifically have an account with it.

This Is My Domain

Managing multiple stand-alone servers on your network means managing multiple lists of user accounts. This can get hairy quickly. Fortunately, there is a way to tell an NT server to go look for user accounts in one central location. Each server that agrees to look in the specified location is said to belong to that NT *domain*. The central list of user accounts for the domain are stored on a computer called the *domain controller*, as shown in Figure 13.2.

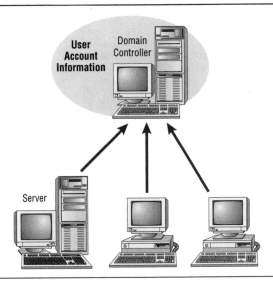

FIGURE 13.2: An NT domain controller consolidates user account information into a single NT domain.

Here are the elements in this type of setup:

- **NT domain controller:** An NT server that maintains a centralized list of user accounts.

- **NT domain**: A group of computers, including an NT domain controller, that depend upon a particular domain controller for account information.

- **Local account**: An account created on an NT server that is not a domain controller. No other servers in the domain will share local accounts.

- **Global account**: An account created on an NT domain controller. Each computer in the domain of the domain controller will be able to grant access to global users, since these accounts are shared by the domain controller with all the servers in the domain.

Servers that are members of a domain can still have local accounts, which are not global domain accounts but are the accounts for that server only. Say you set up a server as stand-alone. You add a bunch of users to that server—local accounts. Later, you add the server to a domain, telling the server that it can look up global accounts on the domain controller. What about those local accounts that you created? They're still there, of course.

> **TIP**   In general, you'll want to minimize the number of local accounts on a server that's a domain member. In fact, you shouldn't have *any* local accounts on such a server, except the built-in administrator and system accounts.

Let's go back to hapless Janie in Purchasing again. This time, you've decided that you're going to have more than one NT server on your network, and so you've set up a domain controller for your company. When you add new users, you add them as *global accounts* on the domain. So now when Janie calls you, asking for access to the new server, you can add her to the access list for that share—and you don't need to (re)create her account on the new server. Janie already exists as a global user on the domain, and the server knows to look in that list of global users when it's looking up accounts. So when it sees Janie in the Access Control List for that share, it will know to ask the domain controller for verification.

Memorize the following: A server in a domain will ask the domain controller for authentication of a global account. As long as a global account appears in a resource's Access Control List, that account will be validated by the domain controller. We'll talk about Access Control Lists in more detail later.

Multiple Domains and Trusts

Domains simplify the situation considerably. We can add more servers to our network, add them to the domain, and have only one list of user accounts to manage.

But in practice, you often want more than one domain. For one thing, users browse through the list of available servers (in the Network Neighborhood, or in the Network Browser when mapping a network drive) on a domain-by-domain basis. If you have 1000 servers in your company, it might become difficult to manage a flat list that includes all of them.

Most of us don't have such large networks. But one could make a real case for decentralizing the administration of user accounts. And even if you can't, you might end up with multiple user account lists anyway. This happened at my company when we merged with another company that had its own Information Systems people and its own list of accounts.

Even if you want to keep one global list of user accounts, you might not want to have just one global domain. Because you must be an administrator of a domain in order to add a server to a domain (you need to have enough authority to tell the domain controller to pay attention to the new server), you will need full administrative privileges on a domain in order to bring up a new server. If you have lots of remote sites, it might make sense to grant administrative access to some of those people out there, but do you want to give an office administrator in San Diego the ability to delete a global user account for a user in Paris?

We'll take a look at some better examples in a moment, but the point is, when you do need more than one domain, how do you get your domains talking to one another? Remember, a domain is a way to consolidate user account information. A computer in a domain will look at the list maintained by the domain controller for user account information. How can you tell a server in a domain to look at another domain's list of users?

Well, one obvious way would be to add the server to another domain—a "multi-domain-ed" server. But (perhaps for your own good) NT doesn't let you do that. Instead, you tell the domain controller of one domain to pay attention to the user account information on another domain; you tell one domain to *trust* another. This situation is illustrated in Figure 13.3.

Don't take the word "trust" too literally. User accounts from trusted domains do not automatically have access to the resources (file shares and other server services) on the trusting domain. A trust simply allows an administrator to grant access to resources in one domain to the users from another domain. A trust allows this to happen, but it does not make it happen automatically. The administrator still needs to explicitly grant access to resources.

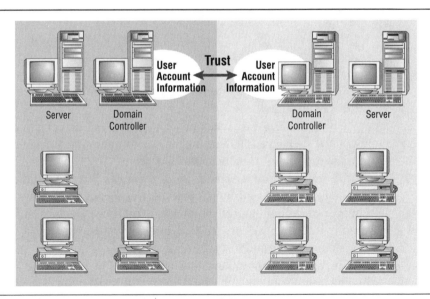

FIGURE 13.3: To share user account information between domains, you establish a trust between them.

Here are some things to remember about trusts:

- **Trusts are one-way**: Telling Domain A to trust Domain B does not mean that Domain B is going to trust Domain A. If you want to do that, you must explicitly tell Domain B to trust Domain A. This trust is referred to as a *two-way trust*, and is often drawn with a two-way arrow (as in Figure 13.3). But it's really two separate one-way trusts (see Figure 13.5 later in this skill).

- **You must have permission to establish trust**: Before Domain A can trust Domain B, Domain B must grant permission to Domain A to trust it. Domain B must say, "Hey, you can trust me!"

- **Trusts can be broken**: You can tell a domain to stop trusting a domain after you've established that trust relationship. Domain A will say to Domain B, "Hey, I don't trust you any more!" You can tell a domain to stop letting a domain trust it. Domain B can say to Domain A, "Hey, don't trust me any more!"

Let's see how user accounts, domains, and trusts can be used to structure a network.

 TIP Don't worry if you don't get it yet. It takes lots of examples to understand these concepts. Take a look at the discussion of domain models coming up for some good examples before giving up!

Understanding Domain Models

Let's take a look at how these pieces can fit together to help you build networks of NT servers. The way in which we join the domains together will result in some very distinct network models. We call these *domain models*.

The Global Domain Model

The first, most basic way to build up an NT network is to have one huge domain, a global domain, to which you add every single one of your NT servers. This is called the global domain model. Everything goes into the domain, as illustrated in Figure 13.4.

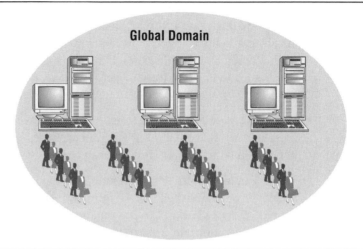

FIGURE 13.4: A global domain contains every NT server and user account in your entire network.

A global domain model seems to make a whole lot of sense. You want to keep your administration as simple as possible. You never want to be forced to create multiple accounts for users in order to grant them access to resources. A global domain model lets you keep the accounts in a centrally administered global list.

One downside to the global domain model is that as the number of servers in your network grows, the browsable list of servers (either the Network Neighborhood in Windows 95 or the Network Browser when you map a network drive) becomes unwieldy. But more seriously, it's very difficult in practice to scale up a global domain in companies that have many remote sites, with lots of decentralized account and resource management. Also, because the domain controller must manage every account in the domain, there's a finite number of accounts that a single domain controller, thus the domain itself, can handle.

WARNING   The maximum number of users per domain has been increased in NT Server 4.0, but it is still not infinite. If you have more than 10,000 users in a domain, you may want to split your network up into multiple domains.

We'll talk about some hard numbers when we discuss the setup of NT domains in the next section. For now, just understand that you might be forced to abandon a single, super-domain at some point.

The Complete Trust Model

The easiest way to scale up the global domain model is to simply add another "global" domain, and then another, and another. Each time you add a domain, you create a two-way trust between the new domain and each of the existing domains. This setup is shown in Figure 13.5.

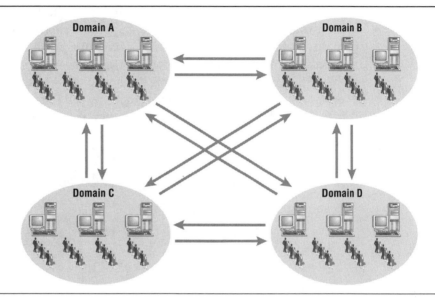

FIGURE 13.5: Scaling up the global domain model by adding multiple, "global" domains requires two-way trusts between each of the domains in the enterprise.

As far as the users are concerned, their account is global to the entire enterprise, because they can be granted access to anything, no matter where it is, no matter what domain it's on.

As far as the administrators are concerned, maintaining a complete trust model requires the maintenance of $N \times (N-1)$ trusts, where N is the number of domains. This gets hairy quickly, because the number of trusts grows geometrically.

In practice, it's very difficult to maintain a degree of global control over your network. You'll need to make sure your user account is a member of the Administrators group on each of the domains. It's likely that you'll occasionally find yourself locked out of an important operation—granting access to a user, or backing up a server—because someone forgot to grant you membership to the

Domain Administrators group of one of the domains. With four domains, as shown in Figure 13.5, this might not happen very often, but it sure is annoying when it does!

The Master/Resource Model

We can solve some of the issues related to the complete trust model by going with an alternative scheme. If the motivation for multiple domains is the local administration of servers at remote sites, we can compromise: Have multiple domains for the servers, or *resources*, and have one single, global domain for the user accounts. We get the best of both worlds here—we keep the user accounts global to the enterprise, with one big list, and it's easy to add sites to the enterprise by adding a resource domain for that site, and then establishing a *one-way* trust between the resource domain and the account domain. This model is shown in Figure 13.6.

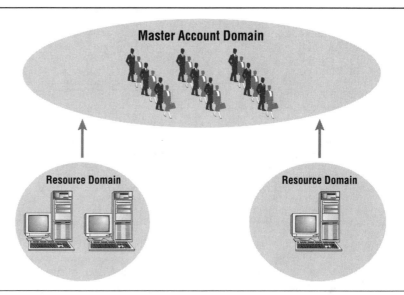

FIGURE 13.6: Splitting out the network resources into resource domains permits us to provide the advantages of local server administration to remote sites. We keep one big user account list in a master account domain (or user domain).

The key to this model is that we've turned the geometric proliferation of trusts in the complete trust model into a linear one. There is a single one-way trust associated with each resource domain: For *N* resource domains, you have *N* trusts. Because the list of user accounts is centralized in the master account domain, as long as a resource domain trusts the master account domain, every user in your enterprise can be granted access to the resources in that domain. It's a hub-and-spoke arrangement for simple scalability.

WARNING   Don't add any users to a resource domain. If you do, those users will have access to only the resources in that domain. You grant trusts from a resource domain only to the account domain—not between two resource domains. If you start granting trusts between resource domains, you'll be halfway back toward a complete trust model—a complete mess!

Another advantage of the master/resource model is that you can provide logical names to your resource domains, such as CHICAGO, NYC, or EUROPE. This gives users browsing the network some idea of where to look to find the network resource they desire.

The Multiple Master Model

The master/resource domain model is about the best you can do, but you still have that limitation on the number of users a single domain can hold. You can carefully mix the complete trust model and the master/resource model in order to scale up your network. As you gain more users than a single domain can handle, add a second account domain with two-way trusts between the account domains, and keep your resource domains trusting each of the account domains with a one-way trust. Whew! Take a look at Figure 13.7 to see what I mean; it's actually very simple.

The multiple master domain model is the model that Microsoft itself uses. It has four account domains: North America, South America, Europe, and Asia. But your network probably isn't big enough to justify a multiple master domain model. Start with the master/resource domain model and scale up to the multiple master model only if necessary.

TIP   You don't need to think too much about geography at this point. You can set up master account domains so that multiple remote sites have access to the same account domain. It's important to keep in mind that domains are not limited by geography. We'll see why in a moment.

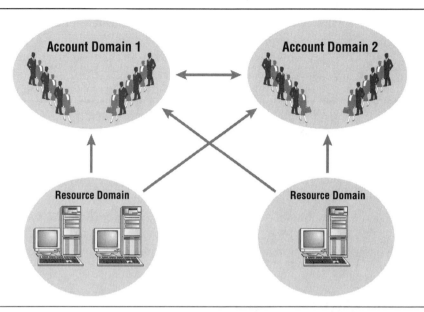

FIGURE 13.7: You can scale up your global user account domain by adding account domains as necessary. Two-way trusts occur only between account domains.

Choosing a Domain Model

Now that you've seen some common domain structures, you'll need to figure out what you want to do with your NT network—which domain model you want to implement. Deciding which domain model is right for you generally boils down to two parts:

- Partitioning your user accounts—identifying the account domains
- Defining relationships between those partitions—identifying the trusts

Identifying the Domains

You need to decide how you will break out your list of users, if at all. If you're planning to split up your user lists into separate name spaces (user account domains), you'll need to figure out what the boundaries are.

East Coast/West Coast might be a good boundary. This is not because the implementation of your domains will depend upon geography, but because (in this example) the people on each coast tend to know one another and work on the same projects. Try to find out what the boundaries are going to be, based on people needs and business needs. My CIO (Chief Information Officer) calls this "performing an affinity analysis." (Go to lots of departmental parties—tell your boss you are performing an affinity analysis.)

Seriously, think about your network and the procedures that are already in place to handle network administration tasks. You won't be able to come up with a good reason for splitting out your user accounts into multiple domains, but on the off chance that you do (or that it has been mandated), keep those divisions as logical as possible.

As for splitting out the domains for network resources, think about how each server will be managed. You might want to go with functional groupings; for example, put all the file servers in one domain and all the number-crunchers in another. Our company decided to go with geography because that's what determined the hands-on administration of the server machine.

Once you've identified your groups of people and machines, or perhaps to help you in this exercise, take a big piece of paper and draw blobs with the people and resources in them. This is your *domain map*. Figure 13.8 shows an example.

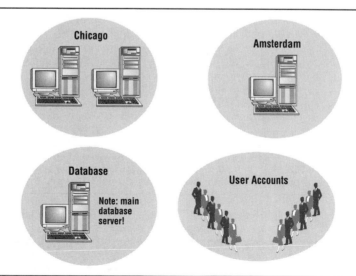

FIGURE 13.8: Step 1 of domain planning: Draw your resources on a piece of paper, and draw circles around them.

Identifying the Trusts

Once you've drawn the boundaries, if any (after you've performed your affinity analysis), you'll know which people need which resources. On your domain map, draw arrows *from your resources to the people*. This might seem backwards, until you realize that the resources will be looking toward the user account domains for the trusts. The resources trust the people; the people don't trust the computers (at least, they shouldn't).

Now take a look at your domain map. It should have circles and arrows on it, as you see in the example in Figure 13.9. This is a very good sign. Compare your domain map to the domain models that we've discussed, and find the domain model that best fits your needs.

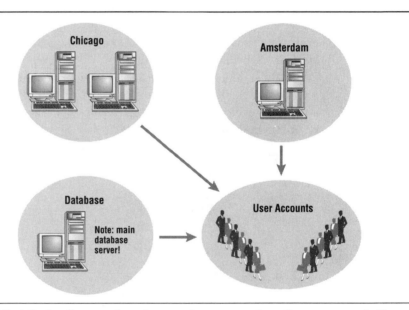

FIGURE 13.9: On your domain map, draw arrows from the resources to the people that need them. For most domain designs, this is the hard part.

Choosing Your Domain Model: Final Notes

If all this seems really easy to you, that's a good thing. It wasn't easy for us, and I'll warn you that the process of drawing your domain map is going to take you about sixteen times as long as you think it will. This is because, of course, the decisions about which things go in which domains are only partially technical. There are sound business reasons, and some not-so-sound political reasons, why certain items belong together. With any luck, you'll precipitate a huge battle over the color printer that ends up creating a new graphic arts department...well, you know how it is.

Consider your domain map and your choice of domain model tentative at this point. Domain models have implications about how the security access rights will play out among the servers in your network. Read the "Managing Network Security" section later in this chapter before making a final decision.

In practice, most organizations have chosen the master/resource domain model, because it offers a good balance between network flexibility and centralized user account administration.

Setting Up NT Domains

One of the first questions that the NT Server Setup program asks you is which role you would like your computer to play on the network. You are offered three choices:

- Primary Domain Controller (PDC)
- Backup Domain Controller (BDC)
- Stand-Alone Server

Let's see how these selections fit into your domain model.

Primary Domain Controllers

A primary domain controller (PDC) is an NT server that maintains the account information for a domain; a PDC defines a domain. As a consequence, you will need one PDC per domain, or one NT server per domain in addition to any NT servers that you already have indicated on your domain map.

You specified the domain name for the PDC when you set up NT. The account information on a PDC is used to define the account information for the domain. When you run the User Manager for Domains and manipulate user account information, you're changing the account data on that domain's PDC.

Yes, a PDC can act as a "normal" NT server, with file, print, and other network servers (I'm writing this on my PDC right now—PDCs do a great job of running Microsoft Office!). However, you probably won't want to do this in a production environment, because the PDC gets hit every time an account needs authentication. On real networks, the PDCs tend to stay busy.

PDCs need lots of RAM—even more than "normal" NT servers, if possible. If you filled out the Hardware Design worksheet in Chapter 4, and took the huge numbers for required RAM seriously, you should be in good shape. Refer to Table 13.1 for Microsoft's recommendations for server RAM for PDCs, and keep in mind that Microsoft RAM recommendations tend to be on the small side. I would double the numbers you see listed in the table.

TABLE 13.1: Microsoft Recommendations for PDC Server RAM

Number of Users	Page File Size (MB)	RAM (MB)
3,000	32	16
7,500	64	32
10,000	96	48
15,000	128	64
20,000	256	128
30,000	332	166
40,000	394	197
50,000	512	256

PDCs are different from "normal" NT servers at a low level—the security database on a PDC is used to define the account information for the entire domain. This affects the implementation of a great deal of the security behavior of the system. For this reason and others, there's no way to create a PDC out of a "normal" NT computer, short of reinstalling NT.

And since the PDC is the definition of the domain, you can't have more than one PDC on a domain. You can't have the possibility of more than one definition of the domain's security information.

But this presents a problem: If you can't have more than one PDC on a domain, then the PDC is a single point of failure for the entire domain. You need to talk to the domain controller for your user domain in order to log in. You need to talk to the resource domain's domain controller in order to gain access to a file server on that domain. If the PDC is so important, and you can't have more than one, and you need to reinstall NT software to get a PDC, what do you do when the PDC goes down? How can you get your network back up quickly, or indeed ensure that the network never goes down at all? Enter the backup domain controller.

Backup Domain Controllers

A backup domain controller (BDC) shares all of the essential characteristics of a PDC, in that it publishes the account information on the network that helps define the domain. However, a BDC cannot be used to modify account information.

A BDC gets all of the domain's account information from the domain PDC. If you need to make changes to an account on the domain, you do it on the PDC. When you run the User Manager for Domains and manipulate user account information, you're changing the account data on that domain's PDC. You never modify anything on the BDC directly. This way, the BDCs don't interfere with the PDC's definition of the account information for the domain. Periodically, the security information is replicated from the PDC to the BDCs on the domain (yes, you can have as many BDCs on your domain as you like).

Then, if the PDC goes down or is otherwise unavailable, you can promote a BDC to PDC status. It will assume the role of PDC and will start replicating the security information back down to the (remaining) BDCs.

You promote a server from BDC to PDC status through the Server Manager. The Server Manager is listed on the Administrative Tools menu (choose Programs from the Start menu to get to this submenu). In the Server Manager, select the computer and choose Promote to Primary Domain Controller from the File menu.

TIP Normally, security information is replicated from the PDC to the BDCs on a periodic basis. If you've just made a whole lot of changes to the accounts—say you just went through the Human Resources termination list and locked out a bunch of accounts—you can manually force a replication to occur from the Server Manager by choosing Synchronize Entire Domain from the File menu.

Establishing Trust Relationships

You establish trust relationships between networks with NT's User Manager for Domains program. Well, I guess this makes sense if you keep in mind that the motivation for domains is the administration of user security. But since all the other domain administration stuff, such as synchronizing the PDCs and BDCs, is in the Server Manager, that's where I looked. But nope—although the Server Manager online help was great, it actually was referring to the User Manager program, without making this clear. This may be cleaned up in a later version of NT Server.

Keep this example in mind while we discuss trusts: A resource domain trusts the master account domain. Here are the terms you need to know:

- A *trusting domain* is the domain that does the trusting. In this example, the resource domain is the trusting domain. It gets the tail of the trust arrow on the domain map that you created.

- A *trusted domain* is the domain that permits the trusting. In this example, it's the account domain. It gets the head of the arrow in the domain map.

Adding a Trusted Domain

If you are an administrator in both the trusted and trusting domains, complete all of the following steps to add a trusted domain. Otherwise, the administrator of the trusted domain should complete steps 1 through 6, and then tell the password to the administrator of the trusting domain, who will complete steps 7 through 10.

1. Fire up the User Manager for Domains (choose it from the Administrative Tools menu, under the Start menu's Programs menu).

2. Switch to the trusted domain (the account domain).

3. Choose Trust Relationships from the Policies menu. This will bring up the dialog box shown in Figure 13.10.

4. Click on the bottom Add button, next to the Trusting Domains list box.

5. Type the name of the trusting domain (the resource domain), and enter the password that will be required to establish the trust. Click on OK.

6. Close the Trust Relationships dialog box.

7. Switch to the trusting domain (the resource domain).

8. Choose Trust Relationships from the Policies menu to display the Trust Relationships dialog box (Figure 13.10).

9. Click on the top Add button, next to the Trusted Domains list box.

10. Type the name of the trusted domain (the account domain) and the administrator password, and then click on OK.

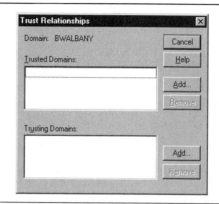

FIGURE 13.10: Creating trust relationships

See the online help for the Server Manager for details on establishing trust relationships.

Setting Up Your Domain Controllers

Domains don't need to be limited by geography. Careful placement of BDCs can ensure successful logins, even when the connection to the home office is slow or not always available. Here are some tips for setting up your domain controllers:

- Place the PDC in the same location as the primary managers of the domain. For example, Microsoft locates the PDCs for both their North America and South America domains in Redmond, Washington, where the main bulk of the Information Systems people live and work.

- For each remote location that participates in the domain, deploy a BDC. For example, each location of my company has a server that's a BDC for our master account domain. Logins occur through the BDC on the local LAN, and user account administration occurs back at the main office, on the PDC.

- Keep in mind that for domains with more than 10,000 accounts, Microsoft recommends a dedicated server for the domain controller. Measure the performance of your BDCs at the remote locations. If you find that you don't need a dedicated BDC, well and good. Following Microsoft recommendations, my company deployed a dedicated BDC server at each remote location (and we bought lots of NT Server licenses). The best advice is to measure, measure, measure.

Managing Your Users

The User Manager for Domains is the tool that you use to modify the account information of a domain. Here are some tips on using this program:

- Make sure that you're creating users in the proper domain. If necessary, choose Select Domain from the User menu.

- Use groups to tag users with similar attributes. The power of groups as a user and security administration tool cannot be overstated. Since a user can belong to any number of groups, it's a good idea to use groups to your fullest advantage. See the "Global and Local Groups" section later in this skill for details.

- Create a Template user and then copy that user to create others. To ensure that you set up group membership and policy information correctly for everyone, concentrate on creating the perfect user sometime when you have the peace and quiet. Okay, never mind—don't wait for the peace and quiet, just do it. Create a user with all the settings you might want, all the group memberships that you're always forgetting to set, and give that member a meaningful first name and the last name Template. For example, you might name this user FinanceDept Template.

- To create hundreds of users at a time in previous versions of NT, you could use an Adduser command-line utility available via the Windows NT Resource Kit. At the time of this writing, there is no such tool that's officially for NT Server 4.0, but the Adduser utility from the NT 3.51 Resource Kit seems to work. Microsoft's official line is to copy and paste users in the User Manager.

Managing Network Security

The entire motivation for all this user account/domain stuff is to ensure that the appropriate people get appropriate access to the proper network resources. In this section, we'll discuss NT security permissions and how those permissions are applied in the context of a master/resource domain model.

Using Visual Test As an Administration Tool

There's another trick you can try. Although this is way beyond the scope of this discussion, it's too cool to keep to myself. Microsoft sells a tool called Visual Test that, among its many other functions, lets you "record" windows operations and then play them back. It's sold to developers as a way for them to perform exhaustive test runs against their Windows programs before they ship (an alternative to training pigeons to peck at the keyboard a certain way).

I used the record feature of Visual Test to track my actions while I fired up the User Manager and created a user. This is the program that it generated:

```
'$INCLUDE 'RECORDER.INC'
SetDefaultWaitTimeout(Timeout)
Scenario "add a user"
    Minimize the Visual Test window.
    If GetHandle(GH_HWNDCLIENT)
    Then WMinWnd(GetHandle(GH_HWNDCLIENT))
    Check the resolution that this script was recorded on.
    CheckResolution (1280, 1024)
    WTaskbarStartClk(VK_LBUTTON)
    WMenuSelect("@5\@16\@14")
    Sleep(9)
    CurrentWindow = WFndWndC("User Manager - BWALBANY", "BltClWin",
                            FINDWINDOWFLAGS, Timeout)
    WMenuSelect("&User\New &User...")
End Scenario
```

Get this tool and see what you come up with. You can see how it lets you script any application you want, just by example. This is like the old macro recorder in Good Old Windows, but on super-steroids. It might help you out!

Access Control Lists and NT Permissions

Each network resource has an Access Control List, or ACL, that lists the accounts that have access to the resource, and what the access level is for each of these accounts. Each entry in the ACL is called an Access Control Entry (ACE). And thus the fine art of NT security devolves into "minding your ACLs and ACEs."

From the Windows Explorer, it takes four mouse operations to bring up the Permissions dialog box for a file or directory, from which you can view or modify the ACL:

1. Right-click on the file in the Explorer.

2. Select Properties from the pop-up menu.

3. Select the Security tab of the file's Properties sheet.

4. Click on the Permissions button to see a dialog box similar to the one shown in Figure 13.11.

NOTE   I think that needing to perform four mouse operations to view something as fundamental as file permissions indicates a certain level of immaturity in the product. But it's not that surprising, since this is the first version of NT with this sort of user interface. Stay tuned for improvements.

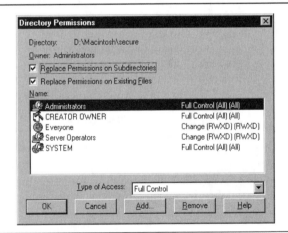

FIGURE 13.11: An Access Control List as displayed in the Explorer

From this dialog box, you can:

- Remove a user or group from an ACL by selecting it and clicking on the Remove button.

- Modify an entry in the ACL by selecting it and changing its type of access in the drop-down menu.

- Add new entries to the ACL by clicking on the Add button.

Files are not the only items that have associated ACLs. Each resource on the network—be it a data file, a printer, or a server—has an ACL. For example, you may want to grant limited access to an expensive color printer.

Table 13.2 explains the different levels or access that are available with NT Server.

T A B L E   1 3 . 2 : NT File Permissions

Permission	Effect on Files	Effect on Directories
Read	View the file contents	See the list of files and subdirectories in the directory
Write	Modify the file contents	Write files to the directory
Execute	Execute the file, if it's an application	Pass-through
Delete	Delete the file from the system	Remove the directory and its contents
Change Permissions	Modify the ACL for this file	Modify the ACL for the directory
Take Ownership	Become the owner of the file	Become the owner of the directory

The Execute permission on directories might need some explanation. Unix folks are used to Execute permission on a directory; Banyan folks are familiar with the Scan permission.

Say that you have a directory called Users that contains the private subdirectories for every user on the server. You've set all this up so that when a user is created, you create a subdirectory for that user on the server as well. Janie wants to access her personal directory. Instead of creating hundreds of shares on the server, one for each user, you've created one User share. You give everyone Execute permission on the User directory, and you give each of the users Read, Write, and Execute permissions on their his or her directory.

You don't want to give everyone Read permission on the Users directory, because they shouldn't be able to see the other users' directories. If they didn't have Read or Execute permission, they would be denied access to the share, even though they have permission to use a directory within Users. That's why we refer to the Execute permission on directories as "pass-through"—you're telling the system that you're just passing through that directory, on the way to a subdirectory to which you have access.

Global and Local Groups

You provide a list of account/permissions pairs for each network resource. But if you were required to enter all the people in the Purchasing department for each of the resources they might share, things could get tedious quickly.

NT allows you to define groups of users that share a common trait or that need access to a common resource. Create groups that are global to the domain: global groups that have global users as members. Then when you add entries to a resource's ACL, make sure that you add the Purchasing group, for instance, instead of listing all the members of the group.

TIP   Don't think about groups too narrowly. In my company's design review, there was a predisposition to think of user groups as business departments. That's a great start, but why can't there be a group for all the bicyclists or all the Macintosh users? There is no hard limit to the number of groups to which a user may belong, so don't limit yourself. Think of membership in a group as an attribute of the user.

You maintain groups with the User Manager for Domains program. Here are the steps for creating a new global group:

1. Fire up the User Manager for Domains program.

2. Verify that you're looking at the appropriate domain. If not, select Select Domain from the User menu and choose the appropriate domain.

3. Select New Global Group from the User menu.

4. Enter a name and description for the new group.

To create a new local group, follow the procedure above, and in step 3, select New Local Group from the User menu instead of New Global Group.

You should try to emulate the group-naming scheme that is followed by NT. Because you can't delete or rename the built-in groups (for example, Domain Admins), it might make sense to follow suit by using mixed case for group names and descriptions. For example, a group used to maintain administrative privileges for a Thing can be called Thing Admins. You can come up with your own conventions, but try to keep the names consistent.

Groups are very powerful tools for managing NT security, but at this point, you might not understand how this all plays out in practice. Let's look at an example of how groups allow you to exert control over access rights in a complex domain environment.

Managing NT Security: Examples

To bring all the concepts together, let's walk through a real-world example—one that I've personally experienced.

I'm an administrator of an NT network that's built on the master/resource domain model. I set up a new NT computer, and I add it to the resource domain. Then I restart the computer, and when it comes back, I try to log in to the server with my named account (as opposed to the local Administrator account that I set up when I installed the NT software). It says here that any administration should be done under our named accounts, so that we can log changes (read, "know who to blame"). But the computer always answers, "The local policy of this computer does not allow you to log on locally." Huh?

This is an effect of the domain authentication interacting with NT security. There are three levels of authentication going on:

- The accounts on the local server machine

- The resource domain, of which the server is a member

- The account domain, which the resource domain trusts

Now, when an NT server joins a domain, it adds the Domain Administrators global group from that domain to its Administrators local group. The local Administrators group *on the server* has *as a member* the Domain Administrators global group from the resource domain of which it's a member.

And my named user account, from the account domain, doesn't show up in there anywhere. Oops, I did it again. I forgot to add the Domain Administrators group *from the account domain* to the *local* Administrators group on the server.

With multiple domains, you want the Administrators local group on each of your servers to contain as a member the Domain Administrators global group from your account domain. Follow this rule:

User → Global → Local → ACL

This says, "Users belong to global groups, which are members of local groups, which are entries in the Access Control Lists of network resources."

Here's another example: I have a couple of NT servers that are used to provide file services to Macintosh clients for cc:Mail. I need the cc:Mail team to have the authority to kick people off the server so that they can perform their routine (and much needed) maintenance of the cc:Mail post offices.

Now, these folks know cc:Mail like nobody's business, but do I want them to be administrators of my NT enterprise? No, and fortunately, they don't need to be.

Instead, I created a global group called "cc:Mail Admins" in the master account domain. Then I added this cc:Mail Admins group to the Administrators local group on each of the three servers being used as cc:Mail servers.

When someone in the cc:Mail team leaves and is replaced, I make the change—once!—in the cc:Mail Admins global group, and the administrative privileges of all three cc:Mail servers happens for me, automatically.

The whole point of the master/resource domain model is the centralization of user account administration. You want the user account information, including group membership, in one place. If I had added each of the cc:Mail team members as *users* to the Administrators local group on each of the servers, I would have a lot more typing to do!

Remember that group membership indicates something about its members. Say that the Finance and Human Resource departments need to share file and print resources. Create a Finance department group where? In the master account domain as a global group, since membership in the Finance department is an attribute of a user, and all user information is kept in the master account domain.

On the file server, we've created a number of file and print resources. We create a group called Finance and HR where? On the server, as a local group, because this group is an attribute of an administration strategy, of our NT system. It says nothing about users. We add the Finance and HR group to the ACLs of the various shared resources on the server. If there is only one such resource, you could dispense with the Finance and HR local group, because it's there only to streamline administration on the local server. If there's only one shared service on the server, then membership of the global group Finance and HR in the shared item's ACL is an implicit grouping.

Are You Experienced?

Now you can...

- ☑ tell an NT server to look for user accounts in one central location

- ☑ allow a server to look at another doamin's list of users by telling one domain to trust another domain

- ☑ decide which domain model best suits your network: a global domain, complete trust, master/resource, or multiple master model

☑ configure your domain controllers (the PDC and BDCs)

☑ use the User Manager for Domains program to set up and change users and groups

Setting Up NT Services for Microsoft Windows Clients

- ❏ Windows 3.1 and DOS client setup
- ❏ Windows 95 client setup
- ❏ File share setup and management
- ❏ Network printer sharing and management

It's likely that most of your NT network clients are Microsoft Windows and DOS computers. With the introduction of LAN Manager, years ago, Microsoft started developing its networking systems. The networking capabilities of NT Server are an extension of the services offered in LAN Manager.

Here, we'll discuss the file and print services for Microsoft networking clients, such as the DOS, Windows 3.1, and Windows 95 clients. You'll see that setting up the file and print services on the NT server is easy. The more difficult operation is configuring your network clients. NT Server includes the Network Client Administrator, which facilitates the creation of installation floppy disks for the Microsoft client computers.

Microsoft Networking Explained

Microsoft networking is built on top of the NetBIOS application programming interface (API). Using NetBIOS as a foundation, a higher-level protocol for inter-computer messaging was developed: Server Message Block, or SMB, networking.

Nodes on a Microsoft network maintain their connections to one another by means of SMB exchange. I call such networks "SMB networks" and use the terms *Microsoft network* and *SMB network* interchangeably.

NetBIOS most often uses NetBEUI as the transport protocol. However, since NetBEUI is not routable, many networks are using TCP/IP or IPX as NetBIOS transports instead of using NetBEUI. See Skill 8 for more information about these transport protocols.

Installing the Network Client Software

Windows for Workgroups and Windows 95 come with the client software for NT. You'll need to configure DOS and Windows 3.1 clients with additional software. The Network Client Administrator, one of the administration tools that come with NT Server, facilitates the creation of software installation floppy disks for Windows 3.1 and DOS clients.

Creating Installation Disks for Windows 3.1 and DOS Clients

You can find the Network Client Administrator with the rest of the NT administration tools—on the Administrative Tools menu, accessed from the Start menu's Programs menu. To begin, log on to an NT server and fire up the Network Client Administrator. Make sure that you have the NT Server distribution CD-ROM mounted.

As you can see in Figure 14.1, the Network Client Administrator gives you two choices for network client setup: Make Network Installation Startup Disk and Make Installation Disk Set.

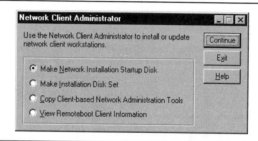

FIGURE 14.1: The Network Client Administrator allows you to create client installation disks.

Making a Network Installation Startup Disk

You can create a floppy disk that will boot the client computer with default configurations, connect to an NT server via the NetBEUI transport, and download all the necessary client system files. The advantage of this method is that you will have only one floppy to carry around. The disadvantage is that it works only if the default configurations work. For example, the default configurations for some Ethernet cards will interfere with the operation of the PC serial ports. And it's the rare network that has identical configurations for every single client.

However, you could use the setup boot floppy as a starting place for making your own setup boot disk. Use the Network Client Administrator to create the floppy, and then edit the INI settings in the files on the floppy to match your network clients' needs.

Making an Installation Disk Set

The other Network Client Administrator option is to create floppy disks that run an installation program on the client computer, and will set up the SMB networking clients under DOS or Windows 3.1. This method is more commonly used, so we'll go through the steps.

Log in to the NT server as an administrator, start the Network Client Administrator (choose it from the Administrative Tools menu), and choose Make Installation Disk Set. You'll see the Share Network Client Installation Files dialog box, shown in Figure 14.2.

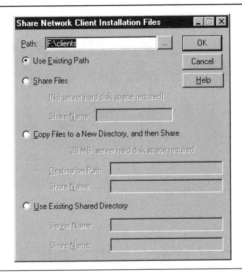

FIGURE 14.2: The Share Network Client Installation Files dialog box appears after you choose to make an installation disk set.

In this dialog box, choose the Use Existing Path option, and then click on OK. You don't need to create a share for the installation disk sets, because all of the required files will be copied to the floppy disks. This dialog box is really for the other installation options. Of course, you can copy the files to your server's hard disk if you want to; this will save you from hunting down the CD-ROM later.

The next dialog box you see is named (appropriately) Make Installation Disk Set. Choose Network Client v3.0 for MS-DOS and Windows, as shown in Figure 14.3. Check the Format Disks checkbox if you would like to format the floppies (and erase any data on them) before copying the installation files, but note that this takes a long time. Make sure that you've selected the proper floppy disk destination drive; this will almost always be drive A. And you already know that you need to create floppies that will fit the drives in the client computers—if you need to create 5.25-inch disks, then use a 5.25-inch drive.

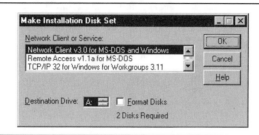

FIGURE 14.3: The Make Installation Disk Set dialog box lets you choose the kind of disks to make.

Click on OK to start the copy process. Keep in mind that floppy drives are slow, and you'll be creating two floppies for the Network Client 3.0 for DOS and Windows 3.1. This will take about three minutes.

Setting Up DOS and Windows 3.1 Clients

After you've created the installation diskettes, you need to run the installation program on each of your network client PCs.

Be sure to note the computer resources that are in use on the client computer, such as the IRQs, I/O ports, and DMA channels. You should also know the make, model, and revision number of the client's network interface card. Some network adapters will require a driver diskette from the manufacturer. Be aware if you need such a disk, and if so, have it available.

Follow these steps to run the installation program on a client computer:

1. Insert the first disk of the installation program into drive A and type **A:\SETUP** at a command prompt.

2. Read the informational screen, shown in Figure 14.4, and then press Enter.

3. In the next screen, type the destination for the network client software on the local computer's hard drive. You'll need to change the default of A:\NET, which is on the installation floppy and shown in Figure 14.5. At least change the drive letter to a local hard drive, such as C:\NET.

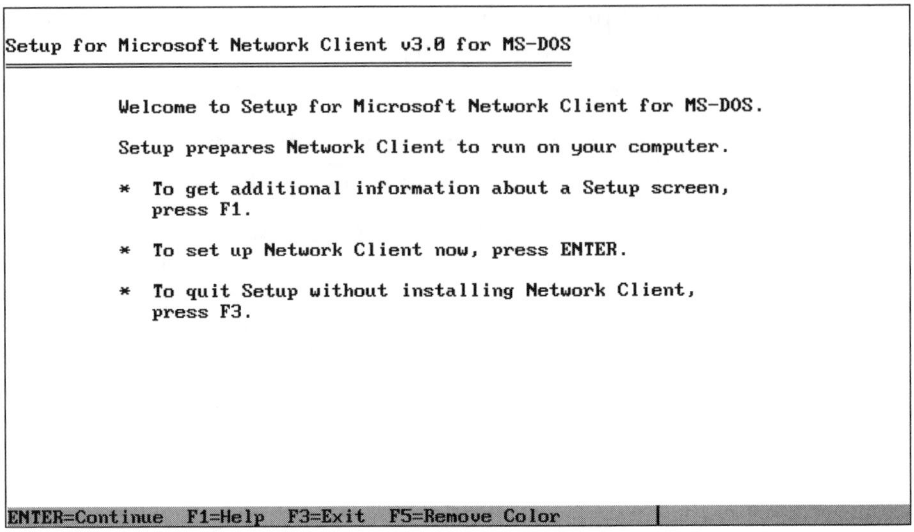

```
Setup for Microsoft Network Client v3.0 for MS-DOS

        Welcome to Setup for Microsoft Network Client for MS-DOS.

        Setup prepares Network Client to run on your computer.

        *  To get additional information about a Setup screen,
           press F1.

        *  To set up Network Client now, press ENTER.

        *  To quit Setup without installing Network Client,
           press F3.




 ENTER=Continue  F1=Help  F3=Exit  F5=Remove Color
```

FIGURE 14.4: This screen welcomes you to the Setup program.

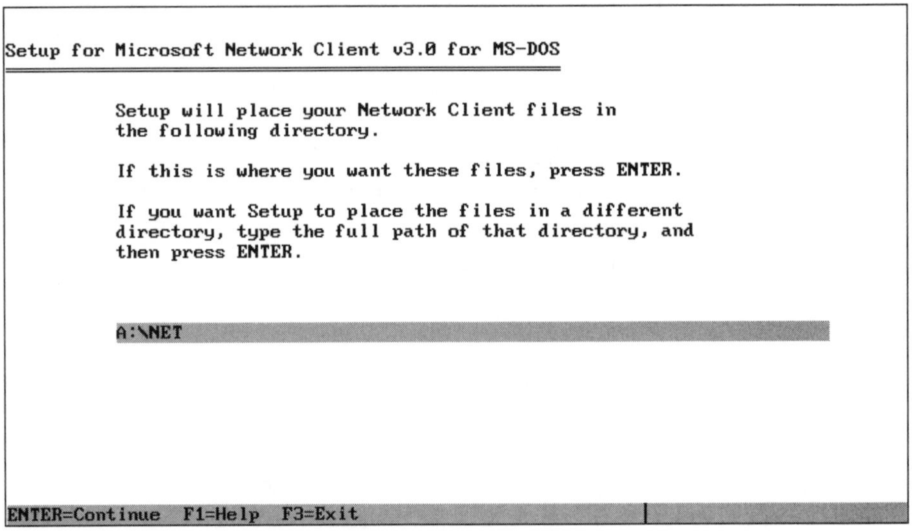

```
Setup for Microsoft Network Client v3.0 for MS-DOS

        Setup will place your Network Client files in
        the following directory.

        If this is where you want these files, press ENTER.

        If you want Setup to place the files in a different
        directory, type the full path of that directory, and
        then press ENTER.



        A:\NET



 ENTER=Continue  F1=Help  F3=Exit
```

FIGURE 14.5: Enter the destination for the client software in this screen.

4. The next screen, shown in Figure 14.6, allows you to change names, setup options, and the network configuration. Make sure that these settings are correct before you accept them. To select a setting on this screen, highlight it with the arrow keys and press Enter.

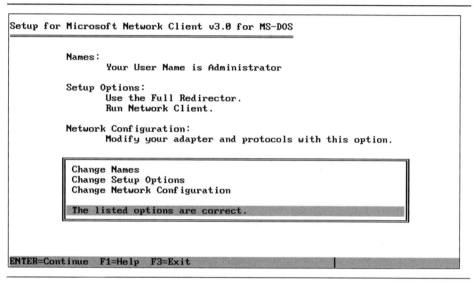

```
Setup for Microsoft Network Client v3.0 for MS-DOS


        Names:
                Your User Name is Administrator

        Setup Options:
                Use the Full Redirector.
                Run Network Client.

        Network Configuration:
                Modify your adapter and protocols with this option.

        ┌──────────────────────────────────────────────────────────┐
        │ Change Names                                               │
        │ Change Setup Options                                       │
        │ Change Network Configuration                               │
        │                                                            │
        │ The listed options are correct.                            │
        └──────────────────────────────────────────────────────────┘



ENTER=Continue   F1=Help   F3=Exit
```

FIGURE 14.6: From this screen, you can change client settings.

5. Select Change Names to see the screen shown in Figure 14.7. Make any necessary changes. When you're finished, highlight the line that says "The listed names are correct" and press Enter.

- **Change User Name:** Match the NT logon name of the primary user of this network client.

- **Change Computer Name:** Use a name that's meaningful to you. For example, you might standardize on a three-letter city code, followed by a number based on the workstation's serial number. You might also consider room locations for client PC names.

- **Change Workgroup Name:** Use a meaningful workgroup name (if you use workgroups). If not, set the workgroup name to the same name as the domain name.

- **Change Domain Name:** The domain name should be the name of the domain to which you wish to add this client PC. For example, you may want to add your computers to the appropriate resource domain.

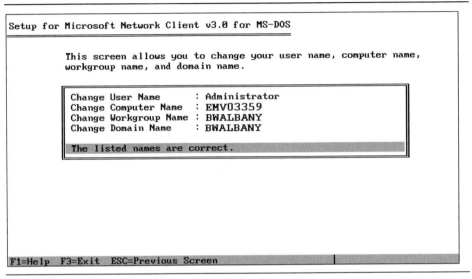

```
Setup for Microsoft Network Client v3.0 for MS-DOS

        This screen allows you to change your user name, computer name,
        workgroup name, and domain name.

        ┌─────────────────────────────────────────────────────────────┐
        │ Change User Name      : Administrator                        │
        │ Change Computer Name  : EMV03359                             │
        │ Change Workgroup Name : BWALBANY                             │
        │ Change Domain Name    : BWALBANY                             │
        │ The listed names are correct.                                │
        └─────────────────────────────────────────────────────────────┘




F1=Help  F3=Exit   ESC=Previous Screen
```

FIGURE 14.7: Changing name settings

6. Select Change Setup Options to see the screen shown in Figure 14.8. For the Change Logon Validation setting, make the setting Logon to Domain if you already have your NT domains set up. Keep the default Redir and Startup options unless DOS memory is really tight. You also have the option of installing a network "Hot Key" TSR, but I think it makes it too easy for naive users to change their drive mappings. When you're finished, select the line that reads "The listed options are correct" and press Enter.

7. Select Change Network Configuration to see the screen shown in Figure 14.9. Change any of the settings as necessary, and then select "Network configuration is correct" and press Enter.

    • Check that the Setup program has the appropriate network adapter listed. If you have a setup disk from the network adapter card manufacturer, select Add Adapter and press Enter. Select "Not shown in the list below" and press Enter. Eject the setup floppy disk, insert the manufacturer's floppy disk, and enter the path to the network interface card's setup files, or otherwise follow the manufacturer's setup instructions.

    • Set up the information appropriate for the network interface card that is installed on this computer, such as the IRQ and I/O address information.

- Set up the network protocols appropriate for this network client. For example, you might want to configure your PCs with TCP/IP.

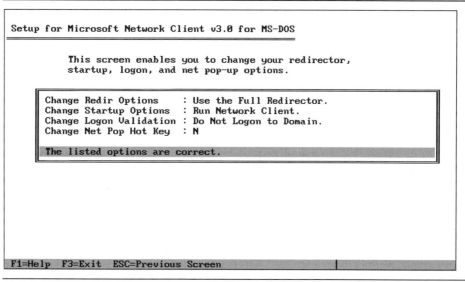

```
Setup for Microsoft Network Client v3.0 for MS-DOS

           This screen enables you to change your redirector,
           startup, logon, and net pop-up options.

    Change Redir Options     : Use the Full Redirector.
    Change Startup Options    : Run Network Client.
    Change Logon Validation  : Do Not Logon to Domain.
    Change Net Pop Hot Key   : N

    The listed options are correct.




 F1=Help   F3=Exit   ESC=Previous Screen
```

FIGURE 14.8: Changing setup options

```
Setup for Microsoft Network Client v3.0 for MS-DOS

           Use TAB to toggle between boxes.

           Installed Network Adapter(s) and Protocol(s):

           Intel EtherExpress 16 or 16TP
                   Microsoft NetBEUI

           Options:

           Change Settings
           Remove
           Add Adapter
           Add Protocol

           Network configuration is correct.



 ENTER=Continue   F1=Help   F3=Exit
```

FIGURE 14.9: Changing network configuration options.

8. After you've checked the settings and made any necessary changes, choose "The listed options are correct" and press Enter. Setup will copy files to the local computer, edit the AUTOEXEC.BAT and CONFIG.SYS files, and save the old versions of these files in the root directory of the C: drive.

9. When the Setup program is finished, you'll see the screen shown in Figure 14.10. Remove all floppies from the drives and press Enter to reboot the computer.

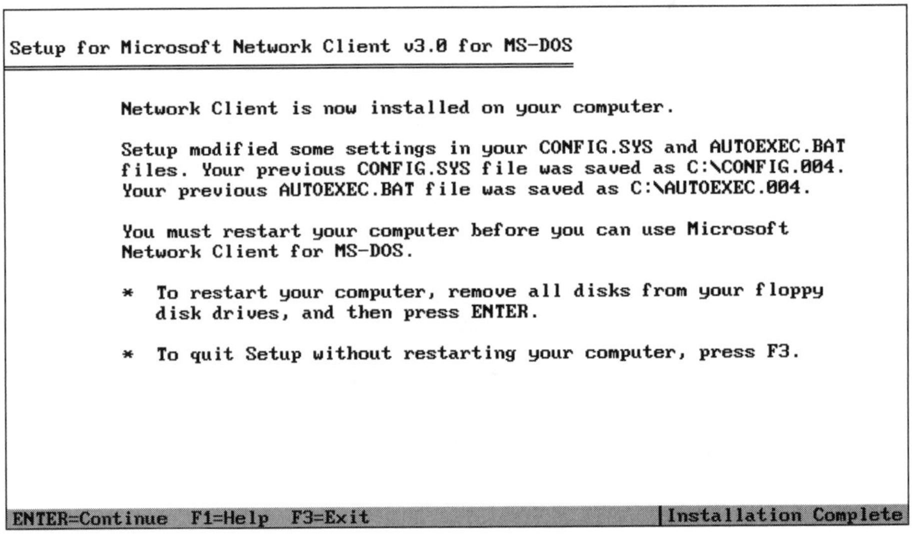

```
Setup for Microsoft Network Client v3.0 for MS-DOS

        Network Client is now installed on your computer.

        Setup modified some settings in your CONFIG.SYS and AUTOEXEC.BAT
        files. Your previous CONFIG.SYS file was saved as C:\CONFIG.004.
        Your previous AUTOEXEC.BAT file was saved as C:\AUTOEXEC.004.

        You must restart your computer before you can use Microsoft
        Network Client for MS-DOS.

        *  To restart your computer, remove all disks from your floppy
           disk drives, and then press ENTER.

        *  To quit Setup without restarting your computer, press F3.




ENTER=Continue   F1=Help   F3=Exit                    Installation Complete
```

FIGURE 14.10: The Setup program tells you when client installation is complete.

Setting Up Windows 95 Clients

You set up Windows 95 clients through the Network Control Panel. Follow these steps:

1. Open the Network Control Panel and click on the Configuration tab. You'll see the dialog box shown in Figure 14.11.

2. Click on the Add button and select Adapter, as shown in Figure 14.12.

3. In the Select Network Adapters dialog box, shown in Figure 14.13, select the appropriate network adapter. If your adapter is not listed, click on the Have Disk button and enter the path to the network adapter setup files.

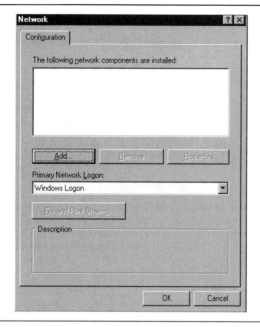

FIGURE 14.11: The Configuration tab of the Windows 95 Network Control Panel

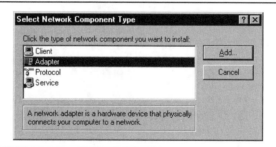

FIGURE 14.12: Choosing the network component to add

4. After you've selected your network adapter, click on OK. Windows 95 will install the default protocols, NetBEUI and IPX, and the default clients, Microsoft (NT) networking and NetWare. Figure 14.14 shows the Configuration tab with the protocols and clients installed. If you need to remove a protocol at this time, select it and click on the Remove button.

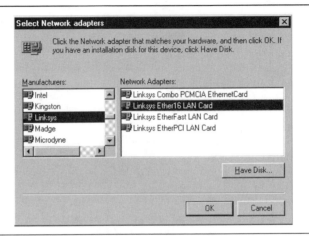

FIGURE 14.13: Selecting your network adapter

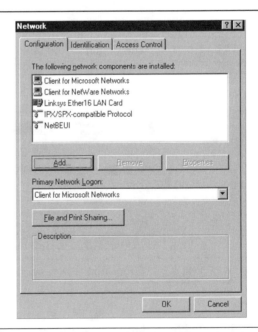

FIGURE 14.14: Windows 95 installs the default protocols and clients.

5. Click on the Identification tab to see the dialog box shown in Figure 14.15. Enter the computer name in the Computer Name field and the name of a workgroup for the computer in the Workgroup field. (You'll configure domain membership in the next step.)

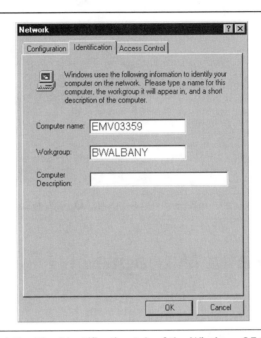

FIGURE 14.15: The Identification tab of the Windows 95 Network Control Panel

6. In the Configuration tab, double-click on the Client for Microsoft Networks to edit its properties, as shown in Figure 14.16. For Logon Validation, check the Log on to Windows NT Domain checkbox, and enter the name of the domain in the text box.

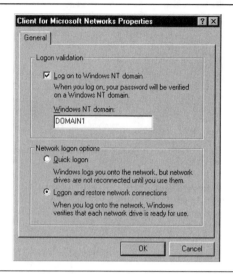

FIGURE 14.16: Setting the Microsoft network client properties

Creating and Managing NT File Shares

It's really easy to set up a file share for Microsoft clients with NT Server 4.0. There are two main ways to do it:

- From the computer's console, through NT's Explorer
- From a remote computer, using the Server Manager

An advantage to setting up the shares on the local machine using the Explorer is that you can simply point to the desired directory; when you use the Server Manager to set up the share remotely, you must specify the whole path.

Setting Up a File Share from the Local Machine

To create a file share while logged in at the console of the computer, follow these steps:

1. Select a folder in the Explorer. If necessary, create a folder (directory) in the desired location.

2. Right-click on the folder to bring up the pop-up menu and choose Properties.

3. Click on the Sharing tab of the directory's Properties sheet. Enable sharing on the directory by choosing the Shared As radio button and completing the share information in the text fields, as shown in Figure 14.17.

4. Click on the Permissions button and set the permissions on the new share.

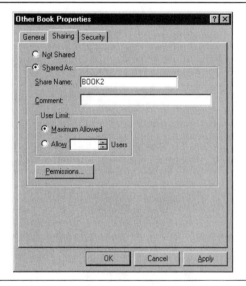

F I G U R E 1 4 . 1 7 : Setting up a share volume through a folder's Properties sheet

 NOTE   DOS-compatible share names are limited to eight characters. The Comment field is optional, but filling it in can be helpful if you are using eight-character DOS-compatible share names.

Setting Up a File Share from a Remote Computer

You use the Server Manager utility to create a share volume on a server from a remote location. Follow these steps:

1. Fire up the Server Manager (choose it from the Administrative Tools menu, under the Start menu's Program's menu).

2. Select the appropriate domain for the desired server.

3. Highlight the server and choose Shared Directories from the Computer menu.

4. A list of current shares appears, as shown in Figure 14.18. To create a new share, click on the New Share button.

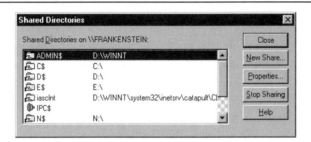

FIGURE 1 4 . 1 8 : Using the Server Manager to create a new share

5. The New Share dialog box appears, as shown in Figure 14.19. Enter a name for the new share. Note that you need to specify the full path on the server to the share.

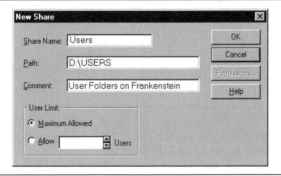

FIGURE 1 4 . 1 9 : Specifying new share information remotely

6. Click on the Permissions button and set the permissions for the share.

Remember that the full path name of an NT file or folder is limited to 260 characters. Keep your directory names short, and don't nest directories too deeply! You might be able to create a folder, but then your users will not be able to nest

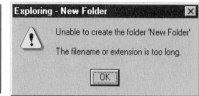

files very far inside the shared folder, and they won't know why. They may see cryptic error messages, similar to the ones shown in Figure 14.20.

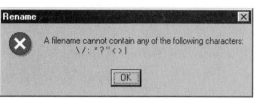

FIGURE 14.20: Creating nested folders with a total path that exceeds 260 characters can lead to strange error messages.

Viewing File Shares in the Server Control Panel

You can use the Server Control Panel to examine the usage of the shares on your server. Figure 14.21 shows this Control Panel.

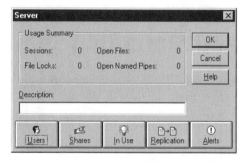

FIGURE 14.21: The Server Control Panel lets you monitor network client connections by share volume, user, and open files.

With the Server Control Panel, you can do the following:

- **To see a list of connected users:** Click on the Users button in the Server Control Panel. You'll see a list of connected users, the files that they have open, and the elapsed time for which they've held the file open.

- **To disconnect a particular user:** Click on the Users button, select the user from the Connected Users list, and click on the Disconnect button.

- **To send a message to a user:** Click on the Users button, select the user from the Connected Users list, and click on the Send Message button. Type a short message, and then send it to the selected user or to all connected users.

- **To see the connections by share:** Click on the Shares button. You'll see a list of the defined shares, and the list of users connected to each one.

- **To disconnect all users connected to a particular volume:** Click on the Shares button, select the network share from the list of the defined shares, and click on the Disconnect All button.

- **To disconnect all users connected to a particular file:** Click on the In Use button, select the file from the list of the open files, and click on the Close Resource button.

- **To change the description for your server that appears in network browsers:** Type a new description in the Description text box.

NOTE   You don't remove file shares through the Shares dialog box. To remove a file share, go to the Volumes list, and click on the Remove button.

Creating and Managing Shared Printers

NT Server provides Microsoft networking clients with powerful printer-sharing capabilities. Printers are easy to set up with the Add Printer Wizard. Clients are easy to administer, because NT Server will download the appropriate driver if necessary.

Adding and Sharing a Network Printer

To add a new network printer, follow these steps:

1. Choose the Printers option from the Settings menu of the NT server to open the Printers folder.

2. Open the New Printer template. This starts the Add Printer Wizard. You'll see the opening screen shown in Figure 14.22.

3. Select My Computer to specify that this server will act as the print spooler. The "My Computer" terminology is a hold-over from the NT Workstation and Windows 95 clients; My Computer refers to this file server.

4. In the next screen, shown in Figure 14.23, choose which port(s) you want to use for this logical print spool. Note that you can create a printer spool that works for multiple physical printers. The spool will print to the next available physical printer.

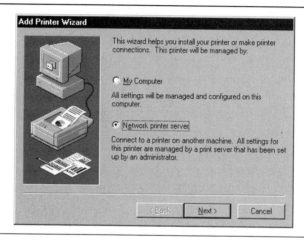

FIGURE 14.22: The Add Printer Wizard guides you through shared printer setup.

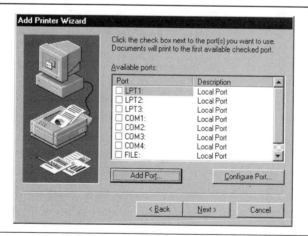

FIGURE 14.23: Choosing the port for the logical print spool

5. If the physical printer is not directly connected to the NT server (via a serial or parallel port), you need to define a logical port for that printer that points

to the printer's network location. Click on the Add Port button to see the dialog box shown in Figure 14.24.

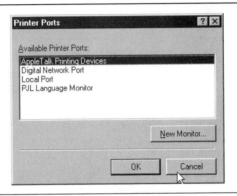

FIGURE 14.24: Defining a logical port

6. Choose your printer from the next Add Printer Wizard screen, shown in Figure 14.25. If your printer is not listed, and you have a driver disk from the manufacturer, click on the Have Disk button and specify the path to your printer's drivers.

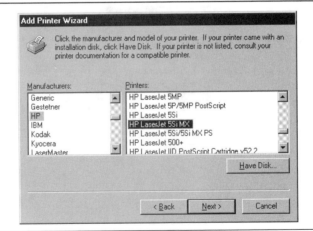

FIGURE 14.25: Choosing your printer

7. Next, the wizard asks for a name for your printer, as shown in Figure 14.26. Specify the name of the printer in the Printer Name text box. Also, choose

whether or not to make this the default printer (most likely, you won't want to set this as the NT server's default printer).

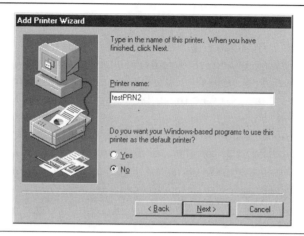

FIGURE 14.26: Naming your printer

8. In the next screen, select the Shared radio button, as shown in Figure 14.27. Select each of the Microsoft operating systems that will be using this printer from the list. This tells the Add Printer Wizard to install these printer drivers, which can be downloaded to the clients if they do not already have the appropriate driver.

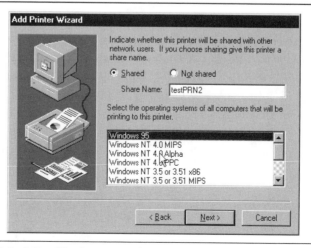

FIGURE 14.27: Sharing your printer

9. The Add Printer Wizard will copy the required files to your hard disk. You might need to be insistent on the location of the NT distribution files; regardless of how many times you tell the system where the NT distribution is located, it may always present you with the same (and often incorrect) suggestion at this point.

10. By default, the wizard will print a test page. This is always a good idea, if you have access to the printer, or can call someone who does. Once you know that the test page has printed correctly, you can let NT know, so it can proceed with the installation and setup of the printer.

In order for network users to be able to access the printer, the appropriate services must be installed for that type of printer. Refer to Table 14.1 for the required network services that must be installed to access various types of network printers.

T A B L E   1 4 . 1 : Required NT Network Services for Network Printers

Printer Type	NT Service Required
Unix LPD	Microsoft TCP/IP Printing
AppleTalk PAP	Services for Macintosh
HP network printer	DLC Protocol
NetWare printer	Gateway Services for NetWare

Setting Printer Properties

You can edit a printer's properties at any time by right-clicking on the printer in the Explorer and choosing Properties to display the printer's Properties sheet. This sheet is also presented to you at the final stages of a new printer setup, so that you can fine-tune the behavior of the printer spool.

The two tabs of interest in this Properties sheet are the General tab and the Scheduling tab.

The General tab is shown in Figure 14.28. Here you can enter a comment for this printer, which will show up in the Printer dialog box of the client computers. Add some descriptive comments on the intended use of this printer. Also specify the location of the printer, so that people will be sure to choose the most convenient printer. You can set up the print job separator page and the print processor in this tab, as well. Don't change these settings unless you need to; and if you do, refer to the online help.

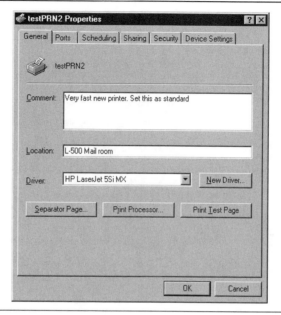

FIGURE 14.28: The General tab of a printer's Properties sheet

The Scheduling tab is shown in Figure 14.29. You can specify the priority of the print spool in this tab. It's possible, and perhaps even desirable, to set up multiple spools on the same physical printer, and give one spool a higher priority. This is an easy way to make sure that important jobs (or important, impatient people) get through quickly. You may also set availability times for this printer spool. For more information about the other options, see the online help.

Managing Printer Shares

Each of the printers defined on a server is shown in the server's Printers folder, which appears when you choose Printers from the NT server's Settings menu. Figure 14.30 shows an example of a Printers folder.

To manage a printer share from the server, double-click on the spool you wish to manage. You'll see a list of spooled jobs, with their print status and size, as shown in Figure 14.31. You may reschedule a print job, stop or restart the print spool, or delete a job from the spool.

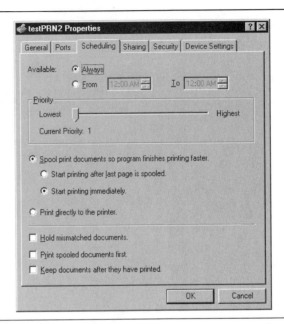

FIGURE 14.29: The Scheduling tab of a printer's Properties sheet

FIGURE 14.30: The Printers folder of the NT server shows all the printer spools currently defined.

To manage a printer queue from a remote client, establish the network connection, just as you do to use the printer from that workstation. In the Printers folder, double-click on the desired printer to bring up the queue. You'll be able to manage the queue, just as if you were at the server (as long as the account you used to connect to the network has the appropriate permissions).

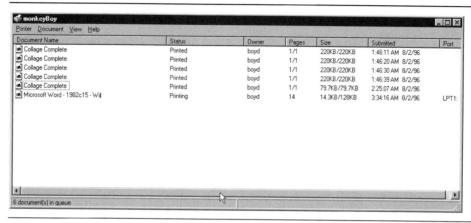

FIGURE 14.31: Double-clicking a print spool in the Printers folder opens it, so that you can manipulate the print jobs in the spool.

Are You Experienced?

Now you can...

☑ for DOS and Windows 3.1 clients, use the Network Client Administrator to make a network installation startup disk or an installation disk set

☑ set up your Windows 95 and Windows for Workgroups clients through their client software for NT

☑ create NT file shares from the computer's console by using NT's Explorer, or from a remote computer by using Server Manager

☑ use the Server Control Panel to monitor network client connections by share volume, user, and open files

☑ set up shared printers by using the Add Printer Wizard, and set printer properties through the printer's Properties sheet

☑ manage a shared printer from the server or a remote client by double-clicking on its print spool in the Printers folder

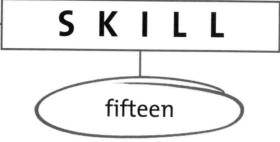

S K I L L

fifteen

15

Setting Up Macintosh Clients for NT Server

- ❏ NT Services for Macintosh Installation
- ❏ Macintosh client software Installation
- ❏ NT Services for Macintosh management
- ❏ Macintosh File Server and Print Server setup

Macintosh computers have been working in corporate LANs for more than ten years now, but sometimes that's hard to believe. If you're expected to integrate Macintosh and PC clients on your corporate network, then NT Server is good news. You get Macintosh connectivity with every NT Server package, right out of the box—there are no extra pieces to buy. And these services are fast; a properly configured NT server can really fly when serving up files to Mac folks, while keeping those PCs happy as well.

Here, we'll take a look at the NT Services for Macintosh, which let you use an NT server to support Macintosh file and print services on your network.

Macintosh Networking Basics

Macintosh computers can run a number of different network protocols. The primary protocol for Macintosh computers is AppleTalk, used to implement file sharing, printing, and many other networking operations.

LocalTalk versus EtherTalk

All Macs can utilize LocalTalk—a cheap, serial-port connection—to give them a workable network. This serial port is capable of more than 100 Kbps on healthy, real-life networks, so that's about as fast as an ISDN connection. In most places, LocalTalk is implemented over the same type of cable as ISDN: a single twisted pair of wires. With PhoneNet connectors like the ones that Farallon sells, Local-Talk mixes right in with normal phone cabling, so it used to be really popular.

 NOTE   Rule 1: AppleTalk is a network protocol. LocalTalk is a type of cabling.

These days, network speed is everything, and most places have spent the extra money to run some kind of Ethernet cabling all over the place. Depending on the network and the application, performance increase can range from 50 to 1000 percent with the upgrade from AppleTalk over phone wires (LocalTalk) to AppleTalk over Ethernet (EtherTalk).

Most everyone who has implemented Ethernet recently has done so with unshielded twisted-pair cabling (UTP). UTP is just like phone cable, but there are two pairs (four wires). This cabling scheme is called 10BaseT, and the phone-like wide modular connector on the end of 10BaseT cable is called an RJ-45 connector, as opposed to the standard phone connector which is an RJ-11. Now that all Macs come with an RJ-45 connection on the back of the unit (finally!), making twisted-pair Ethernet connections for Macs is easy.

Macintosh Network Addressing

On an AppleTalk network, every device on the net—computer, printer, network modem, and so on—has a network address that uniquely identifies it. AppleTalk network addresses are numbers that are three bytes long, split up into the network number and the node number. The network number is always the top two octets (bytes), so we get network numbers ranging from 0 to 65535. The extreme top few network numbers are reserved by AppleTalk; I always make sure my network numbers are below 16383, just to be sure. The bottom octet is the node number, from 0 to 255, so each AppleTalk network can have about 250 nodes on it. (This is a little bit like simplified TCP/IP addresses.)

You tell your AppleTalk routers what the network numbers are going to be. Since it's easy to get more than 250 or so nodes on a network, you're able to assign a *range* of networks to a cable segment. The range must be contiguous. Just estimate how many node numbers you'll need on a network cable segment and divide by 250—that will let you know how many networks you're going to need in your range.

 NOTE   **Rule 2: All AppleTalk routers on a network segment must agree with one another.**

You don't ever assign node numbers, however. AppleTalk assigns node numbers automatically at boot time. Roughly, the way it works is that when the Mac boots up, it grabs a node at random in a network that's way up there in network number space, somewhere in the network number 65,000 range (remember the reserved network numbers?). Then it looks in its nonvolatile parameter RAM (P-RAM) to see what it used for a network and node number last time. If it has a valid number saved away, it then looks on the net to see if that address has been taken by something else while it was sleeping. Usually, that address has not been taken, and the Mac happily uses the same number it used last time. But sometimes, that address is taken, so it backs off with a number that's pretty much random, and then tries again.

Usually, the Mac can get a network address in about 750 milliseconds or less. On saturated networks, it will take longer—sometimes a lot longer.

NOTE   I've seen Macs that would freeze at boot time, and none of the techs could figure it out. I would walk over there, pull the network connection out of the wall, and boom! The Mac would boot right up. It had been trying to find a network number that wasn't taken, and it couldn't find one.

Be generous when assigning cable ranges to your network segments. Think of the networks as parking lots, each with 250 parking spaces (the node numbers). You don't want Macs driving around looking for a parking space at boot time. It's okay to have empty parking spaces, so overestimate the number of nodes you'll need to support on a cable segment.

AppleTalk Names—Discovering Devices on the Network

AppleTalk was meant to be easy to use, self-configuring, and to require little or no central administration. The Macs look everything up by *name*, not by *number*, so the network addresses of a node can change around as needed without any human intervention. A Mac can dynamically reassign its node number and things will still work.

Because AppleTalk devices can query the network to bind a network name to a net address, there is no central address table. When your Mac is looking for its printer for the first time, it will send out a broadcast message: "Hey, are there any printers out there named Larry?" And the printer will hear that and reply: "Yeah, I'm Larry. My network address is 300.28."

The network language—the *protocol*—used when querying the network to get a network address that corresponds to a name is called the Name Binding Protocol (NBP). This process is called an *NBP lookup*. When Macintosh users browse the network with the Chooser, they are using an NBP lookup tool to take a look at the state of the network in real time. They are not asking for a report from a centralized database of network information.

NOTE   This is an important point: AppleTalk discovers things by *name* rather than by network *number*. There is no centralized naming server, like DNS for TCP/IP or WINS for Microsoft networks.

AppleTalk Zones—Partitioning the Name Space

Now all this "Is anybody there?" "Yeah, I'm here" stuff can make for a lot of network traffic. But as it turns out, you don't always need to search the entire network for the thing that you are looking for. There's a way to define a subset of the network in such a way that this subset probably has what you need: an AppleTalk *zone*.

The designers of AppleTalk realized that people almost always print to the same printer or share information among the same computers. And these devices are probably all in the same department or team, grouped together in some way that makes sense to people, not just to computers. These AppleTalk architects wanted to be able to capture this idea of a logical grouping of devices in their protocol, to be able to work with this group as a real network thing.

You, the network administrator, can tell the routers which zone names correspond to which networks. Once you've set up the zones, these zones appear in the Chooser (the network browser) on the Macintoshes, and network devices appear to be contained in these zones. Instead of looking through all the printers in your network, for example, you could just look for printers in the Administration department. Figure 15.1 shows an example of how this appears in the Chooser.

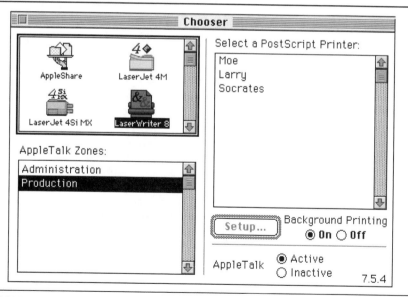

FIGURE 15.1: Macintosh users browse the AppleTalk network with the Chooser, which lists devices of a particular type in each AppleTalk zone.

Note that zones are *not* networks. That is to say, many different networks can be in a zone, and a network range might have many different zones. Take a look at Figure 15.2 and notice that the Production zone is on networks 100, 101, and 300-310; one zone spans many different networks. At my company, we have one network range on our backbone fiber, and a number of zones on that network (Fax Servers, Net Admins, and No Parking) that we use for various things.

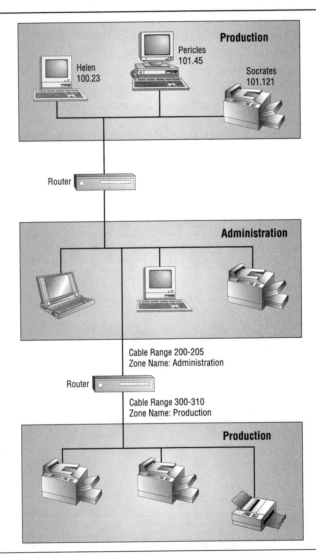

FIGURE 15.2: An AppleTalk network, with three networks, two zones, and nine nodes

Think of AppleTalk zones as a way to provide meaningful filters on your network. For example, you might filter on all the printers in the Administration department.

As the network administrator, you'll set up the list of zones on each network of your AppleTalk routers.

AppleTalk Router Configuration

Okay, so now you know that you need to configure a router on an AppleTalk network to know about the *network range* on the cable segments, and the *zones* which are on the cable segments. These items make up the *zone list*. Since all information from all routers on a cable range must agree, you're in trouble if you don't know what the information should be. How do you keep it straight?

NOTE

Rule 3: Ask your network administrator before adding an AppleTalk router to your network. If you are the network administrator, ask yourself for permission.

Fortunately, you don't have to keep track of all this information. AppleTalk routers can be configured to *discover* this network information from the other routers already on the network. Such a router is said to be a *non-seed* router, as opposed to a *seed* router, which is a router that "seeds" the network with the initial information. A seed router won't ask other routers on the net what the network numbers or zone lists should look like; it will simply start advertising its own information that is in its configuration. You told it to be a seed router, so you must know what you're talking about.

The first router that you set up on a network will almost certainly be a seed router. The second router that you set up on that segment will almost certainly be a non-seed router on that segment. Why would you want to repeat the configuration when the router will find out about it anyway?

Once a router has been configured, either by you or by the process of discovering the configuration from another router, the router becomes a seed router for that network. It doesn't care how it got its correct information, and now that it knows, it will be happy to tell any other router that wants to know.

NOTE

Rule 4: If you don't know, choose non-seed routing when adding a new router, to ensure that the new router agrees with the others on your network.

Skill 15

Once I had a rather, uh, *interesting* weekend, upgrading the network configuration on my network. I had taken all of the AppleTalk routers in my enterprise off-line for the duration, or so I thought. It turned out that our Banyan Vines servers were also AppleTalk routers, and were not remotely manageable (at that time, about three years ago). Even though I thought I knew what I was doing, I got to watch my network melt down, just like any newbie network administrator, because as I reconfigured the new routers, they would get into a fight with the routers that were already seeding the network!

To avoid these "router wars," a consortium of AppleTalk router vendors and system administrators, the AppleTalk Networking Forum, proposed a third mode of router configuration: *soft-seed*. Soft-seed is an intermediate state between seed and non-seed. A soft-seed router is manually configured, but it will verify that manual configuration with another seed router on its network when it first boots up. If the soft-seed router's configuration is different from the seed router's, it will defer to the seed router; the existing network configuration is the final word. So if I had soft-seed routers when I tried to reconfigure my network that weekend, the network would have stayed up. My network changes would have been blown away by the Banyan Vines servers (since they were seeding the old network configuration all the while), but my network wouldn't have melted down.

I'll say it again: Know your AppleTalk routers. AppleTalk routers need to agree on the basic state of the network, such as what the network numbers are. If they don't, they can be flaky. Some vendor's routers will quietly go off-line and not participate in the ensuing battle, leaving the remaining routers to duke it out about which of them has the "real" configuration.

The lesson is to keep a list of every—and I mean every—AppleTalk router on your network. In the list, include the name, type, physical location, and Apple-Talk network numbers for the router. See Table 15.1 for an example. Note that you might want to include additional information, such as physical location, router software revision number, and TCP/IP information.

TABLE 15.1: An Example of an AppleTalk Router List

Name	Type	Seed?	EtherTalk Network Range	LocalTalk Network Number	LocalTalk Zone
Shiva-03	Shiva FastPath 5	Seed	300-399	18	Building 12
Gator_1	Cayman GatorStar	Soft-seed	300-399	21	Administration
Frankenstein	NT Server	Non-seed			

Installing NT Services for Macintosh

Here, we'll go over the steps for installing NT Services for Macintosh, which comes with your NT Server 4.0 package.

Before You Begin

Before you start the actual installation, make sure you're prepared. Here are some tips:

- You'll need to reboot your server after you install the Services for Macintosh, so make sure to schedule a time when you can do this.

- You must have at least one NTFS partition on your server. The Macintosh file services require NTFS.

- Make sure that your NT Server CD is in the CD-ROM drive, or that you're connected to a network file server with the NT Server distribution files on it. In this installation example, we'll assume you're using the CD-ROM.

- Make sure at least one network interface card (NIC) is properly installed on your server.

- You can check the operation of your NICs in the Network Control Panel under the Adapters tab.

- Decide what the name of the AppleShare file server is going to be for your Macintosh users. By default, this name is exactly the same as the name of the NT server. As an option, your server can present a different name to the Macintosh AppleTalk network.

- Are you going to use your NT server as an AppleTalk router? Usually you won't want to use your server as a router. However, you might want to use your server as a router if:

  - You don't already have an AppleTalk router on this network segment, and you need one to provide zone and network number information.

  - You want to connect two different AppleTalk cable segments using your NT server. For example, you might have some printers on a ThinNet (coax cable) Ethernet, and the rest of your Macs on twisted-pair Ethernet. With two different Ethernet cards installed in your server, you could run AppleTalk on each of them, and route between them with AppleTalk routing.

If you're not going to use your server as an AppleTalk router, you can proceed to the installation instructions. If you will use your server as a router, read the following information before you begin installation.

Routing Information

Are you going to use seed routing on your NT server? You will want to use seed routing if there is no other AppleTalk router on your cable segment.

WARNING   **Don't use seed routing unless you know it's okay! Check with your network administrator first.**

If you're not going to use seed routing, you'll use non-seed routing. You can proceed to the installation instructions.

For seed routing, make sure to:

- Note the network number range you want on each of the cable segments that are attached to your server.

- Note the zone list for each of the cable segments that is attached to your server.

- If there is more than one zone on the network cable attached to your server, decide on the AppleTalk zone in which you want your server to appear.

- Complete the AppleTalk Routing worksheet (Worksheet 15.1).

Refer to the diagram shown in Figure 15.3 as you are completing the worksheet in Worksheet 15.1. Complete the worksheet for *each* of the network adapters installed on your server.

The Installation Procedure

Once you've collected all your materials and information, you're ready to install the Services for Macintosh. In this section, we'll walk through the installation procedure, step by step. Have your filled-out AppleTalk Routing worksheet at hand, so you can answer the configuration questions.

1. Open the Network Control Panel, go to the Services tab, and click on the Add button. Figure 15.4 shows this step.

WORKSHEET 15.1   AppleTalk Routing Worksheet

Line	Item	
1	Other AppleTalk router already on this network segment?	
2	If line 1 is Yes, skip to line 8; if no go to line 3	
3	Choose seed routing	
4	AppleTalk network range	From ____ to ____
5	AppleTalk zone list	
6	Default zone	
7	Seed routing setup done (lines 3–6)	
8	Choose non-seed routing	

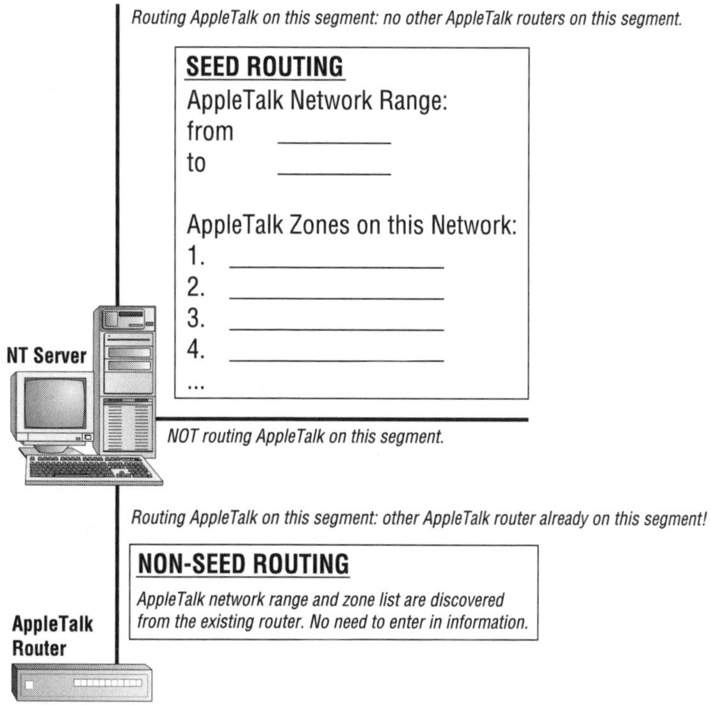

Routing AppleTalk on this segment: no other AppleTalk routers on this segment.

SEED ROUTING
AppleTalk Network Range:
from _____
to _____

AppleTalk Zones on this Network:
1. _____
2. _____
3. _____
4. _____
...

NT Server

NOT routing AppleTalk on this segment.

Routing AppleTalk on this segment: other AppleTalk router already on this segment!

NON-SEED ROUTING
AppleTalk network range and zone list are discovered from the existing router. No need to enter in information.

AppleTalk Router

FIGURE 15.3: AppleTalk routing with NT Server

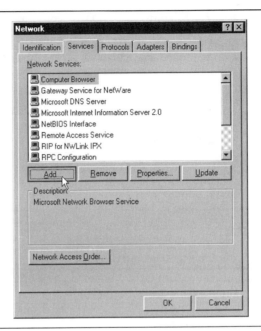

FIGURE 15.4: Choosing to add network services

2. NT will build a list of the services that you can install. Scroll down in this list and select Services for Macintosh, as shown in Figure 15.5. Then click on OK.

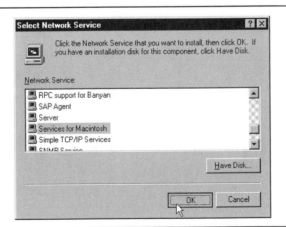

FIGURE 15.5: Selecting to install Services for Macintosh

3. The Setup program may get confused at this point. You need to tell it where the NT distribution files are. Since we're using the CD-ROM in this example, give it the path to your NT Server distribution files on the CD-ROM. In Figure 15.6, I've entered **G:\i386**, because my CD-ROM is on drive letter G and I'm using an Intel computer. Enter the correct path for your drive and server. For example, if your CD-ROM is on drive E, and you're using an Alpha server, enter **E:\alpha** here.

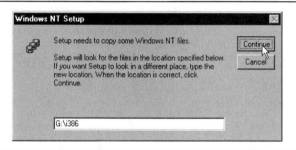

FIGURE 15.6: Telling the Setup program where to find the NT distribution files

4. The Setup program will copy the files to the appropriate places on your system. Once the files have been copied, click on the Close button at the bottom of the Network Control Panel.

5. NT will organize the newly installed network software, and then ask you for the AppleTalk network information, as shown in Figure 15.7. Choose the network adapter on which you're going to run AppleTalk services in the Default Adapter drop-down list box.

6. If this network has been seeded by another AppleTalk router, there will be a list of zones to choose from in the Default Zone drop-down list box. Select the zone in which you want your server to appear.

7. If you wish to use your NT server to route AppleTalk, click on the Routing tab of the dialog box and check the Enable Routing box.

8. If you chose Seed Routing in your AppleTalk Routing worksheet, check the Use This Router to Seed the Network box.

9. Enter the network range information in the Network Range text boxes.

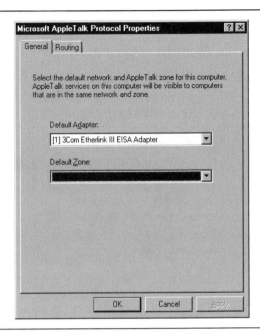

FIGURE 15.7: Configuring the Services for Macintosh

10. Add AppleTalk zones to your network by clicking on the Add button at the bottom of the dialog box.

11. Once you're finished adding zones, verify that the proper zone is listed as the default. If not, select the zone in the zone list box and click on the Make Default button.

12. Verify the information as it appears in the dialog box. Figure 15.8 shows an example of my AppleTalk Protocol Properties dialog box when I set it up for seed routing, and Figure 15.9 shows the dialog box when I set it up for non-seed routing.

13. The Network Control Panel will ask you to restart the server. If it's okay to do so, go ahead and reboot.

14. When the server comes back up, open the MacFile Control Panel and set the attributes for your file server (see the section "Managing Services for Macintosh" later in this skill).

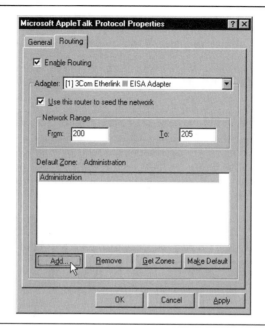

FIGURE 15.8: Setting up for seed routing

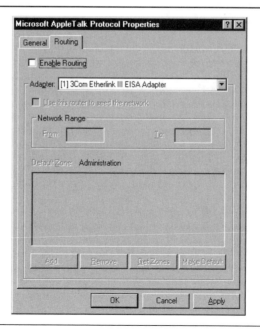

FIGURE 15.9: Setting up for non-seed routing

Installing Macintosh Client Software

There really is not much client software to install on the Macintosh workstations. In fact, there's absolutely none that's required, unless you want to take advantage of NT security and server-to-client notification.

Using the Microsoft User Access Module

The AppleShare specification states that server vendors can extend the normal login procedures with drop-in software modules called User Access Modules (UAMs). If you're already running a NetWare-based Macintosh network, you're probably familiar with the NetWare UAM.

Take a look at Table 15.2 to see the features that the Microsoft UAM provides.

T A B L E   1 5 . 2 : Feature Comparison of the Built-in Apple and Microsoft UAMs

Feature	Apple UAM	Microsoft UAM
Aliases	✔	
Login from programs	✔	
Encrypted password		✔
Password length	8	15
Domain qualification		✔
Notification		✔

It's important to note the trade-offs:

- The Microsoft UAM encrypts the passwords sent from a Macintosh workstation during a login session. The built-in procedures will send the NT user password as clear text, which is easily intercepted with network monitoring software. You might consider this a security hole, especially for Mac clients that are connecting to NT servers across a WAN connection.

- Macintosh file-system aliases (similar to shortcuts) will not resolve across a session initiated by a Microsoft UAM-mediated login. Translation: If a user connects to an NT server with the Microsoft UAM, creates an alias of a file on the server, and copies that alias to the local computer, the alias will not open the file unless the server volume is mounted. The normal behavior for aliases is that they retain network information, and will initiate the connection to the server if necessary. But Mac aliases don't know about NT authentication, so the user gets an error message saying that the file cannot be found on the network.

• Mac clients will not get notices from the system administrator unless they are connected to a server via the Microsoft UAM.

These trade-offs are significant. Although you can require Macintoshes to use the Microsoft UAM to connect to your server, realize the limitations of such a scheme.

Installing the Microsoft UAM

When you install Services for Macintosh, a Mac file share, called the Microsoft UAM volume, is created automatically. Anyone can connect to this file share.
Installing the Microsoft UAM on a client Mac workstation is a simple procedure:

1. Open the Chooser and find your NT server (select AppleShare, the appropriate AppleTalk zone, and double-click on your server's name).

2. Log in to the server as a Guest.

3. Mount the Microsoft UAM volume.

4. There is one item in the volume: an AppleShare folder. If you don't already have another UAM installed, simply drag the AppleShare folder to the Macintosh's System folder. If you have another UAM, like the Novell UAM, already installed, an AppleShare folder already exists in the System folder. Simply open the AppleShare folder on the NT Server volume and drag the Microsoft UAM file to the AppleShare folder inside the Mac's System folder. You only need that one file.

5. Once the copy is done, you can log out of the NT server by dragging its volume icon to the trash.

You don't need to restart the Mac. The new Microsoft UAM will be loaded dynamically the next time the Mac logs in to an NT server.

Managing Services for Macintosh

When you installed Services for Macintosh, a MacFile Control Panel was added to your server's Control Panels. This Control Panel is shown in Figure 15.10.

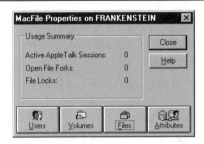

FIGURE 15.10: The MacFile Control Panel is your starting point for most Macintosh administrative tasks.

The MacFile Control Panel allows you to:

- View a list of connected Macintosh users.

- Disconnect selected users or all connected Macintosh users.

- Send messages to connected users.

- View the Macintosh connections by volume.

- Set Macintosh file server attributes.

Viewing and Disconnecting Individual Macintosh Users

Click on the Users button in the MacFile Control Panel. You'll see a list of connected users, the files that they have open, and the elapsed time for which they have held the file open.

To disconnect a particular Macintosh user, select the user from the Connected Users list, and click on the Disconnect button.

Sending a Message to a Macintosh User

In order for a Macintosh client to receive messages sent via Microsoft network messaging, the Macintosh user must be connected to the NT server via the Microsoft UAM, which we discussed in the previous section.

Click on the Users button in the MacFile Control Panel. Select the user from the Connected Users list, and click on the Send Message button. Type a short message, and then send it to the selected user or to all connected Macintosh users.

TIP   Sending messages to all connected users is good practice before shutting a server down. However, be aware that in practice, only those users connected via the Microsoft UAM will receive your warning. For this reason, it's also a good practice to schedule server downtime and give people plenty of advance notice.

Viewing and Disconnecting Macintosh Connections by Volume

An AppleShare volume is a server share (we'll see how to create those in a moment). Click on the Volumes button in the MacFile Control Panel to see a list of the defined shares and the users connected to each one.

To disconnect all users connected to a particular volume, select the volume from the list of the defined shares, and click on the Disconnect All button.

Viewing and Disconnecting Macintosh Connections by File

To see a list of open files, click on the Files button in the MacFile Control Panel. To disconnect users connected to a particular file, select the file from the list of the open files, and click on the Close Fork button.

NOTE   The Macintosh file system originally kept two actual files on the disk for each logical file in the file system: a *data fork*, which is the traditional file, and a *resource fork*, which held the file system information. With the advent of the PowerPC and the continuing need for portable, cross-platform file formats, many of the uses of resource forks are being phased out, but they will continue to hold the file system information for the foreseeable future. NT maintains the resource forks for Macintosh files in the NTFS at a low level. You don't need to worry about them, but the terminology slipped into the MacFile Control Panel.

Setting the Macintosh Server Attributes

Clicking on the Attributes button in the MacFile Control Panel brings up the MacFile Attributes dialog box, shown in Figure 15.11.

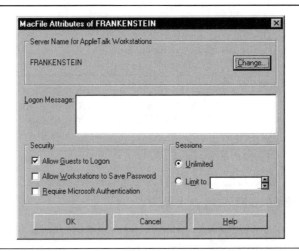

FIGURE 15.11: You can specify the settings for your Macintosh file server in the MacFile Attributes dialog box.

You can set the following attributes:

- **Server Name:** By default, the Macs will see your server as the server's NetBIOS name. If you want to specify a different name for some reason (maybe you want something more descriptive), you can set a separate AppleTalk name for the server by clicking on the Change button.

- **Logon Message:** You can set a message that will appear as a modal dialog box when the users mount volumes from the server. A great logon message is "Welcome to my server. Drag volumes to the trash when you're finished with them or I'll kick you off at midnight. Have a nice day." The logon message is optional.

- **Allow Guests to Logon:** By default, the Macs can connect to your server without a password by specifying Guest instead of a user name at login time. Whether they will be able to mount any volumes depends on the permissions you set on the volumes.

- **Allow Workstations to Save Password:** This is usually a very bad idea. Enabling this option caches the user's login information on the client Macintosh. Anyone who has access to that Mac would have access to all the user's files on your server. This option might be useful in low-security situations, where usage tracking doesn't matter.

- **Require Microsoft Authentication:** This will force the Mac to connect to the server via the Microsoft UAM. See the preceding section on Macintosh client installation for information about the UAM.

- **Sessions:** You can restrict the number of Macs that can hit your server at the same time. This number is a different limit from any licensing-based limits you've set on the server. If you keep the default, Unlimited, the only limitations on the number of simultaneous Macs will be the NT server limits on the number of simultaneous users.

 **WARNING**   I've run into situations where the MacFile Sessions limit becomes set to some low number, such as 1, for reasons we have not been able to explain. If your users get error messages relating to the number of available server sessions, double-check this attribute.

Restarting the Services for Macintosh

We discussed the setup of the AppleTalk routing in the previous sections, so there's not a whole lot to add to the discussion. However, if you ever need to modify the routing configuration, or if you need to kick the print server for Macintosh, you'll need to know how to restart the Macintosh Services on your server.

 WARNING   The AppleTalk protocol does not show up under the Protocols tab of the Network Control Panel, even though every other transport protocol does. As a work-around, you can find every installed protocol, including AppleTalk, in the Devices Control Panel (because protocols are implemented as device drivers). I consider this a bug, but it has been this way since the first release of Windows NT 3.51 and stayed this way through 4.0. I guess we'll learn to live with it.

If you make a change to the Services for Macintosh configuration in the Network Control Panel that requires a restart of the services, the Network Control Panel will let you know with an alert that says something like, "Changes will take place the next time you restart AppleTalk." But there's no mention of how to do that. Here's how (allow 15 minutes for this procedure):

1.   Make sure that there are no Mac users connected to your NT server, using the MacFile Control Panel. As a worst case, you can just go ahead with this procedure without checking for Mac user active connections, and the procedure will still work, but some users will get their network connections yanked. It's always best to warn them first.

2.   Open the Devices Control Panel.

3.   Highlight the AppleTalk Protocol in the Device list, and click on the Stop button, as shown in Figure 15.12.

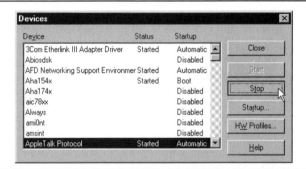

FIGURE 15.12: To start or stop the AppleTalk protocol, use the Devices Control Panel.

4.   The system will warn you that you're about to jerk the rug out from under the file and print services for Macintosh. You'll see the Stopping dialog box shown in Figure 15.13. If you want to do this, click on OK. The system will stop the print service, and then the file service, and then the AppleTalk protocol. This may take a few minutes.

5.   To start the services back up again, open the Services Control Panel, highlight the File Server for Macintosh service, and click on the Start button, as shown in Figure 15.14. The system will first start the AppleTalk protocol

(without giving you any indication that it's doing so), and then start the File Server for Macintosh. This may take a couple of minutes.

6. After the File Server is started, you can scroll down to the Print Server for Macintosh and start that up, too.

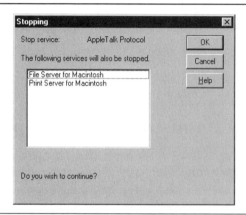

FIGURE 15.13: When you stop the AppleTalk protocol, you'll also stop the File Server and Print Server for Macintosh.

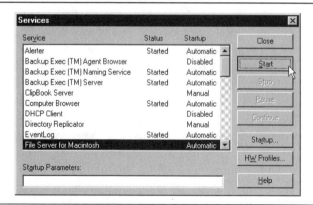

FIGURE 15.14: Manually starting the File Server for Macintosh from the Services Control Panel. This will automatically start the AppleTalk protocol if it has been stopped.

NOTE   You don't need to run the File Server and Print Server for Macintosh together. You can run either of them without the other. But you can't run either of these services for Macintosh without the AppleTalk protocol.

To wrap up, the order of operations is as follows:

- Stop AppleTalk, which will bring down the File Server and Print Server.

- Start the File Server or the Print Server for Macintosh, which will automatically restart the AppleTalk protocol.

Remote Administration of Macintosh Services

You can administer the Services for Macintosh on every NT server in your enterprise (assuming you have administrative privileges everywhere) from an NT server on your desk using the Server Manager. In order to administer Services for Macintosh remotely, you'll need a server with Services for Macintosh installed.

 Once you've installed the Services for Macintosh, Server Manager has a new menu in the menu bar, named MacFile. The Properties menu item on the MacFile menu brings up the MacFile Control Panel of the selected computer. See the previous section for tips on using the MacFile Control Panel.

 You can bring up the Services Control Panel of the selected computer by choosing the Services option from the Computer menu. From the Services Control Panel, you can start and stop the File Server or Print Server for Macintosh.

Managing the AppleTalk Protocol Remotely

There's no "official" way to bring up the Devices Control Panel of a remote server, so you won't be able to stop and restart AppleTalk, as discussed in the previous section, without being at the server's console. However, there is a possible work-around.

The Windows NT Resource Kit for Windows NT Server 3.51 includes a service and a command-line utility for getting a remote command shell connection to a remote NT server. With this setup, you simply type REMOTE and the name of the server, and you'll get the C: prompt at that server. From there, you can issue NET commands. In this case, you would type NET STOP APPLETALK.

For more information about the Windows NT Resource Kit, buy it, or point to ftp://ftp.microsoft.com/bussys/winnt/winnt-public/reskit/nt351/. For more information about the command-line NET commands, type NET /? at any command prompt.

WARNING   The Windows NT 3.51 Resource Kit is not (officially) supported under Windows NT 4.0, but many of the tools work for me. Use it at your own risk.

NT Server and AppleTalk Networks

NT Server can do three things for your Macintosh AppleTalk network:

- **AppleTalk router:** NT Server can act as an AppleTalk router, providing both AppleTalk zone and network number information to your net. As a router, NT Server can also connect two different AppleTalk networks together. We discussed setting up an AppleTalk router earlier in this skill.

- **AppleTalk file server:** NT Server can act as an AppleTalk file server, appearing to the Macintosh clients just like any other AppleShare server.

- **AppleTalk print server:** NT Server can act as an AppleTalk print server, taking in print jobs and spooling them to the appropriate printer. NT can also understand the PostScript page-description language, and output Macintosh print jobs to printers that normally would not be able to talk to the Mac.

File Server for Macintosh

NT Server provides the following features to deliver a solid Macintosh file server:

- **AppleTalk protocol support:** Macs need to speak to file servers and printers via the AppleTalk network protocol. NT's AppleTalk implementation is really solid and fast.

- **Long filenames:** Mac filenames can be up to 32 characters long. NT's filenames can be up to 255 characters long, so NT has the Macintosh long filenames covered. Barring the various illegal characters, the filenames on the Mac are exactly the same when stored on an NT server. There is no radical translation of filenames.

- **Transparent support of Macintosh resource forks:** The Macintosh file system maintains a separate file "fork" to store the file's resources, such as file system attribute information and program code. When writing to an NT server, the server stores these files as one file on the server, and it's all transparent.

- **Integrated file system security:** You can create and modify AppleShare shares from the NT File Manager or from the MacFile Control Panel. AppleShare permissions on a file share are determined by the share's NT Access Control List, just as if it were an NT Server share. We'll see how the Macintosh and NT permissions compare in the next section.

Setting Up Macintosh File Shares

Creating a network share for Macintoshes is easy. In fact, since you've installed Services for Macintosh, you've already created one: the Microsoft UAM volume. But the default volume is read-only, so it isn't very interesting. Here's the best way to create the first Macintosh volume of your own:

1. From the NT Start menu, select the Run command. In the Run dialog box, type **winfile**, and then click on the OK button.

 NOTE   **Winfile is the name of the old, Windows 3.1–style File Manager for Windows. The File Manager has some shared-drive management tricks up its sleeve that the current Windows Explorer lacks.**

2. In the File Manager, select the disk that you want to use for your Macintosh share. You can select the active disk in the File Manager by pressing Ctrl+<*drive letter*>. For example if you want to make drive D your active drive, press Ctrl+D.

3. Usually, you'll want to create a subdirectory dedicated to your Macintosh share. You can create directories in the File Manager by choosing the Create Directory command from the File menu. The directory will be created in the

active directory, which is the one whose contents are shown in the right pane of the File Manager window.

4. With the appropriate directory selected, choose the Create Volume command from the MacFile menu, as shown in Figure 15.15. This will bring up a dialog box where you can specify the AppleTalk name for the volume, set a volume-level password (not commonly done for Mac volumes), limit the number of users, and set share permissions (discussed in the next section).

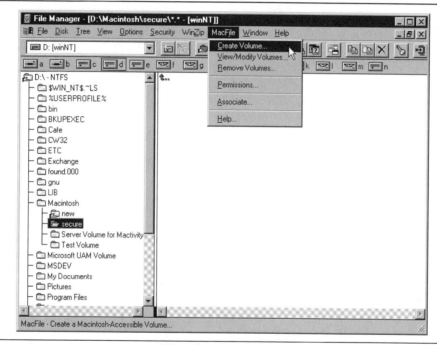

FIGURE 15.15: Creating a Macintosh volume

 WARNING   You can't create "nested" Macintosh shares. For example, if you have a shared folder called Projects, it can't contain a shared Macintosh folder called Important Project Number 2. A Mac server volume cannot contain other Mac server volumes.

Macintosh versus NT Permissions

See Table 15.3 for a sample of the way that the Macintosh file permissions map to
NT permissions.

T A B L E   1 5 . 3 : Comparison of Macintosh and NT Permissions

See Files	See Folders	Make Changes	NT Permissions
X			Read (RX)
	X		Read (RX)
		X	Special (WD)
X		X	Change (RWXD)
	X	X	Change (RWXD)
X	X	X	Special (RWXD)
X	X	X	Full Access (Administrators)
			Read-Only (No Execute)

Note that NT makes no distinction between security on files and security on
folders. In fact, you can't set Macintosh permissions on individual files; permissions can be set only on the folders that contain them. This is an AppleShare
specification.

 TIP   Play around with some dummy files and folders in the File Manager (Winfile),
changing the Macintosh and NT security permissions. You'll get a feel for how
the two systems interact.

File Type Associations

A big part of any cross-platform file sharing scheme is the issue of filenames and
file format types. Since NTFS supports long filenames, filename limitations are
less of a problem. The real problem lies in indicating the proper file format for
documents. Users need to be trained to use the appropriate three-letter extensions.

Every Macintosh file has a file type and file creator associated with it. These
associations are invisibly maintained by the Macintosh file system (if only
Microsoft operating systems would do this!).

The File Server for Macintosh maintains a translation map of three-letter DOS extensions to Macintosh file type and creator. You can edit this list of translations by choosing Associate from the MacFile menu in the File Manager (Winfile). This command brings up a dialog box in which you can view and edit the three-letter extension translations, as shown in Figure 15.16.

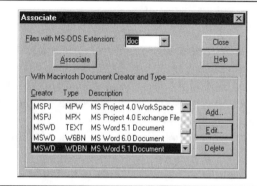

FIGURE 15.16: Three-letter DOS extensions are mapped to Macintosh file type and creator information. Access this translation list by choosing Associate from the MacFile menu in the File Manager.

Although NT and Windows 95 support long filenames, including long extensions, the MacFile association map still insists on three-letter extensions only. For example, although NT registers the type for files with an html extension, your Mac users won't be able to double-click on them and have them open properly, unless the files were created on a Mac.

WARNING The mapping of file type information is only one-way: from three-letter extensions to file type and creator. A Macintosh file written to an NT share will not have its file type and creator parsed out, and an appropriate three-letter extension attached. This kind of automatic renaming of files would cause lots of problems.

Print Server for Macintosh

NT Server can act as a print spooler for Macintosh printers. An NT server can "capture" an existing AppleTalk printer, hiding it from the network, forcing the Macs to spool through the NT server. Or the NT server can simply add another way to print to the printer, coexisting with the printer itself on the AppleTalk network. Interestingly, NT can print Macintosh files to any printer it can see, including non-Mac, non-PostScript printers.

WARNING   Despite the promise of this powerful feature set, the Print Server for Macintosh has problems. We'll talk about those problems at the end of this section. Most administrators have tried to use it, and have stopped doing so. We'll wait until they get the bugs out.

In its basic operation, the Print Server for Macintosh is deceptively easy to use. After the Print Server for Macintosh is installed, when you set up a shared printer, the NT server will share that printer on the Macintosh network as well. You set up printer sharing by choosing the Shared option in the Sharing tab of the Printer Properties sheet.

NT will accept jobs from Macintoshes for this printer, and it will convert the PostScript to an NT print job appropriate for the printer if necessary. For example, I have an HP LaserJet 5L printer—a PCL-only printer—hooked up to my desktop NT server. My Macintosh prints to the printer share, and the NT server renders the PostScript into PCL for the printer.

TIP   It's computationally expensive to use the NT server as a PostScript RIP (Routing Information Protocol). And the image quality of graphics that undergo this type of translation can be poor. However, for straight-text documents, even with some fancy formatting, it works surprisingly well. This might give you an option you didn't think you had.

Setting Up the Mac Client to Print to an NT Spool

Macintosh printer drivers get confused when connecting to NT spools. They attempt to query the printer for the printer type, and NT does not respond. However, there is a work-around: When you are selecting the printer from the Macintosh, hold down the Option key while clicking on the Setup button in the Chooser. This will bring up a manual printer configuration dialog box. Choose any of the PPDs (printer description files) installed on the Mac. If you can't find a printer description that matches the printer that's hooked up to the spool, use the generic LaserWriter PPD.

Creating a Spool for a Mac Printer

With Services for Macintosh installed, NT can print to any Macintosh printer. To create a spool for a Mac printer, follow these steps:

1. In the Printer Properties sheet, click on the Ports tab, and then click on the Add Port button.

2. This brings up the Printer Ports dialog box. Choose AppleTalk Printing Devices, as shown in Figure 15.17.

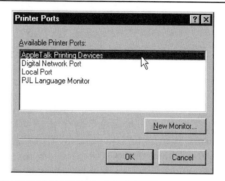

FIGURE 15.17: Creating a port on an AppleTalk printer

3. A Network Browser dialog box appears; you're browsing the AppleTalk network. (Hey, this is cool—a Chooser for NT!) Select the desired AppleTalk printer and click on OK. A port, named after the printer, will be created.

Once you've created a port on an AppleTalk printer, any print spool can print to it.

Capturing an AppleTalk Printer

Capturing an AppleTalk printer will disable the printer's advertisement on the Macintosh network—it will disappear as far as the Macs are concerned! Do this *only* if you have print devices that absolutely must go through a print spooler for auditing or security reasons (like an expensive color printer). You will break the existing connections that Mac clients have to the AppleTalk printer when you capture it!

If you must capture an AppleTalk printer, after a port has been created on an AppleTalk printer, you can select it in the list of ports in the Ports tab of the Printer Properties sheet. Click on Configure Port to bring up a dialog box that gives you the option of capturing the printer, as shown in Figure 15.18.

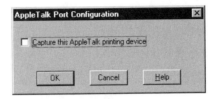

FIGURE 15.18: The AppleTalk Port Configuration dialog box (Danger! Danger!)

 **WARNING**   Remember, if you capture an AppleTalk printer, you will break the existing connections that Mac clients have to that printer! In previous versions of NT, printer capture was enabled by default. This did not make NT popular with AppleTalk network administrators.

Problems with the Print Server for Macintosh

In addition to the problems alluded to so far, many Mac administrators are having trouble with two-way communication between the printer and the Mac client. The NT server does not handle errors from the printer in the same way as a Mac client would, often with disappointing results.

In normal operation, AppleTalk printers can send sophisticated error messages back to the Macintosh client. In some PostScript operating environments, these error messages are commonly encountered when the printer can't understand some PostScript code. Apparently, the NT implementation of PostScript causes such problems often. When the printer signals a PostScript error back to the NT server, the server says, "Oh, this job failed. I'll try to print it again."

The upshot of all this is that the printer keeps printing the job, up until the error occurs, again and again and again—usually until the printer is out of paper. The Mac client never gets any notification that there's a problem.

Also, as I mentioned previously, the NT server does not properly respond to printer type queries from the Macintosh, resulting in configuration errors on the

Mac client. You must use the Option key and Setup button combination to force a manual configuration of the printer type on the Mac client.

The bottom line is that the AppleTalk print server needs work. I wish we could say otherwise, but NT's Print Server for Macintosh, while feature-rich, needs some refinement before it can be used in a production environment. Your mileage may vary, and by the time you read this, Microsoft may have a few refinements in place. That would be a good thing, because flexible printer management is something typically lacking in Macintosh networks.

Are You Experienced?

Now you can...

- ☑ install NT Services for Macintosh, which comes with NT Server
- ☑ install the Microsoft client software on the Macintosh computers in your network
- ☑ perform management tasks from the MacFile Control Panel
- ☑ manage the Macintosh services on remote NT servers
- ☑ start or stop the AppleTalk protocol from the Devices Control Panel
- ☑ set up Macintosh file shares and printer shares

S K I L L

sixteen

Integrating NT and NetWare in Your Network

- ❑ IPX/SPX protocol installation

- ❑ NT's Migration Tool for NetWare

- ❑ NT's Gateway Service for NetWare

- ❑ Directory Service Manager for NetWare

- ❑ File and Print Services for NetWare

No matter how much NT is taking the corporate LAN by storm, the reality is that Novell owns the market. Every LAN has at least one NetWare server somewhere, and most LANs are predominantly NetWare.

So NetWare is the reality. Given this reality, how can NT fit in and stand out? Microsoft has attempted to make it easy to get NetWare and NT environments working together, but they are both complex systems, with different security models and network design issues.

We can't present a comprehensive rundown on all things Novell here—it is too large a topic. But we'll point you in the right direction. Fortunately, the tools are indeed fairly easy to use. The hard part will be developing your interoperability plan. Here, we'll talk about the "nuts and bolts" of Microsoft's family of NetWare interoperability tools, and we'll take the time to present scenarios that emphasize where each tool might be appropriate. After you've completed this Skill, you should know which tools will work for your NT/NetWare integration task and be ready to design a migration plan.

Introducing the NT/NetWare Services

The tools that you can use for a network that integrates NT and NetWare include some that came with NT and others that you can get from Microsoft:

- **Migration Tool for NetWare:** This tool is installed with every copy of NT Server. Microsoft would certainly love for you to migrate from NetWare to an NT LAN, but the Migration Tool only partially achieves this. It lets you accomplish two major tasks in moving servers from NetWare to NT: migrate user accounts and migrate data shares.

- **Directory Service Manager for NetWare:** A step up from the Migration Tool for NetWare, this product is available from Microsoft at additional cost. The Migration Tool for NetWare lets you perform a "one-shot" transfer of NetWare account information to NT; the Directory Service Manager actually tracks account changes between the NetWare and NT systems, keeping those systems in sync.

- **Gateway Service for NetWare:** This service comes with NT Server, and it can be installed as an option. The Gateway Service for NetWare builds a bridge between Microsoft SMB (Server Message Block) networks (Windows for Workgroups, LAN Manager, and NT) and NetWare networks. With the Gateway Service for NetWare, clients of Microsoft networks don't need any Novell client software to access NetWare file services. In effect, the network looks like one monolithic NT network.

- **NetWare File and Print Services:** The flip side of making NetWare networks look like NT networks to Microsoft clients is making NT networks look like NetWare networks to NetWare clients. This is the mission of the NetWare File and Print Services for NT. Available as a separate product, the NetWare File and Print Services product completely wraps up the NT file and print services as their NetWare counterparts. No NT client software is needed to access the server.

Each of the tools depends on Microsoft's implementation of the IPX/SPX (Internetwork Packet Exchange/Sequenced Packet Exchange) protocol used by Novell NetWare networks. You may install the NWLink transport and use it as a native NT transport, independently of the NetWare services. If you are going to use the Novell NetWare services, you'll need to install the NWLink IPX/SPX transport first.

When to Use the NetWare Tools: A Few Scenarios

Now that you've been introduced to them, let's see how these tools might be put to use. In this section, we'll illustrate the use of the various NetWare integration tools by presenting typical NetWare/NT integration scenarios. We'll get to the details of installing and using the integration tools later.

Outgrowing NetWare 3.x Networks

Many sites have outgrown their NetWare 3.x or 2.x servers, which are limited to a maximum of 250 users. Instead of moving up to a new version of NetWare, which could involve significant migration costs for all the clients and servers, these companies are opting to go with NT servers.

As we saw in Skill 7, NT servers can be scaled up to clusters of RISC mini-computers, if necessary, while NetWare is still wedded to the Intel architecture. And as new applications technologies emerge, some companies may move their clients over to Microsoft NT SMB-based services.

Gateway Service for NetWare —An Easy Way Out

Using the Gateway Service for NetWare, you can do an end-run around the technical limitations of NetWare 2.x and 3.x—the 250 users per server limitation. (Of course, you must still remain in compliance with your NetWare license agreement.) Here are the steps:

1. Deploy an NT server running Gateway Services for NetWare.

2. As new workstations come onto the network, set them up as Windows networking (SMB) clients of the NT server.

3. Attach to the NetWare server from the NT server.

4. Use the Gateway Services for NetWare to publish this attached NetWare volume to the SMB networking clients.

Figure 16.1 illustrates the NetWare, NT, and SMB network configuration.

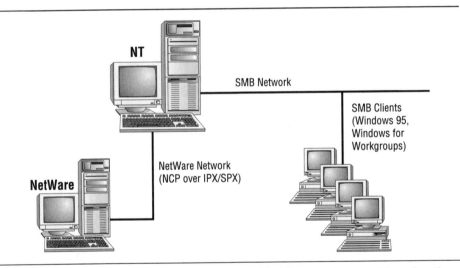

FIGURE 16.1: You can add users to your NetWare environment by using the Gateway Service for NetWare. One user connection is used to attach the NetWare volume, which is then published to the SMB networking clients.

Using the Gateway Service for NetWare might be less than entirely satisfactory. The SMB client computers will probably run into trouble trying to run client applications that require Novell APIs. There is no NetWare software loaded on the client computers, so these types of applications will not work. And from an administrative standpoint, you're now faced with supporting at least two client configurations: NetWare clients and SMB clients. For these reasons, the Gateway Service for NetWare is probably a simple, interim solution.

NetWare File and Print Services—A Drop-In Replacement

A step up in integration and functionality is to deploy an NT server running the File and Print Services for NetWare, which you'll buy as an add-on to the normal NT Server software distribution.

NT servers configured with NetWare File and Print Services will appear to be NetWare 3.1 servers to the NetWare clients, but are not inherently limited to any particular number of client connections.

NT servers configured with the NetWare File and Print Services can act as a "drop-in" replacement for a NetWare server in some cases. For the client computers, there is no software to install. For the system administrator, once the server has been set up, SYSCON can be used to administer user accounts on the NT server.

For simple file and print services, this is a great solution. The server can support some programs that require NetWare, as well as many of the common DOS-based command-line Novell commands; however, you won't be able to run NetWare Loadable Modules (NLMs) on the NT server. As we discussed in Skills 1 and 3, NT is a beast unto itself when it comes to application execution. NLMs simply won't work on an NT server. However, many companies have found that by off-loading file and print services onto the NT computer, they can consolidate the NLM applications servers more effectively.

Consolidating Your Servers

Did you ever put the big fish in the same tank as all the little fish? You come back in the morning, and there's just one big(ger) fish.

You have your big NT server up and running in your NetWare environment. Now it's time to retire some of the dual-486 servers out there, after long and faithful service. Instead of replacing the servers, your team decides to move the NetWare server's information over to NT servers.

Skill 16

Migration Tool for NetWare

The Migration Tool for NetWare allows you to move users and data shares from a NetWare file server to an NT server, while retaining security information, as illustrated in Figure 16.2. And with File and Print Services for NetWare installed, the NT servers will look like the old NetWare servers to the NetWare clients, but those NT servers will be faster.

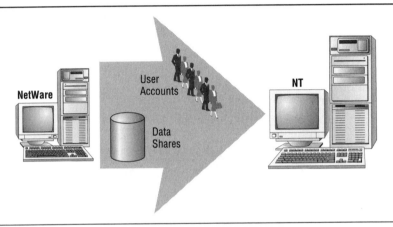

FIGURE 16.2: The Migration Tools for NetWare can be used to move NetWare server resources over to the NT server, consolidating your server environment.

You can use the Migration Tool for NetWare to move from a NetWare server to "straight" NT servers; you don't need the File and Print Services for NetWare to make the migration happen. We'll discuss the ways in which security is mapped between the two systems later.

Slow Migration to NT

For NetWare 2.x and 3.x servers, consolidated account management can be a real challenge. Once a number of NT servers have been deployed in a NetWare network environment, there should be enough NT "critical mass" in place to justify the creation of an NT domain architecture, as we discussed in Skill 13. If you're moving to NT, you can take advantage of your NT domain design to apply some structure to the NetWare user accounts.

The most straightforward way to do so would be to migrate everything over to NT, using the Migration Tool for NetWare. However, it's rarely feasible or even desirable to take such a "blitzkrieg" approach to your network operations. Most migrations will happen over time.

The Directory Service Manager—Applying NT Structure to Your NetWare Networks

The Directory Service Manager for NetWare can buy you the time you need. The Directory Service Manager is a step up from the Migration Tool for NetWare. Use the Migration Tool to get the same user accounts set up on the NetWare and NT networks. Once that's done, the Directory Service Manager tracks the accounts on both networks, noting changes made to the accounts (such as password changes or changes to user privileges) and keeps the NetWare version of the account in sync with the NT version. Figure 16.3 illustrates how the Directory Service Manager for NetWare works.

FIGURE 16.3: The Directory Service Manager for NetWare maintains coherency between the NetWare and NT instance of a migrated user account.

NWLink IPX/SPX Setup

The IPX/SPX transport is the workhorse of the NetWare integration tools, providing the connectivity between NT and NetWare environments. If you're adding an NT server to an existing IPX network, your configuration task will be straightforward. If you would like to take advantage of the network scalability features of NT, as discussed in Skill 7, read on!

Before You Install

Before you install the NWLink transport, you should answer the following questions:

- **How many network interfaces are in your NT server?**

You should have this information handy from your Hardware Design worksheet (Worksheet 4.7 in Skill 4). If you don't know how many interfaces are installed that can be bound to the NWLink transport, you can check the Network Control Panel, which will indicate this when you install NWLink. In general, you can bind NWLink to any LAN network card, such as an Ethernet or a Token Ring NIC.

- **Which network interfaces will support IPX/SPX?**

This is a design decision you need to make. You'll be able to specify the cards bound to NWLink in the Network Control Panel. Make your decision based on the network design for your server. See Skill 13 for some ideas about network design and performance optimization.

- **Which frame types will be supported on each interface?**

The *frame type* specifies the order in which the bits from the network stream are interpreted by the network interface. Token Ring uses a different encoding scheme than Ethernet, and different versions of various Ethernet protocols use slightly different frame types. If you have more than one NIC in your server that will be supporting NWLink, or if you want to support multiple frame types on a single NIC, you must specify the frame types manually. Otherwise, NWLink will auto-detect a frame type for the interface.

- **What are the IPX network numbers of the network segment on each interface?**

If an IPX network is already in place on the network segments to which you're attaching your NT server, the server will discover the network numbers automatically. Otherwise, you'll need to come up with a unique network number for the network segments that don't have IPX yet. Upon installation, NWLink will attempt to discover what it can, and set everything else to the network number 00000000. You can change this later.

- **What is your internal network number for the server?**

If you'll be supporting IPX on more than one NIC, or if you're supporting more than one frame type on a single NIC, your server will be routing IPX among these different interfaces. In order to do so, the server will need an internal network number that's unique to that server. As with IPX network numbers, NWLink will attempt to discover what it can when you install it, and then set everything else to the network number 00000000. You can change the internal network numbers later.

For more information about these topics, take a look at the *Windows NT Server Services for NetWare Networks* manual.

 NOTE   You'll need to reboot the server after installing the NWLink transport, so schedule some server outage time.

Installing the NWLink Transport

You install the NWLink transport in the same way that you install any other transport protocol:

1. Open the Network Control Panel's Protocols tab and click on the Add button.

2. Select NWLink IPX/SPX Compatible Transport from the list, as shown in Figure 16.4.

3. Specify the path to the NT distribution files. For example, if you are installing an Intel server from a CD-ROM mounted on the G: drive, type **G:\i386.** The system will set up the NWLink protocol, copying files to your computer.

4. If the Remote Access Services (RAS) is installed on your server, NWLink will attempt to bind to it, so that your dial-up connections will be able to handle IPX as a transport. You'll see a message that says:

```
Setup has discovered that you have Remote Access Services installed. Do
you want to configure RAS to support the NWLINK protocol?
```

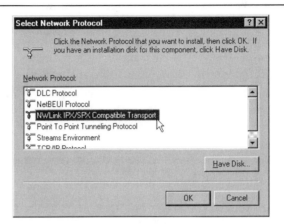

FIGURE 16.4: Choosing to add the NWLink transport

Choosing Cancel here does not cancel the entire installation of NWLink; it simply prevents RAS from binding to NWLink.

5. When the system setup process is complete, you are returned to the Protocols tab of the Network Control Panel. You need to close the Control Panel to initiate any further action, although this is not obvious. Click on the Close button.

6. The system will recognize the new transport, and bind any appropriate services to it. This binding analysis may take some time. A progress bar will indicate what is happening, as shown in Figure 16.5.

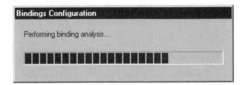

FIGURE 16.5: Watching the progress of the binding analysis

7. Once the system has performed the binding analysis, it will ask you to reboot the server. If you've scheduled downtime, and no one is connected to the server, go ahead and reboot now.

Configuring the NWLink Transport

After you've installed the NWLink transport and rebooted your server, you'll be able to log back into the server and configure the NWLink protocol. Since most of the NWLink transport is self-configuring, there's not much to do. However, if you're already attached to an IPX network, you'll want to set up a unique internal network number for your server.

As you would expect, you configure the NWLink protocol through its Properties sheet:

1. In the Protocol tab of the Network Control Panel, double-click on the NWLink entry (or click once and click on the Properties button) to bring up the NWLink Properties sheet, shown in Figure 16.6.

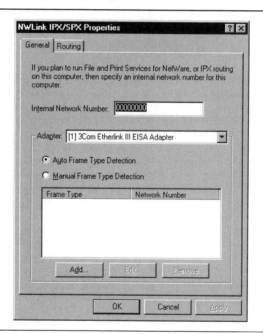

FIGURE 16.6: The NWLink IPX/SPX Properties dialog box

2. If you're already attached to a network segment that has an active IPX network, enter an eight-digit hexadecimal number that's unique to your server in the Internal Network Number field.

3. If necessary, manually specify the frame types for each of the installed network interface cards, by clicking on the Manual Frame Type Detection box and adding frame types to the list. If you have only a single NIC, you can leave this setting on Auto Frame Type Detection.

4. If you wish to use your NT server to manage the IPX numbers on the network segments attached to your server, make sure the Enable RIP Routing checkbox in the Routing tab of the NWLink IPX/SPX Properties sheet is checked, as shown in Figure 16.7. If you have another IPX router on this network segment, and you have a single NIC on the server, you can disable IPX routing by unchecking this box.

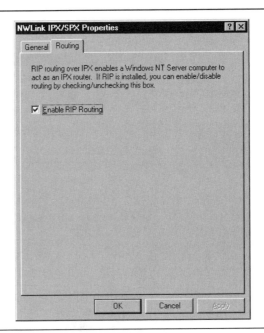

FIGURE 16.7: Enabling IPX routing

5. After you're finished configuring the NWLink transport, close the NWLink Properties sheet, and then close the Network Control Panel.

6. You may need to reboot your server again. If the Network Control Panel asks you to reboot the server, follow its advice.

NT and NetWare Security Compared

NT and NetWare offer similar security features, but there are important differences between the two systems. Make sure you understand the differences before attempting any large-scale integration.

NetWare-Enabled NT Accounts

"NetWare-enabled" NT accounts have an additional password associated with them: a NetWare password. The NetWare password is used to provide access to NetWare services.

The Directory Service Manager and the File and Print Services for NetWare each extend the NT Server software so that it understands NetWare-enabled NT accounts and maintains the NetWare security features of the account.

If you would like to manage your NetWare-enabled accounts on a global basis, which is a very good idea, you should install the File and Print Services for NetWare on the master account domain's PDC (primary domain controller). You don't need to activate the File and Print Services for NetWare on the PDC; simply installing the software will extend the server so that it understands NetWare-enabled accounts.

User Account Security

User account security for your NT/NetWare integration involves the Supervisor account access, account restrictions, and operator and manager groups.

Master Account and Supervisor Access

The master account for a NetWare server is the *Supervisor*. The comparable NT account is the *Administrator*. This account is a built-in account for the system, and it has maximum privileges.

In NT, accounts are granted Supervisor access by simply adding them to the Administrators group. You may optionally add NetWare server Supervisors to the NT Administrators group when migrating users.

Account Restrictions

Most of the user account restrictions, such as required password length and login time restrictions, are common to both systems. However, NT typically supports account restrictions in the global policy for all accounts; in NetWare, every account restriction is on a per-user basis. NT maintains these account restrictions on a global policy basis:

- Password required
- Minimum password length
- Maximum password age
- Password uniqueness
- Intruder detection/lockout

Login time restrictions in NetWare are specified on the half-hour; in NT, the restrictions are for whole hours only. When migrating this information, the NT tools will set the NT login time restrictions on whole-hour boundaries that give the user the most login time. For example, a NetWare login time restriction of 8:30am–6:30pm is transferred to NT as 8:00am–7:00pm.

Expiration dates are generally specified in NetWare as the *first* day for which a particular item is invalid. In NT, expiration dates are the *last* day for which the item is valid.

User Disk Quotas

User disk quotas are not supported by the system under NT. Third-party tools are available for this function, but none of the NetWare migration tools preserves user account disk quota information.

Account Groups and Server Operators

Some account groups under NetWare have similar account groups under NT, but in practice, the use of these groups is different because of the centralized administration model provided by NT domains.

For example, in an NT domain model, user account information is consolidated in the account domain. Domain administrators can add accounts to the domain, and these accounts can be used immediately to access any server in the domain itself or in one that trusts the domain. So there's no reason to delegate account supervisor authority to individual server operators.

 NOTE   For more information about NetWare and NT security features, see the online documentation or the *Windows NT Server Services for NetWare Networks* manual.

Using the Migration Tool for NetWare

The Migration Tool for NetWare is a starting place for NetWare/NT integration. This tool performs two main functions:

- Copies over disk volumes, keeping the file-system security settings intact. You won't need to reset all the security for each file or directory tree manually.

- Reads all the user account information from the NetWare server's bindery and sucks it into the NT domain system. You won't need to key in the information for all those users to create NT accounts for them. This tool gives you a head start.

 TIP   Create shares on an NTFS partition on your NT server, so that you can migrate and maintain effective access rights.

Importing NetWare Accounts into NT Domains

Before you import accounts from NetWare into an NT server, it's important to make sure you understand which server should get the imported accounts.

If you've set up your NT domain architecture, make sure that you're importing NetWare accounts into the PDC of your master account domain. Otherwise, you'll just be moving local accounts from one server to another. When you move accounts from your NetWare servers into the PDC of the account domain, in one step, you've effectively added the users to every NT server in your enterprise! Figure 16.8 illustrates this situation.

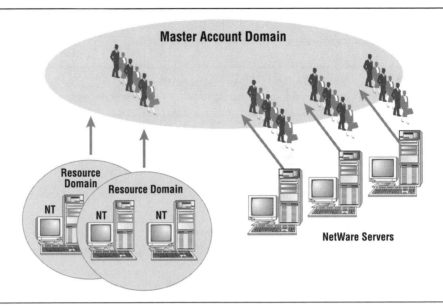

FIGURE 16.8: When importing NetWare accounts into an NT domain model, make sure that you import the accounts into the user account domain.

If you're simply adding a single NT server to an existing NetWare environment, you might not yet have a domain architecture in place for your NT network. But if you're planning on bringing in more than a couple of NT servers, you should seriously consider the advantages of centralized administration offered by a good NT domain model. See Skill 13 for details concerning NT domains.

 TIP   For maximum interoperability with NetWare, you'll want to be running File and Print Services for NetWare on the PDC. See the discussion on File and Print Services for NetWare later in this Skill.

Creating a Migration Map File

When migrating users, you may wish to use a control file called the *migration map*, which specifies which users to migrate and how to handle conflicts between existing accounts.

NetWare user names can be up to 30 characters long. NT user names are currently limited to 20 characters. User names longer than 20 characters cannot be migrated. You'll need to use a migration map file to map the long user name to a user name that can be supported by NT.

NT cannot read the encrypted NetWare passwords for users, so the passwords must be changed to something known by the system. Without the migration map file, you can have the Migration Tool set the password to a single known password for all migrated users, or to the users' account names. With the migration map, you have an additional option of specifying for each user what the new password is going to be. You may also want to use a migration map file as a "filter" to specify which users to migrate, and only those users will be moved over to the NT server.

The format for the migration map file is simple, and you usually will use a spreadsheet to set it up. There are three columns: the user name in NetWare, the user name in NT, and a password for the new NT user account. If no new name is specified in the second field, the old user name is used for the new NT user name.

TIP   You could use a spreadsheet program to generate random passwords, and use the migration map file as a mail merge document to generate a memo to each person, giving that user his or her initial, randomly generated password.

Here is a sample migration map file:

```
BobS,              ,        peaches
AliceB,      Alice,         orange
FredJ,       Sales12,       plums
```

Note that when this migration map file is used, only these three users will be moved over. If a user account is not specified in the migration map file, that account will not be migrated.

The Migration Process

After you've figured out which NT server should get the NetWare resources and created a migration map file (if necessary), you're ready to migrate. Here are the steps for using the Migration Tool for NetWare:

1. Choose Programs from the Start menu, then Administrative Tools, then Migration Tool for NetWare.

2. Specify the NetWare and NT server pairs. Choose a NetWare server and the NT server to which you want to migrate the resources.

3. Specify the resources on the NetWare server that you want to move over.

4. For user accounts, indicate if you want to use a migration map file to specify user accounts to transfer. If so, indicate the path to the migration map file.

5. For disk shares, indicate which volumes on the NetWare server you want to move over.

6. Perform a trial migration to write out the log files, which indicate the effect of the operations you've specified.

7. Check the logs to make sure that the migration operations you've specified result in the effects that you want.

8. Once you have the settings set up the way you want, save the settings. You'll be able to bring up these settings later.

9. Schedule server outage time. You don't want to be moving large server volumes on a production server during peak usage hours.

10. At the scheduled time, perform the actual migration.

The online help for the Migration Tool for NetWare is actually pretty good. You can refer to the online help as you're going through the migration procedure.

Installing and Using the Gateway Service for NetWare

The Gateway Service for NetWare is built on top of the Client Services for NetWare that ship with NT Workstation. After you've installed the Gateway Service for NetWare, you've just turned the NT server, that huge 80-pound beast, into a NetWare *client*—it's now able to attach to NetWare shares, provided that it can give the NetWare server a valid user name/password pair.

If this were an NT workstation, setting up the NetWare login information on a per-user basis would be great; you would attach to NetWare shares when you logged in to the workstation. But this is a *server*, which means that you are not going to stay logged in to the box. Instead, the Gateway Service for NetWare will store the user name/password pair and use it to log in automatically when the service starts.

To share NetWare volumes with SMB clients, you attach a drive letter to a NetWare network share, and then set up an SMB share name on this drive letter through the Gateway Service for NetWare Control Panel. You can set up only as many NetWare shares as there are available drive letters on the server: at most 23 NetWare shares (26, minus one each for primary volume, floppy, and CD-ROM).

To share NetWare printers with SMB clients, you set up a printer defined as a NetWare network printer. We talked about network printer setup in Skill 14.

Setting Up the Gateway Service Account

In order for the Gateway Service to connect to a NetWare server, it must be provided an account and password for that server. On each NetWare server to which you want your NT server attached, follow this procedure:

1. Set up a group called NTGATEWAY. Give the group appropriate trustee rights, if required, to attach to the required NetWare shares on the server.

2. Add an account to the NTGATEWAY group.

TIP   It's a good idea to name the account for the NTGATEWAY group after the NT server, with some standard prefix to signify an NT gateway account. For example, I call my gateway accounts "robots," to signify that they are used by the system and should not be used by users. So my gateway account for server Frankenstein is named RobotFrankenstein.

3. Set up this gateway account in the same way—with the same name and password—on each of the NetWare servers you want to attach.

4. Make sure that the gateway account has appropriate trustee rights to attach to the required shares.

Installing the Gateway Service for NetWare

You'll need to reboot the server after installing the Gateway Service for NetWare, so schedule some server outage time before you begin.

Skill 16

You install the Gateway Service for NetWare in the same way that you install any other NT network service:

1. On the NT server, open the Network Control Panel, click on the Services tab, and then click on the Add button.

2. Select Gateway Service for NetWare from the list.

3. Specify the path to the NT distribution files. For example, if you're installing to an Intel server from a CD-ROM mounted on the G: drive, type **G:\i386.**

The system will set up the Gateway Service for NetWare, copying files to your computer, and then perform a network services binding analysis, which should not take too long. Finally, the system will prompt you to reboot the server.

Using the Gateway Service for NetWare

When the server reboots, the Client Services for NetWare will be enabled on your computer. The first time you log in to the server from the console, you'll be prompted for your NetWare account information.

Don't use the Client Services. Just choose Cancel through the dialog boxes, so that you can set up the Gateway Service. Then follow these steps:

1. Open the Gateway Service for NetWare Control Panel, which is shown in Figure 16.9.

2. Click on the Gateway button or press Enter to see the Configure Gateway dialog box, shown in Figure 16.10.

3. In the Configure Gateway dialog box, check the Enable Gateway checkbox.

4. Enter the gateway account name and password. You're asked to confirm the password to verify that it's entered correctly.

5. Click on the Add button to attach to a NetWare share. You'll see the New Share dialog box, shown in Figure 16.11.

6. Enter the share name and network path. The network path to the share is entered as a UNC. For example, to attach to the SYS volume on NetWare server SALES, type \\SALES\SYS.

7. Associate a drive letter and SMB share name for the share. For DOS compatibility, limit the share name to eight characters.

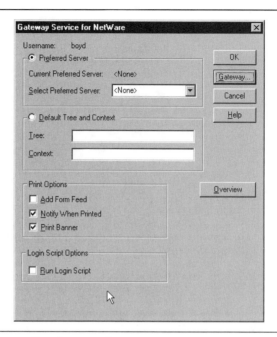

FIGURE 16.9: The Gateway Service for NetWare Control Panel

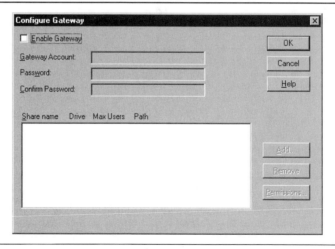

FIGURE 16.10: The Configure Gateway dialog box

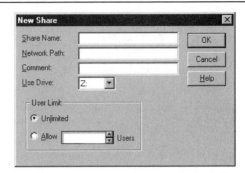

FIGURE 16.11: Attaching NetWare shares to your gateway

8. You can leave the share available to an unlimited number of users, or click on the checkbox next to Allow and specify the number of users.

9. Click on OK to return to the Configure Gateway dialog box.

 NOTE You can set NT permissions on the gateway volumes by clicking on the Permissions button in the Configure Gateway dialog box. These permissions are in addition to the trustee rights that the gateway account and the NTGATEWAY group have on the NetWare server.

Note that SMB clients go through three layers to attach to the network share:

- The NTGATEWAY rights on the NetWare server

- The gateway account (such as RobotFrankenstein) rights on the NetWare server

- The NT permissions on the gateway shared volume

See Skill 14 for more information about setting permissions on SMB shares.

 TIP Where possible, I give the maximum rights to the NTGATEWAY group and my robot accounts, to simplify troubleshooting, but I keep an eye on them, since I don't want them abused. Of course, the rights that are available to your gateway accounts depend on your ability to coerce your NetWare administrators.

Using the Directory Service Manager for NetWare

The Directory Service Manager for NetWare is a service available from Microsoft that can facilitate the interoperability of NetWare and NT network environments by permitting selected NetWare servers to participate in an NT domain.

The Directory Service Manager extends the NT Server software so that it understands "NetWare-enabled" NT accounts. For NetWare 2.x or 3.x networks, which do not have Novell's NetWare Directory Services (NDS), the Directory Service Manager can really help out by applying the NT domain structure to the NetWare network.

You specify which NetWare users and groups on the participating NetWare servers are to be added to the domain. Once these accounts and groups are members of the domain, they are full NT accounts, and you manage them using the NT User Manager for Domains. Changes to the accounts and groups made by means of the NT User Manager are tracked by the Directory Service Manager, and are propagated to the participating NetWare servers.

With an appropriate domain model, domain accounts are effectively global to every NT server. Adding the NetWare servers to the domain gives you the advantage of a single user account that can be used across your entire network!

However, it's important to note the following caveats and limitations:

- You must use the NT-based User Manager for Domains to manage the users and groups on the NT domain, and then let the service propagate the changes down to the NetWare servers. If you use the NetWare tools on a server itself, the changes affect only that particular server, and they cannot be tracked by the Directory Service Manager.

- The Directory Service Manager is limited to 32 participating NetWare 3.x servers.

- The Directory Service Manager cannot interoperate directly with NDS.

- You can propagate up to 2000 user accounts to the NetWare servers.

If you have Workgroup Managers or User Account Operators groups set up on participating NetWare servers, you'll probably want to get rid of them. This is because all changes to user accounts and groups must be performed on the NT domain in order for the changes to remain synchronized. Members of the User Account Operators and Workgroup Managers groups are not automatically added to the Administrators group in NT. You'll need to add users to the Domain Administrators global group manually.

Domain Design Options for the Directory Service Manager

I'm a strong advocate of the centralized, master account domain model, which we explored in Skill 13. With this model, a user can be global to your entire NT network and be managed in just one place.

However, the Directory Service Manager is limited to maintaining 32 NetWare servers, and it must be run on a PDC. Because of this limitation, and because of the complexity inherent in maintaining synchronization between the two environments, I consider the Directory Service Manager to be a temporary solution, or a migration tool. Scaling up the Directory Service Manager is not necessarily a good thing to do.

If you must maintain more than 32 NetWare servers with the Directory Service Manager, it can be done. For each group of 32 NetWare servers, deploy an NT PDC. Maintain a complete trust relationship between these domains and your NT master account domain, as explained in Skill 13.

 WARNING   It's crucial that you really understand NT domains before installing and using the Directory Service Manager for NetWare. See Skill 13 for more information about NT domains.

Reliability Issues for the Directory Service Manager

In order to keep track of the account changes on the various participating servers, the Directory Service Manager maintains an *account synchronization database* on the PDC. In the event of a PDC failure, you're going to need a backup of that database.

You can get the Directory Service Manager working by installing it on just one NT server, a PDC. However, in order to handle the loss of the PDC, you need to have installed the Directory Service Manager on at least one of the BDCs (backup domain controllers).

When you install the Directory Service Manager on a BDC, set the service for Manual startup. Enable backup of the account synchronization database to the *systemroot* \ SYSTEM32\SYNCAGNT\BACKUP directory of this BDC. Then if the PDC fails, promote this BDC to be the PDC. Start the Directory Service Manager service on this newly promoted PDC by issuing the NET START MSSYNCH command from a command prompt.

NOTE   For more information about the Directory Service Manager for NetWare, see the online documentation and the *Windows NT Server Services for NetWare* manual.

Using File and Print Services for NetWare

The File and Print Services for NetWare package, a separate product available from Microsoft, provides the ultimate in NT/NetWare interoperability. With File and Print Services for NetWare installed on an NT server, NetWare users can access the server as if it were a NetWare 3.1 server.

We've already discussed how the File and Print Services for NetWare lets your NetWare users access NT shares, in our "Outgrowing NetWare 3.*x* Networks" scenario. As an additional benefit, using NT servers with File and Print Services for NetWare can greatly enhance the manageability of your NetWare user accounts.

The master account domain model presented in Skill 13 provides a way of giving users global access to NT resources across your entire NT enterprise network. By migrating NetWare users to the master account domain, you can create a global, NetWare-enabled NT user account for every NetWare account. Since these accounts are NT accounts, they can have global access to all NT resources, including the NetWare shares on NT servers with File and Print Services for NetWare installed. Figure 16.12 shows an example.

You'll need to install File and Print Services for NetWare on the PDC of your master account domain to manage NetWare-enabled global accounts. The services do not need to be actively running; simply installing the services updates the User Manager for Domains for NetWare-enabled users.

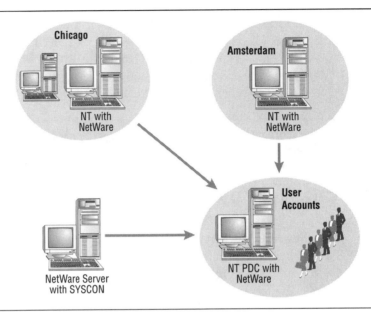

FIGURE 16.12: With File and Print Services for NetWare installed on the PDC of your master account domain, you can use the SYSCON utility to administer NetWare-enabled, NT domain accounts.

 NOTE   As for the other NT/NetWare interoperability products, you can find more information about the File and Print Services for NetWare in the online documentation and the *Windows NT Server Services for NetWare* manual.

Are You Experienced?

Now you can...

- ☑ decide which NT/NetWare integration tool suits your network

- ☑ install the NWLink transport protocol through the Network Control Panel

- ☑ use the Migration Tool for NetWare to migrate account information to an NT server

☑ install the Gateway Service for NetWare to bridge between Microsoft SMB and NetWare networks

☑ use the Directory Service Manager add-on package to keep NetWare and NT systems in sync

☑ use the File and Print Services for NetWare add-on package to let NetWare users access an NT server as if it were a NetWare 3.1 server

Skill 16

S K I L L

seventeen

17

Designing Your Network

- ❑ Domain model selection
- ❑ Domain structure design
- ❑ Network resource organization
- ❑ Network design implementation

We've covered a great deal of network theory and practice in this part of the book. It's more difficult to put this network information into formulas and numbers, as can be done with server design material, but we can zoom in on the most important concepts.

Here, we'll review some of the issues that face you when you're planning your NT network, while still focusing on the big picture. Scanning through this design review should help you put all the pieces in perspective.

In the time of Julius Caesar, Gaul was split into three parts, and so it is with the network design review: domain planning, resource organization, and implementation. In three sections and ten easy (well, maybe not so easy) steps, we'll bring it all together.

Domain Planning Review

Remember from Skill 13 that the most difficult part of NT network design is planning your resource and account domains. Once you're able to enumerate your resources, and then put them into groups, you're home free.

Step 1: Identifying Network Resources

Identifying your resources is the easiest part. Chances are you're all too familiar with your network resources. Write down a list of the major ones, and for each one, keep track of the information presented in Worksheet 17.1, the Network Resource record. Of course, you might have other information regarding the resource. Write down anything about the resource that will help you organize the resources into groups.

WORKSHEET 17.1   A Network Resource Record

Resource Name:				
Resource Type:	Server	Printer	Database	Other
Resource Location:				
Resource Owner:				
Resource Purpose:				

Step 2: Grouping the Network Resources

This is where it gets tougher. Now that you have all the resources enumerated, think about putting them together in groups that make sense for your network. For many resources, it will help you to think about who needs access to the resource: Which users are common to each resource? For other resources, geographical location might be the most significant property. Printers tend to be used by virtue of their location; corporate databases tend to have geographically dispersed, logical groups of users.

Step 3: Mapping the Resource Domains

Once you've identified the resource groups, your next step is to map them. Draw your resources on a piece of paper and put circles around them, signifying groups. Figure 17.1 shows an example.

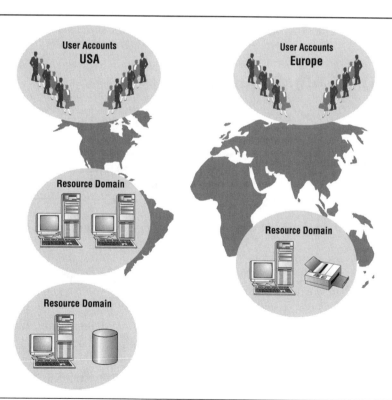

F I G U R E   1 7 . 1 : Draw your resources on a piece of paper, and put circles around them.

Step 4: Mapping User Account Domains

Most NT administrators have found that it's easiest to keep user accounts in domains separate from the resources. We went into the reasons for this in some detail in Skill 13. For most networks, keeping *all* the users in one account domain is your best option. However, in the following situations, you might want to break up your account domain:

- You have more than 10,000 users. Don't go over 15,000 users in a domain. Depending on your network, you may want to keep your user domains even smaller.

- You have administratively distinct locations. If your company is a loose conglomeration of divisions, each with its own Information Systems group, you'll probably have jurisdiction over only a subset of the servers in the company. Note that this is *not* the same as geographically distinct groups. It's not necessary to split user domains in order to accommodate remote sites.

Your fourth main step is to add the user domain(s) to your domain map.

Step 5: Identifying the Trusts

On your domain map, draw arrows from the resources to the people that need them. For most domain designs, this is the hard part. Figure 17.2 shows an example.

NOTE   Remember, draw arrows from your resources to the people. The resources trust the people; the people don't trust the computers.

Step 6: Identifying Domain Controllers

Each domain will need an NT server that's set up as a PDC (primary domain controller). If a domain spans remote sites, or has many users, you'll also want BDCs (backup domain controllers). Keep track of the information presented in Worksheet 17.2.

The account domain will probably have the greatest number of BDCs. Because you want user account domains to be as global and reliable as possible, you'll need one account domain BDC for each site. You don't want the users to depend on WAN connections for login authentication. If the link between the remote site and the PDC goes down, the remote site's network will still chug along, because the users can be authenticated through the BDC on-site.

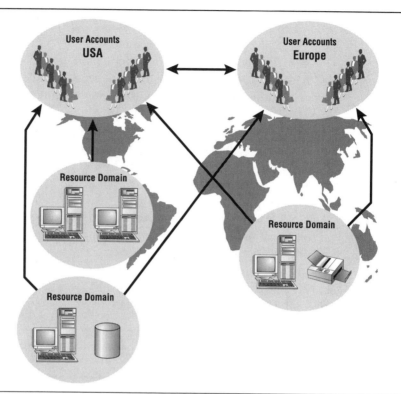

FIGURE 17.2: On your domain map, draw arrows from the resources to the people that need them.

WORKSHEET 17.2   Domain Record

Number of Account Domains:	
For each account domain:	
Domain Name:	
Number of Users:	
Primary Administrative Location	
Number of Resource Domains:	
For each resource domain:	
Domain Name:	
Resources in the Domain:	
Primary Domain Location:	

Resource domains tend to be limited in geographic scope, but the same certainly applies to them: If you have domains that span geographic locations, you'll want a domain controller in each remote site.

Put the PDCs where the network administrators are. Microsoft's South America PDC is located in Redmond, Washington, because that's where there is the highest concentration of network administrators for that time zone.

Put the BDCs wherever you need them. At this point, get out a map of the geographic area you need to cover—a map of the building, city, country, or world—and start marking the areas that will participate in your NT network. This is where you should think about geography and physical connectivity. Make sure that your network guru attends this meeting, and verify the quality and speed of the connections to the remote locations.

Ask the network guru for a network map, showing a diagram of all the routers and their location. At this point, you're trying to figure out where you need domain controllers. We thought that we needed a server at the site across town to act as the account domain BDC, and we found that, as far as the network topology was concerned, it didn't matter; the PDC was just as close to the folks across town as it was to the users on the floor above us.

 TIP   When you think *geography*, think about *network topology*. It's the network topology that matters!

Organizing Network Resources

Your organization of network resources involves two major steps: network optimization and user group identification.

Step 7: Optimizing Network Resources

As long as you're thinking about network topology, remember the network optimization tricks that we discussed in Skill 8. You can put servers on multiple network segments, if necessary.

If applicable, this is the time to think about your intranet, Macintosh, and Novell NetWare requirements:

- How do the resource domains interoperate with the TCP/IP network segments? With the AppleTalk networks and zones? With the existing NetWare services?

- Can you consolidate network resources provided by existing AppleShare or NetWare servers with a larger NT server?

- If you're planning on building an intranet server with NT, will your system be able to interoperate with required mainframe database systems?

Step 8: Identifying User Groups

It's generally fairly easy to identify groups of users. Presumably, your company already has some kind of departmental structure in place, so for a first cut, you can use department names as groups.

Create these groups as global groups in the user account domain with NT's User Manager for Domains utility.

For a second pass through grouping the users, keep in mind that users can belong to many groups.

Now that you have identified the network resources, keep in mind that *any* users who need to share network resources are good candidates for a group.

Groups are the best way to add descriptive tags to the users so that they can be managed collectively. Since groups are an administrative fiction, you need only please yourself and your network when it comes to creating and maintaining user groups.

Here are some examples of possible groupings for users:

- Department names

- Project teams

- Special-interest groups

- Any users who need to share a resource

TIP   Should a user group be global to the account domain or local, in the resource domain or on the server that holds the resource? Keep this rule in mind: If a group *describes a common property of the users* (such as a department, or the group of people who ride bikes to work), create a global group in the account domain. If the group *aggregates a list of users who need to share a resource*, it's probably a local group. For details on setting up user groups in a master/resource domain model, see Skill 13.

Implementing Your Network Design

The final two steps in our review are to decide which protocols and name services your network design requires.

Step 9: Identifying Required Protocols

Once you've decided which services and resources belong on which servers, you'll know which network segments need to carry the required network transport protocols.

For example, TCP/IP is required for FTP, WAIS text searching, and Web server services. NetWare services require the IPX transport protocol, and Mac services need AppleTalk. See Skill 8 for more information about network transport protocols. Table 8.1 lists the transport protocols required for network services.

Step 10: Implementing Name Servers

The last piece of the network puzzle is the name servers. If you're running the SMB (Server Message Block) network using NetBEUI as the transport protocol, you don't need to worry about this. But most large sites will want to use TCP/IP for the native SMB network transport, since TCP/IP is routable, commonly used, and well-supported by the router vendors.

If you decide to use TCP/IP as your transport protocol, you need WINS, the Windows Name Service, running on at least one of the servers in each of the TCP/IP network segments in order to resolve the NetBIOS names that SMB requires. Otherwise, your PC clients will not be able to find your NT servers on the network.

WINS is similar to domain controllers in how it affects your network planning. Keep in mind that you need at least one NT server running WINS on each TCP/IP network. In practice, you'll want a server running WINS at each location. Often, the account BDC and WINS server are on the same computer at the remote site.

Are You Experienced?

Now you can...

- ☑ design your resource and account domains
- ☑ optimize your network resources
- ☑ identify your network user groups
- ☑ identify the transport protocols your network requires
- ☑ implement name servers for the TCP/IP transport protocol

PART IV

BackOffice and Internet Systems

eighteen

Developing Distributed Client/Server Systems

- ❏ Client/server defined
- ❏ NT Server features for client/server applications
- ❏ Database setup in Microsoft Access
- ❏ Database migration to SQL Server
- ❏ Front-end application design with Visual Basic

Computers have become a ubiquitous part of the office environment. These days, companies issue a computer to every employee as a matter of course. Most everyone uses the computer for word processing—what we used to think of as "desktop publishing"—and few companies would be able to operate for very long without their e-mail systems.

But once we get beyond the word processor and e-mail workstation, most desktop computers are underutilized. When everyone has a computer, attached to a network, we should be able to share all kinds of information using sophisticated computational tools.

Now that you've gone to all the work of building your NT network, you have a very powerful set of tools available to you. After all, NT was designed from the ground up to be the workhorse for client/server applications. Here, we'll present an example of what can be done with two popular desktop applications, Access and Visual Basic, when you connect those programs to a full-featured database engine, SQL Server.

A caveat: We're going to show some pretty quick-and-dirty uses of some sophisticated tools. The focus is on jumping right in and getting to a starting place as quickly as possible. We could invest weeks of our time to refine the sample presented here, and there are probably more elegant uses for the tools. But we'll make a start of it here, and survey some of the tools that are available. By the end of this Skill, you should know what it's like to develop simple client/server applications and have ideas about designing your own applications.

Client/Server Explained

Client/server systems are business applications that are implemented as a set of communicating, cooperating programs. Typically, the various programs of the application run on different computers, such as a mainframe for the database engine and a Windows-based PC for the data display and query generation, and these computers communicate across a network connection.

Currently, the most common client/server applications are database applications, which are systems for managing and analyzing large amounts of indexed data. As personal computers with GUIs have become more and more common in the office environment, people have grown accustomed to powerful, "user-friendly" tools. This has raised their expectations of computer systems in general, and they have started to demand the same capabilities from their business database applications.

This created a conundrum for corporate database administrators: The databases needed to be centralized, but the computing power supporting the user community had to be distributed, so it could be placed on every desktop.

The Motivation for Client/Server Systems

In order to be useful, most business data must be consolidated into definitive repositories. For example, it would cause confusion and needless work to have a separate list of company employees for every business application. Updates made to the Human Resources database (such as to record a new hire) would need to be manually synchronized with the Phone Gnomes database (for a new phone number), and with the Information Systems people (for a new computer account), the Facilities department (a cube to put them in), and so on. I'm sure this type of problem is familiar to you. It's far better to have one definitive list of employees.

But the "One Big List" will do no one any good if only a few people (those with proper, restricted access, or those with the necessary computer skills) have access to the data in the list. A good client/server system can make the big, important lists readily available and easy to use, while preserving data integrity.

Three-Tier Client/Server Systems

This need for data integrity adds some complexity to the situation. It's easy to understand the big server-to-graphical workstation model as a two-tier client/server model. There are two things that need to be done: store and index the data, and display it to the user. With two computer systems, there's no problem.

When we add the need for data integrity to the mix, we might need another computer system that simply enforces data integrity rules. The rules for data integrity depend on the business application, and they are often a reflection of the procedures that the business follows to complete a task.

As an example, say that George is transferring to another location. We don't want to delete his record in the One Big List, but we certainly want to ensure that his computer account has the appropriate access rights, that he gets a new phone number if necessary, and that the Facilities departments of the different locations are aware of the change. Tracking all of these updates might not be feasible with traditional database integrity constraints.

For this simple example, you could probably come up with a solution using stored database procedures and triggers on the database server. However, the conceptual distinction should be clear. In a client/server system, you typically want to do three things with the data:

- Store the data in an indexed repository for easy retrieval.

- Query the repository and analyze the resulting data sets.

- Run procedures against the stored data to enforce integrity constraints and business rules.

These make up a three-tier client/server system.

NT Support for Client/Server Systems

We saw in the first part of this book how NT supports sophisticated applications with its mutlithreaded architecture, protected memory, and interprocess communications. NT also supports database connectivity and object-oriented distributed processing.

Interprocess Communications

The interprocess communications (IPC) support in NT is the key to distributed applications. NT is very good at helping programs on one computer talk to programs on another computer across a network. The interprocess communications architecture in NT is largely compliant with the industry-standard Distributed Computing Environment (DCE).

You've already used DCE-compliant interprocess communications; they're the network underpinnings for the NT administration tools that we've discussed throughout the book. Remote server administration couldn't happen without communicating applications.

Database Connectivity

Standard database connectivity, the Open Database Connectivity (ODBC) system, is built on top of low-level IPC. NT's robust support for IPC makes it a great ODBC database server. Since common graphical office applications use ODBC for data transfer, a database on an NT server with ODBC support can provide users with database access from tools that they use every day, like their word processor or spreadsheet.

ODBC support in the end-user applications and in the NT Server system renders the process of connecting to a remote database easy enough for sophisticated users to do it themselves. Certainly, it's easy enough to build database systems very quickly. We'll show an example of this later in this Skill.

Object-Oriented Distributed Processing

A significant new feature of NT Server 4.0 is the support for a networked version of Microsoft's object architecture, OLE (object linking and embedding). The thing to remember here is that where ODBC makes two-tier client/server database access an easy, end-user proposition, Distributed OLE enables programmers to create applications that can run across the network.

 NOTE   Distributed processing used to be a very esoteric subject, and talking about it invariably makes people's eyes glaze over. But everyone is really excited about Java, the programming language designed for distributed computing that has caught fire on the Internet. We'll talk more about distributed computing when we talk about intranet systems in Skill 19.

Skill 18

The First Steps in Developing Our Client/Server Application

A practical example will help you understand the support that NT provides for client/server applications. Now we'll develop a client/server application using SQL Server, Visual Basic, and Microsoft Office. We'll begin with an introduction to our problem and the first steps in solving it.

The Problem: Facilitating Employee Car Pools

We've mentioned a common problem in many office environments: the multiplicity of employee database lists. For our example, we decided to develop a practical employee database that everyone can use. We're still not finished with it, but after six hours of work, we're off to a good start.

Our company has lots of data that we want to track concerning the employees. Some of the data, such as compensation levels and performance evaluations, is highly confidential and needs to be kept secret. Some employee data, like phone extension number and office location, needs to be as widely distributed as possible. And some data, like personal phone number and address, falls somewhere in the middle—some people might want such data to be made public, while others might want to keep this information private.

Keeping data secret is no big deal; well, it's a different big deal. Broadcasting data, so that everyone has access to it, is more challenging.

We ran into the middle ground—sharing different amounts of data for different people—when we started a ride-sharing initiative at our company. We're hiring lots and lots of people, and parking space is becoming a real problem. In our highly congested industrial area, it makes a lot of sense for people to car pool whenever possible.

We would like for people to be able to sign up for the ride-share program, and then have their name, home phone number, and street address made available to the other employees in their area. We want the system to be accessible from every computer in the company. Everyone has to get to work. No one should be left out.

A First Cut: Designing the Database

For this quick-and-dirty example, we're not going to solve the whole problem. But we'll make a start, and we'll show how the various tools fit together.

To start with, we will keep data in a set of tables. One of the tables will have employee "core information," which is the information that's needed by every system that will use employee information. Take a look at Table 18.1 for the information in the Core Employee table.

T A B L E   1 8 . 1 :   Core Employee Data

ID
First Name
Last Name
Office Extension
Office Location

The Core Employee database table is pretty small, but that's okay. We'll expand on the data in our database system by adding other tables. Let's add some personal information that will be optionally public or private: the employee home address information. This is our Address Data database table, with information keyed on the employee ID, as shown in Table 18.2.

T A B L E   1 8 . 2 : Employee Address Data

ID
Area Code
Phone Number
Street Address
City
State
Zip Code

Finally, we'll split out all the ultra-secret stuff, like salary and number of dependents, into an Employee Tax database table, as shown in Table 18.3. Perhaps the Finance or Human Resources department would have access to this data.

T A B L E   1 8 . 3 : Employee Tax Data

ID
Taxpayer ID Number
Salary
Number of Dependents

Building the Database on the Desktop with Office Tools

Now that we have a very simple database model put together, we want to build on it. The easiest thing to do is to start with some common end-user tools and scale the system up.

Skill 18

For this sample database, I created some dummy data using Microsoft Excel, as shown in Figure 18.1. Excel is actually a very powerful tool for the manipulation and analysis of tabular data. For example, once the database is built, we could connect to it, perform a join to get salary data by address, and then plot that in Excel using the Data Map control. Here, we'll just create some tabular data.

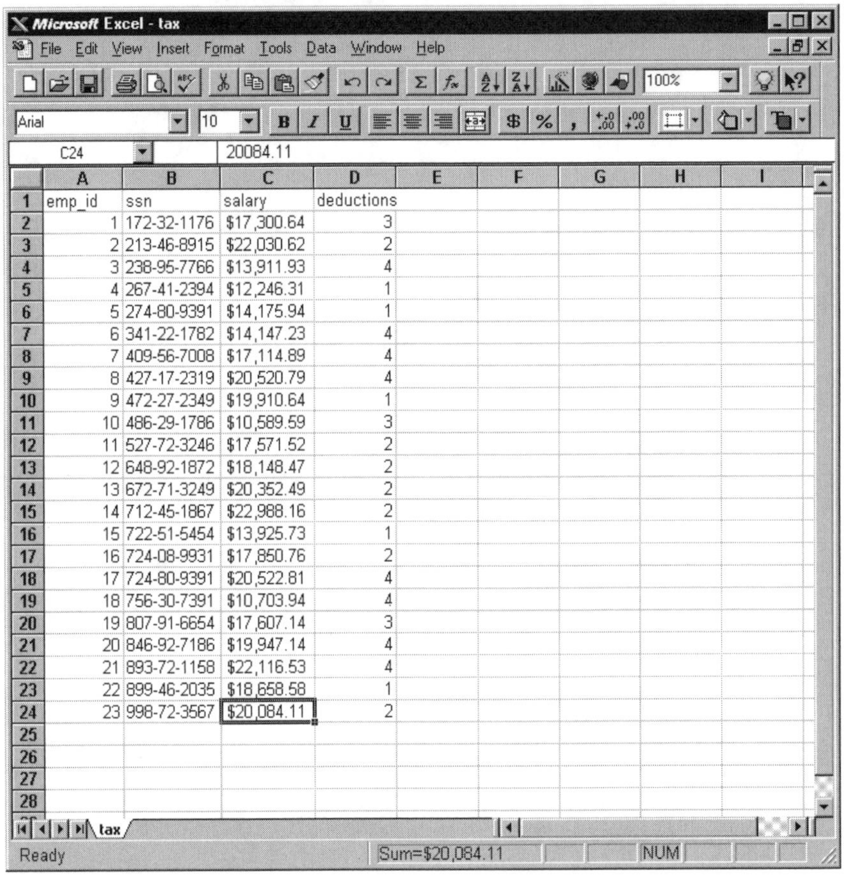

	A	B	C	D
1	emp_id	ssn	salary	deductions
2	1	172-32-1176	$17,300.64	3
3	2	213-46-8915	$22,030.62	2
4	3	238-95-7766	$13,911.93	4
5	4	267-41-2394	$12,246.31	1
6	5	274-80-9391	$14,175.94	1
7	6	341-22-1782	$14,147.23	4
8	7	409-56-7008	$17,114.89	4
9	8	427-17-2319	$20,520.79	4
10	9	472-27-2349	$19,910.64	1
11	10	486-29-1786	$10,589.59	3
12	11	527-72-3246	$17,571.52	2
13	12	648-92-1872	$18,148.47	2
14	13	672-71-3249	$20,352.49	2
15	14	712-45-1867	$22,988.16	2
16	15	722-51-5454	$13,925.73	1
17	16	724-08-9931	$17,850.76	2
18	17	724-80-9391	$20,522.81	4
19	18	756-30-7391	$10,703.94	4
20	19	807-91-6654	$17,607.14	3
21	20	846-92-7186	$19,947.14	4
22	21	893-72-1158	$22,116.53	4
23	22	899-46-2035	$18,658.58	1
24	23	998-72-3567	$20,084.11	2

FIGURE 18.1: Creating and analyzing tabular data in Microsoft Excel

After I developed the raw data, I saved it to a series of separate worksheets and then imported that data into Microsoft Access. Access and Excel understand each other's file formats, so I didn't need to worry about anything. When the tables had been created in Access, I created a simple query to indicate a join on the tables and to test the success of the data import. Figure 18.2 shows the database as depicted by the graphical query editor in Access.

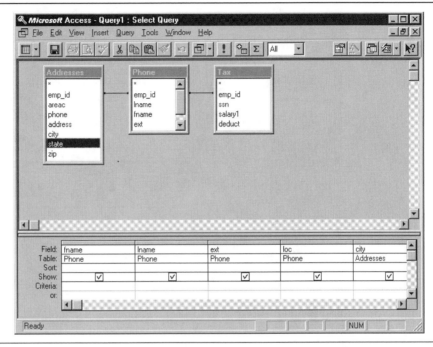

FIGURE 18.2: After I imported the data into Access, I created a query with the tables to set up a relation between them, just to test the success of the import.

Simple Options for Scaling Up

At this point, we could go ahead and start developing a front end. An NT or a Windows 95 computer on the network running Microsoft Access might be used as a simple database system.

Or we could simply share the database file on the file server. We could define an ODBC data source on the Access database files, and point any front-end program to that data source, as shown in Figure 18.3. A Microsoft Access database file is itself a valid data source, and it doesn't require a huge server.

However, none of these alternatives are real options for a large-scale, company-wide client/server system. We need something bigger—something like Microsoft SQL Server.

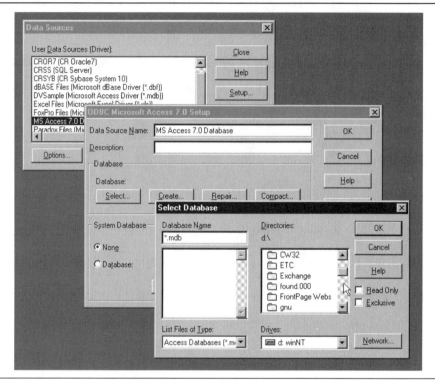

FIGURE 18.3: Defining ODBC data sources

Scaling Up to SQL Server

If Microsoft Office is the tool set for end users, Microsoft BackOffice is a tool set for client/server application designers. Microsoft SQL Server is a member of the BackOffice suite. It was initially developed by Sybase and Microsoft. As such, it inherits a legacy of industrial-strength database engine functions and incorporates enhanced interoperability with Microsoft products by fully supporting the ODBC standard.

Installing SQL Server

You'll need to reboot your server after you install SQL Server, so make sure you schedule the server outage. You'll need about two hours to install, if your server's hard disk system is ready to go.

We won't walk through the entire installation of SQL Server, but I do want to mention some things.

Before You Install

You should keep the following in mind before you install Microsoft SQL Server on an NT server:

- The computer name for a server running SQL Server cannot contain any dashes (-) or spaces. In general, keep your server names as simple as possible.

- You'll need at least 45 MB of free disk space to install SQL Server. Of course, you'll want more storage than that.

You'll also want to review the Hardware Design worksheet at the end of Skill 4 and the Server Performance worksheet in Skill 12. For my sample system, I defined a database device for the MASTER database on my RAID 5 array, with an initial size of 75 MB. You'll probably want a larger system; but then again, you'll probably want to define separate databases for your different systems.

Licensing

SQL Server implements the licensing standard consistent with NT Server. From the License Manager, SQL Server appears as a Microsoft BackOffice component, as shown in Figure 18.4. We briefly discussed the License Manager in Skill 2. Once installed, the Microsoft SQL Server product licensing can be centrally managed, just as with NT Server.

When you're installing Microsoft SQL Server, you'll be asked to specify a licensing mode for the product, as shown in Figure 18.5. We discussed these licensing modes in Skill 4.

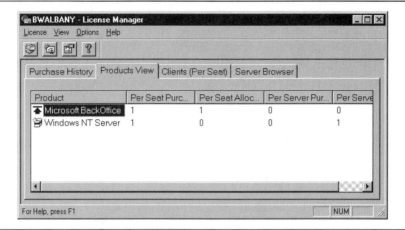

FIGURE 18.4: Microsoft SQL Server is compatible with the centralized software license management included in NT Server.

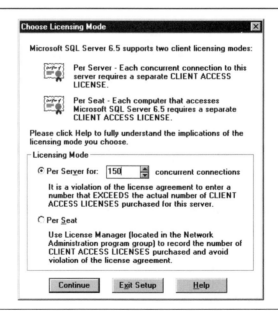

FIGURE 18.5: Specifying a licensing mode for Microsoft SQL Server during installation

Setting Up SQL Server

After you've installed SQL Server, you will want to set up its administration, your user logons, and the permissions for those logons.

Administration Setup

SQL Server is designed to be easy to use. Administration of SQL Server generally takes place with the SQL Enterprise Manager tool, which lets you manage every SQL Server system on your network.

1. Fire up the SQL Enterprise Manager. You'll be presented with the Register Server dialog box, shown in Figure 18.6.

FIGURE 18.6: Registering the new server with SQL Enterprise Manager. Use the "sa" account to initially connect to remote servers, or the Trusted Connection to connect to a server on the same computer.

2. Select your server from the Server drop-down box.

3. Initially, you probably will want to use standard security and logon with the System Administrator account, so type **sa** in the Logon ID box.

4. Initially, the sa account does not have a password. Leave that field blank, and click on the Register button.

You'll open a connection to the newly installed server, and it will be added to the list of servers in the Enterprise Manager.

Adding Database Logons to SQL Server

Database systems generally maintain their own security— their own list of user accounts and permissions. Before you do a lot of work with SQL Server, you should set up some users.

 NOTE   SQL Server logons are independent from NT user accounts.

The SQL Enterprise Manager is primarily a hierarchical list of SQL Server objects. To add a logon, right-click on the Logons folder and select New Logon from the pop-up menu. Figure 18.7 shows this process.

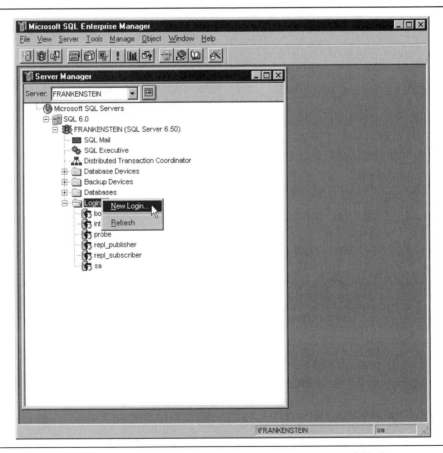

FIGURE 18.7: The SQL Enterprise Manager presents your SQL Server systems as a hierarchical list of objects. Right-clicking brings up a context-sensitive pop-up menu.

You'll see the Manage Logons dialog box, as shown in Figure 18.8. Fill in the logon name, password, and default database. When you're finished adding users, click on Close.

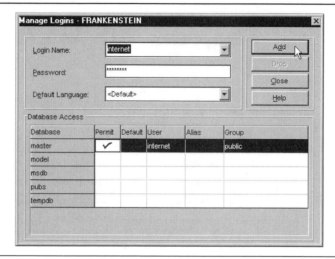

FIGURE 18.8: Adding a new logon. Make sure to set permissions on at least one database, and to specify a default database.

 **WARNING**   It's easy to "drop" a user in the Manage Logons dialog box. Be careful not to drop a logon unless you really want to delete it.

Granting Logon Permissions

Once you've added logons, you need to define the permissions that a logon has for each database. For example, some logons might have read-only access to certain databases, while other logons can create and drop tables.

To set permissions on a database, right-click on it and choose Edit Database from the pop-up menu. Then you can modify the logon permissions in the Permissions tab of the Edit Database dialog box, shown in Figure 18.9.

 NOTE   For more information about SQL Server administration, see the SQL Server documentation.

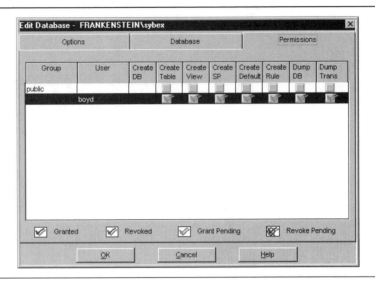

FIGURE 18.9: Adding database permissions to a logon

Migrating the Database from Access to SQL Server

An add-on option to Access, called the Microsoft Access Upsizing Wizard, can perform complex analyses on your existing Access databases and perform a faithful migration to SQL Server. For our simple database, the Upsizing Wizard provides an easy way to define a new database schema in SQL Server and populate it with data, without needing to resort to SQL commands.

Using the Access Upsizing Wizard

Here are the steps for upsizing the sample database using the Access Upsizing Wizard:

1. In Access, open the database you want to migrate, choose Add-Ins from the Tools menu, and then choose Upsize to SQL Server.

2. In the Upsizing Wizard's first dialog box, choose Create New Database, as shown in Figure 18.10.

3. Specify a SQL Server logon with database creation permissions, as shown in Figure 18.11.

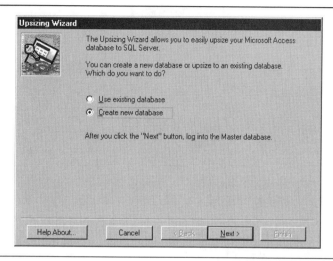

FIGURE 18.10: Choose Create New Database in the Upsizing Wizard's initial dialog box.

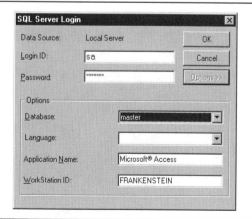

FIGURE 18.11: Creating a SQL Server logon

4. Choose the default database device, as shown in Figure 18.12.

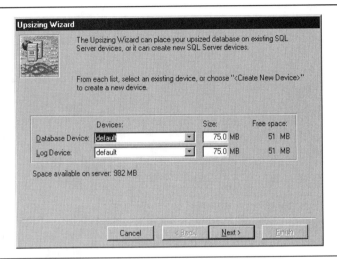

FIGURE 18.12: Choosing the default database device

5. In the next Upsizing Wizard dialog box, name the database. I named this sample database "sybex," as you can see in Figure 18.13.

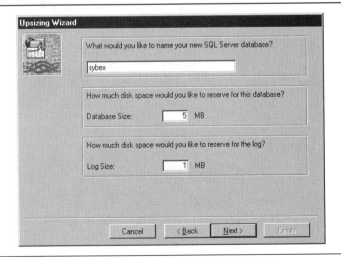

FIGURE 18.13: Naming the database

6. Export all three tables in our sample database, as shown in Figure 18.14.

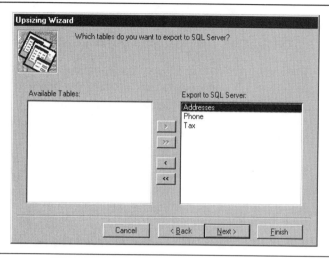

FIGURE 18.14: Exporting the tables to SQL Server

Skill 18

7. In the final Upsizing Wizard dialog box, choose to create an upsizing report, as shown in Figure 18.15.

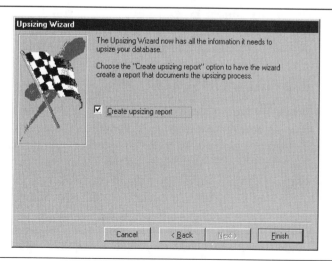

FIGURE 18.15: Finally, choose to create an upsizing report.

The Upsizing Wizard is slow and may take a long time to complete its tasks, depending on the load on the server and on the SQL Server system. Don't worry if it takes a while to migrate your database tables.

Verifying the Database Migration with ISQL/w

The Upsizing Wizard will generate an upsizing report for you, but I don't trust such things. It can be difficult to find errors in the upsizing process by reading the wizard report, and sometimes errors are not reported. The definitive test of the validity of the upsizing procedure is the queries that are run against the upsized database.

If you're familiar with common commercial SQL databases, then you've probably used a tool called ISQL (for Interactive SQL) to talk to the database and get quick answers. The Microsoft SQL Server package comes with an ISQL tool that maintains an interactive SQL session.

Simply fire up the ISQL/w application from the SQL Server menu, accessed from the Programs menu. After you give ISQL a logon ID and password, it will connect you to the server.

Once you're connected, you can verify that you're accessing the proper database. For this example, this should be the sybex database that we created with the Upsizing Wizard. You can choose the database from the drop-down combo box in the toolbar.

Simply type a SQL query in the big text area of the Query tab. Figure 18.16 shows an example. When you're ready to run the query, click on the green right triangle (the Go button) in the toolbar. ISQL will switch to the Results tab and display the results of the query, as you can see in Figure 18.17.

More Fun with ISQL/w

You can save a query or the results by clicking on the disk icon in the toolbar or by choosing Save from the File menu. You can work with multiple queries; instead of replacing the text of an existing query, click on the document icon on the toolbar, or choose New from the File menu. You can switch between queries with the Queries drop-down list in the toolbar.

For complex queries, it might be useful to profile the query performance to see what's taking so long. There's usually more than one way to do it in SQL, and most of the ways are pathological. The Statistics tab can give you a rough idea of which databases are being used by a query, as shown in the example in Figure 18.18. The Showplan tab will show you the tables used and indexes created for each step of execution of your query, as in Figure 18.19.

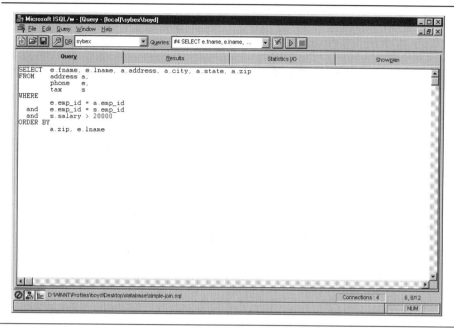

FIGURE 18.16: A sample query in the ISQL interactive query tool

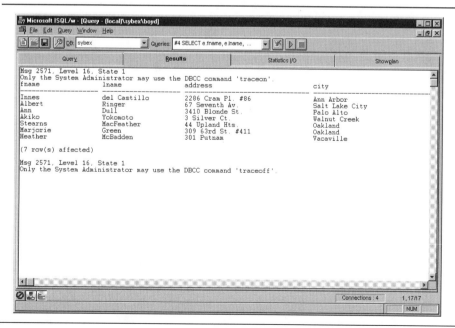

FIGURE 18.17: The results of a query are displayed in the Results tab.

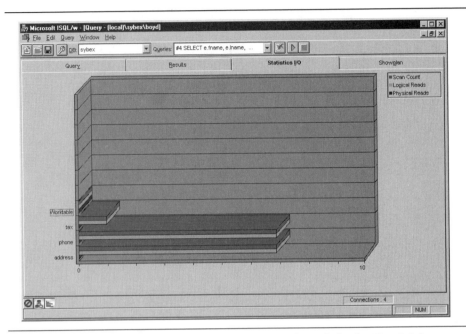

FIGURE 18.18: With ISQL/w, you can view I/O statistics for the databases used by your query.

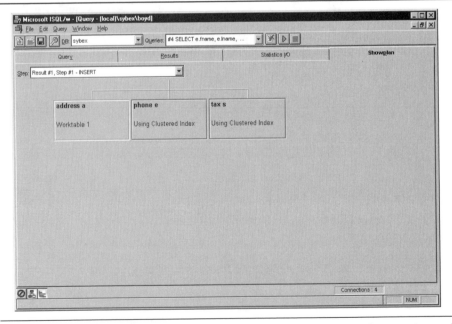

FIGURE 18.19: You can profile the index and table usage of query steps with ISQL/w's Showplan tab.

Developing a Front-End Tool with Visual Basic

Creating a client tool in Visual Basic is so easy it's almost embarrassing; that is, once you know what you're doing. The Data Control included with Visual Basic will let us connect to any ODBC data source, including a SQL Server database. We developed a nice little client tool for our employee information database in about three hours. If we invested more time, we could have used more of the features of Visual Basic and SQL Server to get better performance.

Setting Up the Employee Finder Application

In our example, we want our users to be able to connect to the employee database and get two pieces of information:

- By entering the name of an employee, the user should get the employee's office extension.

- The user should be able to browse the list of employees participating in the company car-pool program, and search this list by the city of the home address.

Here are the basic steps for developing the front-end application:

1. Define an ODBC data source for our sample sybex database on the SQL Server in the ODBC Control Panel of the clients.

2. Use the Data Control in Visual Basic to define a query on this data source.

3. Use the Data Grid Control and the Text Controls to display the data.

4. Create an executable file once we're finished, and give it to the users as a canned application.

Fortunately, using Visual Basic is fairly simple. All the real work happens in the controls, which are written for you. Creating a Visual Basic application is pretty much just plopping controls onto a form and getting things to look right. Figure 18.20 shows the arrangement of controls for locating phone numbers.

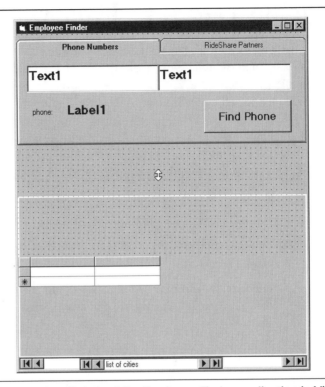

FIGURE 18.20: "Painting" the Employee Finder application in Visual Basic design mode. You can generate simple Visual Basic tools like this one with almost no programming.

The hard part about using Visual Basic is figuring out which controls to use and what they can do for you. Every control can be modified by changing its properties. A solid understanding of the control properties is all you need to develop a simple query tool.

The Key: The Data Control

The key to the Employee Finder application is the Data Control, which you simply drag onto the form. At run-time, this control is not visible; it's there simply to mediate the connection to the database.

For our example, there are two properties that we can use to tell the Data Control about our database:

- **Connect property:** This property points the Data Control to the appropriate data source. For my application, the Connect property was set to:

```
ODBC;DSN=Local Server;
UID=sa;PWD=;APP=Visual Basic 4.0;
WSID=FRANKENSTEIN;DATABASE=sybex
```

- **RecordSource property:** This property defines which data is to be retrieved from the database. I set this property of my Data Control to the following SQL query:

```
SELECT e.fname, e.lname, e.phone, a.address, a.city, a.state
FROM address a, phone e
WHERE e.emp_id=a.emp_id
ORDER BY a.zip, e.lname
```

 NOTE   **Both of these properties should be all on one line; ignore the word wrap shown here. And the case in which you enter them doesn't matter.**

Other Controls

Once the Data Control has been set up properly, adding the other controls is not difficult. The *Data Grid Control* gives a spreadsheet-like display of the query results. Clicking on a row in the Data Grid will set that record as the active record, which will update the display of the other fields at the top of the screen. I dragged a Data Grid Control onto the form, and defined its Data Source property to point to the Data Control. Remember, the Data Control manages the connection to the database system. When another control wants some data, it just asks the Data Control.

I set up a *Tabbed Dialog Control* for the two primary applications of this query tool: finding employee extensions and finding car-pool buddies.

The *Text Controls* were set to point to particular fields of the Data Control, so that when a user selects a record in the Data Grid, these fields are updated.

For the Phone Numbers tab, a *Command Button Control* executes a query based on the name that the user types in the text fields. Here's the code for that:

```
Private Sub Command1_Click()
 Dim strQry As String
 strQry = "select fname, lname, phone from phone" & _
```

```
         " where fname ='" & firstName.Text & "' lname = '" & _
         lastName.Text & "' order by lname"
      Data1(0).RecordSource = strQry
      Data1(0).Refresh

   End Sub
```

The code builds a query based on the values in the text fields. This is a crude query because you must enter both the first and last name. But it's just a quick example. For your application, you could check for the empty text fields and query on just the things that are specified. See Figure 18.21 for a look at the Phone Numbers search.

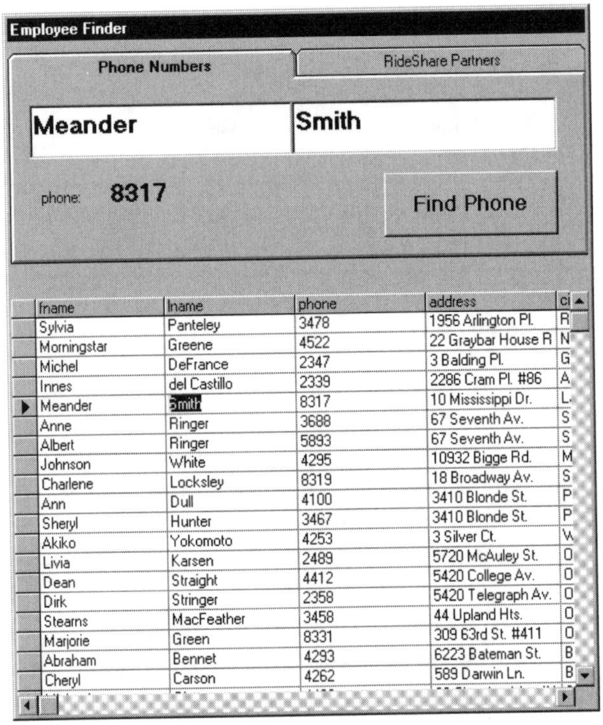

FIGURE 18.21: Searching for employee phone numbers in the Phone Numbers tab

For the RideShare Partners tab, I used a *Drop-Down Box Control* to allow users to select the city. I used a second Data Control (with the same Connect property as the first Data Control and the RecordSource property set to "select city from address") to get the list of cities in the database, which I used to populate the drop-down list. That was the hardest part of building the application, but the procedure is well-documented in the Visual Basic online help. See Figure 18.22 for a picture of the RideShare Partners tab.

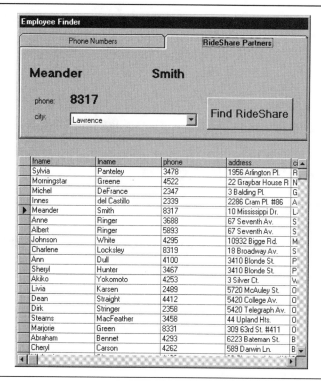

FIGURE 18.22: Searching for car-pool buddies in the RideShare Partners tab

Limitations of Visual Basic

Our Visual Basic application is a great start, but it does have several serious limitations:

- It's yet another application for people to learn. We could get around this limitation by implementing the query in an Excel spreadsheet perhaps, but then people might get confused when their word processor program is used to look up data, because they expect a separate tool. It should be something little and easy, but it's still yet one more application.

- Installation is a big deal. We need to distribute some OCX files (that implement the controls we dragged to the form) and the executable file itself to every Windows client in the company. We need to ensure that the files are installed properly, and that the SQL Server ODBC data source is set up properly.

- This works only for Windows users. In our company, 25 percent of the users have Macintosh computers. Excel could be used perhaps, but we also have people who use Unix workstations. This defeats our purpose of having this tool be as pervasive as e-mail.

We'll see how to overcome these limitations while preserving the client/server advantage in Skill 19, where we'll port this tool to an intranet implementation.

Are You Experienced?

Now you can...

- ☑ design a database for a client/server application

- ☑ build a database with common end-user tools, such as Microsoft Excel and Access

- ☑ scale up a database to Microsoft SQL Server, part of the BackOffice suite

- ☑ develop a front-end application with Visual Basic

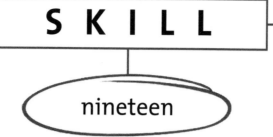

S K I L L

nineteen

19

Developing
Intranet Systems

- ❏ Intranet defined
- ❏ How Web technologies are used in intranet applications
- ❏ Internet Information Server installation
- ❏ Internet Information Server and SQL Server integration
- ❏ Emerging Internet technologies

Many companies have multiple networks, with multiple computer platforms; their networks resemble the worldwide Internet. These diverse corporate networks and the Internet have similar problems, and tools that were developed to solve Internet problems can be of considerable value in corporate environments. When you use Internet technologies to implement or replace a traditional client/server system, you have an *intranet*—an internet that's internal to an organization.

The client/server application that we developed as an example in Skill 18 was easy to create, but it has a number of limitations. With the explosion of technology that the Internet has brought to business computing, we can overcome many of these limitations by abandoning the proprietary Visual Basic front end and using a Web browser as the front-end application instead.

Microsoft's Internet Information Server provides an easy way to link SQL Server databases with any Web client on your intranet. Internet Information Server is now an integral part of the NT Server 4.0 installation process, and it is supported by NT's security and MIME file type file-system information. Coupled with SQL Server and ODBC connectors, Internet Information Server becomes a powerful, easy-to-use, client/server intranet system.

Here, we'll take our ride-share client/server application from the previous chapter and implement the system using the easy connectivity between Internet Information Server and SQL Server.

Limitations of Traditional Client/Server Systems

In Skill 18, we saw how NT and its associated technologies facilitate the development of client/server applications, enabling you to consolidate information into centralized databases while preserving the end-user interaction advantages of graphical desktop systems.

In our example, SQL Server, which runs under NT, made it easy for us to scale up a simple database from a desktop-based system to one that could handle multiple users on the network. We saw how easy it is to set up and maintain SQL Server, which provides graphical tools with enterprise-wide management capabilities. SQL Server on an NT machine can interact with existing desktop programs such as Microsoft Access. With limited knowledge of SQL (Structured Query Language), we can create SQL databases on the server.

However, the method we used for implementing the front end, Visual Basic, had some serious limitations. In order to deploy a Visual Basic application, we need to distribute the application—the application's executable file as well as the libraries that implement the application's controls—to every desktop in the enterprise. Even if you use an installer program, the "installation event" must occur. Visual Basic programs with the requisite controls do not run (at the time of this writing) on DOS, Macintosh, or Unix workstations, limiting our "company-wide" database system to those who use Windows-based PCs.

A client/server development system, such as PowerBuilder, won't completely insulate you from the complexities of cross-platform development. The way in which Macintosh and Windows computers typically connect to back-end databases is different for each platform. Although the systems are getting better, the Macintosh implementations typically lag behind the Windows ones, and setting up such a system requires a degree of sophistication on both Windows and Macintosh platforms. You need to translate the documentation into something that makes sense, and this can be a challenge.

In my experience, cross-platform client/server tools add a great deal of complexity to a project, in terms of development, training, and deployment. For most simple systems, there is now a better alternative, based on Internet technology: an intranet.

Intranets Explained

With the proliferation of the Internet, and most particularly the World Wide Web, rich tools have become available. These tools provide the functionality of traditional client/server systems while avoiding many of their limitations. The main advantages of using Internet tools are:

- Universal implementations

- Easy deployment

It is now possible to provide the functionality of the Visual Basic program, including a graphic interface, using standard Web browsers. These browsers are available from a number of vendors and run on every platform. The "Windows-only" rule no longer applies.

Once you have set up a Web browser infrastructure, with a TCP/IP network and Web browsers installed on the client computers, deploying a new Web-based application is almost trivial. You simply add a link to you company's home page, and let people know about the new service. All they need to do is click on the link to "launch" the new program. You don't need to touch the client computers at all.

Internet Basics

The Internet is a large collection of computer networks that are all interconnected. If you have a multisite, corporate WAN (wide-area network), you have your own "internet."

The worldwide Internet is comprised of computer networks that speak the TCP/IP protocol and follow conventions regarding the assignment of computer names and network addresses. We could fill up a book talking about these conventions. Suffice to say that when you're using the Internet network, you're relying upon a whole bunch of networks to get your data from point A to point B, using the best route available at the time. Using this connection is like skateboarding from Los Angeles to San Francisco: You start at your office building in L.A., cut across a couple of parking lots to avoid the one-way streets and busy intersections, get on the highway for a while, and eventually make your way to your destination. In order to get where you're going, you might take a really complex route.

These days, you lease Internet connectivity from your Internet access provider, who in turn leases transit bandwidth from a big carrier such as Sprint or MCI. It's best if your service provider is not "downstream" from a smaller bandwidth reseller, because you don't want too many hops between you and the big backbones, the superhighways.

You can find out how your data is getting from point A to point B on the Internet with the Traceroute function. On a Unix system, type **traceroute** and give an IP address or hostname. You'll see how the Internet routes your data to establish the connection. You can get a program for NT that includes the Traceroute function, WSPING32, from the Internet at http://204.71.8.24/JUNODJ/wsping32.htm. Figure 19.1 shows an example of the result of using the Traceroute function of the WSPING32 tool.

Understanding Web Technology

The Internet, when used in the context of intranet application development, typically signifies the interaction between Web browsers and servers. Understanding World Wide Web technology is crucial to successful implementation of intranet systems.

The World Wide Web (WWW) is the product of a number of key standards:

- HTML: Hypertext Markup Language
- HTTP: Hypertext Transfer Protocol

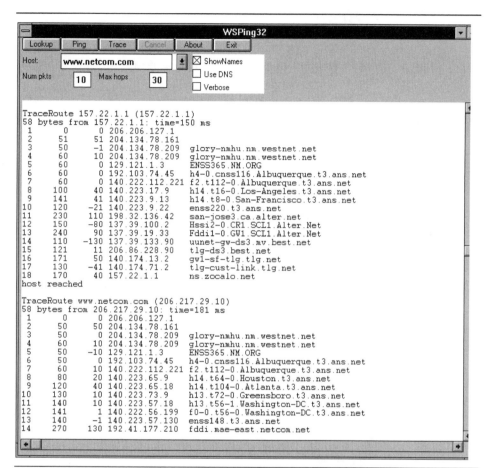

FIGURE 19.1: Using a common Traceroute tool, we can see that the Internet is comprised of a cooperative tangle of multiple networks.

- URLs: Universal Resource Locators

- MIME file types: Multimedia Internet Mail Extensions

- GIF and JPEG: Standard graphics file formats

HTML (Hypertext Markup Language)

HTML is a way of adding properties to lines of text, such as "major heading" or "underlined" or "this text is a link to another page" or "put a picture here."

HTML also describes various elements of the document, such as pictures, text, and sounds, and tells the Web browser where to find each element. The Web browser is a program on the client computer that interprets these notations—these text mark-ups—and renders the page appropriately. Figure 19.2 shows how a Web browser interprets HTML.

The best way to gain an understanding of HTML is to compare HTML code to the page that it describes. Some Web browsers allow you to see the underlying HTML codes with a View Source command. See Table 19.1 for the meanings of some of the most common HTML tags.

T A B L E   1 9 . 1 : Some Common HTML Tags

HTML Code	Meaning
<H1>	Heading 1
<H2>	Heading 2
<p>	New paragraph (typically, with space in between)
 	Line break (typically, with no space in between)
<EM>	Emphasized text (typically bold)
<IMG>	Insert picture
<A HREF=source>	Hyperlink to source

NOTE   Table 19.1 is by no means a complete list! Take a look at Web pages in your browser and choose the View Source command to see what is really happening with HTML.

It's important to understand the distinction between this method of text annotation and page-description languages such as PostScript, which completely determine the appearance of a page. Initially, HTML was designed with the idea that the Web browser would make decisions about the appearance of the page on the screen. A tag like "Heading 1" doesn't say anything about the size or style of the type; it's up to the Web browsers to decide how to represent these styles. Presumably, a heading 1 style will have a larger text face than a heading 2 style, but that's not part of the specification.

FIGURE 19.2: Web browsers interpret HTML code and render sophisticated pages.

Recent extensions to HTML give a page's designer more control over the ultimate appearance of the document. Microsoft and Netscape have proposed HTML tags to specify text color and font size, and Microsoft has been promoting the use of TrueType fonts in HTML pages. The HTML 3.0 specification defines the use of style sheets, which are referenced at the beginning of an HTML document. A style sheet explicitly describes the font, size, style, and alignment of particular tags. If your browser understands style sheets, you can design pages with HTML tags and specify the appearance of the text. For example, you could say that the H1 tag means right-aligned, 30-point Arial Bold underlined.

HTTP (Hypertext Transfer Protocol)

HTTP defines the interaction between the Web browser on the client computer and any number of servers out there on the Internet. HTTP is the language that the Web browser uses to ask for the HTML documents and any included elements (like pictures). A program that responds appropriately to HTTP requests can act as a server to any Web browser.

The most basic HTTP interactions are a series of HTTP requests made by the client computer, which are answered by HTTP responses from the server. For example, a client might ask the server to send a particular document, and the server might respond with the document itself, an indication that the user lacks file permissions to receive the document, or an error indicating that the document cannot be found.

HTTP specifies important information about documents. Last modification times are used by the Web browser to determine if the document is the same document that has been visited before. The Web browser might choose to retrieve the document from a local cache, rather than request the entire document from the server again. For this reason, it's possible for the Web browser to ask the server for a document *header* only. The header contains the document's attribute information, rather that the entire document body.

HTTP also specifies the document's type, so that the browser can handle the document appropriately. The type specification uses the MIME standard, discussed shortly.

Recent extensions to HTTP allow for the secure transfer of data utilizing encrypted connections.

URLs (Universal Resource Locators)

HTTP clients would not be able to find anything if they could not request specific documents from the servers. URLs provide a standardized way to refer to a local file, a file on an HTTP server, or a file on an FTP server. Here are some examples of URLs that specify HTTP, FTP, Telnet, and Gopher servers:

http://www.w3.org/pub/WWW/Protocols/HTTP-NG/Overview.html

ftp://ftp.cdrom.com/

telnet://starwars.arcade.com:4442

gopher://gopher.dartmouth.edu

UNCs or URLs?

If you're familiar with Windows networking UNC (Universal Naming Convention) notation, you'll see a remarkable similarity between the purpose of URLs and UNCs. Indeed, in a future revision of NT and Windows 95, you'll be able to use URLs most anywhere you can currently use UNCs.

Here's a UNC that specifies a program on my computer:

\\FRANKENSTEIN\C$\WINNT\SYSTEM32\notepad.exe

And here's a UNC to read an executable file on a remote computer, have that program load onto the local computer, and get the program to display a text file on a third computer:

\\POOH\LanTeam\programs\wordpad.exe \\EMV02\pub\showplan.txt

Because the Microsoft Internet Explorer for Windows understands UNCs, if you have peer file sharing enabled in Windows 95, you can create pages with links to files specifying the UNC, and have any Windows 95 computer (or NT workstation or server, for that matter) act as a Web server.

Skill 19

MIME (Multimedia Internet Mail Extension) File Types

MIME permits the association of file types and applications on the Internet. A MIME type is simply a text tag with a major and minor category. For example, the MIME type for a Microsoft Word file is application/msword.

To tag a file with the MIME type, the first line should contain the text "Content-type:" and the MIME type. The second line should be a blank line, and then the rest of the document is the file itself. For example, a Microsoft Word document would begin with the line:

```
Content-type: application/msword
```

followed by a blank line, followed by the Word document.

This method of encoding the file type in the first few characters of the file itself is common in the Unix world, but is not so common for PCs running Microsoft software. Such computers use the filename extension to specify the file type. The Netscape Web browser lets you maintain a mapping of file extensions to MIME file types in the Helpers tab of the Preferences dialog box. Figure 19.3 shows an example.

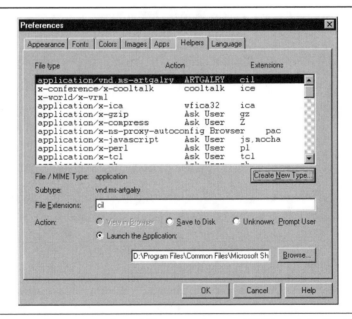

FIGURE 19.3: A mapping of file extensions to MIME types in the Helpers tab of Netscape's Preferences dialog box

NT 4.0 maintains the association of file extensions and MIME types in the file system. Internet Explorer and other applications can use this system-wide data to obtain the appropriate MIME file type information. Figure 19.4 shows the list of file type associations in NT.

FIGURE 19.4: NT 4.0 keeps a list of file extensions and MIME types.

GIF and JPEG Graphics File Formats

Just as HTML gives the standard for normal text files, GIF (Graphics Interchange Format) and JPEG (Joint Photography Engineering Group) are standards that define picture file formats on the Internet.

GIF is a file format developed by CompuServe. It's appropriate for computer-generated bitmaps with limited color palettes (say, less than 1000 colors). The GIF format compresses the data using a run-length encoding scheme. For example, if the bitmap has large regions of blue in it, instead of storing a thousand blue pixels, the GIF format stores a single tag which means, "the next 1000 pixels are blue." Virtually all Web browsers capable of displaying graphics can render GIF images.

JPEG is a graphics standard developed for high-level compression of photographic images, and it generally does a better job than GIF at storing digitized photos. Most modern graphics-capable Web browsers can render JPEG images. You care about the image compression specified in these graphics file formats if you're downloading an image across a slow data link (like a modem). Most slow connections use compression on the data stream. PPP specifies this automatically, and modems or ISDN adapters typically use compression to increase apparent data-transfer rates. But since the GIF file is made up of compressed data, the data compression used on your connection won't make much difference; that 130 KB GIF file is going to come across your 28,800 kbps connection in 7 to 10 seconds (on a really good day, taking into account the protocol overhead), whether or not your connection is using data compression.

WEB BROWSERS AND GRAPHICS

With Netscape as the corporate standard, and Internet Explorer capturing some of the market, you might think that you don't need to worry about the graphics capabilities of browsers. However, at some of the companies that I've helped to deploy intranet services, many of the people were using text-only browsers on terminals connected to mainframe computers. Because a major motivation for developing an intranet system is the universal distribution of (usually textual) corporate data, you should design your pages so that they make sense when viewed on these types of browsers.

Even if you know that only Netscape or other graphical browsers are going to be used with your intranet system, unless graphics are essential to the system (for example, in a chemical structure database), you should design the pages for text first. This is because the user may choose to turn off the picture downloads (which a graphical browser allows), in order to render the pages more quickly.

Use graphics to emphasize the data, as navigational aids, and to make the use of your system more pleasant. But unless you have to, don't require graphics displays in order to use your system.

Web Server Scripting

Web technology would not be interesting if it were not for the ability to add program logic to the server with the addition of server programs, or *scripts*. Instead of specifying an HTML document, a URL might point to a program that can generate the data on the fly. Scripts that can be called by an HTTP server conform to a specification called the Common Gateway Interface, and they are referred to as CGI scripts.

Here is an example of a very simple CGI script, written for a Unix C-shell:

```
cat << EOF
Content-type: text/html

<html>
 <head><title>This is a test</title></head>
 <body>
 <h1>This is a test of the emergency CGI scripting system.</h1>
 <hr>
 Uh, this is only a test...
 </body>
 </html>
EOF
```

When this file is invoked, it simply sends the HTML text to the standard output. (Of course, this CGI script is not particularly useful, since you could simply use a static HTML document instead.)

Here is another CGI script, which returns the date and time of the script's invocation:

```
#!/bin/sh

DATE=/bin/date
echo Content-type: text/plain
echo

if [ -x $DATE ];  then
        $DATE
else
        echo Cannot find date command on this system.
fi
```

Now we can start to consider useful applications. How about a CGI script that returns the formatted result of a SQL query? We'll do this in just a moment, after we install NT's Internet Information Server.

Skill 19

Installing Internet Information Server

You can use Internet Information Server to link SQL Server databases with the Web clients on your intranet. If you didn't install Internet Information Server when you installed NT Server, you can do it now.

Before You Begin

Before you install Internet Information Server, keep the following points in mind:

- Internet Information Server requires the TCP/IP protocol. If you don't have TCP/IP installed and configured, you need to set up your TCP/IP connection first (refer to Skill 8).

 NOTE   If you need to install the TCP/IP protocol, you'll need to reboot your server after installation and configuration. Be sure to schedule the appropriate server outage, if your system is in production use. If your server already has TCP/IP installed, you won't need to reboot the server after installing Internet Information Server.

- Install Internet Information Server onto an NTFS partition in order to utilize NT security. You'll be able to control access to various Web sites by simply setting the appropriate file permissions on the Web files and directories. NT security is Web security.

- The default location for Internet Information Server is inside the *<systemroot>*\ SYSTEM32 directory. Make sure you have enough room on your system partition, or otherwise decide where you will keep the Web files. You want an NTFS partition for security, and you need enough space to hold all your Web files.

- Make sure you have your NT Server 4.0 distribution CD-ROM.

For the final word, refer to the *Internet Information Server Installation and Planning Guide*.

Internet Information Server Installation

Follow these steps to install Internet Information Server:

1. Make sure the TCP/IP protocol is installed and configured correctly.

2. Insert the NT Server 4.0 distribution CD-ROM into the CD-ROM drive of the server.

3. From the Services tab of the Network Control Panel, click on the Add button. Choose the Microsoft Internet Information Server from the list of network services.

4. You may need to tell the Setup program the location of the NT distribution files. For example, if you have your CD-ROM on the G: drive, and you have an Intel machine, tell Setup to look in G:\i386.

5. The Setup program will ask you which components of Internet Information Server you would like to install. For an intranet server, you need the World Wide Web Service and the Internet Services Manager. You also need the ODBC services, which should already be installed if you installed SQL Server on your NT computer. If you have not installed SQL Server on the computer that is to be your Web browser, go ahead and install the ODBC drivers.

6. Choose the location for the Internet Information Server. By default, the Setup program will install the server program files in a subdirectory of *systemroot*\ SYSTEM32\.

7. When you need to specify the "root" directory of the services, make sure that you enter a path that is on a volume that has enough free space to hold all your Web sites. Generally, this won't be a problem. A larger issue is security; make sure that you specify an NTFS volume so that you can set file security permissions on your Web sites. The defaults are generally suitable.

8. The Create Internet Account dialog box will prompt you for a user name and password for the anonymous account that the Internet Information Server system will use to access files. The default is to name the user IUSR_*servername*, which is generally fine.

9. The Setup program will install Internet Information Server. If you've opted to install the ODBC drivers, select the SQL Server driver.

Skill 19

WARNING   The Internet account password here is important. If you change the password of the IUSR_*servername* account, you'll need to tell the Internet Information Server service about it. Use the Internet Service Manager, under the Administrative Tools menu (a submenu of the Start menu's Programs menu), to change the password. Until you do, the server will not have access to the Web files, and any users of your sites will get an "Access Denied" error.

Integrating Internet Information Server with SQL Server

Now that we've discussed how you can take advantage of Web technology in conjunction with SQL Server and Internet Information Server, it's time to see how all this actually works. After a quick rundown of the components, we'll return to the ride-share application we developed in Skill 18, and transform it into the new, improved version.

The Cast of Players

The connection between Internet Information Server and SQL Server is managed by the following pieces:

- **The Internet Information Server Database Connector:** A filter program that ships with Internet Information Server, and is installed with it, is able to interpret special Internet Database Connector (IDC) files.

- **An IDC file:** The Internet Database Connector program is driven by an IDC file, which specifies the data source (the name of an ODBC data source), the user name passed to the data source, the HTML template file used to format the results of the query, and the SQL query itself.

- **An ODBC Data Source:** Since you installed SQL Server, there should already be a System DSN defined for the SQL Server. If not, you'll need to create a System DSN in the ODBC Control Panel of the Web server.

- **An HTML template file:** The Internet Database Connector will format the results of the SQL query according to the HTML template provided. Such template files have a file extension of .HTX. Template files are similar to HTML files, with a number of additional special directives that indicate where the SQL query results are to be inserted in the file.

NOTE **Remember from Skill 18 that System DSNs allow the system processes to connect to databases via ODBC without an active user session. This is very desirable for a Web server, since you'll want the server to be making connections to the database, but you really don't want to leave a user logged in at the console of the NT server in order for everything to work.**

Note that the SQL server and the Web server can be two different computers. A single Web server can query a different SQL server for each IDC file defined. Each IDC file would specify a separate ODBC connection for each of the desired SQL Server systems. However, for performance reasons, it's usually desirable to have the SQL server running on the same machine as the Web server. You don't want the (potentially large) set of results moving across the network to the Web server, only to have to make another trip from the Web server to the client. Don't move the data any more than you have to—keep the SQL server local to the Web server.

Our Intranet Application

As you'll recall from Skill 18, our ride-share application is intended to help employees of a company find a car-pool buddy. Employees sign up for the ride-share program, giving permission to have their home address and phone number made available to other people in the program. Using the ride-share application, employees are able to search by city and find the employees who live close by.

Implementation Structure

Our Visual Basic program essentially wrapped a canned SQL query in a nice graphical browser. You'll recall that we have three tables in our sample employee database. The Core Employee table holds the name, office location, and office extension of the employees. This is the central table of the relational system—an arbitrary design decision. The Employee Address table holds the home street address and phone number information for the employees, keyed to the Core Employee table on an employee ID. The Employee Tax table was included in the discussion as an example of some very restricted information regarding the employees. It contains their salaries and tax ID information.

To make this implementation better meet the system's goals, I've added another table, Riders, which lists the employees who have signed up for the ride-share program. The improved ride-share system will check against the Riders table to verify that an employee wants to share a ride before listing that employee as a candidate.

In these sample IDC files, the System DSN, "Web SQL," is used as the ODBC data source, and the master SQL Server account, "sa," is used as the data source user. In a real production environment, you would want to create a robot user on the SQL server, specifically for this system. The Web SQL ODBC system DSN was created using the ODBC Control Panel.

For more information about SQL Server and ODBC connectors, see Skill 18, as well as the SQL Server documentation.

The City Query Screen

The first screen that the user will see is a pretty barren query screen, which asks the user to specify a city to search. You could do this a number of ways, such as by getting the name of the user, and then presenting the user with a list of employees in the same city. I decided to simply query on the city name.

Our Visual Basic application used a drop-down list box that listed all the possible cities. This drop-down box is a Visual Basic data-aware bound control. We specified a data source for the drop-down box, which returned the list of cities in the database, which we used to populate the list. All this stuff happened behind the screens for us via the magic of Visual Basic data-aware controls.

To accomplish the same feature with a Web-based implementation, we'll use an IDC file to specify the data source for the Web page. An IDC file specifies the ODBC data source, the HTML template used to format the query results, and the SQL query itself. To create a drop-down list that's populated with the list of city names in the database, we'll write an IDC file that has a SQL query of SELECT CITY FROM ADDRESS... for all of the employees who have signed up for the ride-share program:

```
Datasource: Web SQL
Username: sa
Template: form1.htx
SQLStatement:
+SELECT distinct city
+FROM   sybex.boyd.address a, sybex.boyd.rideshare r
+WHERE  r.rider  = 1
+AND    r.emp_id = a.emp_id
+ORDER BY city
```

The IDC file's query will return a list of all the cities. The HTX (HTML format template) file that we use to format this list of cities will create an HTML form, the action of which is to fire off our primary query (which ride-share employees live in the specified city?). The HTML page will display some explanatory information and the list of possible cities that results from the query in the IDC file. Note how we display each city name with a hyperlink to the "buddies.idc" database query:

```
<HTML>
<HEAD><TITLE>Find a RideShare Buddy</TITLE></HEAD>
<BODY>
<H1>Find a RideShare Buddy</H1>
This is a form that gets data from the database in order to build a
list of choices.
<p>
<p>
<%begindetail%>
<%if CurrentRecord EQ 0 %>
<b>Find RideShare Employees from:</b>
<p>
<%endif%>
<A HREF="buddies.idc?selected_city='<%city%>'"><%city%></A><br>
<%enddetail%>
<p>
<hr>
</body>
</HTML>
```

When the user clicks on a city name, the name of the city is passed to the "find a ride-share buddy" query as determined by the hyperlink:

```
<A HREF="buddies.idc?selected_city='<%city%>'"><%city%></A>
```

The IDC lets you express the value of variables with the <%variablename%> syntax. Note how the hyperlink for each city is set to the successive values of the list of cities with the <%begindetail%>...<%enddetail%> loop.

 NOTE   For more information about the syntax and use of the HTML templates in the IDC file, see Chapter 8 of the Internet Information Server documentation.

See Figure 19.5 for a shot of our City Query page in action.

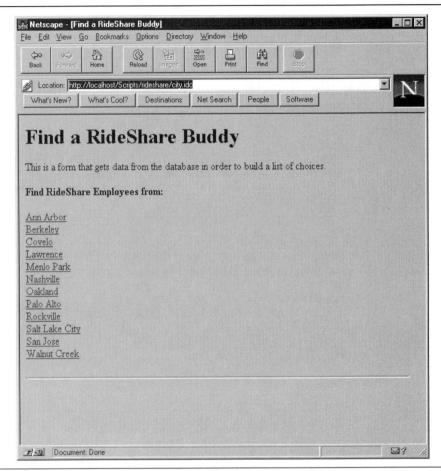

FIGURE 19.5: Users specify the desired city for the ride-share application by choosing the city from a list. The list is populated by the results of a SQL query, which returns all the cities inhabited by program participants.

Ride-Share Buddies Results Screen

After the user has specified the desired city, the city name is passed to the second IDC file, which queries the SQL database again, asking for all ride-share employees who live in the specified city.

```
Datasource: Web SQL
Username: sa
Template: buddies.htx
SQLStatement:
+SELECT fname, lname, e.phone extension, address, a.phone
hphone, areac
+FROM    sybex.boyd.phone e, sybex.boyd.rideshare r,
sybex.boyd.address a
+WHERE        r.rider   = 1
+AND r.emp_id = e.emp_id
+AND e.emp_id = a.emp_id
+AND a.city   = '%selected_city%'
+ORDER BY e.lname
```

After the data is returned, the HTML template file simply displays the data as an HTML table. There is nothing fancy here:

```
<HTML>
<HEAD><TITLE>Rideshare Buddies in
<%idc.selected_city%></TITLE></HEAD>
<BODY>
<h1>Rideshare Buddies in <%idc.selected_city%></h1>
<hr>
<TABLE>
<%begindetail%>
<%if CurrentRecord EQ 0 %>
<TR BGCOLOR="#DDDDDD" FONT="Arial" SIZE=+1>
    <TH>Name</TH>
    <TH>Extension</TH>
    <TH>Home Phone</TH>
    <TH>Street Address</TH>
</TR>
<%endif%>
<TR>
    <TD><%fname%> <%lname%></TD>
    <TD><%extension%></TD>
    <TD>(<%areac%>) <%hphone%></TD>
    <TD><%address%></TD>
</TR>
<%enddetail%>
</TABLE>
<hr>
<A HREF="city.idc">Choose another city</A>
</body>
</html>
```

Note the way in which we check the record number. If we have not yet displayed any of the returned records, then the CurrentRecord is zero, and we'll display the table heading row. For each of the returned records, we write out the data, one row per returned record. See Figure 19.6 for an example of the query results.

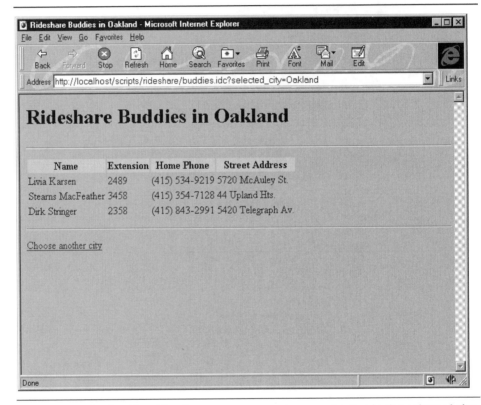

Figure 19.6: The ride-share program employees who live in the selected city are displayed in an HTML table.

Summary: The Ride-Share Application

In this example, we were able to integrate SQL Server and Web server systems on an NT Server 4.0 system to produce a simple application that allows anyone in the company to query the employee database in a well-defined fashion. You may have noticed from the screen shots that the application is equally accessible to PC and Macintosh users, running any of the standard Web browsers.

Aside from the TCP/IP protocol and the Web browser software, there is no configuration necessary on the client computers. We saw how simple it is to set up the server as well, because the ODBC connector makes it easy to get the data from the SQL Server database.

The example given here can be fleshed out in a number of ways. One feature that could be easily implemented within the framework of the current system is to have employees indicate preferred working hours, so that people would know which schedules could be accommodated.

It's dubious to restrict queries on the city name, since cities can border on one another, and someone just up the street might have an address in a different city. A better query would be to display a map, based on the user's name. The system would know the street address of the user performing the query, and could center the map on that street address, indicating ride-share partners on the map. With the ability to dynamically generate Web pages that may contain graphical data, the sky is the limit!

Future Internet Technologies

This is a wild time to be in the computer industry. The Internet technologies spewing forth from the software industry are whizzing by very, very quickly. Internet standards are the best thing that ever happened to Microsoft, a company that's masterful at co-opting technology trends. The company has undergone a dramatic realignment recently, and the effects of that shift are still emerging. But you'll see familiar Internet-inspired standards pervading the newest pieces of Microsoft technology.

On the Server

The IDC file that we played with is but one example of a standard Internet Information Server extension. These extensions are implemented in a programming language like C++, and are written to a specification called the Internet Server Application Programming Interface (ISAPI).

Earlier, I implied that the IDC file was a CGI script, a program that Internet Information Server called in response to an HTTP request. I lied. The IDC file is an ISAPI extension to Internet Information Server, and ISAPI extensions are qualitatively different from the CGI scripts. Instead of running as a completely separate process, ISAPI extensions are loaded into the server's process memory space and are invoked like a simple binary function call. It's as if you were able to rewrite and recompile the Web server program; the extended functionality can be just as fast as the "core" Web server binary program. (You Apache-server programmers should feel right at home with this.)

Obviously, ISAPI extensions are not limited to SQL Server integration. With ISAPI, you are able to extend the Web server so it can look more and more like a standard applications and file server, if you wish.

On the Desktop

The most dramatic changes effected by Internet technologies are occurring on the client PC desktops.

Document Objects

The most widely significant of the Microsoft Internet technologies on the desktop is the ability of the Microsoft Internet Explorer to act as a full Office application when displaying files that conform to the Document Object specification. DocObjects are files that know how to render themselves; they maintain a reference back to the application that created them. When a DocObject is displayed in a DocObject-compatible viewer, the viewer launches enough of the creating application to allow users to display and edit the document.

The end result is that when Microsoft Internet Explorer opens a Word document, the Word application fires up, right in the Internet Explorer window. As far as the user is concerned, there is only the super-application, Internet Explorer, which knows how to display all the toolbars and menus appropriate to the current document. Figure 19.7 shows an example of Microsoft Word running inside the Internet Explorer window (note the Internet Explorer navigation buttons at the top).

Using DocObjects, you could use the Web server as a file server, as a document-management system. The user queries the system for the appropriate document, which is retrieved from the SQL database and then forwarded to Internet Explorer. When Internet Explorer receives the document, it's immediately displayed for editing in the Internet Explorer window.

The reference that the document maintains back to the creator application is *not* a file association; it's an OLE signature. Future versions of the NT file system will use OLE to maintain relationships between files and the applications that created them. This will clean up a lot of problems that currently exist with file types (maintained by filename extension associations) and file creators (which are not maintained at all in current versions of Microsoft operating systems).

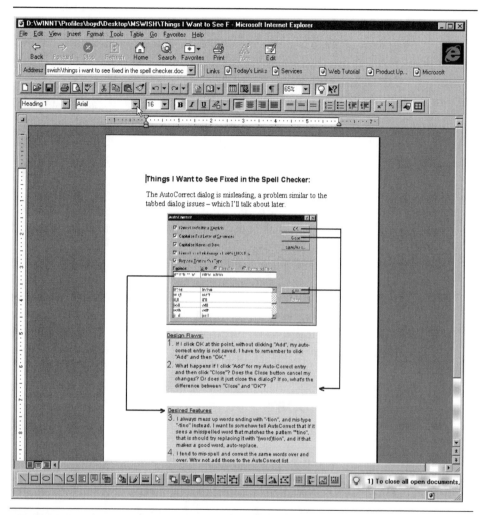

FIGURE 19.7: The Microsoft Internet Explorer is a Document Object container, so the Web browser can host standard desktop documents without switching to a separate application. Here, Microsoft Word is running inside the Internet Explorer frame.

The Document Object idea is one of the most far-reaching because Microsoft folks claim that they're committed to delivering this technology to the Macintosh platform as well as the PCs. If a Mac has Microsoft Office and Internet Explorer installed, it will be able to participate in the theoretical document-management system described here. We'll have to see if the Macintosh implementation of Document Objects actually occurs. Currently, Microsoft Office for the Mac lags behind the Windows version by about a year.

Ubiquitous Web Explorer

The Windows Explorer and Internet Explorer are being folded together to yield one program: Explorer. You will be able to "surf" your computer, or your Network Neighborhood, in precisely the same fashion as you currently surf the Web.

We've already used HTML template files to format the display of SQL query results. The next release of Windows will use an optional HTML template file in each directory of the computer to format the display of that directory's contents. A directory window could have any and all of the characteristics of an HTML page, including hyperlinks to other files or directories, embedded graphics, and even ActiveX Controls.

Note that HTML can create multiple-frame displays. You could set the Desktop to have many panes. For example, a long, narrow pane at the bottom might point to an "actual" Web site on the Internet, which could display stock price information (see http://www.pointcast.com). A pane in the upper-right corner might render an HTML file of your favorite places, or point to the corporate home page on the LAN, with links to important messages of the day (good-bye to junk e-mail and phone messages!).

For the Developer

And of course, the emerging Internet technologies give application developers a whole new set of tools.

ActiveX Controls

Currently, all you can display on an HTML page is some formatted text, graphics and simple animations, and the few user-interface goodies that are necessary for the creation of Web forms: radio buttons, checkboxes, pop-up menus, and text-entry fields. If you want users to enter a number within a specified range by using a slider control, you're out of luck.

And there are more limitations. Three-tier client/server applications need to be able to validate data entry according to business rules. Currently, people using a Web form must submit data to the Web server and have it parsed out before they're rewarded with the error message that indicates an inappropriate entry. This is very bad—there's no way to check the data as it's being entered, and the lack of feedback frustrates people.

Microsoft wants you to be able to create HTML pages and forms that contain any custom control that can be contained by a Visual Basic form. So with ActiveX technology, we could take all the pop-up menus and data grids from our application in Skill 18, plop them onto a Web page, and have that page served up from the server. This gives you all the benefits of Visual Basic program development, with the freedom from the deployment issues that keelhauled our Visual Basic implementation.

Microsoft is committed to delivering ActiveX technology to the Macintosh clients. We'll need to see if any ActiveX control vendors are willing to jump into Mac development. The Java programming language may make that easier.

Integrated Java Development

All of the cool emerging Microsoft technologies are based on Microsoft's object-oriented software component model, the Common Object Model, or COM. Programmers who wish to take full advantage of all this technology have had to get comfortable with COM programming, and this can be an onerous task for the C++ developer.

Java to the rescue! The design of the Java programming language is apparently ideally suited to the development of COM objects. Microsoft has integrated COM support into its implementation of Java, so that you'll be able to create ActiveX controls and other Windows applications in Java.

To that end, the Microsoft implementation of Java is completely integrated into the Developer Studio programming environment, as you can see in Figure 19.8.

FIGURE 19.8: The Microsoft Developer Studio screen

Are You Experienced?

Now you can...

- ☑ install Internet Information Server from the NT Server 4.0 distribution CD-ROM
- ☑ integrate SQL Server and Web server systems on an NT Server system
- ☑ create platform-independent intranet systems
- ☑ find other Internet technologies to use for developing intranet applications

Index

Note to the Reader   Page numbers in *italics* refer to figures; page numbers in bold refer to significant discussions of a topic.

b

C

g

h

sample query, *423*

Showplan tab, *424*

to verify database migration, 422

ISQL/w, saving query in, 422

j

Java, 407, **459**

JPEG file format, **443–444**

k

Kernel, 74

and threads, 68, 71

kernel mode, 7, **72–80**

keyboard, **109**

l

LAN Manager, 304

Last Known Good Menu option for server installation repair, **142**

level 2 cache, 101, 103, 116

in Pentium Pro, 93

licensing

client, 53, **85–86**

for SQL Server, 413, *414*

licensing mode, 135

linear scalability, 153, 160

LNK extension, 35

load calculation, for UPS, **204–205**

local accounts, 278

on domain server, minimizing, 279

local administrator account, password for, 135

local computer, file share setup on, **316–317**

local groups, **298**

vs. global groups, 397

LocalTalk, vs. EtherTalk, **330–331**

log file

exporting data from, **168–169**

from Performance Monitor, 167–168

Log Options dialog box, 167, 168

logical port, for printer, 321–322, *322*

logical print spool, port for, *321*

logon message, for Mac server, 348

logon permissions, granting for SQL Server, **417**

Logon Validation setting, for DOS or Windows 3.1 client, 310

logs, 51

long filenames, 32

for Macintosh, 353–354

m

MacFile Attributes dialog box, *348*, 348–349

MacFile Control Panel, **346–353**, *346*

Files button, 347

Users button, 346

Volumes button, 347

MacFile menu (File Manager), Associate, 357

MacFile menu (Server Manager), 352

Create Volume, 355

Macintosh. *See also* Services for Macintosh

ActiveX technology for, 459

and Document objects, 457–458

network addressing, **331–332**

t